The Devil's Anvil

A corpsman bandages the hand of a wounded Marine under enemy fire. (USMC)

The Devil's Anvil

THE ASSAULT ON PELELIU

James H. Hallas

 PRAEGER

Westport, Connecticut
London

Library of Congress Cataloging-in-Publication Data

Hallas, James H.
    The devil's anvil : the assault on Peleliu / James H. Hallas.
       p.   cm.
    Includes bibliographical references and index.
    ISBN 0–275–94646–0 (alk. paper)
    1. Peleliu Island (Palau), Battle of, 1944.   I. Title.
D767.99.P4H3   1994
940.54′26—dc20   93–13532

British Library Cataloguing in Publication Data is available.

Library of Congress Catalog Card Number: 93–13532
ISBN: 0–275–94646–0

First published in 1994

Praeger Publishers, 88 Post Road West, Westport, CT 06881
An imprint of Greenwood Publishing Group, Inc.

Printed in the United States of America

∞™

The paper used in this book complies with the
Permanent Paper Standard issued by the National
Information Standards Organization (Z39.48–1984).

10 9 8 7 6 5 4 3 2 1

Contents

Maps

Preface

On the morning of 15 September 1944, over 16,000 Marines of the U.S. 1st Marine Division waited off an obscure speck of coral in the Palaus Islands group roughly 500 miles east of the Philippines.

The name of that speck was Peleliu.

Also waiting, hidden deep in Peleliu's caves and coral ridges, were some 10,000 Japanese soldiers, sailors and laborers, their backbone provided by members of the proud 14th Division. The Japanese had been digging in for months in anticipation of this day.

Morale was high, although the garrison commander, Colonel Kunio Nakagawa, had few illusions about the sheer weight of firepower and materiel his men would face; his ambition was to make Peleliu as costly as possible for the young U.S. Marines then standing off the landing beaches.

By contrast, the commander of the 1st Marine Division, General William Rupertus, was filled with brash optimism. He expected a tough fight but was confident enough to go on record with a prediction: Peleliu would be secure in two days, three at the most, he told officers and news correspondents. He was wrong by 68 days.

Nearly 1,500 American soldiers and Marines died in the battle for Peleliu. Thousands more were seriously wounded. Except for a handful of prisoners, the Japanese garrison fought to the death in the best traditions of Bushido.

Tragically, the prize, 6,400 acres of upheaved coral, proved to be of dubious value. Seized to protect General Douglas MacArthur's flank in the drive on the Philippines, it contributed little to that victory. The war in the Pacific moved on too quickly; enemy capabilities were far less than assumed; Peleliu became a backwater almost before it was invaded.

Adding to the bitterness of this historical assessment, the Peleliu campaign was largely overlooked by the American public at the time and generally ignored by historians in years after. Overshadowed by events in Europe and the Philippines, deprived of the publicity that made Guadalcanal, Tarawa and Iwo Jima household names, it became, in the words of one historian, "the forgotten battle."

Ironically, in modern times, the Palaus have taken on a strategic significance which may ultimately surpass that of 45 years ago. With the abandonment of the huge U.S. base at Subic Bay in the Philippines, the Palaus are being eyed with new interest as a potential naval base, to the mixed feelings of the native islanders. Such are the vagaries of world politics.

This book owes much to many. My gratitude goes to the staff at the U.S. Marine Corps Historical Center for their help in locating documents and other material relating to the campaign. Thanks also go to the Naval Historical Center and the U.S. Army Military History Institute in Carlisle, Pennsylvania. Nicholas Oresko of the Congressional Medal of Honor Society was kind enough to help me locate the two surviving Peleliu Medal of Honor winners and provide information on other awards. My friend Tom Leahy, formerly of the 5th Marines, was instrumental in helping to locate dozens of Peleliu veterans.

My deepest thanks go to those veterans themselves. In the course of my research, I interviewed officers and privates, Marines and GIs: men who landed with the first wave and were wounded within minutes, and men who fought through the entire campaign without bodily injury. Another veteran was among the troops that helped repatriate thousands of bypassed Japanese in the Palaus after the war.

Many of these combat veterans poured their hearts out to me—a stranger—confiding memories they had tried to forget for over 40 years, remembering friends who died almost before their lives had begun . . . sometimes finding those memories so painful they were unable to continue. They are proof that courage is not limited to the battlefield. Without them, this book would not have been possible.

I have tried in these pages to show Peleliu as it appeared to the rifleman as well as the planner, to convey something of the terrific heat, the primal fear and the bone-numbing exhaustion that come with combat, while still demonstrating how events unfolded.

But the rifleman's war is not a civilized chess match. Combat is a confused situation at best, intensely personal and emotionally chaotic—any effort to impose order on the experience can be only partially successful.

Even the official record can demonstrate confusion and ambiguity. A notable case in point concerns the Japanese tank attack across Peleliu's airfield on D-Day. Sources disagree on how many tanks were involved and just what happened. Time and study have done little to shed more light on the incident.

In each such instance I have tried to resolve discrepancies of time, place or action to my own satisfaction. Any resultant errors are mine alone.

Today Peleliu is much different in appearance than when Marines and GIs fought for possession. The island is home to a handful of natives who survive by fishing and know little of the events that took place there 45 years ago. The heavy jungle growth has returned to the island's once naked ridges; the taxi strips and secondary runways of the airstrip that was the primary objective of the assault have been swallowed up by scrub.

The cemetery once located behind the Orange Beaches is gone, the bodies returned to the United States after the war. The remains of a stone monument lie forlornly in the undergrowth. Atop Hill 300 stands another abandoned and decaying monument, this one to GIs of the 81st Infantry Division who ultimately annihilated the last Japanese resistance. For 40 years, until 1984, there was no marker to the 16,000 men of the 1st Marine Division. Today, a modest granite tablet, erected by a handful of Peleliu veterans, stands below Bloody Nose Ridge, with a brief inscription to those who gave their lives in the campaign. Few Americans will ever see it.

It is my hope that this book may stand as some small tribute to all who fought on Peleliu ... to those who died and to those who will never forget. *Semper Fidelis.*

The Devil's Anvil

Chapter 1

Rough but fast.

That was the scuttlebutt in the 1st Marine Division, training on Pavuvu in the Russell Islands in August 1944. Their next island assault would be tough, but it would also be of short duration.

Veteran Marines greeted this rumor with some satisfaction. Created in early 1941—built around the nucleus of the 1st Brigade based at Quantico—the 1st Marine Division had seen much war in the previous three years. It was the original, the Old One, the mother of Marine divisions to follow, and its men were very proud, even for Marines.

Guadalcanal, the division's first campaign, had lasted four months, from August to December 1943. After a memorable respite in Australia, the division had gone back into action in the Cape Gloucester campaign in early 1944—four more months of jungle hell with mud, rain and Japanese in a climate that rotted the dungarees right off a man. With those memories all too fresh, the idea of a short campaign—even a very rugged one—came as a relief of sorts to the men of the Old One.

Then there was Pavuvu.

Pulled off Cape Gloucester in April 1944, the Marines had expected to return to Australia. To their complete disgust, they ended up on Pavuvu, the largest of the Russell Islands, lying only 60 miles northwest of their old battlefields on Guadalcanal. "Why the very name sounded like a gag!" wrote the division historian of their new home.

Ironically, it was the view from the air that landed the 1st Marine Division on Pavuvu in April 1944. Staff officers of the III Amphibious Corps (IIIPhib) had flown over the island, surveyed the graceful shoreline and the neat palms and decided to let the worn-out division recuperate there.

Unfortunately, Pavuvu, so tidy from the air, turned out to be a ten-mile-long "rain-soaked, rat-infested hunk of real estate." "If you were gonna give the world an enema, that's where you would put it," a Marine private first class recalled sardonically. Virtually nothing had been done to prepare for the division's arrival.

The former site of a large Unilever coconut plantation, the island had few roads, no housing or other amenities. The trees concealed a carpet of rotting coconuts, green ferns and rich topsoil. It rained continually. Men and vehicles rapidly turned the whole area into what one officer described as a "deep stinking mush." Guards had to be posted to protect what little lumber there was on the island—any piece left untended promptly disappeared as men tried to keep their gear out of the mud.

Morale hit an all-time low. A sergeant remembered one teenaged sentry who plodded stoically for hours, back and forth, in the ankle-deep muck, lugging his M–1. Upon being relieved, the youngster stopped by the last tent, quietly put the muzzle of his rifle in his mouth and blew the top of his head off.

Teetering on the edge of his own personal breaking point, another man rushed out of his tent at dusk and pounded his fists against a coconut tree, sobbing angrily, "I hate you, goddamit, I hate you!"

"Hit it once for me," came the sympathetic call from a nearby tent.

On top of all of Pavuvu's personal discomforts, it proved grossly inadequate for field maneuvers. Because the island was so small, maneuvers had to be scaled down. Even company-sized exercises frequently saw units getting in each other's way, skirmishing through the company streets and tripping over the guy ropes of their own tents. "It was funny to see a company move forward in combat formation through the groves and become intermingled with the rigid ranks of another company standing weapons inspection, the officers shouting orders to straighten things out," recalled a Marine. With no place to execute artillery problems, the gunners had to fire out to sea, while observers worked out of boats or DUKWs.

Despite these handicaps, the 1st Tank Battalion managed to spend a full day with each infantry battalion, practicing teamwork with rifle squads and fire direction by visual signals and over the tank/infantry telephone. Emphasis was also placed on small unit exercises.

Gradually, as the camp took shape and training progressed, complaints lessened. Men began to pay new attention to their weapons and gear. "It was as if some common instinct told them that the time had come to prepare for the next battle," recalled an officer. That "common instinct" may have resulted from a sudden rise in "chicken discipline"—a rash of weapons and equipment inspections, work parties and petty work details.

Not long afterward, the division learned the name of the island it was slated to take: Peleliu in the Palaus Group. It had a nice sound to it, wrote one Marine. *Pel'e loo*. He would come to learn that there was nothing nice about Peleliu.

Lying just north of the equator, roughly 500 miles east of the southern Philippines, the Palaus Group extends about 100 miles northeast to southwest and covers approximately 175 square miles. The principal islands in the chain, from north to south, are Babelthuap, Koror, Arakabesen, Urukthapel, Eil Malk, Peleliu and Angaur. There are scores of others, many little more than uninhabited dots in the ocean. All would have been considered almost impossibly remote under any other circumstances.

Most of the islands are hilly, but they range from flat atolls in the north, to volcanic central islands, to coral limestone islands in the south. Vegetation is heavy.

Annual rainfall on Peleliu, where the Marines would land, normally exceeds 140 inches, the bulk of it coming in the summer and early fall. Mean temperature for the islands varies from 80 to 83 degrees F, the hottest months between June and September. Humidity is high, with a yearly mean of 82 percent. The Japanese on Peleliu used large cisterns to collect rainwater since there are no freshwater springs on the island.

Babelthuap is the largest of the major islands, roughly 20 miles by 5 miles, bigger than all the others combined, larger even than Saipan in the Marianas. Just north of Babelthuap lies Kossol Passage, a spacious, well-protected fleet anchorage.

The logic behind seizing the Palaus seemed eminently clear in 1944. As General Douglas MacArthur approached the Philippines, the island group appeared to pose a serious threat to his line of attack. As Admiral Chester Nimitz put it, U.S. seizure of the Palaus—occupied by Japan for some 30 years—would serve "first, to remove from MacArthur's right flank, in this progress to the Southern Philippines, a definite threat of attack; second, to secure for our forces a base from which to support MacArthur's operations."

The suggestion to seize bases in the Palaus had been broached as early as August 1943 at the First Quebec Conference (QUADRANT), attended by high Allied officials. At this top-level meeting, the date for an assault was tentatively set for 31 December 1944. The campaign would be launched following seizure of the Marshalls and Truk, but precede the invasion of the Marianas.

Within a few months of that decision, the American drive in the Pacific reached a critical juncture. In the southwest Pacific, forces under the command of General MacArthur had driven Japanese troops from eastern New Guinea, western New Britain and the Admiralties. Naval and Marine forces had seized the Solomons and neutralized the enemy fortress island of Rabaul.

Meanwhile, Admiral Nimitz had driven across the central Pacific, seizing Tarawa, Kwajalein, Makin and other islands in a push through the Marshalls and Gilberts in late 1943 and early 1944. Strategic considerations had allowed U.S. forces to bypass the big Japanese base at Truk.

These developments allowed planners to speed up their previous time frame. A new schedule was formulated by a Joint Chiefs of Staff directive of 12 March 1944. Now Nimitz and MacArthur were to coordinate their offensives in a series of moves culminating in the recapture of the Philippines, occupied by Japanese forces since the fall of Corregidor in 1942.

Map 1.
The Palaus Islands

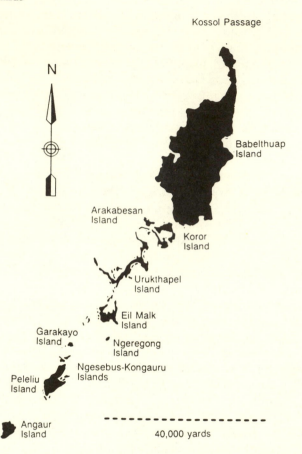

MacArthur would push northwest from New Guinea and seize Morotai and Mindanao in the long-planned thrust into the Philippines. Nimitz would drive west through the Marianas, seizing Saipan and Guam, then continue the push through the Carolines and the Palaus.[1] As plans subsequently gelled, MacArthur's forces would invade Mindanao in the Southern Philippines on 15 November. Leyte, in the Central Philippines, would be invaded on 20 December.

The timetable for the Palaus operation was now pushed up to September 1944.

Planning for the Palaus operation was conducted by a provisional planning staff detached from IIIPhib and later designated X-Ray Provisional Amphibious Corps. By then IIIPhib itself was heavily engaged in the Marianas campaign, where fighting on Saipan and Guam had dragged on beyond expectations. This forced numerous alterations and variations in the Palaus planning, which took second place to the current preoccupation with the Marianas. Early plans, somewhat prophetically code-named Stalemate, called for the seizure of the entire Palaus Group, beginning with Babelthuap and moving south. However, Stalemate planners soon discarded this proposal when intelligence indicated that Babelthuap, the second largest island in Micronesia, was heavily garrisoned, offered difficult terrain and would exact too high a price in U.S. casualties. It was also felt the rugged terrain would be less than ideal for airfield construction. The lone airstrip then being built on the island was not very prepossessing, even by Japanese standards.

In mid-June the Joint Chiefs of Staff queried the top Pacific commanders on the feasibility of bypassing the Western Carolines completely. Such a course, it was suggested, could allow an earlier move against Formosa or even Japan itself. However, the general consensus among Pacific commanders was that the Western Carolines operation could not be completely abandoned, although the scope of the Palaus invasion could be more limited than originally proposed, particularly in light of the information about Babelthuap.

Consequently, Nimitz decided to neutralize Japanese forces on Babelthuap by isolating them. According to subsequent planning, only the three southernmost islands in the group—Peleliu, Ngesebus and Angaur—would be seized: Peleliu and tiny Ngesebus for their Japanese-built airfields, Angaur for its suitability as a site to build U.S. bomber fields. Kossol Passage would be taken for use as an emergency anchorage.

Also to be seized in the Western Carolines was Japanese-held Yap, 240 miles east of the Palaus, site of an enemy air base and considered a softer target than Babelthuap. Ulithi, located just east of Yap, would be taken for its exceptionally deep and spacious anchorage.

The new plan was issued on 7 July 1944 under the code-name Stalemate II. According to its timetable, the 1st Marine Division and 81st Infantry Division would invade the southern Palaus commencing with a Marine landing on Peleliu on 15 September. Yap and Ulithi would be seized by the 7th and 96th Infantry Divisions, under command of the army's XXIV Corps, in early October.

Mild, bespectacled Major General Julian Smith, who had led the 2d Marine Division at Tarawa, was designated Commander of Expeditionary Troops. In August, General Roy Geiger was named corps commander of the troops slated to go ashore at Angaur and Peleliu.

In the midst of the Stalemate planning, one discordant voice arose. As early as May, when he first learned of Stalemate I, Admiral William "Bull" Halsey, who would hold overall naval command of the operation as Commander, Western Pacific Task Forces, questioned its necessity. His objections, formally broached a month later—he was the only Pacific commander to recommend bypassing the Western Carolines in response to the Joint Chief's query in mid-June—were all the more jarring in light of his reputation as an aggressive, grab-'em-by-the-throat fighter. It was Halsey's slogan, "Kill Japs, kill Japs, kill more Japs," that adorned signs and buildings throughout the Pacific Theater. It was the blunt-spoken Halsey who declared, "My ambition remains to populate hell with yellow bastards."

Now, disturbingly, it was Halsey who questioned the wisdom of invading the Palaus. The fighting admiral felt that, of the proposed objectives, only Ulithi was worth seizing, valuable because of its deep water anchorage. Yap, useful only as a minor staging point for aircraft, seemed of little value to him. As for the Palaus, Halsey felt their airfields would not be worth what he predicted would be "a prohibitive price in casualties."

Halsey's fears were noted and dismissed. The operation would proceed as planned.

The target of the 1st Marine Division was a six-mile-long chunk of upheaved coral and limestone lying just north of the equator. About two miles long at its widest extremity, Peleliu is shaped roughly like a lobster claw with a long upper pincer and a shorter lower one separated from the main body of the island by swamp.

Toward the southern hinge of the pincers, where the island bulges out to a width of about two miles, the Japanese had constructed an unusually good airfield with complete servicing facilities. Surfaced with hard-packed coral and capable of handling fighters and bombers, the main runway was over 1,000 yards long, with a shorter fighter strip intersecting at a 90-degree angle. An auxiliary fighter strip was also under construction on tiny Ngesebus, lying just to the north of Peleliu and connected to the larger island by a wooden causeway.

Unlike the flatter southern section, the central and northern parts of Peleliu consist of cliffs and steep-sided gorges all lumped together in a sort of geological goulash. This terrible terrain is especially characteristic of central Peleliu, where the ridge system rises 556 feet to Umurbrogol Mountain. Unfortunately for Marine planners, the true extent of this geological nightmare was masked by heavy tropical growth which made topographic evaluation difficult. The island is surrounded by a coral reef up to 1,000 yards in width.

First claim to the Palaus had been made by Spain, with an authenticated visit to the group made in 1712 by Spanish missionaries from the Marianas. The Spanish had done little with the islands, and in 1899, following the debacle of the Spanish-American War, they sold them to colony-hungry Germany.

Japan seized the islands at the outbreak of World War I, a possession legitimatized by a League of Nations mandate in 1920. In subsequent years, a cloak of secrecy descended on the Palaus. Japanese restrictions on foreign visitors to the group and to other Japanese-held possessions in the Pacific raised widespread suspicion that the islands were being fortified in direct violation of the original League mandate.

These suspicions appear to have been largely exaggerated, although a Marine lieutenant colonel who tried to investigate Japanese activity died under mysterious circumstances on Koror in 1923.[2] Considerable effort was expended to develop mineral resources and agriculture. Some attempts had been made to mine phosphate deposits in the islands, with mixed success. Harbors were dredged, roads improved and airfields built, all of which could double as military facilities in the event of war. However, aside from a seaplane ramp and an airfield, there appears to have been no attempt to construct fortifications or to position troops on the Palaus. This changed in 1939, as the Japanese decided to prepare their Pacific mandates for war. Military development of the Marshalls, Marianas and Carolines shifted into high gear.

Construction on Peleliu was limited to completion of the airfield started in 1938, a fuel storage area and improvements to the harbor. Even so, the island was hardly overdeveloped. Main roads ran up the east and west coasts from the airfield; they converged in the north and ran on to the village of Akalokul, site of a phosphate crushing plant and a hand-operated narrow-gauge railroad. On Ngardololok, off the eastern peninsula, the Japanese later set up a radio direction finder, a power plant and some miscellaneous military installations.

As war loomed, the Palaus were used as a base for reconnaissance missions and as a staging point for amphibious forces. In the early days of the war, a Japanese naval force from the Palaus attacked the Southern Philippines, and troops from the Palaus landed in the Central and Southern Philippines. In subsequent months, the Palaus served primarily as a staging and training area for Japanese troops passing through on their way to the south and southeast. Many of these troops ended up in New Guinea and the Solomons, where they encountered the 1st Marine Division in 1943.

However, by late 1943 the tenor of the war had changed. Now the United States was on the offensive. The great Japanese defensive perimeter had begun to crumble, with defeats in the Solomons, eastern New Guinea and the Aleutians. Pressed hard, the Japanese decided to move the fleet to the Palaus until more permanent facilities could be constructed in the Philippines. This plan was hastily scrapped when, on 30 and 31 March, U.S. carriers struck the Palaus, decimating Japanese airpower with the destruction of an estimated 160 planes in the air or on the ground and sowing mines in Kossol Passage.

Passing through Babelthuap, a stunned Japanese warrant officer confided to his diary, "The pathetic sight of our sunken warships in the harbor was enough to throw doubt on the future of the Imperial forces." His doubts were well-founded. Following the raids, the Combined Fleet stepped up its retirement to the Philippines. The Japanese Navy considered the Palaus as good as lost.

On the night of 11 August a low dark silhouette broke the surface off Peleliu, as the submarine USS *Burrfish* hove to offshore with a special reconnaissance team aboard. On her third war patrol, the *Burrfish*, commanded by Lieutenant Commander W. B. Perkins, had been lurking among the Palaus since 30 July. A combination of bright moonlight and very active Japanese radar had hindered the sub's activities. The closest scare came the night of 4 August, when an enemy plane came "out of the moon" and dropped a stick of three bombs which exploded not far from the surfaced sub.

Despite this Japanese activity, the *Burrfish* collected data on offshore currents, took photos of the beaches and marked visible enemy defenses. "No evidence of activity on the islands or beaches was noted," reported *Burrfish*. "All beaches observed were well covered with beach defenses consisting of barbed wire and sullies. What appeared to be sandbag pillboxes and other unidentified camouflaged positions were observed on the southeastern coast of Peleliu in the vicinity of the beaches."

Not until 11 August were conditions suitable to attempt an actual beach reconnaissance. UDT men Lieutenant (junior grade) M. R. Massey and Chief Howard Roeder picked their five-man boat teams as if choosing sides for a baseball game. Roedner, a gutsy Californian, cut high card for the right to make the first reconnaissance. He and three men swam in to the beaches on the southeastern shore, while the fifth team member tended the rubber raft just offshore.

The reconnaissance team returned safely with its report on beach defenses and other information. "This beach was found to be satisfactory for LVTs, DUKWs, and possibly LCTs," reported the team. "Any smaller landing craft would have difficulty in the surf." The swimmers also discovered that what appeared in photographs to be "sullies" were actually log supports for a smooth wire fence.

This proved to be the first and last reconnaissance landing on Peleliu. Plans to investigate other beaches were scrapped when Lieutenant Commander Perkins and Lieutenant C. E. Kirkpatrick, who was in charge of the special recon team, agreed the risks were too great to attempt another landing. Due to strong enemy radar activity, both felt there was less than a 50 percent chance of recovering the recon party if another mission was attempted.

Burrfish proceeded to Yap.[3] No further attempts were made to land reconnaissance parties on Peleliu.

Early U.S. intelligence on the Palaus was not good. There were no coast watcher or displaced Europeans to interview. Old navigational charts, a few reports dating back to the German occupation, a handful of old scenic photographs and a scattering of more or less random aerial observations conducted earlier in the war made up the bulk of available information. As late as April 1944, a joint Army/Navy intelligence study included the notation that "sources disagree as to the coastal outline of Peleliu Island."

Intelligence gathering on Peleliu began in a systematic fashion during the carrier strike against the Palaus on 30 and 31 March. Photographic coverage at this time was not considered adequate for planning purposes, so subsequent sorties were flown starting on 2 July and continuing into late August. Photographs included high- and low-level shots, both vertical and oblique.

Using this material, along with photos shot by the submarine USS *Seawolf* in late June, the 64th Engineer Topographical Battalion completed a map on a scale of 1:20,000. With a target-area grid superimposed, this became the standard map used during the Peleliu operation, some portions being blown up to 1:10,000 and 1:5,000 for the use of unit commanders operating ashore.

This map later came in for considerable criticism for reasons largely beyond the mapmakers' control. First Marine Division photo interpreters were unable to spot many ground installations. Heavy jungle growth obscured the incredibly rugged terrain north of the Japanese airfield—an oversight that would come back to haunt the Marines later—and there was no way of recognizing just how deeply the Japanese were dug in. According to the assistant division commander, photo interpreters listed no caves in their report; in fact, there were hundreds on Peleliu.

The map showed the southern part of the island to be generally flat, as was the lower pincer of Peleliu's "lobster claw." The airfield, completed only three years before the outbreak of the war, was well constructed with fighter and bomber strips of hard-packed coral with large turning circles and disposal areas. Just to the north of the airfield was a large sprawl of barracks, hangars, machine shops, a radio station and a large two-story administration building.

North of this zone, the ground appeared to rise sharply, but thick scrub jungle made it difficult to be certain of details. The eastern side of the airfield was bordered by a dense mangrove swamp; scrub jungle lay to the west and south. The northeastern peninsula—the shorter prong of the "lobster claw"—was also reasonably flat. A small village named Ngardololok contained a radio direction finder, power plant and other installations, all in the open and tastefully landscaped.

Planners were more concerned with the jungle-masked high ground to the north of the airfield. "There was never any question in the minds of the 1st Division planners but that the high ground north of the airfield was the key terrain feature of the island," recalled Assistant Division Commander O. P. Smith.

Despite this deduction, not a single defensive installation of any significance could be spotted in the area, although experience should have told the planners there were plenty of them. Profile photos taken by submarine confirmed the existence of the elevation but gave no reliable indication of its true height or ruggedness.[4] The area was finally drawn on the map as one generally continuous ridge line extending two thirds of the way up the upper pincer. At the northern end of the island were another enemy radio station, a recently abandoned phosphate refinery and several steep hills, one of which accommodated a radar installation.

Some 500 to 700 yards beyond Peleliu's northwestern tip were the smaller islands of Ngesebus and Kongauru, joined to the main island by a wooden causeway. Photo reconnaissance revealed the Japanese were building a fighter strip on Ngesebus.

Peleliu offered a number of possible landing beaches consisting of coarse coral sand, rubbly with much coral debris. The island was surrounded by a reef ranging from 400 yards to a mile wide on the western coast, but narrower on the east. Surf was usually light to moderate during the fall months. The mean range of the tides was from 3.3 to 3.9 feet.

Thanks to the fortunes of war and the Japanese penchant for keeping voluminous records, the enemy order of battle in the Palaus was no mystery to U.S. intelligence. Saipan, captured by two Marine and one army division in July, had been the headquarters of the Japanese 31st Army. Among the booty captured there was a major part of that organization's files, complete with an enemy intelligence officer to help explain the fine points.

Documents found in this trove "provided a source of information which may be unparalleled in future operations," exulted General Geiger's intelligence officer. Through these documents, U.S. intelligence was able to identify units stationed in the Palaus, determine their approximate numbers and glean enough clues to deduce their dispositions. Their information was later substantiated by the ULTRA intercept of a 28 July 1944 message sent by the Japanese 14th Division entitled "Disposition of Forces." The intercept also revealed the presence of a battalion-sized mobile reserve force on Koror, which could be used to reinforce the Peleliu garrison.

The combination of information proved almost uncannily accurate as far as Peleliu was concerned. U.S. intelligence missed only three minor units: a temporary mortar company, a machine cannon company and some sort of heavy rocket unit, all probably improvised on the spot from personnel detached from infantry units.

Defense of the Palaus rested primarily on the 14th Division, previously stationed in Manchuria and shifted to the island group while en route to New Guinea earlier in the year. The bulk of the division arrived at Koror on 24 April 1944, while a tank company and a heavy mortar outfit were diverted to the Marianas, where they were subsequently destroyed in the summer fighting with U.S. landing forces.

The 14th was no second-string organization. It was one of the oldest and finest units in the Japanese Army, with a long tradition dating back to the Sino-Japanese War (1894–95) and the Russo-Japanese War (1904–5), where it figured prominently in the seizure of Port Arthur, the most notable land campaign of the war. More recently, the 14th Division had formed part of the crack Kwangtung Army in Northern China. Made up of three infantry regiments—the 2d, 15th and 59th—its troops were experienced and morale was high. The division was recruited primarily from Ibaragi Prefecture on the coast north of Tokyo and mountainous Gumma Prefecture farther inland.

Commanding the 14th Division was Lieutenant General Sadae Inoue, who was also chief of the Palaus Sector Group, which included all the Palaus and Yap. Commissioned in 1908, Inoue had risen to the rank of colonel in command of a regiment by 1936. After the outbreak of war with China, he commanded units and served as a staff officer in Taiwan and northern China. He was promoted to lieutenant general in 1942, just over a year before receiving command of the 14th Division. Stable and competent if uninspired, Inoue would carry out his duties whatever happened.

Those duties were clear enough. Before leaving for the central Pacific, he and his brilliant chief of staff, Colonel Tokuchi Tada, met with the prime minister and War Minister Hideki Tojo in Tokyo to discuss plans for the defense of the Palaus. Simply stated, the major islands were to be defended to the death.

Inoue located his headquarters on Koror, long the administrative seat of the Palaus, just south of Babelthuap and 25 miles north of Peleliu. The bulk of his troops—estimated to total 35,000 in the Palaus, with another 8,000 on Yap—were stationed on the largest of the Palaus, Babelthuap. U.S. intelligence estimated that Inoue had about 25,000 men there, where the Japanese general later admitted he expected any major battle for the Palaus to be fought. To the south, Peleliu was garrisoned by an estimated 10,500 troops. Of these, approximately 6,500 were trained combat infantry.

Japanese units assigned to Peleliu included the 2d Infantry with mortar, signal and a tank unit with 17 light tanks; a battalion of the 15th Infantry; an infantry battalion of the 53d Independent Mixed Brigade; and various other elements. Naval forces on the island totaled 4,100, only 700 of whom were first-line combat troops; they included the 144th and 126th Antiaircraft units and the 45th Naval Guard Force. There were 1,400 naval air personnel, all of them maintenance men. The remaining 2,000 were labor troops, including an all-Japanese labor battalion, the rest composed largely of Koreans and Okinawans.

The Japanese had at least one battalion of 75 mm artillery and one mortar company with 81 mm mortars. The naval contingent possessed some large-caliber guns for defense, too. The Marines would also suffer considerable casualties from huge 155 mm mortars incorporated into the island's defense.

Command on Peleliu was held by Colonel Kunio Nakagawa of the 2d Infantry. He would prove to be a resourceful and dangerous enemy.

Detailed planning for the Peleliu assault began on 2 June, when the 1st Marine Division got the word from CiCPOA (Command in Chief Pacific Operations Area). More than the usual share of tactical planning fell on division headquarters. This was partly due to the drain of the Marianas campaign and partly to the long distance between division headquarters and Julian Smith's X-Ray Provisional Corps in Hawaii. Division Commander Major General William H. Rupertus being absent in Washington at the time, Assistant Division Commander Brigadier General Oliver P. Smith immediately got the planning stages underway.[5] A viable plan was ready by the time General Rupertus returned on 21 June.

Compiling the available information, planners ultimately considered four possible landing beaches:

(1) Purple Beach on the southeast coast offered the most natural advantages to a landing force. The fringing reef was only 200 yards wide off this area, and at one point it seemed possible to bring in vessels as large as LSTs. These assets were also clear to the Japanese, who had fortified the area with some of their strongest beach defenses, including three gun casements and numerous pillboxes. Also a drawback was the presence of a large mangrove swamp which limited egress from the beach area to the main island. The entrance to this swamp was covered by a 37 mm gun in still another casement.

(2) Scarlet Beach on the extreme south was seriously considered in conjunction with Orange Beach on the opposite shore. This proposal, the last alternative discarded, was abandoned when further information revealed the beach was dominated by fortified promontories and the reef between was crowded with concrete tetrahedrons and mines. A UDT lieutenant put the cap on any effort to land men or guns on Scarlet when he explained that pillboxes ringing the cove would make it suicidal for frogmen trying to carry out demolition work on the reef and for any force trying to land.

(3) Amber Beach on the northwestern peninsula had the disadvantage of a wide reef and possible enfilade from the northern outlying island of Ngesebus. The beach itself was dominated by high ground 100 to 300 yards inland and located far from the airfield, which was the primary objective of the assault.

(4) The last option was to land on the 2,200-yard-long White and Orange beaches on Peleliu's southwestern shore. Crossing the 700-yard reef, the Marines would drive straight across the island, quickly seizing the airfield and splitting the Japanese defense. This plan was ultimately chosen as the most sound since it would allow a landing on a wide front on ground suitable for the use of tanks. Once seized, the southern end of the island would provide room to emplace artillery, along with adequate beaches to bring in supplies.

It would not be easy. Enemy defenses along the southwestern shore included anti-boat guns protected by casements, pillboxes, anti-tank ditches, mines and barbed wire. General Rupertus originally intended to assault these defenses with two of his regiments, holding the third afloat in reserve. However, General Julian Smith, assault force commander, recommended stiffening the punch by landing all three regiments at once. An army regimental combat team from the 81st Infantry Division would be held in reserve.

As finally formulated, the planners decided to land the 1st Marine Division's three regimental combat teams abreast. The 1st Marines (code-named "Spitfire"), would land at the extreme left with one battalion on White 1, one on White 2 and one in regimental reserve. Driving inland and helping secure the upper part of the airfield, the regiment would pivot left and attack the high ground north of the airfield.

The 5th Marines ("Lonewolf") would land in the center on beaches Orange 1 and Orange 2. The battalion on the left would tie in with the 1st Marines; the other would push straight across Peleliu to the eastern shore. The support battalion was scheduled to land at H plus 1. Passing between the first two battalions, it would attack across the southern end of the airfield, then join in a turning movement to the north. Once the airfield had been seized, the 5th Marines would clean up the flat northeastern pincer and the small outlying islands.

At the southern end of the beachhead, the 7th Marines ("Mustang"), leaving their 2d Battalion aboard ship as a floating division reserve, would land at Orange 3 with 3/7 in the van, followed by 1/7. They would push to Peleliu's eastern shore on the flank of the 5th Marines, then turn south and mop up Japanese units cut off on the southern end of the island.

It was clear, even in the planning stages, that the 1st Marines had drawn the toughest assignment with the mission to push inland and seize the high ground just beyond White 1 and 2. So long as the Japanese held the dominating ridges, the Marines on the low ground would remain vulnerable to large-caliber guns. However, it was assumed that the 7th Marines would finish mopping up southern Peleliu on the first day of the assault and could then be thrown in to stiffen the 1st Marines in the attack to the north. Plans also called for Marine artillery to land quickly and be prepared to mass fire on the ridges north of the airfield.

Meanwhile, in corps reserve would be a regimental combat team of the 81st Infantry Division. This outfit, nicknamed the "Wildcat Division" while serving in France during the First World War, had yet to see action in World War II but was considered well trained and capable. It was commanded by 51-year-old General Paul Mueller, a 1915 graduate of West Point who had won the Silver Star as a battalion commander in France during World War I. Later referred to by Douglas MacArthur as "brilliant," Mueller also inspired respect and affection and had done a fine job of getting his division in shape for combat.

The 81st would seize Angaur, seven miles off Peleliu's southern tip, but only after the situation on Peleliu was clearly under control. The Navy had previously suggested seizing Angaur first, but this was scrapped for fear the Japanese would then be given time to reinforce Peleliu from the northern islands. Only about half the size of Peleliu, Angaur was believed to be defended by two Japanese battalions—about 2,500 men. If all went as hoped, the 81st would throw two regimental combat teams against the Angaur garrison soon after the 1st Marine Division hit Peleliu. On the other hand, if things went badly on Peleliu, the Wildcats would be committed to help the Marines.

At least one Marine seemed confident that this exigency would never come to pass. The balding but dapper 1st Marine Division commander, William Rupertus, 55, was predicting a quick victory. An old China hand with 30 years experience in the Corps, he had served as assistant division commander in Guadalcanal, succeeding to command of the 1st Marine Division in July 1943 in time for the campaign on New Britain. He was also a personal friend of former 1st Division commander, now Marine Corps Commandant General A. A. Vandergrift, who had picked him as his assistant before the division shipped out for the Pacific and who thought highly of his energy and ability. There were those who thought Vandergrift was grooming his protégé to one day succeed him as commandant.

Many of Rupertus's subordinates were less enthralled with their leader. They had come to know their neatly mustachioed commander as a moody individual, prone to sometimes fickle behavior in his relationships with his officers. There were those who thought this moodiness stemmed from the loss of his wife and two daughters in a scarlet fever epidemic in China years before. Whatever the case, he seems to have inspired little personal loyalty from his subordinates, some of whom referred to him as "Rupe the Stupe" or "Rupe the Dupe." His critics also questioned whether his performance had really merited the Navy Cross he received for leadership in the Solomons campaign or the Distinguished Service Medal he was awarded for Cape Gloucester.

During maneuvers in preparation for the Peleliu campaign, Rupertus had broken his ankle when he fell out of an amtrac, but his optimism remained strongly intact. He expected to take Peleliu in a matter of a few days. Only three lines marked the operational maps, so certain was he of a quick campaign.

One evening, General Rupertus stopped by the tent of Colonel Lewis "Chesty" Puller, the 46-year-old commander of the 1st Marines, who would take on the toughest part of the initial assault. "Lewie," said Rupertus expansively, "you should make general on Peleliu. It's tailored for you. Your performance of duty should bring you another Navy Cross and a brigadier's star, too."

Puller, a three-time Navy Cross winner, had joined the Marine Corps in 1918, before most of the men he now commanded were even born. Colorful, aggressive, outspoken and unquestionably brave, he still carried a piece of steel in his leg, courtesy of a Japanese artillery shell on Guadalcanal. No one would expect him to back down from anybody or anything. But Rupertus's brimming optimism worried Puller. The reason was numbers. The safe ratio for an amphibious assault was generally conceded to be three invaders to one defender. There were 17,490 troops organic to the 1st Marine Division. With the addition of 10,994 troops, the reinforced division would field a total of 28,484 men, bringing the ratio of Marines to Japanese close to the optimum 3:1. What the statistics did not reveal, however, was that of those 28,484 Marines, only about 9,000 were combat infantrymen. The rest were specialists, added to handle the many complexities of a modern amphibious assault.

General Rupertus could expand as he pleased, but Puller did not like those odds.

Puller was not the only Marine officer to question Rupertus's brash optimism. Also among the skeptics was the assistant commander of the 1st Marine Division, Brigadier General Oliver P. Smith. A quiet, gentlemanly Californian, Smith, at age 50, was known for his brains. He had been an instructor at the Marine Corps School in Quantico, attended the Ecole Superieur de Guerre in Paris and served as executive officer, Plans and Policies, before being sent to the Pacific, where he commanded the 5th Marines on Cape Gloucester. He had been appointed assistant division commander in April 1944 and had yet to enter a campaign in that capacity.

Smith's relations with Rupertus were not close. "I was never consulted about anything tactical, or anything like that," he recalled. "I went around, inspected the training, and periodically I'd come in and tell the general what I saw. Our relations weren't buddy-buddy, but there was no bitterness or anything like that." Now, though he doubted Rupertus's projections, which he termed "very, very optimistic," he was obviously in no position to try to temper that optimism.

Also dubious was IIIPhib commander General Roy Geiger. Almost 60 years old by the time of the Peleliu operation, Geiger's main experience was in aviation, but he was equally qualified to handle large ground units in combat. Famed for his frigid "twenty-foot stare" and inevitable cigar, he was described as "thickset, poker-faced, chilly-eyed . . . a Marine's Marine."

Wrapped up with the Guam operation, Geiger did not assume command of IIIPhib until 15 August. By then, judging from what he had seen on Guam and from the type of opposition encountered on Saipan, he felt General Rupertus's optimism was misplaced. Among his main concerns was the small size of the division reserve for the Peleliu assault: one lone rifle battalion. Ironically, the original plan drawn up by X-Ray called for all three

Marine regiments to land abreast, with one regimental combat team of the 81st Division in division reserve. This was the setup favored by Expeditionary Forces Commander General Julian Smith.

General Rupertus, however, showed a "marked reluctance" to rely on army troops, so the reserve was reduced to one battalion of the 7th Marines. This decision was made palatable only by the fact that a Wildcat regiment had been assigned to corps reserve, and it was agreed that the 81st Division would not hit Angaur until the situation on Peleliu was well in hand. Though not one of Rupertus's biggest fans, Geiger decided not to interfere for the time being. The plan was adopted by IIIPhib and confirmed as a corps order.

In fact, it was not a bad plan. Attacking inland over the flat ground, the Marines would be able to employ their tanks, quickly overrun the southern part of the island and obtain plenty of maneuvering room for the division as well as for artillery. Seizing both coasts would provide multiple points to unload the materiel needed to feed the assault.

Once the critical airfield had been seized—on the first day, if all went according to schedule—the 2nd Marine Air Wing (MAW) would bring in its aircraft from Espiritu Santu in the Northern Solomons. Scheduled to land with the assault units at Peleliu were the ground echelons of Marine Squadron 114 (VMF–114), VMF–121, VMF–122 and Marine Night Fighter Squadron 541—VMF(N)–541—of Marine Air Group 11 (MAG–11). Other units would be flown in as soon as practicable, followed by wing headquarters.

The only obvious drawback to the assault plan was that the Marines would be attacking across low ground dominated by guns in the Japanese-held ridges. Marine planners had accepted this risk in the belief that the 7th Marines would quickly seize southern Peleliu and then be available to beef up the assault on the high ground. Seizure of the southern part of the island was expected to take only one day.

NOTES

1. These plans followed an acrimonious debate between the Navy, which proposed bypassing the Philippines in favor of invading Formosa, and General Douglas MacArthur, who insisted upon reoccupying the Philippines. President Roosevelt ultimately decided in favor of MacArthur.

2. The Marine officer was the brilliant, but eccentric, Lieutenant Colonel Earl Ellis, who predicted the details of a Japanese attack on the United States with startling accuracy—20 years before Pearl Harbor. Traveling as a businessman, he died on Koror in 1923; whether he was murdered by the Japanese, committed suicide or died of alcoholism has never been satisfactorily established.

3. During a beach reconnaissance the night of 18 August on Gagil Tomil in the Yap group, three UDT men, including Chief Roeder, failed to return to the raft. It was later discovered they had been captured. Sent to Peleliu, they remained there

until 2 September, when they were placed aboard a Japanese subchaser for transfer to the Philippines. Nothing more was ever heard of them.

4. There is some evidence that more detailed information failed to filter down to the division, possibly because of the considerable geographical distance between X-Ray in Hawaii and the 1st Division on Pavuvu, the speed of the planning and the fact that the bulk of the planning was done on the divisional, rather than corps level.

5. The general's absence at such a critical time has been cause for some speculation. It appears that his close friend Commandant A. A. Vandergrift appointed Rupertus temporarily to minor duty stateside to give him a chance to visit with his new wife and infant son.

Chapter 2

Nearly 1,600 miles from Guadalcanal, General Sadae Inoue was prepared to make any U.S. assault on the Palaus as costly as possible. His orders from Superior Headquarters were blunt: "The islands must be held to the very last as the first position barring the enemy from penetrating the Pacific. Peleliu and Angaur must be fortified as important air bases."

Ironically, following the American capture of the Marianas and the northern coast of New Guinea, strategists at Imperial General Headquarters recognized the possibility that the enemy might bypass the Palaus altogether and proceed directly to the Philippines. Some thought was apparently given to evacuating General Inoue's men from the Palaus, but sufficient shipping was not available, and the idea had to be abandoned. In any event, prowling submarines would have made any withdrawal an expensive proposition at best. The 14th Division would stay where it was, and if the Americans invaded, it would do its duty and fight to the death.

As the summer wore on, this possibility seemed more and more likely. An American carrier strike in mid-July was followed by stepped-up attacks by land-based aircraft during August. B–24s of the U.S. 5th Air Force had begun a concerted effort to pulverize Japanese defenses throughout the Palaus. Night flights from 8 August through 14 September dumped 912 tons of fragmentation and incendiary bombs on the island chain. Beginning on 25 August, American bombers based in New Guinea and the Admiralties took on Japanese fighters and heavy flak in daylight runs over the target.

One of these air raids caught General Inoue on an inspection tour of Peleliu, his second since the 14th Division arrived in the Palaus. He had just finished circling the island by barge when U.S. planes struck. "From the northern end of the island, I saw smoke rising from the airfield sector," he recalled. "I landed on the north side and immediately went to the airfield to ascertain the damage. The naval headquarters had suffered a direct hit, and all of the navy staff officers had been wounded...the fuel depot had been hit and was burning fiercely, blackening the sky with smoke." Inoue, who was not injured in the raid, left Peleliu the next morning.

In 394 sorties, the bombers dropped nearly 800 tons of explosives on Japanese defenses, while "we hid in the shelters like field mice," recalled a warrant officer on the receiving end of the raids. Over 500 buildings in Koror Town, General Inoue's headquarters, were completely flattened. By 5 September, U.S. reconnaissance found only a dozen enemy fighters, 12 float planes and three observation planes still in the Palaus. Enemy airfields were so badly cratered that only a major overhaul could put them back into operation, even if aircraft were available to use them.

U.S. ships and aircraft also made a concerted effort to destroy enemy ships, barges, and sampans which might be used to reinforce the garrisons on Peleliu and Angaur. A Japanese antiaircraft crewman passing through Babelthuap expressed shock at the destruction. "When I saw the ships that had been sunk within the harbor and the area containing the warehouses along the piers that had been turned into a wasteland, I felt very conscious of how fighting was nearing the mainland of Japan," he confided to his diary.

On 3 September, Inoue's superiors in Southern Army Command Head-quarters in Manila alerted the Palaus garrison that an American invasion could take place any time. Inoue alerted his troops, although five days later he conceded that the American carrier strikes might be a diversion to distract attention from a pending assault on another target.

If the Americans came, General Inoue expected the main battle for the Palaus to be fought at Babelthuap, with secondary thrusts at some of the more important islands. The invaders would find that the Japanese had discarded the basic tactical doctrine used previously in Pacific island fighting. The original doctrine had called for an all-out defense of the beaches to defeat an amphibious landing. However, under the tremendous punishment of American pre-invasion shelling and bombardment, this tactic had been consistently unsuccessful. More recently, the Japanese experience on Biak Island and on Saipan had persuaded planners to adopt an alternative strat-egy. At both those battles the Japanese defenders had preserved most of their strength to fight from dug-in positions inland. The battles had been prolonged, and American casualties had risen sharply.

As a result of that experience, Imperial General Headquarters issued a new procedure for combating enemy amphibious assaults. Delaying actions would be fought on the beaches, but the bulk of the defense would be located inland, beyond the heaviest smash of American naval gunfire. The defense would be organized in depth, and reserves would be used for con-ventional counterattacks, rather than the blind banzais the U.S. Marines had consistently chopped to bits with their superior firepower.

On 11 July, General Inoue issued a directive titled "Palau Sector Group

Training for Victory." Postwar evidence indicates the document was mainly the work of his able chief of staff, Colonel Tokechi Tada, considered one of the most capable staff officers in the Imperial Army. Stripped of its bombast, the document outlined a practical means for conducting a determined defense, based in large part on the lessons learned on Saipan.

The directive took for granted that Japanese soldiers were willing—even eager—to sacrifice their lives for the Emperor, but noted that it was important to preserve personnel and ordnance. Dying was not enough. "The ultimate goal of this training is to minimize our losses in severe enemy pre-landing naval and aerial bombardment and, on the very night of the enemy landing, to take advantage of the fact that their equipment is not yet fully consolidated to destroy their bridgehead in one blow," it stated.

American naval and air bombardment was powerful—but had limitations, emphasized the directive. By taking advantage of the terrain and lulls in the bombardment, casualties could be kept to a minimum. "It is most advantageous to be able to repel groups of landing craft before their arrival at the beach by means of strongly prepared beach positions, but we cannot expect to accomplish this completely," it conceded. Strong, well-organized counterattacks would be launched. Japanese troops in overrun positions should "lead the enemy to destruction and confusion by concentrating rapidly disappearing firepower in his midst, even though partially trampled underfoot by landings."

American material power was great, but proper discipline could negate much of that power. "The only fearful thing next to great physical power is the psychological effect upon ignorant and inexperienced personnel," declared Inoue.

In a dugout on Peleliu, an anonymous Japanese soldier posted a sign found many weeks later by U.S. Marines. "Defense to the death," he wrote. "We will build a barrier across the Pacific with our bodies."

25 AUGUST 1944

The 1st Marine Division was moving out. Down through Pavuvu's coconut groves, the sweating men filed two by two, bent forward under the weight of their battle gear. "Most of us were silent," recalled Captain George Hunt, "but a few were talking in subdued tones." At the beach, a snarl of trucks and tanks and tractors sent up a deafening roar. Men pointed and beckoned, invectives going unheard in the din. Soon the tangle would straighten itself out, and the troops would board ship.

Despite the lack of talk, the mood among the Marines was upbeat. Scuttlebutt that the campaign would be quick contributed to the general optimism. There was also the irrepressible optimism of youth. The Marines were young: at least 80 percent were between 18 and 25, with the average

age probably about 20 among the combat infantrymen. More than a few had no real need for the razors in their packs.

At the other end of the spectrum were the old-timers like Gunnery Sergeant Elmo "Pop" Haney, who had fought in France in World War I. Haney was pure "Old Corps": a young enlisted man recalled pausing in wide-eyed awe in the shower as Haney nonchalantly scoured his testicles with a stiff-bristled GI brush, an instrument more conventionally applied to floors and web gear. "I felt that he was not a man born of woman," recalled the private, "but that God had issued him to the Marine Corps."

Few had Haney's vast experience, but even with rotations home, 30 percent of the division had been overseas two years or more and served through the previous two campaigns. Another 30 percent had 12 months and one campaign; the rest were replacements in various stages of seasoning.

Leading these men were two of the most famous regimental COs in the Corps, along with a third of great potential. Heading up the 1st Marines was Chesty Puller, a Virginian of blunt speech and a no-nonsense, straight-ahead approach to combat—an approach that had already earned him three Navy Crosses and a reputation for complete fearlessness. Somewhat odd looking physically—one officer compared him to the cartoon character Snuffy Smith—he inspired fierce loyalty from his men.

The 7th Marines was also led by a strong-jawed mustang of wide experience, Lieutenant Colonel H. H. Hanneken. Then 51, "Hard-Hearted" or "Hot-Headed" Hanneken, as he was sometimes called, was also Old Corps. He had won the Medal of Honor as a sergeant in Haiti in 1919 for almost single-handedly penetrating guerrilla territory and killing Charlemagne Peralte, a key rebel leader. Older than most of his fellows and less flamboyant than Puller, Hanneken tended to be stoic and unsmiling, but he was equally fearless and a fine leader of troops.

Commanding the 5th Marines, Colonel Harold D. "Bucky" Harris was the youngest of the three regimental COs and the only one to have graduated from Annapolis. More cerebral than the others, he had attended the Ecole Superieur de Guerre in Paris and served in intelligence and as executive officer of the 1st Marines on New Britain before receiving command of the 5th Marines just before Peleliu. His leadership there would show him to be a commander who valued his men over medals and spent their lives as frugally as possible.

Qualitative differences between the three regiments were minimal at best, but in the assistant division commander's estimation, Puller's 1st Marines was the most aggressive of the three regiments, followed by the 5th and then the 7th.

By 26 August veteran and rookie alike were loaded aboard ship. Final rehearsals were held off Cape Esperance on 27 and 29 August. Assistant Division Commander Smith had originally chosen another site, an island off the coast of Malaita, as being more suitable for the rehearsals, but the

Australian government objected to its use because the natives would have to be moved. The Marines had to settle for Cape Esperance.

Unable to get into the boat because of his broken ankle, General Rupertus remained on board ship while Smith took the troops ashore and set up a command post. IIIPhib Commander Roy Geiger came by and inquired, "Where is Rupertus?" Smith told him about the general's broken ankle. Geiger was not pleased. "If I had known, I'd have relieved him," he remarked. Smith, who had previously checked with the doctor in charge, said the general's ankle was expected to mend sufficiently over the next two weeks to permit him to carry on with the use of a cane.

The first rehearsal, on 27 August, was marred by communications snafus, but the second, on 29 August, went smoothly—so smoothly, noted Smith, that a critique held at IIIPhib headquarters the next day produced little constructive input because "everybody was pleased with everyone else." Following the rehearsals, the convoy stood off Tetere Beach, while the 81st Division, which had staged out of Hawaii on 12 August and assembled in the area by 26 August, rehearsed on Tassafaronga for its assault on Angaur. On 4 September, LSTs sailed for Peleliu, 2,100 miles to the north. The faster transports followed later.

The preparations had not been problem free. Combat loading had been hampered by lack of facilities, logistics mix-ups and lack of experience among certain naval officers involved in the procedure. In one instance, Marine logistics officers experienced considerable difficulty persuading the tank-landing ship commander to permit "understowage"—stowing equipment in the tank decks as opposed to lashing it topside. While commonplace in Central Pacific operations, the flotilla commander had apparently never heard of it. Only reluctantly did he finally allow items such as rations, barbed wire, pickets and ammo to be stowed below.

Far more serious was the lack of shipping to carry the 1st Division's tanks. Only two 458-foot LSDs (Landing Ship Dock) were provided. Able to carry only 30 tanks between them, this meant 16 had to be left behind. Their absence would be sorely felt in the upcoming fighting.

Equipment shortages were also a major headache. Shortages of amphibian tractors, pack-type flamethrowers, demolitions, bazookas and BARs, spare machine-gun barrels, engineering equipment, spare parts and waterproofing material had been problems right up to the last moment. Lack of space forced engineers and Seabees to leave much road-building and construction equipment behind.

In other instances, what supplies were furnished turned out to be second-rate. Some assault units found that belts of machine-gun ammunition had rotted, powder rings on mortar shells had deteriorated and bourelets rusted, shotgun shells had swollen from moisture. All ammunition had to be unstowed, inspected and much of it replaced and restowed at the last minute.

A full allowance of new dry-cell batteries for the vital TBX radios was also found to be dead. Fortunately, these were replaced the same day.

Yet another difficulty was the 1st Marine Division's lack of experience assaulting a fortified island surrounded by reef. Its previous experience had been almost entirely in jungle fighting on Guadalcanal and Cape Gloucester. Few officers of the division had so much as laid eyes on the newly developed LVT-A "amphibian tank" which had been used in Central Pacific combat. In July it had been decided to form another amphibian tractor battalion in addition to the one already organic to the division. A new armored amphibian battalion was also hastily thrown together. Both organizations suffered severely from a lack of equipment and trained personnel. Some of the men were reduced to makeshift training in Army DUKWs.

All knew the amtracs would be crucial to the assault. In the planning for Peleliu, Marine officers were haunted by the specter of the 2d Marine Division's experience on Tarawa the year before. Like Peleliu, Tarawa had been a small, heavily fortified island protected by reef. Over 3,000 Marines had been killed or wounded in that assault, many because a shortage of amtracs forced the landing waves to wade in over the reef under enemy fire. The 1st Marine Division profited from that hard lesson. At Peleliu, the assault riflemen would all go in over the reef by amtrac. Nevertheless, casualties were not expected to be negligible. Corporal Russell Clay recalled, "When we were having our little critique before the operation, the company commander said, 'Well, we're expecting about 50 percent casualties.' What you'd do is look at your buddy, and he'd look at you, and you'd be thinking, 'Which one of us?' "

The goal of Peleliu was to get 4,500 infantrymen ashore in 19 minutes. The method, following standard operating procedure as developed in central Pacific assaults, was a model of careful planning and logistics. The amphibian tractors (LVTs), which would carry the troops, were loaded onto LSTs along with the armored amphibians (LVT-As), which would lead the troops ashore, holding down resistance with fire from their snub-nosed 75 mm guns. New LVT(4)s with the ramp in the rear (first used at Saipan the previous June) gave more protection to disembarking troops and also made it possible to land 75 mm pack howitzers fully assembled and ready for action. Army amphibian trucks equipped with A-frame unloading devices capable of handling a 105 mm howitzer were also assigned to the landing force. Some cargo had been palletized, a system that yielded mixed results. Pontoon barges bearing cranes would also facilitate the unloading. Six LSTs were to arrive with 175-foot causeways attached, one on each side. When the beach was secure, these would be assembled to form a dry roadway across the reef to deep water, permitting trucks to unload directly from the LSTs.

At Saipan, tanks had landed too late to provide much-needed support to the initial assault troops; at Peleliu, the process would be speeded up. Water-proofed tanks would be shuttled in to the edge of the reef on LCTs, then proceed under their own power to the beach, where they would provide immediate fire support to the infantry. Two hospital transports, armed and claiming no immunity, would be present offshore to take care of the wounded, with four regular hospital ships to arrive as soon as practicable. Three barges at the transfer control line would supply amtracs with gasoline and lubricating oil. Nine others would act as floating supply dumps for water, rations, ammunition and flamethrower fuel.

Among the innovations to be used by the division were amphibious trailers, in quantity for the first time. Fitted with wheels and a watertight metal cover, a trailer could be unloaded from a ship into the water, where it would float. It could then be pulled ashore by tanks, bulldozers, LVTs, DUKWs or other vehicles. About 60 of these trailers were used at Peleliu, loaded mostly with high-expenditure items such as mortar and machine-gun ammunition, flamethrower fuel, medical supplies, signal equipment and similar gear. As it turned out, the trailers were of more limited use than had been hoped, since their low freeboard made reloading at the ship's side impracticable.

The amphibious assault itself would guide on five imaginary lines. Farthest to sea, 18,000 yards offshore, was the transport line, where the ships would halt on D-Day. Next was the initial LST unloading line, where LSTs would pause to discharge small boats with the wave commanders. These would then lead the LSTs to the LST launching line 6,000 yards from the beach. Here the LSTs would open their doors to let out the troop-carrying amtracs. The amtracs would rendezvous at the line of departure 4,000 yards offshore, where the assault waves would gather for the 30-minute trip to the beach. The fifth line, 2,000 yards from the beach, was the transfer control line, where empty amtracs would return after discharging their troops to pick up more men and supplies from small boats.

Two new weapons had also been introduced to the 1st Marine Division in time for Peleliu. One was the U.S. Navy Mark I flamethrower, capable of shooting a jet of blazing napalm 150 yards for 80 seconds. Three of these flamethrowers were mounted on LVTs, with a fourth LVT detailed as a supply carrier for the napalm mixture. Expected to be useful primarily against beach pillboxes in the initial assault, they would actually prove of even greater value during the subsequent fighting inland.

The other new weapon, a 60 mm shoulder mortar adapted to fire from a light machine-gun mount, proved less useful. Designed for flat trajectory fire against pillboxes and cave openings, it was heavy, had a vicious recoil and more or less duplicated the function of the more manageable bazooka. The severe recoil, which made it necessary to replace the gunner after two to four rounds, was highly unpopular with the men who tried it. Twenty-seven were issued to the division for testing purposes.

One other change involved exchanging carbines in the infantry units for rifles and submachine guns. It was generally felt among the infantry battalions that the carbine was an adequate substitute for a pistol, but not for an M–1 rifle with bayonet. Unfortunately, the switch could not be carried out immediately due to shortages of rifles and machine guns.

Meanwhile, any doubts the men might have had about the pending campaign seemed to be lifted by General Rupertus, still upbeat following a critique of the rehearsals at the movie area on Guadalcanal shortly before the division left for Peleliu. "We're going to have some casualties," he conceded, "but let me assure you this is going to be a short one, a quickie. Rough but fast. We'll be through in three days. It might only take two." He expected his men to bring him the sword of the Japanese commander on Peleliu, he concluded.

"It wasn't really a critique at all, it was a pep talk," recalled a staff officer. Nevertheless, the general's optimism was contagious. The news spread quickly. Three days, maybe two. Rough but fast.

Only the more pensive—or morbid—would recall the scene along the beach road on Pavuvu as the division embarked. There, near the engineers' carpenter shop, stood long lines of simple white crosses, all stacked up to be loaded aboard ship. Now, those crosses were stowed away somewhere in the convoy headed toward Peleliu, and they were not being carried just for ballast.

The duty of transporting and protecting the landing force en route to the Palaus fell upon Admiral Bull Halsey's Third Fleet. It was not a minor responsibility. In addition to transport and protection, the fleet was responsible for furnishing naval gunfire and air support, along with related missions such as supplying the troops ashore after the beachhead was seized. Before Stalemate II ended, every major command in the Pacific would participate. The operation eventually involved 800 vessels, 1,600 aircraft and an estimated 250,000 Army, Navy and Marine personnel.

As the largest naval amphibious assault up to that time in the Pacific, the assault force alone included 14 battleships, 16 carriers, 20 escort carriers, 22 cruisers, 136 destroyers and 31 destroyer escorts in addition to numerous types of landing craft and service ships—not counting the support ships designed for the 31st Infantry Division's landing on Morotai. Supplying this huge collection of men and ships strained the logistical support of all Allied commands.

To fulfill all his varied missions, Halsey divided the 3d Fleet into two parts. He retained direct control over the Covering Forces and Special Groups (TF–30). Vice Admiral Theodore S. Wilkinson assumed command of the 3d Amphibious Force (TF–31). Wilkinson's force was further divided into the Eastern Attack Force (TF–33), to provide direct support for the Yap-Ulithi assaults, and the Western Attack Force (TF–32), to cover the

Peleliu and Angaur operation. Command of TF–32 was delegated to Admiral George H. Fort.

The Navy had learned much over the past two years about delivering massed fire during amphibious assaults. For the Peleliu operation, Admiral Jesse Oldendorf's fire support group boasted considerable muscle, including the battleships *Maryland, Idaho, Mississippi* and *Pennsylvania*, along with the heavy cruisers *Louisville, Portland* and *Indianapolis*, the light cruiser *Honolulu* and nine destroyers. Air units would be provided mainly by Rear Admiral Ralph Ofstie's escort carriers; there would be as many as 11 or as few as seven of these baby flattops, depending upon the day.

Plans called for the bombardment of preselected targets to begin on 12 September. Naval gunfire would concentrate on aircraft, airfields, gun positions and enemy troop concentrations. On D-Day, gunfire would concentrate on beach defenses from the "low water line to 400 yards inland" until ordered to lift as the Marine assault waves went in. Minesweepers would clear Kossol Passage to the north and the gap between Peleliu and Angaur on 13 and 14 September. At the same time, UDT teams would clear the beach approaches. Then it would be up to the Marines.

General Inoue was not leaving everything to exhortations and paper directives. The 10,000-odd men on Peleliu had been tunneling into the ground like moles ever since arriving on the island in April. "Day in and day out, all we do is dig," wrote a Japanese warrant officer. The remaining natives on Peleliu and Angaur had been evacuated.

Colonel Nakagawa could have entertained few illusions about the odds he would face in any U.S. invasion of Peleliu. As his superior, General Inoue, subsequently testified, "It was estimated that at least three American divisions would land on either the southern or the eastern beaches."

Whichever beaches the Americans landed on, they would encounter stiff resistance. Nakagawa had divided the island into four sectors, each manned by a reinforced battalion with another in reserve. Practice in advancing under actual bombardment had been conducted during American air raids to reinforce his men's confidence and to prepare them so they could be deployed to bolster the defense at any threatened point, even under heavy naval gunfire.

Detailed plans for counterattacks had been rehearsed, some involving special units. A few companies had been reorganized as special counterattack units. One had been trained to swim out and destroy landing craft with mines and grenades. An infantry platoon had been trained to ride the garrison's 17 tanks into combat. Special two- and three-man infantry close-combat teams were organized to infiltrate and destroy lucrative targets such as tanks, amtracs, and mortars.

All potential landing beaches had also been heavily mined, the belts extending as far as 100 yards inland. Over 1,300 horned anti-invasion mines were placed along the beaches, supplemented by aerial bombs rigged with pressure detonator plates. Anti-boat and antitank obstacles were constructed, antitank ditches dug and artillery meticulously registered on the reef and beach areas.

The southwestern beaches, where the Marine assault was to land, were fairly typical of the enemy's plan to defend in depth. Tetrahedrons were placed offshore along with barbed wire to impede troops, boats and amphibious tanks. Over 300 single- and double-horned mines were laid. The beaches and their exits were choked with tangles of barbed wire and liberally placed mines. Long antitank ditches were dug parallel to the beach, covered by reinforced concrete pillboxes and gun casements mounting 37 mm or 47 mm anti-boat and antitank guns.

Rifle pits and pillboxes were constructed to house two or three infantrymen. Further inland, other pillboxes and defensive positions were built. One steel and reinforced-concrete blockhouse had as many as 16 mutually supporting automatic weapons. Observers could call down artillery and mortar fire from positions in the ridges. Among those weapons was a 75 mm mountain gun which commanded the entire southern part of the island.

On the high ground between White 2 and Orange 1, two casements and a large number of pillboxes were positioned so they could lay down fire on both beaches. Most of these works were in defilade from the sea, including two casements which had been built 30 yards apart and could fire south on Orange Beach and north on White. A Japanese sergeant who survived the battle recalled, "We spent many days and nights constructing the pillboxes, although the thickness of the cement was not up to expectations due to lack of manpower and machinery."

Pillboxes and bunkers also protected the airfield, along with a more peculiar defense: scarecrows. Apparently designed to draw enemy fire, the scarecrows were made of coconut fronds with a coconut stuck on top as a "head"—the nut just visible over the edge of the trench parapet.

Finally, the Japanese took advantage of the upheaved coral and warren of natural caves. This terrain, later described by a Marine veteran as "a monster Swiss cheese, pocked beyond imagination with caves and crevices," was ideal for defense. There were literally hundreds of cave positions: months later, after heavy fighting, a U.S. survey would locate over 500 caves still recognizable as such. Improved by hand and by blasting, these positions ranged from crevices small enough to shield a single sniper to huge caverns large enough to house a battalion among its stalactites and stalagmites.

Cave types W and J were intended to shelter troops and reserves located in the interior valleys; I, L, T and U caves were smaller, designed for combat and clustered together for mutual support. When feasible, caves were built with two or more staggered levels. Multiple entrances, cleverly camouflaged, were provided with sharp turns or niches to protect occupants from concussion and direct fire. The caverns were filled with food and ammunition, and receptacles were built to catch water dripping from stalactites. Caves for mortars and supplies were located on reverse slopes; caves for artillery, some fitted with steel doors, were located on the forward slopes of the southern, western and eastern ridges. Many positions, particularly those sited in sheer cliff faces, were inaccessible to infantry assault and strong enough to withstand even a direct artillery hit.

Caves constructed by naval troops far surpassed army caves in size and complexity, although they lacked the army's careful attention to interlocking defense. Aided by the 214th Naval Construction Battalion, composed of men who had been miners and tunnel workers in civilian life, their caves were large with cross tunnels and saps off the sides to protect the occupants. Hollowed out of the coral limestone, they usually measured ten feet across and six feet high. Some had separate rooms for food, ammunition and living quarters and were equipped with electric lights, ventilation systems and wooden floors. There were eight separate types in all, with the H and E designs used for the larger caves.

With the exception of a few navy caves constructed near army positions for liaison, most of the naval installations were located in the northern part of the island. Among these was the most sophisticated cave installation on Peleliu, a series of intersecting H caves over 500 feet long with five laterals and multiple entrances in three directions, located on the nose of the island's northernmost ridge. On 3 September, when the 1st Marine Division prepared to sail for Peleliu, there were over a thousand men housed in this huge installation, according to subsequent testimony by a Japanese POW.

The difference in cave styles was indicative of a more serious rift between the army and navy, a lack of cooperation that plagued the Japanese throughout the Pacific war. This rivalry was especially bitter in the Palaus, in part because the island group had originally been a naval base. As army troops flooded in and took control, resentment rose among naval personnel.

The lack of cooperation between the services was reflected in the failure to coordinate defenses. The navy refused to release civilian labor for work on army defenses. The navy also declined to make their installations available to General Inoue, which meant army troops had to work that much harder to get their defenses in order before the anticipated invasion. The rift was even more pronounced on Peleliu, where the army commander, Colonel Nakagawa, was outranked by the chief of Peleliu's naval detachment, Vice Admiral Seiichi Itou.

U.S. forces were to learn very little about Nakagawa in the months to come. Extant photos, taken while he was still a staff officer, show a heavyset man in his late 30s, not markedly different from thousands of other Japanese officers. What the pictures do not reveal is that he was considered perhaps the most talented regimental commander in the 14th Division—and possibly in the whole Japanese Army, according to Inoue. General Inoue greatly respected Nakagawa's ability, which is why he gave him responsibility for Peleliu and its valuable airfield, but Nakagawa was severely handicapped by Vice Admiral Itou, who seems to have pulled rank at every opportunity. The admiral's lack of cooperation was summed up by one of the few Japanese to survive the campaign, Second Lieutenant Ei Yamaguchi, who said in a sarcastic commentary on the lengths they had to go to coax supplies from their navy counterparts, "The building materials were rich in the navy area, the army units bowing three times and then nine times received it."

Finally, in July, Inoue sent General Kenjior Murai to Peleliu in the capacity of "tactical adviser" and liaison. Murai, 53, was considered an expert on fortifications. In this case, however, his main purpose was to give Nakagawa the clout to deal with the obdurate Vice Admiral Itou. Despite Murai's higher rank, it appears that Nakagawa retained control of the tactical defense of Peleliu, with Murai on hand for guidance and to assume direct control in the event the colonel was killed or seriously injured.

Meanwhile, supplies to Japanese forces in the Palaus had begun to dry up. U.S. victories in the Marianas had forced a change in strategy. Emphasis was now to be placed on the more strategically valuable Philippines. The Palaus had become expendable. Japanese officers at Colonel Nakagawa's headquarters on Peleliu grumbled that they were expected to defend the island without more generous supplies of ammunition and materiel. "We depended only on our united spirit," recalled a noncom who survived the campaign.

Among the most acute shortages in the Palaus were aircraft. There were not any. By U.S. estimates, the carrier strike of 30 and 31 March had destroyed 168 aircraft in the Palaus, and replacements were not available. The Japanese Imperial staff was carefully hoarding almost every available aircraft for the "decisive battle" to be forced with the Americans in the Philippines. By September, General Inoue reported later, Japanese airpower in the Palaus consisted of only five navy floatplanes.

Stuck with aerial bombs and no way to deliver them, Inoue ordered that the bombs be adapted for use as land mines along the beaches, creating one more menace for attacking Marines.

Across the flat, gray ocean, creeping along at 7.7 knots under a leaden sky, the 30 LSTs carrying the assault companies moved inexorably toward Peleliu. They steamed along in regular, even columns, recalled a Marine, "riding on the sea squarely upright, like cardboard boxes." Seventeen transports and two LSDs were also allotted to the division, but the faster transports (average speed: 12.1 knots) would not leave until 8 September. The ships sailed northwest through the Solomons and the Dampier Straits, crossing the equator above New Guinea and then out across the broad Pacific toward the Palaus. Seas were calm, breezes light.

Crammed aboard the slow-moving LSTs, the Marines could see the outlying columns and the rakish destroyers darting back and forth on the fringes of the convoy to protect against submarine attack. The LSTs were crowded with 15,616 enlisted men, 843 officers, scores of jeeps, tons of ammunition, nearly 250 amphibian tractors, water, gasoline and a thousand other things integral to a modern amphibious assault. The heat was suffocating.

Aboard LST 227, Captain George Hunt's K Company, 1st Marines, found that the sleeping compartments accommodated only 77 men. With 225 men in the company, the surplus spilled onto the main deck, finding what place they could among the jumble of trucks, jeeps, trailers, crates and drums lashed to the deck. Tarps were strung as protection against the blazing equatorial sun, but the heat hung thick and heavy over the plodding ships.

On one vessel the loudspeaker blared tunes from the musical *Oklahoma!*, the Marines singing along, "Oh, what a miserable morning, oh, what a lousy day!" On a more serious note, large-scale plaster of paris relief maps had been issued down to the lower echelons so that each man could get a reasonably good picture of the target area.

Embarking from the staging areas, the 1st Marine Division was 5 percent over strength—excluding, presumably, eight stowaways from the replacement pool on Guadalcanal, who materialized on one of the LSTs carrying the 5th Marines after the division was at sea.[1]

The assault elements carried sufficient rations for 32 days and medical supplies to last 30. Water enough for five days (prorated at two gallons per man per day) was stowed in five-gallon cans, with reserves in scoured-out 55-gallon oil drums. For the assault phase, all weapons were allowed five units of fire—a unit of fire being the amount of ammunition calculated to last through one day of heavy fighting. The unit of fire for the M–1 rifle, for example, was 100 rounds. The division also carried an additional ten units of flamethrower fillers and explosives to deal with the numerous fortified positions anticipated on Peleliu.

The assault troops amused themselves by reading, gambling and "shooting the breeze." On LST 607, Corporal Joe Lommerse and his buddies listened to one young replacement who "held sway on the open deck predicting his death on the first day and quoting from the Good Book." Lommerse and the other old-timers made a mental note to stay away from the doomsayer on D-Day.

The more superstitious Marines might have been alarmed to learn of various other ill omens. Before rehearsals on Guadalcanal, two battlewagons that were supposed to provide fire support for the landing, the *California* and the *Tennessee*, collided. Damage was not serious, but the *California* was unable to participate in the bombardment. As the attack force proceeded toward Peleliu, two oilers also collided, causing minor damage to both. Then, before dawn on 12 September, the destroyer *Fullam* rammed into the stern of the transport *Noa*. The *Noa* went to the bottom, while the *Fullam* was seriously damaged. Although no men were lost, the *Noa*, carrying Team

Able, one of three underwater demolition teams assigned to clear shore obstacles at Peleliu, lost all of its explosives and gear, effectively knocking it out of the battle before it began.

Meanwhile, some of the higher ranking Marine officers were still scratching their heads over General Rupertus's behavior in a conference shortly before leaving Guadalcanal. Rupertus had called his regimental commanders, the division artillery chief, chief of staff and Assistant Division Commander Oliver P. Smith in for a conference.

"You have your orders," Rupertus told them. "I will not be ashore on D-Day and may not be there on D plus 1. It depends on the course of the action. But I want you to understand now that there will be no change in orders, regardless. Even if General Smith attempts to change my plans or orders, you regimental commanders will refuse to obey."

This openly stated lack of faith did nothing to ease Colonel Puller's mind. Never before had he felt such pessimism on the eve of battle. Aboard ship on the way to Peleliu, he studied the maps of his assigned sector until they were committed to memory, but his forbodings only increased.

Doubts about the Peleliu assault also continued to nag at Bull Halsey, who had questioned the operation almost from its inception. On 28 August, Halsey had led TF 38 out of Enewik to blast Yap, the Palaus and Mindanao. He was also to make a diversionary strike on the Bonins. These moves were designed to neutralize possible Japanese opposition to the pending assaults on Peleliu and Morotai and mislead the enemy as to the actual objective. The force hit the Palaus on 6 to 8 September; Mindanao on 9 to 10 September. Noting a complete lack of opposition, Halsey cancelled further strikes on Mindanao and moved on to the Visayas. This sweep destroyed an estimated 200 enemy planes.

Mulling over the Japanese reaction—or lack of it—Halsey concluded that enemy airpower was virtually defunct and Japanese defenses in the Central Philippines were little more than "a hollow shell." This suspicion seemed to be supported by a U.S. pilot who had been shot down over Leyte, rescued by guerrillas and returned to the fleet. The pilot told Halsey the guerrillas reported there were no Japanese aircraft whatsoever on Leyte. Halsey began to wonder if the invasion of the Philippines should be moved up. He consulted his staff and, in his words, decided to "stick his neck out." At noon on 13 September, he informed Nimitz of his thinking in an unusual dispatch.

Basing his conclusion on the lack of enemy opposition encountered in his sweep, Halsey recommended cancelling Stalemate. The timetable for the Philippines assault should be moved up and the original plan to take Peleliu, Yap, Morotai and Mindanao should be scrubbed, he advised. The troops originally slated for these operations should be immediately placed at General MacArthur's disposal for the seizure of Leyte in the Central Philippines, an operation originally scheduled to take place on 20 December.

Nimitz felt the first phase of Stalemate, involving seizure of Peleliu, Angaur and Morotai, had proceeded too far for cancellation. However, he agreed to submit Phase II, involving Yap and the attack on Mindanao (due to be launched 15 November) to immediate review.

General MacArthur was then aboard the heavy cruiser *Nashville* en route to Morotai under radio silence. However, in Hollandia, his chief of staff, Lieutenant General R. K. Sutherland, greeted Halsey's proposal with alacrity, certain MacArthur would agree. If the navy could furnish the necessary air cover against weak Japanese airpower, there was little need to seize airfields in the southern Philippines before assaulting Leyte.

In MacArthur's name, Sutherland expressed willingness to push up the timetable and invade Leyte as early as 20 October, provided the immediate services of XXIV Corps, then scheduled for the Yap operation, could be obtained. At that very moment, the Joint Chiefs of Staff were meeting with their British counterparts in Quebec for the Octagon Conference between President Roosevelt and Prime Minister Churchill. Halsey's suggestion arrived flagged with Nimitz's recommendation that the invasion of Yap and Mindanao be cancelled as Halsey suggested. The seizure of Leyte, the eighth largest island in the Philippines, should be moved up two months to 20 October. The army divisions originally slated to hit the Western Carolines should go to MacArthur for the invasion of Leyte.

Impressed by the agreement between the top Pacific commanders, the Joint Chiefs of Staff needed little time to debate the suggestion. Ninety minutes after receiving the dispatch, they flashed their approval. The Yap and Mindanao operations were cancelled; Leyte would be hit 20 October.

Oblivious to their near salvation, Marines aboard the convoy bound for Peleliu had few illusions. Whether the campaign would be protracted, as Chesty Puller was beginning to fear, or "rough but fast," as General Rupertus predicted, the veterans knew their enemy too well to think Peleliu would be a pushover. "We'll have to kill every little yellow bastard there," one Marine sergeant concluded succinctly.

Four days or 40, that was the hard fact of the matter.

14 SEPTEMBER: D MINUS 1

Day dawned startlingly clear off Peleliu. A strong breeze riffled the water, making it glitter from countless reflections. Throughout the convoy, the assault troops were getting ready. Tarpaulins were struck and folded into squares. Hammocks came down; personal items and excess equipment were rolled up into horseshoe-shaped bundles and stowed away to await their owners' return. Men field-stripped weapons, flicking off imaginary bits of dust with old toothbrushes.

Flamethrowers and bazookas sported newly painted camouflage; here and there an automatic weapon ripped loudly as it was test-fired over the side. Gone was the khaki worn during the voyage. The men had donned their battle dress: gray-green trousers and jackets with the eagle, globe and anchor stenciled in black on the left breast pocket. Helmets, covered with camouflage covers, were near at hand.

Aboard LST 227, Captain George Hunt, a lanky former newspaper man and veteran of the fighting on Guadalcanal, found the activity a relief. Hunt had good reason to be pensive. With two campaigns already under his belt, he had expected to be rotated home from Pavuvu. When that happy event failed to transpire, recalled one of his men, the highly capable company commander disappeared into his tent for a two-day lament with a bottle of Scotch.[2]

Now, however, Hunt had more pressing concerns on his mind. His company had drawn one of the toughest and probably the most important single mission of the initial assault. Landing on the extreme left of the 1st Marines, Hunt's men were supposed to seize a rocky promontory extending 25 yards into the ocean on the regiment's flank. Referred to only as "the Point," the promontory sheltered at least two pillboxes. Aerial photographs had revealed anti-boat obstacles on the coral reef in front of the beach and entrenchments on the beach itself. Enemy troops in the pillboxes—and in any other positions still unspotted—would be able to take the whole beach in enfilade unless they could be neutralized.

Hunt planned to let his 3d Platoon assault the Point. The 1st Platoon would be in direct support, while the 2d pushed in on the right. The scheme of maneuver had been rehearsed and repeatedly traced on the map. Landing about 50 yards down the beach, the Marines would push inland, then turn sharply left and seize the Point. Every man knew exactly what was expected of him—which did not mean things could not go wrong, as Hunt well knew. At best, Hunt hoped the naval gunfire would leave the Japanese stunned and slow to react. At worst, his company would be swept by flanking fire at point-blank range from the dug-in Japanese.

Especially concerned about the Point was Sergeant Wilfred "Swede" Hanson, attached to K Company from Battalion Intelligence. Hanson had a terrible feeling that the Japanese had dug into the Point like "one huge pillbox," but every officer he tried to approach on the subject shrugged off his fears. Plans called for naval bombardment and strafing, he was told. The commander of the armored amphibs on the LST reassured him that his short-barreled 75s would simply "blast the Japs to pieces" if there were any left on the Point. Still, Hanson couldn't shake his doubts.

Now, on the afternoon of D minus 1, only a few hours remained before K Company's assault. Speaking over the ship's crackling PA system, Captain Hunt counseled his men with the same theme he had been trying to pound into them for the past three months. "Hit the beach and drive in fast for one hundred yards and keep driving; clear it for succeeding waves," he told them.

Aboard LST 661, Private Eugene Sledge's unit of the 5th Marines, slated to land in the center, heard much the same advice. "Remember what you've been taught," their lieutenant told them. "Keep your heads down going in on the amtrac . . . get off the beach fast! The Japs will plaster it with everything they've got, and if we get pinned down on the beach, artillery and mortars will ruin us."

After the talk, NCOs issued ammunition, K rations and salt tablets. The salt would be indispensable with temperatures hovering well over 100 degrees. Already wilting under the heavy equatorial heat, many of the men wore no skivvies or shirts. Still the humidity hung over the ships, muffling the clatter of the chow lines until "even the exercise of breathing brought sweat to the brow," recalled an infantry officer.

In Captain Hunt's company, Wayland Woodyard, a newly joined lieutenant, approached one of the veteran officers. Woodyard was a very serious-minded man; he would never play cards with the other officers and was always brushing up on what he was supposed to do. Now, however, he had a puzzled look on his face. "Tell me," he said to the other officer. "I've been reading up on what happens when you land, but what actually is the real scoop? I want to do the best job possible."

"Okay," said the other, "first, don't worry about it. You know everything you've been taught. Once we land, you'll forget most of it. You'll just think about saving your own hide and losing as few men as possible. It'll come natural to you. Wait and see, there's just too damn much confusion to go by the book."

After supper, church services were held on LST 227, conducted by a sailor who was two years short of graduating from divinity school when war intervened. Only about 40 Marines attended the service, giving lie to the old adage about atheists in foxholes. Elsewhere in the crowded ships, Marine troop commanders and civilian news correspondents opened sealed letters from General Rupertus. The letters had been handed out just before the ships left Guadalcanal, with instructions not to open them until D minus 1, at which time the contents were to be broadcast to all hands. Now, much to the astonishment of the recipients, they found that Rupertus had gone on record with his prediction that the fighting on Peleliu would be tough but short, comparable to Tarawa, lasting not more than four days.

It was a prediction he would come to regret.

As evening fell, the men who would be on the leading edge of the fighting tried to appear nonchalant, but bull sessions finally trailed off and the men hit the sack. Lying there on LST 661, Private Sledge broke out in a cold sweat, thinking about what awaited him the next morning. The 20-year-old Alabaman had dropped out of the Marion Military Institute to join the Marines. Now, cursing himself as a coward, he finally fell asleep repeating the Lord's Prayer to himself. Peleliu would be his first combat.

As dusk fell, 25-year-old Corporal Bill Myers found himself standing at the rail of his LSD next to his tank platoon commander, Lieutenant Richard

Kelly. Both men were veterans of previous 1st Marine Division campaigns. Within a few hours their company, numbering 15 tanks, was scheduled to land in support of Chesty Puller's 1st Marines.

A recent graduate of Notre Dame, Kelly looked nothing like the traditional concept of a Marine. One of his men recalled him as "sort of pear-shaped ... a sweet man with family back home." The lieutenant's relaxed style made him popular with his men, but tonight he seemed preoccupied, staring pensively out over the water. He turned to Myers all at once and blurted, "Bill, I'm not going to survive this one."

Myers protested, offering "all the normal platitudes."

Kelly just looked at him. "You don't understand," he repeated quietly, "I'm not going to survive this one."

For the Japanese on Peleliu, the battle had already begun. Carrier planes from the 3d Fleet had begun a final working over of beach defenses and antiaircraft positions on 10 September. Two days later, the battleships, cruisers and destroyers of Rear Admiral Jesse Oldendorf's Fire Support Group joined in, pounding Peleliu with their heavy guns. Minesweepers and UDT teams moved in to clear obstacles.

On Koror, General Inoue knew the moment of decision had finally arrived. He had been informed by the Southern Army on 3 September that an American assault appeared imminent. This was followed by Japanese intelligence estimates that the attack force was probably in divisional strength. The Japanese also managed to learn of Major General Julian C. Smith's involvement. Now, as salvos from American battleships rocked Peleliu, any lingering doubts that the attack might be a feint were dispelled.

"The entire army and people of Japan are expecting us to win," Inoue exhorted his troops. Now was the time to "break the deadlock of the Great Asiatic War" and repay the Emperor's benevolence. "Rouse yourselves for the sake of your country!" Inoue declared. "Officers and men, you will devote your life to winning this battle and attaining your long cherished dream of annihilating the enemy."

For three days, the U.S. bombardment chipped away at Peleliu. Standing offshore, warships fired more than 2,200 tons of ammunition at various targets. None moved in closer than 7,250 yards, and much of the fire was conducted from as far as 8 miles out. Still, to anyone unaware of Peleliu's formidable defenses, the statistics appeared impressive. The fire support group, consisting of 5 battleships, 4 heavy cruisers, 4 light cruisers and 14 destroyers, pounded the island garrison with 519 rounds of 16-inch shells, 1,845 rounds of 14-inch, 1,427 rounds of 8-inch, 1,020 rounds of 6-inch and 12,937 rounds of 5-inch ammo—nearly 2 rounds for each of Peleliu's 10,000 defenders. Adding to the destruction, carrier planes screeched overhead, strafing and bombing the Japanese garrison.

The most obvious result of this pounding was to denude Peleliu of its thick tropical vegetation, turning the island "into a barren wasteland," noted a Japanese diarist. Only now did the startled observers realize just how rugged the island was and the true extent of the high ground north of the airfield. In the planning stages, Peleliu had frequently been referred to as "flat." That misconception—perhaps the most crucial of the campaign— was now all too clear, as the limestone cliffs protruded like old decayed bones from Peleliu's blasted scrub.

Deep in their caves, Japanese soldiers weathered the American bombardment virtually intact, both physically and morale-wise. Writing in his diary, a Japanese soldier observed, "I cannot help feeling that fate is closing in on us who are in the Palau sector. But we will defend Peleliu! We are imbued with the firm convictions that even though we may die, we will never let the airfield fall into enemy hands. Our morale is sky high."

Colonel Nakagawa had divided the island into four defensive zones. The western sector was defended by Major Hoji Tomita's 2d Battalion, numbering slightly over 600 men. The 3d Battalion, commanded by Captain Senkasi and numbering about 750 men, was assigned to the southern sector. Major Michero Hiikino and 550 men of the 346th Independent Infantry Battalion manned the northern sector. Another 600 men commanded by a captain defended the east. Colonel Nakagawa placed the remaining battalion in general reserve in the ridges.

Now, as the pre-assault bombardment continued, Nakagawa ordered the bulk of his forces to withdraw into the safety of the Umurbrogol ridges, leaving Captain Senkasi's 3d Battalion, 15th Infantry south of the airfield to repel any assault from that quarter.

The U.S. gunfire support plan originally called for only two days of softening up by naval bombardment before D-Day. Strong protests by General Geiger had persuaded Vice Admiral Wilkinson, the scholarly, thorough-minded Solomons veteran in charge of providing close support on Peleliu, to add another day. The decision allowed a little more deliberation in target selection, but even so, the effect on the enemy was probably minimal.

Maintaining strict fire discipline, the Japanese guns remained mute under the shelling to avoid exposing their positions to American naval gun spotters. Among the exceptions—and a small indication of things to come—was a coast gun spotted by a gunnery officer aboard the heavy cruiser *Portland*. Peering through his binoculars, he saw the gun poke its ugly snout from a coral cave. The gun fired, then the Japanese crew dragged the piece back out of sight. The *Portland* slammed five salvos of 8-inch shells into the spot, only to watch in frustration as the gun emerged again, unscathed, to fire at the U.S. warships.

"You can put all the steel in Pittsburgh on that thing and still not get it," blurted the gunnery officer in frustration.

On Peleliu, a Japanese soldier reported in his diary that though the American bombardment had turned the surface into a wasteland, only one man in his company had been slightly injured by the tons of steel directed at the island.

Returning from a reconnaissance flight over the island, an American scout plane pilot said, "It was like flying over an immense broken graveyard." There were no signs of life. "I saw plenty of gun emplacements and defense positions, but that was all," the pilot reported ominously.

Eyeing the heavy cloud of smoke and dust hanging over the island, Rear Admiral Oldendorf had no way of realizing that most of the shells had merely pocked vacant coral. On the evening of 14 September, he reported blithely, "We have run out of targets."

Meanwhile, deep in Peleliu's caves and bunkers, over 10,000 Japanese waited, hardly touched by the massive bombardment. Within a few hours, thousands of Marines then tossing restlessly aboard the ships offshore would discover just how mistaken admirals and generals can be in their opinions.

Already in action off Peleliu's southwestern beaches were UDT Teams 6 and 7. Team 7 had responsibility for clearing the underwater obstacles off the northern third of the landing area. The lower two thirds were assigned to Team 6, which had also drawn Team Able's third after the latter's gear went down with the *Noa* just before dawn on 12 September.

The UDT men took their initial plunge the morning of 12 September. While Oldendorf's destroyers tried to keep Japanese heads down with 5-inch and 40 mm fire, landing craft dropped the swimmers into the water. The tide was low on the long shelving reef, leaving it barely awash 100 yards from shore. Snipers popped away at the swimmers, while machine guns rattled from camouflaged pillboxes. Machine gunners on the landing craft fired back, while spotters radioed coordinates to the support ships.

The shallow water made it impossible for the swimmers to go all the way to the beach. They needed at least two feet of water to cover them, and it just was not there. This was painfully apparent to one swimmer on the coral who had been targeted by a sniper in a palm tree. Unable to move quickly or escape under water, he suffered some anxious moments until a 40 mm shell blew his tormentor out of the tree. "It was a very comforting sight," he reported.

Examining the northern end of the beaches where Chesty Puller's men were to come ashore, Lieutenant Richard Burke's Team 7 found a thicket of rusty tetrahedrons on either flank. A double row of wooden posts jutted out of the water 75 feet from shore. On the beach itself, rock-filled log cribs, concrete cubes, a fire trench and antitank ditch would have to wait for Marine demolitionists on D-Day.

Burke's men did report one piece of good news. Earlier air color and stereo photos had shown what appeared to be huge potholes on the reef, an obstacle that could seriously impede the amtracs. Team 7 found that potholes were actually patches of dark moss or seaweed. The reef was flat and smooth, posing no problem to the tractors. Burke reported that work to clear the posts and open the beach could be completed in one day.

To the south, Lieutenant DeEarle M. Logsdon's Team 6 found that both nature and the Japanese had made things more difficult for any landing force. Coral mounds and boulders cluttered the reef, waiting to hang up amtracs and DUKWs. The southern shoal, intended for an LST landing channel, was also studded with obstacles. To these natural obstacles, the Japanese had added obstructions of their own. Inshore were posts such as those encountered by Team 7 further up the beach. Swimmers also found steel tetrahedrons and *cheveaux-de-frises*—massive sawhorses built man-high out of coconut logs strung with barbed wire. Wire fences also paralleled parts of the shore. Spiders—three leaning posts cabled together at the middle—had been set up to channel landing craft into Japanese lanes of fire.

Returning to their ships, Teams 6 and 7 set up a timetable: Team 7 had one day to clear its beaches; Team 6, with more work at hand, had two to do the job.

By 0730 on 13 September, Logsdon's team was back in the water, this time pulling their explosives. Off the southernmost beach, the swimmers set charges against the boulders, blowing two clear lanes for the DUKWs on D-Day. Team 6 also blasted a wide ramp on the drying reef for tank landing ships and pontoons, working right in to shore and setting off a train of explosives to clear the way.

Knocking off at 1530, they swam back to the ship for hot chow and a rest, waiting for the next shift an hour after midnight. Again heading in to the reef, the team worked for four hours—this time without fire support, which would have silhouetted them for Japanese marksmen. Fortunately, the support was not needed: not a shot was fired as the swimmers laid their charges and withdrew. The charges went off with a mighty blast, clearing a line of posts, pyramids and *cheveaux-de-frises* scarcely a grenade's toss from the startled Japanese. The following day was spent blasting ramps, smoothing potholes and clearing remaining boulders.

Meanwhile, Team 7 passed the night before D-Day off the northern beach. Two ten-man squads flippered in and bellied ashore to place charges on the posts strung with barbed wire. Teams also set up tripods and range markers on the flank. Worried about Japanese attempts to intercept them, they devised an identification signal—waving a piece of primacord. No Japanese appeared to contest their work, but nerves remained tight. "You'd be surprised at the number of drifting logs that were stabbed that night," remarked an eyewitness. The poles were blown without trouble, and the UDTs returned on board ship.

Despite Japanese fire during the demolition work off Peleliu, not a single UDT man was killed or wounded during the clearing offshore. The only injuries were the usual coral infection and embedded sea urchin spines.

The way was open. Now it was all up to the Marines.

NOTES

1. The stowaways were "adopted" into the regiment. All were subsequently killed or wounded on Peleliu.

2. Veterans of K/3/1 all speak of Hunt in glowing terms. All also seem to remember, as one remarked, that "he had the longest legs in the world, and when you went on a hike, you were dog trotting and he was walking."

Chapter 3

SEPTEMBER 15: DOG-DAY

Combat artist Tom Lea's watch said 0340 when he woke. Barefoot and still in his skivvies, he went up to stand by the rail. Light flickered on the black horizon, and sick yellow balls of fire flashed low in the clouds like heat lightning, only continuous. The black silhouette of a seaman on watch by the rail turned to him. "Them Japs are catching hell for breakfast," the gob remarked.

It was still dark when NCOs came around and began waking the men. "Okay, you guys, hit the deck." The engines had stopped. Drenched in sweat, Marines still lying in the darkness could hear the creak of davits, the scuffle of hurried feet, voices raised in command.

Up on deck one Marine stood at the rail, peering futilely over the water for a glimpse of Peleliu, until a sailor remarked, "The island's over this way," pointing in the opposite direction. The Marine looked out off the other side and still could not see anything.

"Are you ready?" his buddy asked.

"Yeah, I guess so," said the young Marine.

Breakfast on most of the ships was steak and eggs, although on Private Russell Davis's LST the men received black coffee, dry toast and an orange or apple per man. When Davis, a greenhorn, inquired about the legendary pre-invasion steak and eggs, a veteran sergeant laughed grimly. "It's better not to have much in your stomach in case you get hit," he explained. On one of the other LSTs, Private Eugene Sledge did not enjoy his steak and eggs anyway, because "my stomach was tied in knots."

As day dawned calm and clear at 0552, ships were visible as far as the eye could see on the water off the invasion beaches. Daylight also brought a rise in the tempo of the naval bombardment. Salvo after salvo roared toward Peleliu, the shells shrieking over the water like so many wild birds. Decks trembled under the concussion; the continuous flash-slam of the bombardment made normal conversation impossible. Six miles away from the transports, jets of flame and spiraling columns of black smoke rose over the enemy-held island.

Excited Marines lined the rails yelling, "Burn! Burn!", as the island vanished in a sheet of flame, smoke and dust. "They're givin' 'em hell," shouted a Marine officer jubilantly. "I'd sure hate to be in those bastards' shoes!"

"Goddam right," a captain returned.

It seemed inconceivable that anything could survive such a pounding. "I wondered how many Japs would be left alive to fight," recalled a Marine private, thoroughly impressed by the navy's firepower. Sergeant Walter "Flip" Afflito of 1/5 was also impressed. "We'll be off here by tomorrow," he predicted optimistically.

As the novelty paled, the crowd at the rail thinned out, but the screech of an air-strike brought them back again. The planes dove, strafing and firing rockets. The noise was fearful, recalled Davis. Some of the newer men already had their packs on and rifles slung, but the veterans waited for orders from the ship's speakers. Here and there the men of some outfits had painted their faces with camouflage paint; they looked a ghastly green in the new light.

The assault troops instinctively separated into pairs, each man with his buddy. "You seldom saw three guys together, and never five or six," observed a rifleman. Strained faces revealed their apprehension. "The breakfast didn't sit very well in my stomach, and I was awful weak in the knees," recalled a South Carolina corporal, "but I remember thinking that the swabbies seemed much more excited than we were."

On one of the LSTs carrying elements of the 7th Marines, some disgruntled leathernecks paused to leave a notice on the bulletin board in the ship's officers wardroom. The message expressed their fervent hope that the "U.S.S. *Repulsive* receives a Jap torpedo immediately after the debarkation of all troops."

From down in the bowels of the LSTs, there came a rumble as the armored amphibians started up en masse. The deck plates shook with the vibration, and the veterans moved knowingly toward their packs. A bell rang and a loudspeaker sputtered, "Get your gear on." The men helped each other with their packs, straightening shoulder straps and buckling on cartridge belts. The next bell would signal them to go below and board the amtracs.

On Private Davis's LST, a runner suddenly and completely surrendered to his fear and found himself unable to move from his cot. A sergeant screamed at him and tried to drag him off. Two Marines finally grasped the man under the arms and walked him out to the line waiting to go below. The runner was not alone in his fear—his terror was just more visible. Davis could feel the fear around him like a palpable thing. It affected rookie and veteran alike, although the veterans seemed to conceal it better. Later, Davis was to become all too familiar with fear in all its various forms, but now, in the innocence of his first combat, he was "deeply shamed for them and for myself."

Scheduled to go in the third wave, Colonel Puller went to the bridge of his transport to thank the skipper for his hospitality. The naval officer was aglow with optimism. "Puller," he said, "you won't find anything to stop you over there. Nothing could have lived through that hammering."

"Well, sir, all I can see is dust," returned Puller pessimistically. "I doubt if you've cleaned it out. I know they have underground oil dumps for that airfield. We haven't seen that blow. I've been boning over those maps for weeks, and I believe they'll have pillbox stuff and fortifications like we've never seen before. They've been at it for years."

As Puller left the bridge a few minutes later, the naval officer remained upbeat. "Good luck, Puller," he remarked. "We'll expect you for dinner this evening."

"If we get out of this one, you'll be back in Hawaii long before we're through with this job," replied Puller, prophetically.

Filing down the ladder to the tank deck, Private Eugene Sledge felt a weakness in his knees as he saw the older model amtrac assigned to his unit. Unlike the newer amtracs, the older ones had no tailgates. The men would have to vault over the sides, exposed to enemy fire, when the amtrac hit the beach.

The roar of the engines in the enclosed space was deafening. Exhaust blew over the men despite the big fans whirring overhead. Many Marines were already seasick; some had become sick just at the sight of the small boats. Each had a cardboard sign on a stick with the wave and boat number on it.

As some Marines in the 1st Regiment began boarding their amtracs, a few of the men began yelling, "So long, swabbie" and other good-natured insults at the sailors. "Some of them threw pieces of rope or gear from one amtrac to the other, then the fumes were so bad everybody shut up," recalled a South Carolina private.

Crouched in his amtrac, Private Davis heard the LST's bow doors open. Chains clanked as the bow ramp dropped, but the amtrac did not move. Davis, a battalion scout, opened his map and glanced at the overlay of his landing area. There seemed to be one solid cluster of black symbols for guns and bunkers all the way across the beach. Uncheered, Davis put the map away. Blue exhaust hung in layers overhead. A Marine said impatiently, "Let's go before we die from monoxide."

"We'll go soon enough," another replied grimly.

Wedged in so tightly he could not turn, Davis stared idly at the Marine seated across from him. The man looked miserable, hunched down in his jacket like a turtle, his eyes streaming from the monoxide and his teeth clenched as if he did not know whether to scream or be sick.

In the South Carolina private's LST, a bell finally rang. The amtracs lurched forward and the first one exited down the bow ramp. The men spilled toward the front as the vehicle nosed down the ramp and floated free. The private's amtrac was third in line. "As we went out the ramp, everybody began joking again, and we all had to hold on to each other," he recalled. "As soon as we were in the water, I looked up and I saw these sailors standing up in the bow, and I cursed myself for not joining the navy."

Peleliu was on fire. Wisps of smoke and ash drifted overhead. The air was thick with the stink of high explosives and diesel fuel. Large-caliber shells passed overhead "roaring like locomotives," recalled a Marine. Some of the riflemen were vomiting in the bilges.

Waiting with his tank unit off the Orange Beaches, Captain Jack Munday jotted in his notebook, "It's pretty tense. Everyone trying to act nonchalant. No one looks scared, but they look damned interested."

The metallic concussion of naval salvos slammed into the amtracs, circling like hundreds of pygmies around the hulking warships. "Boy, it must cost a fortune to fire them 16-inch babies," remarked a Marine in Private Sledge's amtrac. "Screw the expense," growled another.

Sledge clung weakly to the side of the tractor, his stomach in knots. It was with a sense of fatalistic relief that he finally saw the wave commander motion his flag toward the beach.

Although the Marines suffering from seasickness in the bobbing amtracs probably did not appreciate it, conditions were ideal for amphibious operations. There was practically no wind, and only a slight surf was running. Visibility was excellent with only a few high clouds.

Starting at 0750, 50 carrier planes bombed Japanese gun positions and beach defenses as naval gunfire continued to slam into the island. The first wave was scheduled to cross the line of departure at 0800. Order of battle from left to right was 3/1 on White 1, 2/1 on White 2 (1/1 in regimental reserve), 1/5 on Orange 1, 3/5 on Orange 2 (2/5 in reserve) and 3/7 on Orange 3, to be followed at once by 1/7 (2/7 in division reserve).

As naval gunfire continued to pound the island, the LVTs carrying the assault Marines proceeded to the line of departure roughly 4,000 yards offshore. Here, the vehicles were formed into waves regulated by patrol craft and subchasers. The LVTs had a waterborne speed of about 4.5 miles per hour. The trip from the line of departure to the beach would take about 30 minutes.

Preceding the first wave, armored amphibians would attempt to suppress enemy fire from the beach area with their 75 mm and 37 mm guns. The armored amphibs would hit the beach at 0830. The assault troops would land a minute later, with the other assault waves following at approximately

Map 2.
Peleliu

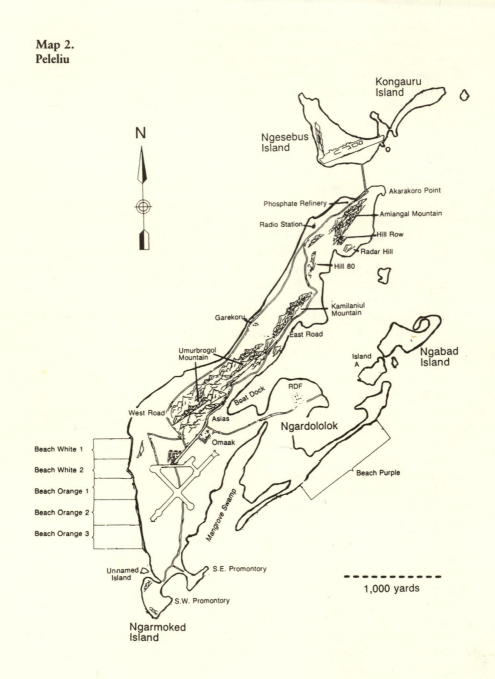

N

Kongauru
Island

Ngesebus
Island

Akarakoro Point

Phosphate Refinery

Amiangal Mountain

Radio Station

Hill Row

Radar Hill

Hill 80

Kamilaniul
Mountain

Garekoru

East Road

Ngabad
Island

Umurbrogol
Mountain

Island
A

Boat Dock

RDF

West Road

Asias

Ngardololok

Omaak

Beach White 1

Beach White 2

Beach Orange 1

Beach Purple

Beach Orange 2

Beach Orange 3

Mangrove Swamp

Unnamed
Island

S.E. Promontory

1,000 yards

S.W. Promontory

Ngarmoked
Island

five-minute intervals. Machine-gun, mortar and forward-command echelons were slated to come in at about the fifth wave. Battalion commanders and their staffs boarded free boats which would bring them in wherever the situation seemed to warrant.

If all went according to plan, five assault battalions—some 4,500 men— would be lodged on Peleliu's beaches within the first 20 minutes. Tanks would then begin coming in over the reef, followed by the regimental weapons companies. By H plus 85 minutes, three more infantry battalions would have landed, bringing a total of 8,000 combat Marines onto the island.

Circling in an amtrac off LST 227, the Marines in Sergeant Wilfred "Swede" Hanson's unit eyed the flag on the LST's mast. When the flag dropped, they would form for the run to the beach. Suddenly, a recording of General Douglas MacArthur's voice blared out over the water from the LST's loudspeakers. The Marines were attacking the last Japanese stronghold barring his reentry into the Philippines. Their victory would allow his landing to proceed more safely, and he was certain the assault troops would carry on in the best traditions of the U.S. Navy and Marines.

As that recording concluded, another began, and the strains of the Marine Corps Hymn blared out over the water. The flag on the LST dropped. The armored amphibians churned over the line of departure and headed for Peleliu's smoke-obscured beaches. It was 0800 on a Friday morning.

In the third wave, Russell Davis saw the amtracs in front form into an irregular line between the picket boats. The line wheeled abruptly, and white water showed in its wake as the amtracs churned toward the beach. The island was now obscured, the result of white phosphorus smoke shell-fired inland to mask the run toward shore. One Marine later described the effect as like being drawn into a vortex.

Minutes later, it was Davis's turn. For a moment, fear disappeared as the amtracs passed the picket line and raced for shore. The Marines were up and yelling excitedly. "Drive! Drive! Drive!" they chanted. Only the two veteran noncoms in the craft stayed down and kept quiet.

The Japanese 47 mm Type 1 antitank gun fired a 3.5-pound armor-piercing shell at a speed of 2,700 feet per second. It was capable of piercing 70 mm plate at a range of 500 yards. That latter distinction was purely academic as far as the thin-skinned amtracs were concerned.

Davis saw the amtrac in front of them explode in a shell-burst. He stared, uncomprehending. "Hey, I think they hit him," someone said in surprise. The amtrac went up in flames. Burning gasoline spread over the water. Men leaped out of the stricken vehicle. The driver of Davis's amtrac screamed so loudly at the sight that the Marines in back could hear him over the din.

Another shell missed Davis's amtrac close astern, spraying the Marines with salt water. The men shrank down lower behind the steel sides of the vehicle. Small-caliber fire clattered against the steel. A dark stain suddenly blossomed on a Marine's shoulder. The man clutched at the wound and swore.

The squad leader yelled up at the amtrac machine gunner, a youth still in his teens. "What's going on, kid? Are they reaching us?"

The gunner turned, all eyes. "They're hitting them all," he replied in shock. "What will we do?"

Heading toward Orange 2 was Private Eugene Sledge. The beachline was now marked by a continuous sheet of flame. Great clouds of smoke rolled off the island.

As the amtrac rushed in, a lieutenant produced a half-pint whiskey bottle and yelled, "This is it, boys!" He took a long pull from the bottle and passed it around.

A Japanese shell exploded close by, and the amtrac stalled. The driver fumbled frantically with the controls. Shells geysered all around. A Marine sergeant leaned over and spoke to the driver; the man settled down and got the amtrac started again. They continued toward the beach as water sprayed skyward from near misses.

Preceding the LVTs were 18 LCIs (Landing Craft, Infantry) fitted with 4.5-inch rocket launchers. Moving within 1,000 yards of shore, they began unleashing the rockets in salvos of 22 each. Startled Marines glanced up as the rockets screeched toward Peleliu. Most had never seen rockets before; the sound was new, and it "scared the hell out of us," recalled a tanker.

As the rocket salvos ceased, 48 navy fighter-bombers appeared over the beach. In a coordinated attack which kept at least eight of the planes in action at a time, the pilots worked over the beach area with bombs, rockets and machine guns as naval gunfire shifted inland.

From his amtrac off White 1, Corporal Harlan Murray, a former University of Arizona student, watched the planes diving at the beach. "We're watchin' all this crap goin' on, and I mean that island was smokin'," he recalled. "And then somebody says, 'There won't be anything alive in that place.' And about that time one of these dive bombers went down, and all of a sudden *boom boom boom* around him, and he caught fire, and right straight down he crashed. And I can remember saying to this guy, 'Nuthin' on the island, huh?' Boy, then the navy planes just really started givin' 'em hell."

On the far left of the assault waves, Captain George Hunt's amtrac bumped up on the coral reef. "Goddammit, stick her into second!" the commander, a tall, lean sergeant, shouted at the driver. The driver threaded his way through defense obstacles. The commander swore. "Jesus! That was close. The bastards are firing back."

Hunt identified the incoming rounds as mortar fire. His mouth seemed very dry. The amtrac lurched across the reef, and he heard the quick typewriter staccato of machine gun fire. The fire emanated from the left . . . from the Point. "Son of a bitch," muttered Hunt. "The beach is lousy with the bastards."

The front of the tractor rose up, the tracks ground forward on sand and the amtrac halted. Splintered trees loomed overhead. Hunt rolled over the side and sprinted across the beach.

"I can't get any farther in," shouted the driver of Russell Davis's amtrac as the tracks bumped along the sea bottom. "Get out of here before we get hung up."

"Get in," yelled a young Marine sergeant. "Get on in farther, or I'll blow you into the water."

The driver pleaded but kept going. A near miss scattered fragments across the back of the amtrac, but no one was hit. Another shell slammed into the amtrac alongside. It tilted over, and men spilled out.

"Unload," pleaded the driver. "I can't go anymore. I'll never get off."

The ramp dropped, and a few men jumped out into the water. Terrified, the driver tried to back out before the others jumped. One of the riflemen crumbled as the ramp slammed into him.

"Out," shouted the squad leader. "Get out. They've zeroed in on every amtrac in this line." He started kicking at helmets and men in the crowded vehicle.

"Drive 'em," ordered the young sergeant, "before we get hit good."

Davis was on the edge of the ramp when a shell—apparently a small mortar round, he was never sure—slammed into the amtrac. He came up in waist-deep water, still clutching his rifle. The air all around hummed with bullets. He remembered what his officers had said about moving in fast and started slogging in toward the beach.

If here and there an inexperienced amtrac driver panicked, the great majority of the crews performed superbly amid the carnage on the reef.

An amtrac private first class named Sellers recalled how a shell penetrated his vehicle after it crossed the reef. Over the intercom, he heard the machine gunner, known as "The Kid," crying, "It's my leg . . . they got me in the leg." The Kid propped himself up and continued firing, but as the amtrac left the water and started across the beach, it took another hit, forcing the crew to bail out. When Sellers got to The Kid, he was unconscious, his wounded leg dangling.

Under fire from snipers in the splintered woods behind the beach, the crew administered first aid to their wounded buddy. Sellers stripped a machine gun from the crippled amtrac and fired inland until the blistering barrel burned the skin off his palm. Finally a corpsman got The Kid into another amtrac and back out past the reef to safety. "After that we found foxholes until things cooled off," observed Sellers.

"Why did you call him 'The Kid'?" asked a news correspondent, hearing the story soon afterward.

"Oh, he was only 19," said Sellers. "The rest of us are 20."

Observation planes circled over the beaches, their reports crackling over ship radios. "Playmate, this is Spider," began a report from one of the aircraft. "Resistance moderate to heavy, I'd say. There are amtracs burning on the reef. Repeat. There are amtracs burning on the reef. Over."

"Spider, this is Playmate. Where are our front lines? Over."

"Playmate, this is Spider. Lines well inland on the right and center, but left of Spitfire is still on Beach White 1. They seem to be pinned down. Over."

"Spider, this is Playmate. Can you see what's holding them down? Over."

"Playmate, this is Spider. There's heavy fire from the point just north of White 1. They seem to have both beaches enfiladed. More amtracs are burning on the reef. I'm going lower to try and see what's to their front."

"Playmate, this is Spider 2," cut in a new voice soon afterward. "Spider 1 has been shot down... resistance is heavy behind the White Beaches. Over."

"Spider 2, this is Playmate. How are things on the reef now? Over."

"Playmate, this is Spider 2. Damned bad. Boy, the stuff's sure hitting the fan now! Some big stuff. There's about 20 amtracs burning off the White Beaches, and I make about 18 off Orange 3. They got that one enfiladed ... Oh! I see 'em! Six of 'em with a field gun! Request permission to attack. Over."

"Spider 2, this is Playmate. Your request—negative. Over."

"Playmate, this is Spider 2. Please, just one little strafing. Over."

"Spider 2, this is Playmate. Negative; repeat, negative. You're supposed to be an aerial observer. Stay in the air and observe. Over."

"Oh, goddamn it to hell."

Private First Class Harlan Murray would never forget those scared moments as the amtracs neared the beach.

"We're goin' in, goin' in. And then they say, 'Okay, get ready.' And you have to turn around and face the back. And you have to stoop down. And you have to fix bayonets. The guy behind you had to pull your bayonet out of your pack and then you stick it on your rifle because it's so damned cramped. And God Almighty, there's nothin' going' on... all of a sudden there's a big explosion just behind us and another one nearer...

"At about that time we hit the beach and we... you just go in a little ways... and 'Lower the ramp, goddammit! Lower the ramp!' And all this screamin' and cussin' and finally the ramp falls and out we go."

The armored amphibians lurched out of the water onto the shore at 0832, directing fire on the beach defenses with their 37 mm and 75 mm cannon. At 0833, the first assault Marines landed, scattering hastily across the coral sand. "You still don't see anything other than these big explosions around," recalled a Marine rifleman. "Hell, you don't have time to pay attention... you're runnin'."

No one would ever know for certain the identity of the first Marine rifleman to set foot on Peleliu, but it may well have been Private First Class Joe Moskalczak, K Company, 5th Marines. When the amtrac lurched up on Orange 2, Moskalczak, a 19-year-old former coal breaker from Pennsylvania, dashed down the back ramp, ran 50 yards to the left and jumped in a large shell hole. "I looked to my right and saw no one," he recalled. "I looked to my left and saw a lone figure running in at about White Beach 2."

Moskalczak's buddy, BAR man Frank Minkewicz, also jumped in the hole. "Let's go!" yelled Moskalczak and ran up a sandy incline. Reaching the top, the Marines saw eight or nine Japanese pulling a field gun with spoked wooden wheels. The Marine skirmish line opened up on the artillerymen and knocked them all sprawling. Moskalczak and the others examined the bodies, "Look, he's still breathing," someone remarked, indicating one of the sprawled Japanese. Another Marine promptly ran his bayonet into the wounded Japanese. Unable to extract the blade, he squeezed off a round to blast it free of the corpse.

Leaving the artillery piece and its dead crew behind, the Marines headed inland.

Among the first Marines to land on White 1 was Corporal Bob Anderson of Captain George Hunt's K Company. On the way in, Anderson could see shore guns taking the amtracs under fire. Hitting the beach, he ran a short distance inland, then turned left and struck out toward his company's objective, the Point.

Running "quite a ways" through the downed trees and scrub jungle, Anderson found himself alone. He could hear a beach gun shooting close by and realized he must have made an unconscious note of the position on his way into the beach. Looking out toward White 1, he could see the shells exploding, hitting amtracs he and his company had just left. Suddenly he noticed an air vent sticking up from the top of the nearby bunker.

Still alone, Anderson crawled up on top of the bunker. "I looked around and didn't see any Japs," he recalled, "so I dropped a white phosphorus grenade down the air vent." Listening at the vent, he heard moaning and screaming from down inside the bunker, so he dropped in another. The noise stopped, and Anderson realized the large gun had also ceased firing.

The young corporal turned around and suddenly saw two Japanese pop up from a trench leading away from the gun he had just knocked out. He shot them both dead, then sat down on the bunker to rest. "After a few minutes, the hair on my head started to stand up," he recalled. "I turned around, and there was a Jap coming at me from the front of the gun emplacement with a bayonet in his hand. He was only about six feet from me when I got him. Most of his clothes were burned off, so I figured he had been in the bunker."

Following this encounter, Anderson decided he'd "better get out of there," so he headed on up the shoreline.

Corporal Joe Lommerse, one of the early arrivals on White 2, landed on a beach already crowded with burning amtracs and dead and wounded Marines. Mortar shells walked across the beach, bursting among the Marines "digging for China" or already hunkered in holes blasted in the sand by the naval bombardment. Lommerse's section leader lay off to his right, blood welling from his left shoulder. An officer yelled for someone to help the wounded Marine. Lommerse got up and ran over to the man. Trying vainly to cut the man's pack straps with his commando knife, he finally opened up the wounded man's first aid kit, poured sulfanite into the gaping hole and tried to control his trembling hands as he bandaged the wound.

The man suddenly cried out. While being bandaged, he had been hit again, this time by a bullet through the leg. Finally a corpsman dropped down beside them, and Lommerse ran forward to the cover of some scrub trees and undergrowth. Behind him on the beach, wounded men were calling for corpsmen.

As the smoke obscuring the island began to dissipate, observers still aboard the ships offshore were appalled to see burning amtracs and DUKWs strewn along the length of the reef. The boundary of danger was the reef, for few enemy guns or mortars were registered beyond that protective barrier. Outside the reef, the amtracs were reasonably safe; inside, they were in major peril.

Enemy mortars, preregistered on the reef, seemed almost like a "protective curtain" which followed the assault waves toward the beach. So intense was the shell fire that all but one of the 15 Sherman tanks assigned to the 1st Marines were struck by high explosives during the ten minutes it took to cross the reef. Fortunately, only three were knocked out of action, some of the explosions occurring below the waterline, which prevented serious damage.

The situation was particularly hot on the flanks. High-velocity weapons on the Point enfiladed White I, while others on the southwestern promontory and on a small unnamed island just below the Orange Beaches enfiladed the 7th Marines on Orange 3. At one point, an observer reported 38 LVTs burning simultaneously. The total knocked out, at least temporarily, rose to over 60, according to unofficial estimates by assault unit commanders, although some of these were probably DUKWs which observers mistook for amtracs.

The official report later counted 26 LVTs destroyed on D-Day. Part of the reason for the discrepancy, noted a Marine officer, might have been "the extreme reluctance, short of complete demolition or submersion in over ten fathoms, of any crew chief to regard his vehicle as destroyed."

Waves two through six managed to land on time, but succeeding waves were held up due to the mounting losses of LVTs. The 12th wave was delayed 30 minutes, the 14th was held up 45.

A Marine artilleryman who landed in one of the later waves noticed that when the LVTs were hit by a mortar shell in deep water "they'd go straight down... just boom, straight down. But when they were on the sandbar or on shallow water, they'd burn and all the guys would burn too."

Creeping over the reef in his Sherman tank, Corporal Bill Myers saw a landing craft flame up from a direct hit from a heavy shell. Doomed Marines leapt out, their clothes on fire. Myers knew they were dying, but he felt curiously detached, almost as if he were watching a movie. He later learned that none of the men in the landing craft survived.

Rear Admiral Oldendorf, previously so complacent about the effectiveness of his naval gunfire, viewed the carnage off Peleliu's beaches with "surprise and chagrin" from the heavy cruiser *Louisville*. It was now clear, even to the most dedicated proponent of naval bombardment, that Japanese defenses had been barely touched by the three-day shelling.

Watching from the deck of a transport, a lieutenant colonel of supply found himself turning over a peculiar reaction in his mind. "I'd never seen combat before," he recalled, "and the first thing that struck me was that this was a hell of a way to treat $40,000 equipment."

Chapter 4

Chesty Puller's 1st Marines landed at 0832—only two minutes behind schedule—in a cauldron of enemy fire on the White Beaches. On White 2, 2/1 drove inland against "moderate resistance," pushing 350 yards through heavy undergrowth by 0930. White 1, on the extreme left, was another story. The 3d Battalion—and most particularly Captain George Hunt's K Company on the extreme left of the landing area—was involved in fierce fighting.

"Thirty yards from the beach we were actually catching small arms fire," recalled Sergeant "Swede" Hanson. "Machine guns, pistol fire, rifle fire... the executive officer had his head up looking to see where we were going to come ashore, and we went down into a dip on this coral reef and a 40 mm shell went right over his head. If he had a piece of fuzz on his helmet, it woulda knocked it off. I don't think there can be anybody that ever came closer to getting a 40 mm in the head than he did. Well, he came down in a flash, and I thought sure that it had got part of him, but it didn't."

Lurching up onto the beach, the Marines in Corporal Harlan Murray's amtrac waited agonizing seconds while the man at the rear fumbled with the ramp releases. Shells were bursting up and down the beach, recalled Murray, "and then he got it down, and boy we went out of there like a shot."

Dashing inland, Private First Class Joe Hendley's group hit a concrete pillbox located at the vegetation line. Naval gunfire had not so much as scratched the fortification, which housed a 47 mm gun. The Marines lobbed grenades at the pillbox, hoping to keep the enemy's head down. Finally, somebody tossed a satchel charge through the embrasure. The charge set off all the ammo inside, knocking out the strongpoint.

Hendley ran through knee-deep crushed coral behind the ruined pillbox and tumbled into a huge tank trap that paralleled most of the beach. Murray's group also hit the trap, running down one side and right up the other. "Slow it down! Slow it down!" yelled the noncoms, but it was too late. Coming up over the top into an area of fallen coconut trees, the running Marines were suddenly swept by enemy machine-gun fire "and guys started fallin'," recalled Murray. He suddenly realized the obvious: "Hey, there's other people on this damn island besides us."

Directly to his front, a Japanese 47 mm gun cut loose, so close he was jarred by the concussion. Looking back toward the beach, Murray saw the turret of an armored amphib fly straight up into the air.

Smack in the middle of his first combat, Murray tried to sight in on the Japanese, but he could not see anyone. He and some other men took shelter in some abandoned enemy trenches fronting the tank trap. As bullets buzzed overhead, Murray, "the big shot corporal," crawled out to make contact with I Company. He made the mistake of stopping to shoot back at the invisible source of the fire, and a Japanese rifleman took that opportunity to hammer a slug through his shoulder from no more than 15 yards away. A Marine machine gunner saw the Japanese rise up to see if he had finished Murray and put a burst of fire into the man's chest. Dragging his useless right arm, Murray crawled back to the tank trap, leaving his rifle behind. "I'm hit," he said to the cluster of men in the ditch. A couple of Marines looked him over. "Well, you're not hit," said one. "Yes I am," insisted Murray. The men looked again. "I see a little hole in your shovel," said one.

"They cut my pack off, and sure enough, there was the bullet hole," said Murray, "right through the shovel, through the pack, into my shoulder blade, and it hurt like hell."

Landing on White 1 with the third wave, Colonel Puller scrambled over the side of the amtrac and ran inland as fast as he could for 25 yards before flopping down on the coral sand, his leg aching from the chunk of Guadalcanal shrapnel still embedded there. When he glanced back, he saw five or six shells slam into the amtrac and blow it to oblivion. Some of the slower men died right then and there. Puller's communications officer had also been hit in the early minutes. His leg gone, he lay dying on the white coral sand.

"I looked down the beach and saw a mess—every damned amtrac in our wave had been destroyed in the water by the enemy or shot to pieces the moment it landed," reported Puller. Among the casualties, five LVTs carrying the command group had been badly shot up while crossing the reef, losing most of the communications equipment and expert operators.

The beach itself was already littered with broken and abandoned equipment. Gas masks, helmets, weapons, mortar shell cases and other debris lay among the splinters of coconut log and coral fragments. Numerous dead and wounded Marines also lay strewn on the gray coral. One Marine, new to combat, was surprised at how unobtrusive they were. "They quietly bled and died in the sand without being conspicuous," he recalled.

Despite the chaos on the beach, Puller remained unflappable. An enlisted Marine lifted his head out of the sand long enough to see Chesty confront an excited major. The major had his automatic pistol drawn and "he was just shaking like a leaf on the end of a twig," recalled the Marine. Puller tore the weapon out of the officer's hand, shoved it back in his shoulder holster and snapped, "Keep that goddamn thing there. We've got all these men to do our fighting."

Also caught in the confusion on the beach was Sergeant "Swede" Hanson. He had spent his first few minutes on the beach flattened behind a concrete tank obstacle while a Japanese machine gun chipped away at the top. Now, scrambling to his feet, he dashed out to help a wounded Marine lying at the edge of the water. The Marine looked up as Hanson leaned over him and pleaded, "No, Mac. Please don't touch me. Leave me be."

"Man, I can't leave you here," said Hanson. "You're gonna get hit by a tank." He reached down to lift the Marine out of the water and realized with horror that the lower part of the Marine's body was gone.

"See what I mean?" said the Marine, looking at him. "Please, just leave me here. There's no hope for me. Get some cover for yourself."

"Mac, God bless you," blurted Hanson, and he turned and ran up the beach as hard as he could, trying to run the thought of the dying Marine right out of his mind.

"All of a sudden I'm running by a little fellow whose sitting gook style," recalled Hanson. "He's got a pipe in his mouth, and my God, it's our regimental commander, Chesty Puller. And I can't believe that man is up so close to the front lines observing everything. And as I run by him, he says, 'Give 'em hell, Marine.' It was so damn hot . . . while running I threw off my gas mask. That I knew I wouldn't need. The sun was going to get me before gas did."

Despite Puller's cockiness, the 3d Battalion was in trouble. In addition to the artillery and mortar fire blanketing the entire area, the Marines found themselves under intense small-arms fire from strongly entrenched Japanese. Worse, the lead elements had not pushed 100 yards inland when they came up against a rugged coral ridge to their right front: a ridge that was not supposed to be there . . . at least it had not shown up on any of the advance maps or intelligence reports. About 30 feet high, the long scrub-dotted ridge was honeycombed with caves and dug-in positions manned by determined Japanese infantry.

The Marines could not make much headway against this obstacle, even after tanks were brought up. Marines trying to assault the northern part of the ridge found themselves caught in the long antitank ditch 75 yards inland. Ten feet deep and several hundred yards long, it was cleverly enfiladed and dominated by the Japanese positions.

Meanwhile, enemy mortar and shell fire continued to wreak havoc on the beach as subsequent waves came in. The men burrowed into the sand like so many camouflaged gophers. Wading in from his amtrac, Private First Class Larry Kaloian found cover near a stump 30 or 40 feet inland. Another Marine flopped down beside him, produced a shovel, dug a foxhole, then passed the shovel over to Kaloian. "Here, dig," he said. "I read somewhere you're supposed to dig a hole and get in it when you're in a situation like this." Not knowing what else to do, Kaloian started to dig. The other Marine told how he had been right at the shoreline when a mortar shell killed his buddy next to him.

"Your buddy was right next to you?" asked Kaloian nervously.

"Yeah," said the Marine.

"Excuse me, but I gotta leave," said Kaloian. Scuttling away from the other Marine, he jumped into a nearby bomb crater just as a mortar shell exploded behind him, showering him with dirt and debris. He looked back as the dust settled. The tree stump and the Marine were gone, obliterated by the explosion.

Working his way down White 2, Russell Davis nearly stumbled over a Marine who was just sitting on the sand, watching the blood pump out of his mangled leg. The man had started to tie a tourniquet around the leg before shock had intervened; now he just sat and stared at the wound, making no effort to staunch the bleeding.

Davis was also momentarily mesmerized by the sight, then he reached around, took off the man's belt and cinched it around the leg above the knee. As the bleeding stopped, the wounded Marine wordlessly rolled over on his side and lay there with his eyes open.

Davis managed to attract a tobacco-chewing corpsman, who regarded the whole affair with a cynical nonchalance. "We ought to be getting an evac boat in here soon—I hope," he told Davis. "This guy might just last and make it; then again he might not." With a wave, Davis warned him to pipe down, gesturing at the wounded Marine's wide open eyes. The corpsman shrugged it off. "He can't hear a thing we say. He's miles away in shock land."

As Davis moved off, the corpsman casually spat a stream of tobacco juice on the wounded Marine's shoes.

The problems on the White Beaches were being caused in large part by enemy positions on the Point, just off the left flank. Weapons dug into the jagged coral outcropping poured enfilading fire the length of the beaches, threatening the entire landing.

Captain George Hunt's K Company, charged with seizing the Point, had been shot to pieces after landing about 100 yards to the right of its assigned area. Though Hunt did not know it yet, many of his men remained pinned down in the antitank ditch behind the beach. Now, lying in a shell hole, Hunt was trying to get his survivors organized. Someone nearby was yelling for a corpsman.

One thing was already eminently clear. The Point far surpassed anything the Marines had envisioned when studying aerial photos of the objective. Rising 30 feet above the water's edge, it was a tumbled mass of coral, crevices, caves and fissures. One reinforced concrete pillbox housing a 47 mm anti-boat gun had been blasted into the sheer base of the Point. Four others, covered with up to six feet of coral and concrete, sheltered heavy machine guns and 6 to 12 Japanese. Other Japanese, some with light machine guns, lurked in spider holes blasted into the hard coral.

Although photographs had not revealed these fortifications, Colonel Puller had insisted that the Point be blanketed with fire during the preliminary bombardment. Naval officers had assured him the area would be properly dealt with. Now, to their dismay, Hunt's men found that naval gunfire had apparently made not the slightest impression on the pillboxes.

Hunt's radio operator droned into the instrument. "Hello one, hello two, hello three. This is control, do you hear me? Over."

A colonel slid into the hole. Surprised, Hunt offered him a cigarette, which the colonel declined. "No, thanks, I've got to be moving. Take care of my radio operator, he's been hit."

"No, he's dead, Colonel," said a corpsman.

"Oh." The colonel paused. "Good luck." He scrambled off down the beach.

As Japanese fire built up, Hunt's radioman finally got through to the 1st Platoon commanded by Lieutenant William Willis. Willis reported that the 3d Platoon had been badly shot up neutralizing the defenses leading up to the Point. They had no contact at all with the 2d Platoon, supposed to be on the right.

"Well, push through and take the Point," ordered Hunt. "I'm coming right up."

"Okay, okay," said Willis. "That's what I figured."

There were five pillboxes all told on the Point. Four mounted heavy machine guns, the fifth, blasted into the base of the cliff where it could enfilade the landing area and protected by reinforced concrete, sheltered a 47 mm gun. Spider holes were manned by riflemen and light machine gunners.

Pushing inland past the Point, then turning to hit it from the landward side, the 3d Platoon under Lieutenant Ralph Estey had already cleared the way to the objective itself—but at high cost. Coming up, Hunt saw a swath of dead and wounded, some still "groaning and writhing," others "grotesquely transfixed in the attitudes of death, entrails exposed, chunks of their bodies blasted away." Among the wounded was Lieutenant Estey, shot through the arm.

A dying Marine looked glassy-eyed at Hunt and struggled to speak before his head slumped back, blood oozing from his mouth. Also among the dead was the conscientious Lieutenant Wayland Woodyard. He had barely taken ten steps off the amtrac when a bullet caught him square through the head.

Willis was already on the move. Taking advantage of the 3d Platoon's work, at 1015, what remained of the 1st and 3d Platoons stormed the Point, pushing past dead Japanese killed by Estey's outfit. The corpses lay sprawled around the base of the rise and slumped in cracks and holes in the coral. The Japanese seemed big and healthy, and they had new equipment, observed Hunt.

A Marine private named King took on one pillbox single-handedly, ignoring a bullet that passed through his helmet without touching his skull and another that glanced off his cartridge belt. Squirming behind a large rock, he bobbed up, tossed a grenade through the embrasure and ducked back down. The occupants of the pillbox died in a muffled blast. Two other Marines dodged around a boulder right into three Japanese trying to set up a heavy machine gun. The Japanese reached frantically for hand grenades, but one of the Marines already had one in his hand. He lobbed it into their midst, killing two. The third enemy soldier threw a grenade and started to run; one of the Marines shot him dead. The grenade, which landed directly between the two Americans, was a dud.

As the Marines scrambled among the rocks and shattered stumps to the top of the Point, some of the Japanese could be seen fleeing down the other side. The Marine riflemen lined them up and squeezed them off. Among the Japanese was one man whose pack had apparently caught fire. It left a trail of smoke in his wake as he fled, screaming, down the rocks. A bullet slammed him into the ground, and he did not move again.

The assault on the Point reunited Corporal Robert Anderson with his company. After leaving the knocked-out bunker on the beach area, he had proceeded about 50 yards north to the Point, where he came up on another shore gun shooting at the boats and amtracs offshore. "I couldn't get a very good look at the barrel end of the gun because of a steep drop-off from the bank I was standing on," he remembered. "I grabbed hold of a tree and leaned over the bank for a better look. All of a sudden, I could feel something warm running down by leg. I thought I had been hit. I looked down and saw a bullet hole in my left canteen."

About that time, Lieutenant Willis arrived with the survivors of his platoon. Tackling the big pillbox housing the 47 mm gun, the Marines sidled down from above, leaving a squad to cover the rear exit. The men could hear the Japanese jabbering to themselves inside. Willis tossed a smoke grenade in front of the embrasure. Balls of fire whipped overhead as the enemy gun opened up, scaring Willis half to death.

Anderson put a rifle grenade on his M–1 and tried to line up the bunker opening, but his first round exploded harmlessly against the concrete. He put another rifle grenade on the Garand, hooked his right leg around the tree, leaned out as far as he could over the embankment and squeezed the trigger. The grenade glanced off the barrel of the 47 mm and ignited the ammunition in the pillbox. Flame and smoke spewed out, and the Marines heard the men screaming inside. Shrieking with pain, three enemy soldiers suddenly burst out the rear exit, cartridges on their belts popping off like firecrackers, flames clinging to their spiral-wrapped leggings. The covering squad gunned them down.

As the Marines consolidated on the coral point, word came that they were cut off from the rest of the regiment. A corpsman pitched his empty medical bag into the air. "For cripes sake, somebody give me a weapon," he blurted. Willis walked over and handed him his own M-1 rifle and a cartridge belt. The corpsman looked at him. "Lieutenant, thank you, but what are you going to do?" he asked.

"There are plenty of M-1s around here," replied Willis, "I'll be able to find one."

Isolated from the rest of the regiment, Hunt organized the 32 survivors of his two platoons in an all-around defense of the Point as enemy resistance ceased. The Marines had counted 110 dead Japanese scattered among the coral outcroppings, but American casualties had also been high. If his missing 2d Platoon had suffered as heavily as the 1st and 3d, Hunt estimated perhaps two thirds of K Company had already been killed or wounded.

He had been on Peleliu just over two hours.

Also landing on White Beach 1 that morning was the Sherman tank commanded by Corporal Bill Myers. The young Oklahoman's luck had already been put sorely to the test. On the way into the beach, a Japanese mortar shell had hit the turret ring. The burst miraculously missed Myers, foolishly standing in the open hatch to see what was going on, but drove a three-inch splinter into his gunner's back. The man was alive but in bad pain.

From a combat standpoint, the 30 tanks assigned to the 1st Marine Division had already accomplished a minor landmark. Lurching across the reef in six widely spaced five-tank columns, the Shermans landed on the invasion beaches only 20 minutes behind the first wave. Within half an hour of landing, the infantry had full tank support, a record surpassed only during the Marshall Islands operation.

Grinding up onto the beach, half in the sand and half in the water, Myers opened the pistol port and saw a Marine stretched out behind a stump. "Hey, Mac!" he yelled at the rifleman. "Where's the front lines?"

"Hell," retorted the Marine. "You're twenty feet in front of them."

"Thanks a lot," said Myers, slamming the port shut.

Pinned down on the beach, the tankers waited for something to happen, unable to fire. Bullets splattered against the turret like rain. "It was comforting to be inside," recalled Myers.

Tank Platoon Commander Richard Kelly arrived with a corpsman and a replacement for the wounded gunner. "I've got to get back to the post," said Kelly after the gunner was safely evacuated. Myers warned him to be careful of a Japanese machine gun firing down a trail toward the beach. All morning long, the gun had been rattling away at the beach, but the men had learned it was firing in a pattern and managed to dodge between the bursts.

"I will," said Kelly, trotting off. The gun fired a burst, and Kelly started across the path. It suddenly fired another burst out of sequence, knocking the lieutenant down. Standing in the turret of the tank, Myers heard the cry for corpsmen and saw Kelly being carried down to the boats on a stretcher. The officer looked over at him, and Myers waved. Kelly raised his hand and waved weakly. He died aboard a hospital ship that same night.

Coming in on Orange 1 with A/1/5, Private First Class M. L. "Bird Dog" Clayton was surprised to see an army lieutenant in charge of his amtrac. As the trac hit the coral reef, the lieutenant came unwound. "Get out!" he screamed. "Get out! Drop the ramp!"

Loaded down with a 68-pound flamethrower, Clayton stepped off into a hole and went into water up to his neck. He was still hollering for help when another Marine grabbed him by the collar and pulled him out. Right then and there, Clayton decided he was going to get rid of the heavy flamethrower the first chance he got.

Wading 30 yards to the beach through knee-deep water, Clayton's outfit came ashore by a 10-foot coral ledge. The Marines huddled down at the base as mortar shells plunged down behind them. Clayton slapped the denim-clad back in front of him. "Move out, dammit," he snapped. "Move out."

The other Marine turned and looked at him unenthusiastically. "You SOB," he retorted. "If you want to move out, *you* get up here."

Stung, Clayton raised his head up over the ledge and found out why no one was moving: machine-gun fire was slashing directly overhead. He slid back down and reached for a cigarette, only to find them ruined from the soaking he had taken on the way in.

Also coming in on Orange 1, the 30-odd men in Sergeant Walter "Flip" Afflito's amtrac made it to the base of the ledge, only to be cut to pieces by enemy mortar fire. Afflito had already had one indication it was going to be a bad day. On the way in, his amtrac had gotten hung up on the coral and the frightened tractor sergeant ordered the Marines out. Knowing they wouldn't have a prayer, Afflito stuck the muzzle of his M–1 in the man's throat and snapped, "Get this motherfucker off the rocks, or I'll blow your head off and I'll drive it in!"

The noncom rocked the amtrac free and gunned her onto the beach. "As soon as he let us off, he was in reverse," recalled Afflito. "I think he was in reverse when he lowered the ramp." The Marines went over the side and out the back and promptly got clobbered as Japanese mortar shells plummeted down on them. One of the first to go down was the navy corpsman assigned to the outfit.

Grabbing the corpsman's first aid kit, Afflito started treating as many of the casualties as he could reach. One of the Marines—a man who had been his friend for over two years—had a hole the size of a baseball just under his navel. Afflito tore off the man's burning cartridge belt and threw it in the water. As he sprinkled sulfanide powder on the wound, he could see the intestines moving. The Marine's eyes were already turning back, and his skin was bluish. He died within a couple of minutes.

Another private lay nearby, his arm blown off at the shoulder. "Oh, help, I'm dying," he repeated as Afflito leaned over him.

"You're going to be all right," lied Afflito, straightening the man's head as it lolled against his butchered shoulder. The Marine quickly died.

Afflito later estimated he lost eight or ten men on the beach in a period of about 45 minutes. The New Jersey noncom did not pause to mourn. Stripping a dead Marine of his BAR, he led the survivors inland.

Though subsequent attention focused largely on the ferocity of the fighting in the sector of the 1st Marines, Peleliu's first Medal of Honor was won by a member of the 1st Battalion, 5th Marines who came in on Orange 1.

Pushing inland off the beach, Corporal Lewis K. Bausell, 20, a former apprentice bookbinder from Washington, D.C., was in a squad assigned to clean out one of the many Japanese pillboxes concealed in the scrub. On one side of the position, Lieutenant Jack Kimble of Greenville, Mississippi, and several of his men were using a flamethrower to force the Japanese out through the other side where Bausell and some other Marines waited.

Two of Kimble's men stood at the entrance, firing into the pillbox. A Japanese charged out holding a grenade against his body. The grenade exploded, blowing the man to pieces and injuring several Marines. Another Japanese appeared at the entrance. He was shot. Then a third enemy soldier appeared and threw a grenade among Bausell and the others.

"There wasn't any cover and no place to run," recalled Kimble. "Bausell ran toward the grenade and fell on it." There was a muffled blast as the grenade exploded under the young Marine's body. Still alive, he was evacuated to the hospital ship *Bountiful*, where he later died. "He fought to the end, but he was torn apart in so many places that we couldn't stop the bleeding," a navy surgeon told one of Bausell's buddies.

Just inland from Orange 2 where 3/5 came ashore, Private Eugene Sledge stumbled across the first dead Japanese of his brief combat career: an eviscerated medic and two riflemen. The medic had apparently been rendering first aid when he was killed by a shell. He lay on his back, his abdominal cavity gaping, the glistening viscera speckled with coral dust, his medical instruments at his side. It reminded Sledge of nothing so much as the many rabbits and squirrels he had cleaned on boyhood hunting trips.

As he stared, sickened, two veteran Marines came along, casually field-stripped the corpses for souvenirs and strolled away with a Nambu pistol, flag and other trinkets. Typical of combat veterans, they took only smaller items, leaving the heavy souvenirs for rear-echelon scavengers. "See you later, Sledgehammer," one tossed over his shoulder. "Don't take any wooden nickels."

The scene was indicative of the relative good fortune befalling Sledge's battalion. Leading K Company in over the gray-colored beach, Executive Officer Lieutenant Tom Stanley took the first wave up into the vegetation line, 30 yards away. There were no live Japanese on the beach. Trotting at high port through a small coconut grove, the Marines pushed through some brush and found themselves at the corner of the airfield. Suddenly Stanley heard one of his men yelling, "I got one! I got one!" To Stanley's great amusement, the Marine had slammed the door shut on a bunker after seeing a Japanese soldier dart inside; now the excited hunter stood there with his quarry "trapped."

Meanwhile, the subsequent waves were landing in good shape. The flanking fire and high ground which wreaked havoc among the 1st Marines were not a problem on Orange 1 and 2, so the assault waves suffered less in crossing the reef. And while some units took heavy losses on the beach from mortar and artillery fire, most managed to get inland in reasonably good order.

The regiment also escaped serious losses from mines on the beach, due largely to a whim of nature. The Japanese had made extensive use of double-horned mines on both Orange beaches, laying three rows of the devices in a checkerboard pattern at intervals of about one meter. Each mine contained roughly 50 pounds of explosive. Fortunately for the assault battalions, rough weather before D-Day had deposited almost a foot of sand on the mines, greatly decreasing their effectiveness. In other cases, the pounding of the waves had cracked the horns at the base, letting sea water in and ruining the fuses.

Despite checks by UDT swimmers up until H minus a few hours, type J–13 mines were also found on the reef, 150 yards offshore. Apparently laid in haste before dawn on D-Day, the mines were poorly concealed, and most still had their safety pins in place, rendering them harmless. Also found were aircraft bombs set out in groups of six in deep water on the reef shelf and designed to be fired electrically. Once again nature intervened on behalf of the landing force. Most of the lightweight wires leading to the mines from shore had been broken by the surf.

Unexploded mines were later dragged away with one or more horns broken off by the weight of U.S. vehicles. Some aerial bombs were also found unfused, with the wooden nose plugs still in place. A number of LVTs and DUKWs were disabled by mines and became easy meat for enemy artillery, but it could have been much worse.

3/5 did not get off completely unscathed. Commanded by Lieutenant Colonel Austin C. Shofner, whose exploits included his escape from a Japanese prison camp in the Philippines earlier in the war, the battalion suffered some disorganization after the landing. Shofner's executive officer, Major Robert M. Ash, was killed shortly after hitting the beach, and the LVT carrying most of the communications equipment and personnel was destroyed by enemy fire. Nevertheless, the battalion pushed forward on the left, reaching the first phase line at the same time as 1/5, about 0930.

Meanwhile, on the right, K Company ran into trouble not entirely of its own making. Some elements of K Company, 7th Marines, slated to land on Orange 3, had actually landed on Orange 2, pushed there by enemy fire from the right. Considerable confusion arose as the two identically named companies extricated themselves and tried to advance inland. For at least 15 minutes after landing, K/3/5 was the right flank unit of the whole division landing, while K/3/7 tried to sort itself out.

When the push to the east resumed, K/3/5 soon ran into mutually supporting pillboxes and log bunkers at the edge of the airfield. These were reduced, and K tied in with I Company by about 1000. Soon afterward, 2/5 was committed and the Marines began to advance east in an attempt to cut Peleliu in half.

While the 1st and 5th Marines struck at the Japanese over their beaches, the 7th Marines on the far right sent one of the most ominous messages of the morning: "The assault waves are wading ashore." Faced with the restrictions of a narrow, 550-yard beach, the 7th Marines had intended to land two battalions in column on Orange 3. The lead unit, 3/7, was supposed to drive across to the eastern shore along with the 5th Marines, splitting Peleliu's defenders. The 1st Battalion, landing behind them, was to wheel to the right and mop up the Japanese isolated at the island's southern tip.

It didn't work out quite that simply.

Coming in with A/1/7, Private Tom Boyle knew he was in trouble when 150 mm mortar shells started dropping in the water while the amtrac was still 1,000 yards off Orange 3. Packing 56 pounds of high explosives, the big shells blew some amtracs right out of the water. By Boyle's count, of the five in his formation, three were knocked out crossing the reef.

A former sergeant, busted down to private for the umpteenth time for striking another noncom, Boyle stepped forward to guide the amtrac driver onto the beach. Each time a mortar shell exploded nearby, he directed the driver to steer for the spot, figuring the Japanese would not drop two in the same hole. By this strategy, he gradually worked the amtrac over to a gap he had spotted in the tetrahedrons guarding the beach.

The amtrac entered the gap and moved directly into the fire of a machine-gun emplacement on the beach. "Shit, I've run into it," thought Boyle, just as a machine-gun bullet glanced off his helmet right between the T and the R of the T. R. BOYLE painted on the front. Boyle yanked his head down like a scared turtle, but when the amtrac lurched up onto the beach, he popped up and pitched a grenade at the machine-gun emplacement only 50 yards away. The grenade missed.

Meanwhile, the noncom in charge of ordering the ramp lowered had frozen. Boyle pulled his pistol and told him to give the order. "Drop the ramp," said the noncom. The ramp dropped, and the men started piling out.

Lingering behind, Boyle saw someone had forgotten the spare parts kit for the machine gun. He pitched it over the side, but as he went to get out of the vehicle, he slipped in a pool of vomit and got hung up on the hand crank. Freeing himself, he ran out of the amtrac. A Marine from another outfit was lying on the beach next to the vehicle. Boyle told him to get in off the beach.

"I can't move," said the Marine, paralyzed with fear.

Boyle left him there and ran for a big tank trap just up the beach. He no sooner ducked under cover than a mortar shell obliterated the amtrac, its driver and the frightened Marine lying alongside.

Also landing on Orange 3 was 23-year-old Sergeant Carl Stevenson, who had the unnerving experience of vaulting over the side of his amtrac and landing directly on an anti-invasion mine. His weight broke the horns off, but the device failed to explode.

Stevenson had little time to congratulate himself on his good fortune. Looking up, he saw a Japanese infantryman directly in front of him. He pulled the trigger on his tommy gun, but in his excitement he failed to hold the weapon down and "that damn thing climbed clear to the sky." The Japanese promptly disappeared into a bunker, and the occupants began lobbing grenades out at the Marines. Luckily, the grenades were landing in the soft sand and did little damage, although a close miss left Stevenson's head ringing.

An amtrac stood nearby, but when the grenades started going off the crew ducked down to the bottom. Finally, as Stevenson watched, a Marine climbed up the side of the amphib, turned the 50-caliber machine gun on the bunker and "just flat disintegrated" the strongpoint.

As Boyle and Stevenson discovered, the 7th Marines had the misfortune to encounter the strongest beach defenses of any of the chosen landing areas. These included, according to the regiment's report, "anti-boat barriers, anti-boat mines, antitank mines and antipersonnel mines," along with "extensive and intricate barbed wire entanglements covered effectively by heavy, well-aimed, sustained automatic fire." One Marine recalled seeing "kind of a little ridge sitting out in the water, and they had little rifle slits cut right into the rock inside . . . they had a little fortification there."

The reef was so cluttered with natural and man-made obstacles that the amtracs had to pick their way shoreward in column at various points, making them easy targets. An unnamed island just offshore on the right flank provided an ideal location to enfilade the landing and "direct fire from heavy-caliber anti-boat guns took an extremely heavy toll of landing craft." Other weapons were located on the southwestern promontory sometimes referred to as Ngarmoked Island. On the beaches themselves, "preregistered mortar and artillery fires maintained a steady, unceasing barrage on the landing beaches, causing serious disorganization and inflicting heavy casualties."

Inexplicably, naval gunfire had apparently failed to target these enfilading positions. "During the ship-to-shore move, I did not see a single indication of friendly fire on this target," an infantry colonel noted subsequently. Now Marines trying to wade in from disabled amtracs fell in bloody splashes, as enemy machine-gun fire whipped the water.

Six of the new armored amphibs worked over the beach as the waves approached, and six more fired on the small unnamed island to the right. A Marine officer later saw an amtrac that had rammed a Japanese dual-purpose gun. The bow of the armored amtrac actually rode up onto the muzzle of the gun before the assault vehicle was knocked out.

Despite such efforts, the flanking fire pushed many of the LVT drivers off to the left, so they landed some men on Orange 2 where they became intermixed, causing the K Company imbroglio. Battalion CO, Major E. Hunter Hurst, landed on Orange 2, although his exec, Major Victor H. Streit, came in on the correct beach. The vehicle carrying much of the battalion's communications gear was also destroyed, which complicated control still further.

Somehow the unit managed to get its men on the beach. Among them was *Life* magazine artist Tom Lea. "There was a rattle and roar under my helmet when I undid the chin strap and smelled flaming oil and popping ammunition from the burning amtracs around us," he recalled. Running up the beach for cover, half bent over, Lea fell flat on his face just as a mortar round whispered in.

"A red flash stabbed at my eyeballs," he recalled. "About 15 yards away, on the upper edge of the beach, it smashed down four men from our boat. One figure seemed to fly to pieces. With terrible clarity, I saw the head and one leg sail into the air."

Lea got up and ran a few steps, darting into a small shell hole just as another mortar round showered dirt all over him. Lying there in terror, he saw a wounded Marine staggering toward the amtracs. One half of the man's face had been smashed to a pulp, and the shreds of one arm hung uselessly as he stumbled toward the water. "The half of his face that was still human had the most terrifying look of abject patience I have ever seen," remembered Lea. The mortally wounded Marine finally collapsed just behind him, his blood draining red on the white sand. Mortar shells continued to slam into the beach and reef without any apparent pattern. A Marine artilleryman realized to his horror that he could actually see the big-caliber mortar shells tumbling through the air. "About the size of a 50-gallon oil drum," he recalled. "Spigots all over 'em. The minute they hit, they went boom . . . boy, they'd clear everything out for 50, 60 yards in each direction."

One made a direct hit on an amtrac. Pieces of the vehicle and its occupants sailed in slow motion through the air. Japanese machine guns lashed the reef with fire. Marines wading in from a disabled amtrac slumped into the green water. "The survivors seem so slow and small and patient coming in there," thought Lea, watching from the tenuous safety of his hole on the beach.

One of the Marines in the water off the Orange Beaches was Sergeant Robert Askey. Askey had been up in the driver's compartment, helping guide the driver in, when a shell slammed into the aft end of the amtrac just 100 yards off the beach. "All I can remember is the flash," he recalled later. "The next thing, I was on the beach . . . with all of my equipment." Wet only to the ankles, Askey never knew how he got to shore. Of the more than 20 men in his amtrac, only the driver, co-driver, Askey and one other man survived.

The first casualty in Private Robert Biron's party occurred during their initial seconds on the beach. As the last Marine left the amtrac, the coxswain, unable to see him, swung the vehicle around and ran over the man's foot. The injured man's buddies threw him right back in the amtrac, and he headed straight back to the ships offshore.

On the beach itself, numerous land mines barred the way, reaching about 100 yards inland. As on the other landing beaches, many of these mines were anti-invasion types with twin horns consisting of lead-covered bottles of acid which detonated the explosives when broken. Fortunately, practically all of these mines had deteriorated and failed to detonate, thus averting what could have been a worse disaster for the Marines attempting to land.

Assault troops landing on Orange 3 also encountered quantities of aerial bombs jury-rigged as mines. The 50-kilogram bombs were buried with the tail assemblies down and a pressure-detonating fuse extending about three inches above the ground. They were strewn so thickly on the beach that the lead tank commander got out to scout the area, then led his tank through, leaving a trail of toilet paper to mark the way for other vehicles. An amtrac was less fortunate—or its driver less observant. Rolling over a mine, the vehicle went up in "a shuddering explosion" followed by the wild popping of 50-caliber shells as its ammunition cooked off.

Landing quickly, the tanks, led by First Lieutenant George Jerue, accounted for the main Japanese gun position on the unnamed island off to their right. Jerue first became aware of the gun when he saw a flash. The shell hit his tank and knocked him momentarily unconscious. Coming to, he made his way to another of his tanks, hung on the outside of the turret and directed the gunner's fire on the Japanese emplacement, which blew up after a direct hit. Still clinging to the turret, Jerue then directed fire on several hostile machine-gun positions on the beach, knocking them out and earning him a Navy Cross.

Confusion reigned on the beach itself. Lying in his hole next to another correspondent, Tom Lea sensed someone crawling up behind him. He turned his head to see a corpsman grinning at him. "Christ," said the corpsman, "I thought you were a couple of corpses."

A burly man moved up the beach, walking fast. "Where's the CP?" he bawled at the men he passed. Always the reply came, "Up that way, Colonel." Hanneken pushed on, never bobbing or missing a step as enemy fire came in on the beach.

Plagued by disorganization during the landing, the assault battalions of the 7th Marines took time to reorganize. Fortunately, 3/7 encountered less than 30 live Japanese still on the beach, and these men were so stunned by naval gunfire that they put up little resistance. By 0925, the assault battalions had seized the beach at a cost of 40 Marine casualties. Nevertheless, Colonel Hanneken's early reports to division were not encouraging. A number of his amphibious tanks had been hit on the way into the beach. The assault waves "are wading ashore," he reported.

Reorganization ashore was hampered by mines, barbed wire entanglements and spotty—but stiff—resistance from Japanese infantry fighting from mutually supporting trenches and pillboxes dug into the coral. The bombardment had also stripped away most of the vegetation, changing the appearance of the terrain and making orientation difficult.

Paradoxically, the Marines were aided by a feature originally intended to hamper them: a large Japanese antitank ditch a short distance behind the landing beach. The trench had not been spotted by pre-invasion reconnaissance, but was seen from a support aircraft which radioed a report just before the first wave pushed off. The assault companies were able to orient themselves on this ditch, which crossed the whole width of the sector parallel to the beach, and use it to deploy for the push inland. Battalion Exec Major Victor Streit later credited the ditch with helping 3/7 to pull itself together at least an hour earlier than would have otherwise been possible.

Reorganized, the Marines took up the advance with two companies in assault. Progress was encouraging. By 1045, K Company, attacking on the right, had pushed forward 500 yards, overrunning an enemy radio direction finder in the surge inland, and the 7th was off the beach.

The assault on Peleliu was barely an hour old before General Rupertus recognized at least half of his prediction had already come true: It was rough. Confined by his broken ankle to a folding canvas chair on the open deck of the division command ship *DuPage*, he could see amtracs burning on the beach. Japanese rockets traced erratic white trails across the sky. Most of the rockets seemed to be falling well short of the landing beaches, but the enemy artillery fire hitting the beaches and reef was deadly accurate.

Radios were scattered around the deck of the command ship, each tuned to some element of the operation. They crackled with messages, some of them dire. The situation remained confused; Rupertus grew increasingly restless and worried as order failed to emerge from the chaos ashore.

The general's frustration probably would have reached new peaks had he known how well Stalemate's sister operation—MacArthur's assault on Morotai some 500 miles to the southwest—was proceeding. While Marines battled fierce resistance on Peleliu, two combat teams of the 31st Infantry Division landed on Morotai against negligible opposition.

Forty miles long and 25 miles wide, Morotai dwarfed Peleliu in size but was lightly garrisoned. Although located only 300 miles from the Southern Philippines, the island was held by only about 500 men—mostly Formosans under Japanese officers—of the 2d Raiding Unit. American casualties totaled only seven wounded. Total casualties for the operation would subsequently run to about 30 killed and 85 wounded. The 31st Division had lucked into the combat soldier's dream . . . a walkover.

Peleliu, meanwhile, remained more like a combat man's nightmare. The assistant division commander, Brigadier General Oliver P. Smith, came ashore with a skeleton staff on Orange 2 at about 1130. Watching from the troopship *Elmore*, Smith had seen shell fire landing on the reef; periodically an LVT would go up in flames. The 5th Marines reported successfully landing two battalions; the situation in the 7th's area remained confused; and the 1st Marines had not reported.

Smith finally decided to go ashore in the 5th Marines sector since Bucky Harris's regiment seemed to have made the firmest lodgement. He also decided it would be wiser to go ashore in an LVT and dismissed the DUKW driver who had been standing by. "I do not know whether he was relieved or disappointed," remarked Smith with a touch of humor.

Working through the mortar fire, the driver of Smith's amtrac hit the reef flat out, knocking everybody sprawling. Among the casualties was a thermos of coffee lost over the side when Smith's clerk slipped and fell. Smith noticed the Japanese had marked the reef with small flags, apparently to establish ranges for their artillery and mortars. The driver turned north along a barbed wire fence running parallel to Orange 2. He could have gone right through the fence, but for some reason he did not. Finally, Smith told him, "Look, you are going to run out of beach here pretty quickly, and we've got to move in."

The driver turned toward shore, and Smith landed on the northern end of Orange 2 in the zone of the 5th Marines. The area seemed deserted, although someone had already marked the mines with white or red tape. Setting up an advance command post in the antitank trench behind the beach just below the southern leg of the main airstrip, he was soon in touch with the CPs of the 5th and 7th Marines and with General Rupertus aboard the *DuPage*. Efforts to raise the 1st Marines by radio brought no response. Vehicles rapidly chewed up any commo wire laid on the ground, while an experimental LVT(A) fitted out as a mobile communications center (facetiously dubbed "USS *Fubar*" for "Fucked Up Beyond All Recognition") proved to be less than a complete success.

Dissatisfied with the fragments of information trickling in to his command post, Rupertus toyed with the idea of going ashore himself. According to the original planning, he was to follow General Smith as soon as possible but not later than H plus four hours. Rupertus optimistically assumed his division would have occupied the entire southern end of the island by that time and he could make a decision on how to tackle the terrain north of the airfield.

His broken ankle clearly made such an early landing impracticable, although on the way to Peleliu he had again begun to talk about landing on D-Day. His staff talked him out of it, but now he again "got ants in his pants," as one of his officers put it, and broached the idea of going ashore. His chief of staff, Colonel John Seldon, advised against it. "General, if you go ashore, you'll know less than you do now," he told Rupertus. Seldon pointed out that General Smith was already ashore, and if his reports seemed less than comprehensive, it could only mean the situation was not yet clear.

While unable to make contact with Chesty Puller's regiment at the northern end of the assault line, an early report from a liaison officer seemed to offer some assurance that the 1st Marines were doing well. The officer, who came in from the 1st Marines to the advance CP at noon, told General Smith that Puller had "forty or fifty" casualties.

General Rupertus would later discover that assessment to be too optimistic by far—Puller had actually taken 200 to 400 casualties by this time—but for the moment his concern focused not on the north, where the 1st Marines were butting their heads futilely against the high ground, but to the south, where the 7th Marines, who were supposed to be mopping up Peleliu's flatter southern tip, had apparently lost their initial momentum.

His anxiety was increased by a late-morning message from the 7th Marines reporting, "Heavy casualties. Need ammo, reinforcements." The plea for help would later prove to be premature, although the 7th had been badly shot up during the landing, reporting the loss of 18 LVTs to division at mid-morning. But now, from the available information, it seemed to Rupertus that the 7th Marines were in need of help.

Shortly before noon, Rupertus decided to land the Division Reconnaissance Company on Orange 3 to reinforce the 7th Marines; soon after, he also contacted General Smith onshore about landing the division reserve, 2/7, as well. He apparently hoped this added punch would help Hanneken's regiment attain its ambitious first-day objective: clearing the entire southern end of the island.

Seldon recommended committing 2/7 to the fight, but Rupertus was reluctant to commit his only major reserve. "All right, Johnny, go ahead, but I've shot my bolt when they go in," he finally told Seldon.

Back on Peleliu, General Smith was somewhat puzzled by Rupertus's decision to commit the reserves, as it was clear to all ashore that 2/7 would only take up more room on an already constricted beachhead.

Commanding 3/7, Major Hunter Hurst recalled, "The enemy was groggy, disorganized and devoid of communications, although bitterly defending every step of the way. At no time did we feel him capable of organizing a successful counterattack. We at no time requested reinforcement, and, in fact, recommended against it, since the beachhead was already overcrowded."

Colonel Hanneken, more equaniminous now that some order had evolved from the confusion of the initial landing, agreed that reinforcements were unnecessary. Working out of the captured Japanese antitank ditch just behind the beach, he realized his outfit had not suffered as badly as he had originally feared and was in the process of pushing inland. However, he said if Rupertus insisted, he would find a place for 2/7 to assemble where it would not be underfoot. Rupertus did insist, and orders were subsequently cut to send 2/7 ashore on the southern beaches.

Meanwhile, there had still been no definite word from Puller's 1st Marines.

Chapter 5

There was good reason why Chesty Puller's 1st Marines had not been in contact with General Smith's CP: it lay in the burning and shattered amtracs on Peleliu's reef. All five LVTs carrying the regiment's communications gear had taken direct hits on the way to the beach.[1] Land lines for the field phones had been quickly cut by Japanese mortar and artillery fire plastering the beachhead.

The loss of the regiment's communications equipment was particularly unfortunate because of the situation on the White Beaches. If anyone needed the extra punch of the division reserve, it was Puller, but at that point he apparently did not yet recognize the true extent of his losses.

In eight hours of what was described by experts as "some of the fiercest and most confused fighting in the Pacific war," the 1st Marines had been unable to make any headway against the Japanese entrenched on the pocked coral ridge to their front. Even the arrival of Marine tanks shortly after the initial troop landings made no impression on the obstacle. Hidden in caves and holes amid the blasted scrub, the Japanese infantry continued to sweep the beach with machine-gun and rifle fire.

Commanding 2/1, Colonel Russell Honsowetz lost his adjutant right on the beach. They were running across the sand when a Japanese popped up from a spider hole and shot the officer dead. "They had spider holes everywhere," remembered Honsowetz.

Once off the beach, the Marines found themselves scratching at Peleliu's unforgiving coral. Recalled a private first class with the 1st Marines, "Around this place there's nothin' but sharp coral. I mean, you get down on your hands and knees, you're getting cut. And grenades are going off. And each time this coral is just shattering in small bits and it peppers you. I guess it would be as if somebody turned a sandblaster on you. It just stung you all over."

Oily plumes of smoke rose from the shot-up tractors littering the beach. Now and again, ammunition in one of the abandoned hulks would explode, showering the surviving Marines with burning debris. Hoping to avoid a similar fate, those amphibian vehicles still operating unceremoniously dumped their reinforcements amid the carnage and scurried back for another load.

The 3d Battalion on the extreme left was getting the worst of it. Captain Hunt's 30 or so survivors on the Point were isolated from the rest of K Company by Japanese forces which had pushed into the gap. His 2d and 3d Platoons had been reduced to the size of a couple of squads. Pinned down by Japanese forces on the ridge just inland from White 1, battalion commander Lieutenant Colonel Stephen Sabol ordered his reserve, L Company, into the line in an attempt to push the enemy off the high ground.

The fighting was like nothing the Marines had ever seen. "Five Marines were killed right in front of me before they got this one lousy Jap in a hole in the ground," recalled a dismounted tanker. Every time a Marine came up to pitch a grenade in the position, he would get shot. Finally, someone came up behind the Japanese and roasted him with a flamethrower. "It was like opening a can with a can opener to try to get each of them out," remarked the tanker.

Unable to dislodge the Japanese, Sabol was forced to request help from the regiment. A Company of the reserve battalion was committed early in the day in a futile effort to clear the ground between the Point and the Japanese-held ridge. B Company was similarly committed later in the afternoon. Neither force had the muscle to close the gap on the left, although both took heavy casualties in the effort.

A witness chronicled the fate of the lieutenants trying to get things moving that morning. Raymond W. Mueller of C Company was shot through the head and instantly killed as he stepped onto the beach. John Buss of A Company took a slug in the chest and died later. His replacement was killed by a bullet in the head; then the platoon sergeant was wounded by shrapnel. Cries of "Corpsman!" and "Stretcher bearer!" rose from the scrub. The only cry more disheartening, recalled one Marine, was the addendum, "Never mind the corpsman." Also among those hit was Battalion CO Major R. G. Davis, who took a long splinter from a mortar round in his knee. It bled a lot, he recalled, but was not serious enough to stop him.

The Marines did manage to gain a foothold on the southern slope of the ridge before the attack petered out. A squad from A Company's 1st Platoon got up on the ridge and down the other side, where it contacted I Company on the right and refused its left flank.

With the gap on the left, the flank of the 1st Marines—and the entire beachhead—was now threatened. "It was possible," conceded the 1st Marines report, "that a coordinated counterattack in force along the corridor between the coral ridge and the sea could roll up the line and sweep down on the beaches." The result, on the narrow, congested beachhead, would be disaster. Keenly aware of the danger, Puller organized all available troops to guard against a possible Japanese counterattack through the gap. All men who could be spared, including headquarters personnel and 100 men from the 1st Engineer Battalion, were pressed into service, along with the remnants of the regimental reserve.

It is indicative of the confusion of the landing that artillerymen were reduced to assaulting pillboxes. Private First Class Warner Pyne landed with an artillery observation group amid the litter of Marine dead and abandoned equipment on the southern beaches. Pyne, who had accumulated two battle stars since being thrown out of the Admiral Farragut Academy in 1941 for fistfighting, thought it looked like the landing force was getting the hell knocked out of it.

The group pushed 200 to 300 yards inland, when the captain in charge shouted, "Down, down, hit the deck!" The artillerymen hit the prone as machine-gun fire whipped overhead. Pyne stuck his head up and spotted the enemy gun emplacement—a dug-in pillbox—about 100 yards to the front. Working to the left, Pyne crawled around and then cut in until he was on top of it. Only then did he realize he did not have any grenades— in fact, he did not have a weapon of any kind. "Did I ever feel like a horse's ass," he recalled.

By now a couple of other Marines had also moved out on the flank. One of them tossed Pyne a grenade, and he popped it into the gun emplacement. The captain shouted a Japanese phrase encouraging any survivors to sur- render. After a moment, a Japanese soldier emerged from the pillbox, his hands over his head. He looked dazed, but did not seem to be wounded. An overzealous Marine promptly shot him dead.

A tank clanked up and put a couple of rounds into the box. Pyne, figuring nobody was left alive, looked inside just as a Japanese grenade soared out. Jerking backward, he missed the full blast but caught some fragments in the chest area, knocking him off his feet. Looking down at his bloody front, the 19-year-old New Yorker thought he was dying, but he was lucky: though messy, no vital organs had been hit. An hour later, he was off the beach and on the hospital ship *Bountiful*.

Elements of at least two companies and other strays spent the morning and afternoon fighting from the tank trap behind White 1. "Anytime any- body tried to climb out and keep attacking, he was shot," recalled a teenaged private first class. "Guys with blood on 'em were all over the ditch."

Marine dead littered the bottom of the trench. Sitting against the side, nursing his shot-up shoulder, Corporal Harlan Murray saw his outfit's flamethrower man lying dead, the weapon still on his back. His assistant lay nearby, also dead. Murray's lieutenant sprawled on the ground, the top of his head shot off. "Our machine gunners did everything they could," said Murray. "They'd set up their guns and shoot, and the guy would come sliding down the tank trap dead. And somebody else would get behind the gun and shoot, and he'd come sliding down."

Another man came staggering down the ditch, one hand dangling from a piece of skin, the other also mangled. A corpsman grabbed him. By now, K Company's 2d and 3d Platoons had been reduced to the effective strength of a squad. Some of the Marines were already making their farewell speeches. "We was figurin' we'd never get out of there, and we'd all get it sooner or later," remarked a young private.

Not far from where Murray sat, a slight, freckle-faced, Alabama private first class named Hugh Wiginton took charge. He looked to be only about 17, but he had seen combat on Cape Gloucester. Now he collared a lieutenant sitting idly with a walkie-talkie in his hand. "We need help up here," he told the officer. The lieutenant replied, "I can't get you any help 'cause this damned radio is tuned in to K Company."

"K Company!" blurted Wiginton, grabbing his radio. "That's my company."

Talking on the "spam can," Wiggie worked to get some kind of help forward. The lieutenant (who was not from K Company) just sat there. "That officer was an asshole," announced a witness to the scene. "He didn't know nothing." Further up the ditch a BAR man named Hoffman saw Japanese coming down the trap. He tried to get some stray mortarmen to help ambush them as they came around a bend in the trap, but the response was less than enthusiastic. None of the mortarmen moved. Hoffman was already pitching Japanese grenades back, and his position was clearly perilous. Exasperated, he turned to one of the sergeants and snapped, "Why don't you shoot a couple of 'em? Then they'd move!"

Also fighting in the trap was Jack LaBerge, a K Company machine-gun sergeant. Running northward up the trap, he and another Marine pulled up short as about 25 Japanese trotted across the ditch and up the other side. LaBerge fired at them with his M–1, and the other Marine cut loose with his tommy gun. They killed six. LaBerge was more angry than pained to see the dead Japanese were wearing clean khaki. Some of them had green nets over their helmets. "They hadn't even worked up a sweat," he recalled irritably.

The survivors retaliated with a volley of grenades, and LaBerge felt a stinging pain in his back as a splinter cut into him. He yelled at his machine-gun section to set up their weapons, but they just stood there, looking blank, apparently stunned. "Set up those fucking guns!"

The guns were set up but quickly jammed due to sand kicked into the mechanisms from nearby mortar bursts. Peering over the edge of the trap, LaBerge saw the Japanese running along in file. They were moving away from the Marines in the ditch ... toward the Point.

Out on the Point, Captain Hunt's Marines were consolidating their lines when a Japanese infantryman approached as if he wanted to surrender. The man still wore his pack and was carrying his rifle. Suspicious, the Marines shot him. The enemy soldier blew up before their eyes. He had been loaded with explosives.

Soon afterward, enemy mortar concentrations began to fall on Hunt's 30-odd survivors. Shrapnel richocheted among the rocks. One Marine took a piece that broke his leg. Gray-faced, he was carried down to the water to await evacuation by amtrac.

By late afternoon, amtrac was the only feasible way to get on and off the Point. Hunt's men were still cut off. Efforts to reach the 2d Platoon, still trapped in and around the antitank trench, had failed. Already, Hunt's men were asking for drinking water. Peleliu's incredible heat had them consuming water at a tremendous rate. There were only a few grenades left plus whatever ammunition each man had in his belt.

Swede Hanson approached Captain Hunt and suggested it might be a good idea if he burned all the military maps, message books and other information he was carrying as intelligence sergeant. "Hanson, do what you think is best there," replied Hunt. "I think it's a good idea." Hansen immediately started burning all the papers.

Sweating Marines constructed foxholes out of rocks and fallen logs. Earlier, when Hunt's Exec, Lieutenant Bull Sellers, tried to contact him from further down the beach, a woman had broken in on the radio, jabbering incessantly and drowning out the call. Frustrated, Sellers bellowed into the mouthpiece, "Fuck you, bitch! Get off the air!" Sellers gained a certain immortality among his fellows for this direct approach to the problem, but the jamming continued.

Now, managing to get through by radio, Hunt learned that his machine-gun platoon "had been mowed down on the beach." He was promised resupply and reinforcements by water and told to watch for L Company, which was supposed to move into the gap on the right and establish contact. But as the afternoon wore on, there was no sign of L Company or reinforcements. The gap was crawling with Japanese. Hunt only hoped they did not realize how weak his little force really was.

Farther south, the 2d Battalion had stopped along the edge of the airfield in what was officially termed "moderate" fighting. Under the direction of Lieutenant Colonel Russell E. Honsowetz, a highly respected officer, 2/1 had punched rapidly inland after the landing. The push was not unopposed.

Private First Class Victor Case organized the assault on one of the enemy positions, a pair of adjoining concrete pillboxes. He managed to get a grenade through one of the horizontal slots, killing most of the crew; now, back pressed into the crevice between the two structures, he was unable to get a second grenade into the other pillbox. The enemy machine gunner kept the other Marines at a distance, at the same time traversing as far as he could toward Case to keep him away from the slot.

As the Marines in support watched, Case suddenly dropped down, scrambled under the slot and disappeared around the back of the pillbox. Four or five other Marines worked around to the flank. One was shot in the leg and had to be left behind. The others found Case busily trying to pry open the rear door of the pillbox.

Standing watch while the others joined Case, only the BAR man saw five Japanese burst from the woods and dash toward them. The Japanese in the lead, an officer or NCO with shaved head and wrap leggings, fired a pistol as he came. The other four carried rifles. The BAR man fired a burst from the hip, cutting down the first two men behind the leader. A second burst sent the other two sprawling, but the officer came on, still firing his pistol. The BAR man got off a single shot at close range, splitting the officer's shaved head like an overripe melon.

Meanwhile, Case continued to labor at the pillbox door, finally getting a grenade inside, obliterating the crew. He then went on alone after another pair of pillboxes. None of the other Marines followed. He soon came back remarking that the pillboxes had been taken care of.

Case would be killed five days later, but his actions on Peleliu would earn him a posthumous Navy Cross. He, and many others like him, both recognized and unrecognized, made the Marine beachhead on Peleliu a reality.

Paced by surviving LVT(A)s, the Marines worked forward 350 yards inland through an area of knocked-over woods and occasional swamps, pushing through enemy strongpoints to reach the O–1 phase line by the edge of the airfield by 0930. Unable to advance because of the precarious situation on its left, the battalion tied in with the 5th Marines on the right and waited, facing the open airfield and building area from the edge of the woods.

Some Marines lay at the top of an embankment, observing an enemy blockhouse area across the airfield. A lot of men were digging in behind the embankment; other riflemen and machine gunners moved out over the bank to dig in on the edge of the airstrip itself. Heavy fire from the pillboxes droned overhead, and the Marines could pick out gun flashes in the smoke. Short on water, some of the men scavenged canteens from dead comrades.

Among the casualties of that so-called "moderate fighting" was a popular lieutenant, Gordon "Go-Go" Meyers of Jersey City, who was knocked down by a sniper's bullet as he tried to form a firing line. He fell beyond reach in an area swept by heavy fire. Several of the men started out after him, ready to risk their own lives, but the lieutenant was quicker. He drew his pistol and ordered, "Stay back. Stay back or I'll shoot." He died moments later.

Sometime later, when the tanks came up, the fire seemed to taper off, and some of the Marines began to relax. Private Russell Davis, who had survived his wade onto the beach earlier that morning, became "almost silly," and he noticed many of the young riflemen around him laughing and joking. Only the older men—the veterans—were not laughing or joking. Veteran sergeants trotted by with shiny belts of machine-gun ammunition draped over their shoulders. Noncoms hustled men up over the bank with jerry cans of water, rifle ammunition, grenades and barbed wire.

"Dig it in," a machine-gun sergeant shouted at his men. "Dig it down. Get that wire out."

"We may see a banzai charge," a veteran of other island fighting remarked almost casually.

Davis, his own jovial mood evaporating, suddenly realized the joking and laughter had stopped. The only noise along the line was the sergeants saying, "Dig, dig."

Offshore, the crew of a heavy cruiser watched as an amtrac drew alongside. A haggard corpsman stood to hail the ship. "I've got wounded aboard," he shouted. There were 13 in all, most of them hit hard. The corpsman said he had lost his plasma ashore and soon ran out of morphine due to the many wounded. "They asked me for morphine, and I could not give it to them," he kept repeating as he was led below.

Later, a doctor told the young man he had done a good job, probably saving some of the men's lives. The corpsman could only shake his head. He thought he had failed.

Back on the beaches, Marines continued to die.

Al Geierman's artillery outfit came in with the later waves at the Orange Beaches. Shells continued to splash in the water, but the 19-year-old private first class, participating in his first combat, did not realize at first just how serious the situation really was. As the amtrac churned toward the beach, the top sergeant assigned Geierman and another Marine to lie on either gunnel and watch for mines in the water. "I wouldn't know a mine if it bit me," recalled Geierman, but he dutifully climbed up and stared into the water. Soon, he noticed bodies bumping up against the amtrac. There were scores of them, floating limply just beneath the surface. What the hell are all these Japs doing out here, he wondered, idly watching the corpses float past.

The other Marine suddenly climbed down from his post and sat down with his head between his knees as if he were about to vomit. Geierman waited for the sergeant to reprimand the man, but the noncom remained tight-lipped. He looked back in the water at the floating Japs. Then he suddenly realized they weren't Japs. They were dead Marines.

Up ahead, amtracs were still burning on the reef. Shocked now, Geierman thought there must be 18 or 20 of them. As his own tractor lurched by, he could see bodies in the derelicts. The dead Marines were burned "black as toast," standing fused together like statues, still clutching their rifles and wearing their fire-blackened helmets.

Geierman's complacence vanished in an instant. "It dawned on me what was goin' on," he recalled. "I thought, my God, if we make it in there . . . we'll make it anyplace."

Pushing inland off the beaches, the Marines were learning that Peleliu was far different from anything they had encountered in the jungles of Guadalcanal and Cape Gloucester. Sergeant Flip Afflito was moving along through the scrub jungle when he saw one of his section leaders gesturing at him. The Marine kept pointing toward the ground. "I didn't know what the hell he was talking about—so I think, well, he wants me to get down. 'Cause you couldn't hear. So I laid down and he shook his head, side to side, meaning *no*."

Afflito looked around and suddenly realized he was on top of a mound built up over a pillbox. Crawling around to the side, he found the aperture—an opening about seven inches by thirty—and flipped a grenade inside. The Marines later found two dead Japanese in the position but suspected they had been killed earlier. "Otherwise, I don't think I could have gotten that grenade in there," remarked Afflito.

From that point onward, Afflito began to keep a careful watch for mounds. "These things used to pop up from nowhere," he recalled. "I found out later, everything that looked like a mound was a pillbox . . . if it's not natural to the terrain, it's a pillbox. You consider it a pillbox. You're sort of evening your chance of survival."

Toward noon, 2/5 had begun a strong drive westward in preparation for a turning movement toward the north. Since contact had to be retained with 1/5 on the left, the 2d Battalion soon found itself deployed completely along the southern end of the airfield. It was already feeling a shortage of ammunition due to the heavy loss of LVTs on the beach area, but resupply came later in the day. Further to the right, L Company struck all the way to the eastern shore of the island, splitting Peleliu in two as called for in the plans. K and I Companies also pushed on, overcoming strong resistance from a nest of pillboxes that temporarily halted the advance.

Private First Class Moskalczak found himself crossing a leg of the airstrip about 75 yards from a bomb-damaged hangar. The roof had a large hole in it, and one of the big doors hung to the leeward side, twisted on its bottom hinge. Coming to a small shed, Moskalczak was behind Corporal John Teskevich and Private First Class Seymour Levy when a Japanese grenade went off without warning and a splinter hit Levy in the chin. "I'm hit! I'm hit!" he yelled. Teskevich ran into the shed and sprayed the wooden floor with his submachine gun. On the other side, they found a spot where the ground was worn down as if someone had been crawling in and out under the floor. Teskevich heaved a grenade into the hole and they moved on.[2]

Riding his tank through the scrub, Captain Jack Munday spotted a group of men manning a machine gun near a bunker. They were wearing clean khaki, and he assumed they were Marines until they opened fire on him. The tank replied, knocking the machine gunner back into his hole. Five other Japanese broke out of the bunker, running bent over for cover. The tank machine gun riddled them.

Emerging from the thick scrub under heavy sniper fire, some of the 3/5 Marines found themselves in a clearing overlooking the ocean. To the front lapped a shallow bay choked with barbed wire entanglements, tetrahedrons and various other anti-boat obstacles. More then one Marine issued up a fervent prayer that the landing had not come in over these beaches.

As it was, the enemy was caught. The Marines fired on Japanese soldiers wading along the reef several hundred yards distant. About a dozen were alternately running and swimming along the reef toward a small promontory on the right. Most of the runners went down with a splash under the Marine fire, but a handful made it to the promontory and scrambled away in the rocks.

"You guys couldn't hit a bull in the ass with a bass fiddle," roared a sergeant in disgust.

Several more Japanese dashed out from the shelter of some mangroves in an attempt at the reef. Marine rifles cracked, and every man splashed down. "That's better," muttered the sergeant, somewhat mollified.

Meanwhile, enemy resistance, thick scrub and inaccurate sketch maps had caused 3/5 to lose contact with 3/7 on the right. Units were not where they thought they were, and patrols failed to regain contact, At one point, Lieutenant Tom Stanley, executive officer of K/3/5, glanced over to see some men milling around. He assumed they were from the "adjacent" 7th Marines until he took a closer look. They were Japanese. The 7th Marines was nowhere in sight.

3/7's problems had begun early in the afternoon when I Company ran afoul of Japanese resistance built around a large blockhouse, the concrete ruins of a barracks area, several pillboxes, concrete gun emplacements and mutually supporting gun positions. Marked clearly on the operational map, this opposition had been expected, and a tank platoon had been briefed in advance for this particular mission.

In order to minimize casualties, the Marines stopped to wait for tank support before tackling this tough nut. Unfortunately, in a scene reminiscent of the confusion on the beach earlier in the morning, the Shermans latched up with I Company of the 5th Marines under the mistaken impression it was I of the 7th. By the time the error was recognized, 3/7's timetable had been thrown completely off kilter. The battalion CO, Major Hunter Hurst, later said that this delay was primarily responsible for keeping his battalion from reaching the eastern shore on D-Day.

Further south, 1/7, which had come in behind 3/7 as planned, wheeled south to clean up Peleliu's lower tip. Resistance had been described as "light, except for heavy mortar fire" until about 1200. As 1/7 pushed south, however, the terrain grew more rugged, and enemy resistance stiffened appreciably.

Japanese were all through the area. Scouting ahead of his platoon when it hit the first phase line, Sergeant Carl Stevenson heard a noise in the bushes and dropped into a shell hole just as "the biggest, best-looking, neatest, cleanest Jap I'd ever seen in my life" stepped out in front of him, no more than ten feet away. The man was huge, over six feet tall in Stevenson's estimation, and he was nattily turned out in a pressed short-sleeve khaki shirt, shorts, socks and boots. He had a bag hanging off his back, but he wore no helmet and seemed to carry no weapon.

Amazed, Stevenson's first inclination was to shoo away this parade-ground apparition. His second was to give the Japanese a burst from his tommy gun, knocking him off his feet. The man jumped back up, and Stevenson let him have the rest of the clip, knocking him down again. The Japanese lay there a second. To Stevenson's complete and utter astonishment, he started to get up again. Reversing his taped clips, Stevenson gave him a full 30 rounds, only to see the man—who should have been cut in half—start crawling toward him.

That was enough for Stevenson. The 23-year-old Arizonan scrambled out of the hole and ran back to his platoon, leaving the seemingly indestructible Japanese in possession of their small battlefield.

Among the nastier surprises encountered by 1/7 was a swamp that did not appear on the operational map and blocked a considerable portion of the battalion's operational zone. A single trail along the western edge was well covered by Japanese pillboxes and bunkers constructed from large chunks of coral. Many of the Marine casualties from this push were carried to a temporary aid station working out of a big shell crater about 30 paces behind the Japanese antitank ditch. A doctor at the bottom of the crater sweated over the worst of the stretcher cases amid a litter of spent shell fragments, recalled Tom Lea, who stumbled across the scene.

Aid men, four to a stretcher, arrived continuously with another bloody load. Plasma bottles hung from a broken tree stump, the doctor giving transfusions as fast as he could after rough surgery. Corpsmen handled the less seriously wounded. Some of the hard hit Marines died. Corpsmen placed a poncho, shirt, a rag or whatever was handy over the gray faces of the dead, then carried them to the beach, where they lay in lengthening lines under a tarpaulin until graves could be dug. A padre, armed with two canteens and a Bible, helped where he could. He was deeply moved and looked very lonely and very close to God as he bent over the suffering men, observed Lea.

Meanwhile, in the confusion of the advance, A Company finally managed to feel its way around the swamp to the east. B Company tied in A's flank with C Company, and the battalion halted for the day. Like most of the Marine units on Peleliu, they had fallen well short of the original optimistic projections for D-Day.

Back on Orange 2, General Smith, trying to make some order out of the fragmentary reports filtering in, was astonished to see General Geiger come sliding down into his antitank ditch.

"Look, General, according to the book you're not supposed to be here at this time," blurted Smith, not really wanting to be responsible for the safety of such an important personage.

Geiger, well-known for his nonchalance in the face of danger, serenely replied, "Well, I wanted to see why those amtracs were burning." Then he added, "I'd like to see the airport."

"That's simple," said Smith. "All you have to do is climb this bank, and there it is."

Geiger scrambled up, and the Japanese chose that moment to send a large caliber shell screeching overhead. Somewhat startled, the IIIPhib commander slid back down into the ditch, his curiosity settled insofar as the airport was concerned. Somewhat to Smith's relief, the corps commander moved down the beach to check on the 5th and 7th Marines, but he soon returned, announcing, "Now I'm going up to see Puller."

"Now look, General," Smith protested, "there is a gap of 800 yards above here, and we don't know who's in there and you just shouldn't go up there."

Fortunately, Geiger heeded Smith's protestations and soon went back aboard ship. For his part, General Rupertus, still confined to the *DuPage*, was less than happy to find he had been upstaged by the corps commander.

Up by the airfield, Lieutenant Carlton "Cobber" Rouh decided he should check on his mortar platoon OP. Rouh, a big, soft-spoken 25-year-old from Lindenwold, New Jersey, had been commissioned from the ranks after winning a Silver Star and being wounded on Guadalcanal, and he freely admitted that the new responsibility of being an officer gave him butterflies. "It wasn't the work I was afraid of," he recalled, "but just the idea of giving men jobs to do that might kill them."

Coming ashore on Peleliu with 1/5, his mortar platoon had taken its first casualties seconds after hitting the beach, when a mortar shell whispered in on them as they bunched up, running out of the amtrac. By 1500 hours, the survivors had worked up to the edge of the airfield. Rouh realized they would not be able to get across the strip before dark, so he ventured up to check on his observation post and see about laying a heavier wire to their field phone.

He found his spotters in a Japanese ditch along the edge of the airfield. Closer inspection showed the ditch to be the sloping entrance to a dugout. The coral from the ditch had been piled up along the edge, and his observers crouched against it trying to spot guns in the ridges across the way. There were a few Japanese dead at the bottom, and the mouth of the dugout still smoldered where it had been burned out by Marine flamethrowers.

Rouh didn't like the looks of the position; he decided to inspect the dugout. "It was a hard thing for me to do," he recalled. "I had made it a guiding rule of my life on all those islands out there never to go into a Jap cave. Not even six months after the last Jap in it was presumed dead and even the quartermaster boys had been in there for souvenirs." But he was the only one available to do it; the others were all spotting targets for the mortars.

Sliding down the side of the ditch to keep as far out of the line of fire as possible, he examined the entrance. There were some shelves at the side of the doorway with whisky bottles and some packages wrapped in cloth. He tossed them to another Marine, then stepped deeper into the darkness, lifting his carbine to make sure the safety catch was off. There was a sudden loud *bang*. At first Rouh thought his carbine had gone off by accident. Then there was another *bang* on top of the first, and he felt a sledgehammer blow to his gut. He doubled over. There was a great temptation to fall, but he resisted it, turned and ran out into the light. The others pulled him to the top of the ditch, and he lay there thinking how lucky he had been. The bullet had entered just below the ribs, a serious but not fatal wound.

He was still contemplating his good fortune when one of the Marines gathered around him yelled, "Look out!" While the Marines were trying to tend to Rouh, a Japanese had crept out of the dugout and pitched a grenade at them. Rouh was never completely clear on what happened next. "I got to my feet," he recalled. "I remember that. Then after that I can remember things only in patches with blind spots in between."

What Rouh did was detailed in the subsequent citation for his Medal of Honor. "Quick to act in spite of his weakened condition," noted his citation, "he lurched into a crouching position and thrust both men aside, placing his own body between them and the grenade and taking the full blast of the explosion himself."

The next thing Rouh knew, he was back on the ground, rolling toward the spot where the grenade had just exploded. Suddenly, another Marine appeared overhead, straddling him as he fired down into the ditch. Rouh later learned that 15 Japanese hiding in the dugout had tried to break out. All were killed. But at the time, the New Jersey Marine was conscious only that his whole side seemed to be torn off. He could not take his eyes off the mess.

"Don't look at it," a voice advised.

Rouh leaned back against the bank. His incredible luck held fast as he saw a corpsman walking along the edge. "There's the doc," he said. "Get the doc."

Pumped full of plasma, Rouh survived the trip back to the hospital ship and ultimately recovered from his wounds. A year later, possessing the starred blue ribbon of the Medal of Honor, he was back at work in his family's small hotel in Lindenwold. There, approached by a magazine reporter curious as to what motivates someone to jump on a grenade, the soft-spoken hero mentioned how he had always been afraid of the idea of giving his men jobs that might kill them. "I guess that feeling of responsibility was as much to blame as anything else for what happened on Peleliu Island," he said.

As afternoon waned, Japanese forces were preparing to strike back at the constricted Marine beachhead in accordance with the tactical document drawn up earlier by General Inoue's headquarters. The blow, fortunately, was not aimed at the vulnerable flank of the hard-pressed 1st Marines. Instead, it was to come directly across the airstrip close to the juncture of the 1st and 5th Marines.

A noticeable increase in the volume of enemy mortar and artillery fire at about 1625 tipped the Marines off that an attack was in the works. Twenty-five minutes later, Japanese infantry in approximately company strength was sighted advancing from the northern end of the airfield. The infantry attack was no blind banzai; the brown-uniformed veterans of Manchuria remained well dispersed and took advantage of what little cover they could find during their approach.

Meanwhile, an American air observer from the escort carrier *Marcus Island* spotted enemy tanks forming behind the ridges north of the airfield. This information came as no shock to the Marines with their fine intelligence on enemy units located on Peleliu. Shortly before the division left the Russells, sharp-eyed photo interpreters scanning aerial shots of Peleliu had also noticed what appeared to be tank tracks. The most logical area to use this armor was on the flat open airfield.

Exercising shrewd judgment, Bucky Harris, whose 5th Marines would face the open airfield, had ordered both assault battalions to land their 37 mm guns and heavy machine guns in the assault waves. These guns were to be emplaced in forward positions as soon as the line had been secured— which the Marines did as they settled down on the edge of the airfield. Three supporting Sherman tanks from B Company, 1st Tank Battalion, had also been brought up and placed in hull defilade among the bomb craters, where they could lay down fire in front of the Marine infantry. By early afternoon, a battery of 2/11's pack howitzers had also come ashore and were digging in just to the right rear of 1/5.

Map 3.
The Main Japanese Tank Attack

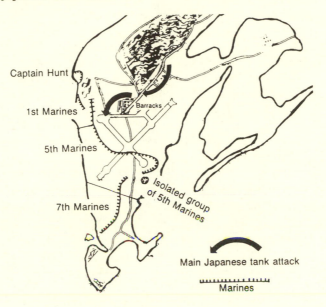

Crouched in his foxhole at the edge of the airstrip, a Marine corporal suddenly heard someone shout, "Here they come!" A moment later, he saw the "ugly snout of a Japanese light tank" emerge from behind a bombed-out hangar at the end of the airfield. Then came another and another, "dodging and swirling crazily about."

To Private Robert Leckie of F Company, 1st Marines, the attack was "startling." The tanks seemed to come out of nowhere. He had a moment's glance at a tank streaking along, Japanese riflemen clinging to its deck. At the same time, a veteran Marine came running to the rear in a panic, shouting, "Tanks! Tanks!" An officer collared the man and kicked him back into the line.

Other men filtered back through the smoke and dust and took up positions along the edge of the field. Two machine gunners came walking in toward Russell Davis's position carrying their gun still mounted. "They never once looked back into the smoke, and they appeared thoughtful rather than scared," recalled Davis.

Despite the appearance of confusion, the Japanese attack started in a systematic fashion. Emerging onto the airfield in two columns, the enemy tanks, probably a dozen all together,[3] began their attack about 600 yards to the left front of 1/5 in full view of the waiting Marines. About half carried from eight to a dozen infantrymen riding tied to the outside. Some had 50-gallon oil drums lashed upright on the deck, apparently as makeshift tubs for infantry. If so, few of the occupants probably survived long; assuming the barrels were full of gasoline, Marine machine gunners immediately riddled them, somewhat disappointed when there was no fire or explosion.

The tanks were Type 95s. Carrying a three-man crew and weighing just under ten tons, they mounted one 37 mm gun, one 7.7 mm machine gun in the rear of the turret and another 7.7 mm in the hull. Equipped with a 110-horsepower Mitsubishi diesel, the tanks were capable of 28 miles per hour—1 less than the U.S. Sherman, which outweighed the Japanese Type 95 by over 25 tons. The Japanese tanks were also very thinly armored— 14 mm maximum, far less than the 76 mm maximum on the Shermans backing the Marines on Peleliu.

The tanks initially made some effort to find cover along the edge of the jungle on the northern edge of the airfield. Then, passing through their own infantry about 400 yards beyond the Marines' lines, the Japanese drivers gunned their engines and raced for the Marines, leaving their own infantry behind in a cloud of dust.

Superficially unsound, this tactic was actually the enemy commander's only real hope of reaching the Marines before being blown to pieces by superior American firepower. Presumably, he hoped to effect a breakthrough with the aid of his tank-borne infantry, which could then be exploited by the foot soldiers following behind.

The thrust of the charge took the Japanese southwest over the open ground diagonally in front of 2/1, which poured devastating fire into the lightly armored vehicles. Two bazooka men balanced on the edge of the embankment near Private Davis and sent a rocket whooshing toward one of the tanks in front. Flame flickered along the tread, and the tank stopped and toppled over. One of the bazooka men cheered like a little boy, "Yay! Yay! That's us!"

Two Japanese squirmed free of the wreck and tried a dash through the smoke. One was hammered against the side of the tank before he even got started; the other, sprinting laterally across the line, absorbed dozens of bullets and went down in what one witness described as "a very dead sprawl."

A machine-gun squad slid over the bank by Davis and started firing without bracing the legs of the gun; the weapon bucked all over. While two Marines tried to hold it down, the gunner swore at them and kept firing into the smoke. Another Marine, running back from somewhere out front, stumbled and collapsed directly in front of Davis's rifle. Davis and a scout sergeant crawled out to find him already dead.

One tank clattered directly at Private Jay C. Blakely, who held his ground and managed to fire a rifle grenade into it. The turret hatch clanged open, and the tank commander popped up. As the tank slowed and started to back up, Blakely dashed forward and climbed onto the deck. The Japanese commander lashed out with his pistol, hitting Blakely over the eye, but Blakely shoved him off the tank and another Marine shot him dead. Blakely then dropped two grenades down the open hatch, blowing the rest of the crew all over the inside of the vehicle.

Despite the volume of fire, two of the enemy tanks veered into the lines of 2/1, hurtled over the embankment and crashed into a swamp just beyond. One of them drove right over a Marine in his foxhole. "It was black and noisy," recalled the shaken Marine. "I just hoped I wouldn't hit my head on the bottom of it."

As one of the tanks rushed over the embankment, a Marine stood up in his foxhole and peppered the vehicle with automatic fire. "The tank was not ten feet away when it burst into flame, leaving a trailing fire as it still rolled forward," recalled a corporal. "The lower half of a twisted and burnt Jap body fell not a pace from me." The burning tank rolled forward over a machine gun, crushing the weapon even as the gunners leapt away.

As the tank lurched to a halt, a flamethrower operator rushed up to hose it down, only to meet a quick death as the turret gun caught him directly in the chest. A Japanese crewman raised his head above the hatch and was promptly shot dead. Another tanker tried to get out the bottom escape hatch and was also killed. A third crewman raised a dirty white rag out of the top hatch. The Marines shot the man's hand off, then threw grenades in on top of him.

Meanwhile, just down the line, the Marines of 1/5 were pounding the tanks with everything they had: bazookas, small arms, support tanks, AT grenades. Even a navy dive-bomber joined in, swooping in at low altitude to drop a 500-pound bomb on the milling tanks. From the southern end of the airfield, four Shermans attached to 2/5 also charged out and opened fire.

The Japanese vehicles could not take the punishment. Actually tankettes by American standards, they could not withstand hits from the heavy weapons the Marines had in abundance, particularly the short-barrelled 75 mms on the armored amphibs. One U.S. tank commander recalled starting out by firing armor-piercing shells at the enemy, but concluded that their armor was too thin to detonate the shells—they were going right through. "I changed to high explosive, and still they came on," he reported. "Finally, I changed the fuses to instantaneous. That stopped them."

Tanks began burning and exploding all along the line. Hit squarely by a high-explosive shell, one of the tanks blew up like a tin toy, its turret flying 40 or 50 feet into the air. Watching from his foxhole, the scene reminded Corporal Russell Clay of nothing so much as an animated cartoon.

Pinned down by another tank, Private First Class Wesley D. Hamilton of Fayville, Massachusetts, thought he was dead meat. Then he heard a BAR rip and turned his head to see an automatic rifleman blazing away at the tank. The vehicle spun around and stopped. Hamilton was convinced the

BAR man had saved his life, although it seems likely the tank was stopped by heavier fire from another source. There was so much U.S. fire, and the damage was so extensive, that it was difficult later to determine just how many tanks had participated in the attack, never mind who hit what.

The surviving vehicles kept coming and several—perhaps as many as six, no one was ever sure—charged over a section of line held by a platoon of 1/5. Lieutenent Colonel Robert Boyd, commanding 1/5, recalled that these tanks "were running around wildly, apparently without coordination, within our lines, firing their 37 mm guns with the riders on those tanks carrying external passengers yelling and firing rifles."

One of the Japanese tanks penetrated B Company's area and stopped not more than 145 feet from Sergeant Flip Afflito's hole. "I didn't even have a chance to say 'Oh, my God.' It happened so suddenly," he recalled.

Seeing two other tanks further down, Afflito's squad played possum. Peering through the cracks of his fingers, Afflito could see the enemy 37 mm gun pointing directly at him. The tank commander stood upright in the open hatch, surveying the ground. A Japanese infrantryman squatted on the deck, a Nambu light machine gun across his knees. After what seemed like hours, but was probably only 10 or 15 seconds, the tank started to move off. "Salonis, get that bazooka!" Afflito shouted to a Marine in a nearby hole.

"It won't work," the bazooka man shouted back.

Afflito sprinted over to him, checked the wiring and stepped aside as the back blast seared off his moustache and sideburns. The shell struck the top of the tank, but failed to stop it. The exposed tank commander and the Nambu-toting rider were already dead, blasted off by Marine riflemen. The machine gunner still hung limply off the side as the tank rolled forward.

One of Afflito's buddies, Brooklyn-born Patsy DeStefano, jumped up on the moving tank and dropped a grenade down the hatch. He caught a back spray of shrapnel in the blast and had to be evacuated, but he killed the tank.

Elsewhere along the line, Marines battled the tanks to a standstill. Two Marines, caught in the path of an enemy tank, were crushed. Another tank, hit by a rifle grenade that failed to explode, rolled over a rifleman crouched in a hole near Corporal Russell Clay before it was hit point-blank by a 75-mm shell from a nearby armored amphib. One of the Marine riflemen climbed out of his hole, jumped up on the burning tank and leaned inside to rummage around for souvenirs. Coming up with a Japanese pistol, he jumped off just as the ammo inside the tank exploded. "He missed getting run over by the tank, and then he almost got his butt blown away when the tank exploded," recalled Clay. "It's amazing what some of these guys would do, especially the new people, you know, that were on their first operation."

A few other Marines were wounded or burned as tanks were destroyed in their midst. One tank, heading straight for the Marine howitzers, lurched to an abrupt halt as a gunner hit it with a single round of direct fire. Bazooka men then blew the stalled vehicle apart. Another tank nearly reached the beach before it was blasted to scrap. Also among the casualties was a Marine Sherman which took three bazooka hits in the confusion of the attack.

The firing peaked, then gradually receded as the two surviving Japanese tanks fled back across the airfield, leaving their comrades burning on the coral runway. The Marines braced for an attack by the supporting infantry, but it never came. The infantry, drawn mostly from the Special Naval Guard Force, had melted away, leaving only dead men scattered across the airfield. In the quiet backwash, cries for corpsmen sounded up and down the line.

One of the derelict tanks attracted Private Robert Leckie, who wandered out to look inside at the dead crew. Dead Japanese riflemen hung limply in nets on the outside "like dolls stuffed in a Christmas stocking." Other scorched and contorted bodies lay on the ground. Leckie turned to go and nearly stepped on a man's hand. Instinctively starting to apologize, he belatedly realized the hand had no body. It lay there, palm up, fingers extended, all alone. Somehow, that one forlorn hand affected him more than all the mutilated corpses scattered about nearby.

The Japanese made two more tank attacks in the airfield sector over the next several hours, each consisting of a pair of tanks and infantry support. All three were easily destroyed, completely annihilating Colonel Nakagawa's tank support.

"The entire airfield is covered with gunsmoke, obliterating the sun," a Japanese soldier with the 33d Independent Machine Cannon Company confided to his diary as afternoon waned. "I crawled into the shelter and could not lift my head because of the explosion of shells and hail of tracer bullets. The enemy appears to be forcing a landing."

Aboard the *DuPage*, General Rupertus's anxiety had not subsided as the afternoon progressed. All day, he had been pestering General Smith on when it would be feasible for him to bring his command post ashore. Smith, who saw little reason for optimism in the developments ashore, continued to advise Rupertus against landing. Finally, however, late in the afternoon, he radioed the division commander that the situation had eased enough to land the CP if he so desired.

Back on the *DuPage*, Colonel Seldon continued to advise against going ashore at this time. The command group was already ashore and functioning, he pointed out. To bring the entire division staff onto such a constricted beachhead under heavy enemy fire was an unnecessary risk of valuable personnel.

Finally, Rupertus agreed to a compromise. Colonel Seldon would go ashore with the bulk of the staff. The division commander would wait until the following morning to go ashore and take immediate command of the situation.

Boarding two LCVPs, Seldon and his staff arrived at the transfer control line off the Peleliu beaches to find elements of the division reserve, 2/7, still waiting to go ashore. The battalion had been ordered to go in to support the 7th Marines earlier in the afternoon, but the lack of amtracs to ferry them across the reef had kept them waiting at the transfer line.

Boarding the nearest control craft, Seldon became convinced that the main need ashore was for more combat troops, not staff. Neither did it seem likely that enough amtracs would be available to transport both groups. More than half of the DUKWs had been knocked out on D-Day; the attrition among the amphibian tractors had also been severe. The shortage had already affected ammunition supplies among some assault companies and delayed evacuation of the wounded.

Twenty-six amtracs were listed as knocked out on D-Day, and many more were put out of commission temporarily. The repair ship was loaded to capacity with amphibian vehicles; other damaged tractors, some under tow, milled around the ship waiting to be taken aboard. Suffering from a damaged hull, one LVT sank alongside the ship before it could be taken on.

As darkness closed in and enemy high-velocity guns began to range in on the control craft, Seldon radioed his views to Rupertus. He was going to bring the staff back to the *DuPage*, he said, giving priority to the reserve battalion to use what amtracs were available to get ashore.

As it turned out, sufficient amtracs never did arrive. Soon after the division staff returned to the *DuPage*—much to Rupertus's obvious displeasure—2/7 was ordered back to the transports.

The return was more easily ordered than accomplished. Many of the boats lacked compasses, boat officers had not been provided with return courses and the transports had moved further offshore. It was after midnight—seven hours bobbing around on the water in small boats—before battalion CO Lieutenant Colonel Spencer Berger located his transport, the *Leedstown*. The captain of the *Leedstown* then balked at taking the Marines back on board, contending he had orders only to land them. Berger finally talked his way on, contacted division and resolved that particular issue, but boatloads of exhausted, seasick Marines continued to trickle in long into the night.

Housed in his command center in the ridges above the airfield, Colonel Nakagawa, for all his ability, was apparently even less in touch with the real situation than his American counterpart aboard the *DuPage*. According to Nakagawa's report, the American landing attempt had been largely foiled. "By 100 hours our forces successfully put the enemy to rout," he reported to Inoue. "At 1420 hours, the enemy again attempted to make the perilous landing on the southwestern part of our coastline. The unit in that sector repulsed the daring counterattack and put the enemy to rout once more."

The only successful landing attempt, reported Nakagawa, had taken place near Ayame (Orange 3), where the Americans had gained a toehold with the aid of several tanks, "although they were encountering heavy losses inflicted by our forces."

In fact, the situation ashore was not that grim, although U.S. gains had fallen far short of the optimistic preinvasion predictions. Those projections had called for the 1st Marine Division to seize all of southern Peleliu below the northern ridges, including the airfield. By nightfall, these objectives remained well beyond reach. Approximately 9,500 Marines—riflemen, artillerymen, dismounted amtrac crewmen and other personnel—held a beachhead 3,000 yards long and about 500 yards deep and were sweating the possibility of major Japanese counterattacks.

The firmest lodgement was from Orange 2 south. To the north, on the White Beaches, Chesty Puller's Marines were hanging on by their fingernails. On the far left, Captain Hunt's K Company remained cut off on the Point. The flank of the 1st Marines remained anchored on the water, while they had not seized any of the high ground before them.

Further south, 2/5 and 3/5 had driven a deep wedge into the southern end of the airfield, having moved into the vacuum after the Japanese tank attack fell apart, but they had become somewhat disorganized in the scrub jungle as dusk approached. Colonel Harris phoned in to General Smith, explaining he was short of water and ammo and asking if the morning attack could be delayed. Smith said the 5th would have to attack, but he promised to try to get the necessary supplies forward.

At the other end of the line, the 7th Marines faced parallel to the southern end of the East Road, its right flank anchored on the beach. Shoulder to shoulder with the infantry some 50 men from VMF(N)–541 landed in a group and formed a second line of defense to protect the 7th Marines' mortar positions. The veterans dug in as deeply as possible. Grumbled one, "It's the fucking nighttime I don't like when them little fuckers come sneakin' into your lap."

By nightfall, most of the artillery of the 11th Marines was ashore, although some units found their assigned positions still in enemy hands. Others were unable to get in on their designated beaches because of congestion and enemy fire. Diverted to other areas, they set up as best they could.

The sight of the guns reassured the Marines already ashore. Watching the sweating artillerymen lift their 75s out of the amtracs, a bystander muttered, "The more of those damn guns they put on there tonight, the better I'll feel."

As for the artillerymen, they quickly found that even some so-called "secure" areas still contained enemy stragglers. Private First Class Al Geierman's outfit climbed out of the amtrac and almost immediately stumbled across a Japanese hiding in a gully. "The guy was shaking on his knees, crouched over," recalled Geierman. "He was scared to death." A noncom strolled over and nonchalantly shot the man through the head with his carbine.

Elsewhere, two 105 howitzer batteries of 3/11 were actually ashore, although still aboard their DUKWs, then they were ordered back to the LSTs because of the congestion on the beaches. During the return, three of the DUKWs, already damaged by coral, sank with the loss of all the howitzers and equipment aboard. The other 105s were landed the following morning along with corps artillery, which could not get ashore on D-Day because of the shallowness of the beachhead.

Enemy mortar and artillery fire continued to fall on the beaches as afternoon waned. A flurry of mortar bursts sent Tom Lea and some passing Marines diving into a hole on top of some shore party personnel. One of the latter stuck his head up and swore, "Goddammit, what are all you bastards in this hole for? Them bursts are a mile off. Scatter, you punks." Just then another shell walloped in close to the hole. The complainer buried his head in the sand and said no more. Somebody grunted, "You're a brave son of a bitch walking around out there, ain't you?"

The beaches were cluttered with men and equipment. "Jagged holes in the scattered stone and dirty sand, splintered trees and tangled vines made a churned, burned wilderness," recalled Lea. "Strewn through this chaos were not only the remnants and remainders of the Marines' advance, but also the new men and new gear that had poured ashore to back up the front line.... These men were digging in, making holes for themselves for the long night ahead. We jumped over foxholes, climbed over and around smashed trees, sidestepped tapes denoting mines and booby traps, walked gingerly around those yet unmarked. Telephone wires in crazy criss-cross mazes were stretched along the broken ground.

"Scattered everywhere were discarded packs, helmets, rifles, boxes, clothes, rubber lifebelts—the rubbish of battle. Lying on the seared leaves and hot sand were dead bodies yet ungathered by burial parties."

Division had projected 500 casualties for D-Day. Actual casualties, in return for disappointing gains, had been more than twice that: 210 killed and 901 wounded, not including combat fatigue and heat prostration cases—a number that was growing. These were very heavy losses, amounting to over 10 percent of the men ashore.

Nearly half of those total casualties—or one sixth of that regiment's strength—had been suffered by Chesty Puller's 1st Marines. White 1 was a slaughterhouse. "When the tide went out that night, you could have walked 300 yards across the beach on the bodies of dead Marines," recalled a tank crewman pinned down at the water's edge.

When Puller finally established contact by field phone with division late in the day, General Smith asked him how he was making out.

"All right," Puller replied.

"Do you need any help?" said Smith.

No, answered Puller. He did not need any help. He made no mention of his heavy losses, the gaps in his front or a need for reinforcements, although some of his officers were already shanghaiing men from the shore party along the beach.

Puller reported that his regiment was firmly established on the beachhead but still well short of the original objective line. Shrugging off the beating his regiment had taken in the last several hours, he informed division he was "ready to resume the attack at 0800." Later that night, he informed the command ship: "Enemy well dug in. Opposition strong. Little damage done by our preliminary fire. A hard fight ahead. Casualties over 20 percent. I've ordered no man to be evacuated unless from bullet or shell wounds."

From his command post on the beach, General Smith informed Rupertus at nightfall that all regiments were in contact and dug in for the night and the attack would resume at 0800 the next morning.

"It was not difficult to draw up an order," he remarked later. "It was simply a question of resuming the attack to capture objectives previously assigned."

Just before dusk, a Japanese mortar concentration slammed down on 3/5's command post. Slightly wounded, the battalion CO, Lieutenant Colonel Austin C. Shofner, went to the rear. The communications officer was less fortunate: a shell burst took off most of his head, leading to an erroneous report that Shofner himself had been killed.

The loss of Shofner could not have come at a worse time. When hit, he had been trying to establish control among the companies of his battalion, which had become disorganized in the scrub jungle during the push across the island. By the time he was evacuated and the general confusion settled down, control of the 3d Battalion was virtually nonexistent.

Lieutenant Colonel Lewis Walt, executive officer of the 5th Marines, took command of the battalion but could not locate even one of its scattered companies until after dark. Accompanied only by a runner, Walt pushed through the Japanese infested scrub, laboriously located each of his units and directed them into a cohesive defense along the airfield facing generally south. The job was not completed until 2300, and even then at least one company spent the night with its flank in the air. Nevertheless, Walt had achieved a near miracle and salvaged a very perilous situation by sheer determination and courage.

The same darkness that complicated Walt's task gave Harlan Murray a chance to escape from the tank trap on White 1. Some Marine tanks came up toward dusk and "were just shooting the hell out of everything," recalled Murray, which relieved some of the immediate pressure. Some of the Marines took that opportunity to get out.

As the able-bodied helped the wounded, a Japanese machine gun raked the trench from directly in front. A small redheaded private climbed out of the trap and began throwing grenades and shooting his rifle at the gun while the badly wounded got out. Still in the trap, Hugh Wiginton yelled at him to come back but received no answer. Wiginton climbed out and saw the little private was dead, "shot up awful bad."

Murray decided that if he was going to die, he might as well get killed running as stay in the tank trap and maybe get bayoneted by some over-enthusiastic Japanese. So he climbed up and ran back toward the rear "as fast as my two little legs would carry me." Stumbling into the battalion headquarters group, he got some cursory treatment, then got up and ran again, keeping his arm tucked inside his dungaree jacket so it would not wobble, until he finally reached an aid station on the beach.

"I'm hit," he told one of the medical men.

"I know it," said the man, eyeing Murray's bloody jacket, hurriedly slashed down the back to expose the wound.

Soon afterward, a DUKW picked up Murray and a load of other wounded to take them out to the auxiliary hospital ship USS *Pinckney*. "They had these mines along the beach," recalled Murray. "These land mines...they look an awful lot like these ocean mines but not as big and they've got these two prongs sticking out on either side of them. We got out in the water and [the driver] says, 'I've got to go down here to pick up some more people.' And he goes in there and he doesn't really secure the boat and the damn thing is bobbing around and I see one of these land mines right there and the bow of the boat is almost rubbing against it and I says, 'Goddammit, you know what you're doin'?' After all this crap I had I don't want to get blown up by a thing like that. I'm not the only one that's bitchin'. There's other guys, too."

Safe aboard the *Pinckney*, Murray and the other ambulatory wounded were led below and told to sit on a long bench. A doctor went down the line of injured men, telling the corpsmen what to do for each. One changed Murray's dressing. He received a tetanus shot and heard the corpsman say something about gangrene. "Oh shit," he thought. "I've got gangrene already." To his relief, the corpsman was only referring to the drop they put in each casualty's eye to prevent gas gangrene. Finally, feeling "weaker than hell," Murray was assigned a bunk and told to get some sleep.

CINPAC COMMUNIQUE NO. 117, SEPTEMBER 15, 1944...OUR CASUALTIES DURING THE FIRST DAY OF THE ASSAULT WERE LIGHT, ALTHOUGH THE LANDING BEACHES HAVE BEEN UNDER SPORADIC MORTAR AND ARTILLERY FIRE...

Night brought no relief to the Marines on Peleliu. Naval shells rumbled overhead. Artillery fire, characterized by its higher whistle, passed over

Marine positions. Worst of all, Japanese mortar shells plummeted down with lethal regularity, followed all too often by the cry, "Corpsman! Corpsman!"

Flares fired from warships offshore cast a flickering, greenish pallor on the shattered landscape as they swung slowly down on parachutes. Now and again, small arms fire crackled down the line as a fire fight flared, then tapered off as the Marines fidgeted and stared into the darkness. Japanese rifle fire could be distinguished from Marine by its lighter sound and higher crack. Their machine guns had a faster rate of fire than the Marine guns, while their artillery sounded more wobbly in flight.

Some of the heaviest gunfire was coming from the Point, where Captain George Hunt's small band of K Company survivors had settled in for a siege. An amtrac with supplies had finally sneaked in just before dusk, bringing much needed cans of water, two light machine guns, case after case of hand grenades, small arms ammunition, rolls of barbed wire and C rations. The tractor crew also parted with two of their own machine guns, which considerably bolstered Hunt's skimpy armament.

So far, Peleliu had exceeded anything most of them had ever dreamed of. "Gosh, Captain, I never expected it to be as rough as this," a young, redheaded Marine remarked to Hunt. "If I live through it, I sure hope I never see another one like it." A few minutes later, he was dead, picked off by one of the Japanese snipers who had crept forward to harass the Marines on the Point. The supply amtrac scuttled back out to sea, Japanese mortar fire landing in its wake. Hunt's men were again on their own.

Two squads of L Company's machine-gun platoon had managed to reach Hunt earlier in the afternoon, but no Marines had arrived to fill the gap on the right. Hunt's radio was on its last legs. Before it faded out entirely, he learned that the 2d Platoon had managed to escape the tank trap inland from White 1. An estimated 150 Japanese had promptly filtered into the hole. A couple of Marines who managed to sneak in just before dark confirmed the area was "lousy with Japs."

Darkness fell, and the Marines lay waiting among the rocks. Some slept uneasily under the greenish glow of the flares as the hours crept by. Hunt woke from an uneasy sleep at about 2335 to hear the radio man calling softly into the radio. The only reply was the blare of martial music as the Japanese jammed the wavelength.

The desultory firing picked up as hand grenades burst in quick succession along the Marine outer line. Japanese mortars began to work over the Point, and the cry went up for corpsmen. The Marines hunkered down, assuming they were being softened up for an infantry assault.

"I'll be damned," a Marine whispered after a close burst. "That one got me in the thigh."

Flares suddenly popped overhead from Marine support units. "There they are, I see 'em, I see 'em," someone cried as the Japanese came in.

"Well, plug the bastards, don't look at them," someone else returned in exasperation.

A machine gun ripped, then BARs and rifles joined in amid the thump of grenades. Muzzles flashed whitely. Bullets ricocheted among the coral outcroppings. Suddenly, the Japanese mortar fire stopped. The Marines braced themselves, but no attack followed. The firing lessened, then tapered off almost completely. All was quiet except for an occasional burst or grenade explosion and the cries for corpsmen from the Marine wounded. Hunt's line remained intact.

Facing the open beach, Swede Hanson had taken up position on a slight reverse slope. Down below, the redoubtable Corporal Robert Anderson set up with a captured Nambu light machine gun behind a low coral bulwark about 10 or 12 inches high. The coral was too hard to dig any deeper. "Whenever someone heard the Japs jabbering, they would call for a star shell," recalled Anderson, "and when it would go off, we could see Japs running out to our front. Then I would open up with the machine gun at the running Japs. I don't know if I hit any or not, but I used up a lot of ammunition."

Recalled Hanson, "You could hear movements going about, and your ears got bigger and bigger because you're wondering, is it a Marine or is it a Jap? And you didn't want to take a chance . . . so I start throwing hand grenades out there in front. And then I waited. Then, *brrrrr*, that Nambu machine gun. So I threw a couple of more hand grenades out there and I heard *brrrr*, but it took a little longer to get that one in."

All night long, Hanson pitched grenades out to his front while Anderson fired the Nambu. Sometime during the night, the Japanese machine gun jammed. Anderson had never seen one before that day, but he field-stripped it in the dark and managed to clear the stoppage. It jammed again toward daylight, this time for good, but by then the Japanese had backed off. Daylight also revealed dead Japanese strewn in the rocks, one only four feet from Anderson's Nambu. Hanson's grenades and Anderson's captured machine gun had played a key role in blunting any Japanese threat to the open flank. "You don't know how many Japs you piled up out there," a Marine told Hanson later. "I never saw so many dead Japs in one place in all my life."

Hanson was also hurt. Sometime during the night, a knee mortar round plummeted down and mangled his right arm. Knowing the corpsman did not have any supplies left, Hanson just held onto the arm and waited for the sun to come up.

Further down the beach, where 2/1 faced the Japanese airfield, Private Russell Davis started nervously in his foxhole as a voice called out from the darkness beyond. "Amelicans. Amelicans. Pigs . . . dogs. Amelican pigs and dogs." The voice sounded louder than life, as if amplified through a megaphone. "Amelican pig," taunted the voice. "You die. You die. You die."

A torrent of profanity rose from the Marine positions. "Hey, Shambo," taunted a Marine rifleman. "Come on in and see what we did to your tanks. We're using them to pack fish in." A machine gunner conversant in Japanese furnished choice expletives, and the exchange continued until officers silenced the men.

Here and there, enemy infiltrators sifted through the lines. Thoroughly familiar with the terrain, the Japanese, some wearing the helmets of dead Marines, moved confidently over the broken ground in the dark. Their primary mission was to reoccupy emplacements already overrun by Marines so they could harass the Americans from the rear. Vicious hand-to-hand struggles occurred throughout the night. Three infiltrators penetrated as far as General Smith's command post before an alert sentry gunned them down.

Another infiltrator made the mistake of climbing into a hole with a big black Marine from one of the ammunition platoons just inland from Orange 3. Other Marines on the line heard him yelling and screaming, "Lord, help me, I got me one! I got me one!" Well versed in night discipline, no one else moved. Daylight revealed the black Marine still clutching the neck of a dead Japanese. "He wasn't going to let go to find out if he was dead or not," chuckled a Marine artilleryman. "As long as he held him, he stayed still."

Several local counterattacks hit the 7th Marines out of the dark. Hunkered in his CP back of Orange 2, General Smith heard one of these assaults develop. "Everything was quiet," he recalled, "and suddenly we heard this banzai, the Japanese shouting, and then everything in God's green earth opened up."

During one of the enemy probes, a Marine manning the edge of the ditch was hit and slid down on top of Smith. The wound was not serious—a small shell fragment had hit the man in the back of the head—and Smith was amused to see how talkative the youngster was. He told Smith he was married and had been overseas for two years. To him, the wound was his ticket home—and a welcome one at that.

Another group some 50 yards south of Smith's command post was less fortunate as a mortar shell made a direct hit on their position. Three men were killed and seven wounded; so close, the spent fragments landed on Smith's group. One man found a piece of hot metal in his pocket.

The most serious attack against the 7th Marines hit C Company at about 0200, when a large number of Japanese swarmed out of the swamp and hit their lines. Some of the screaming Japanese penetrated the forward positions, and a number of beach party personnel had to be called up as a mobile reserve. In four hours of fighting, the 7th inflicted about 50 casualties on the attackers before the surviving Japanese withdrew.

Some men of 2/1 had one more scare before dawn, when they wakened to the sound of a high gurgling cry. The more veteran Marines reassured the rookies, explaining it was only "The Screamer," a man who had terrible nightmares and had been screaming his way through three campaigns. "The guy would drive you crazy if you didn't know about it," remarked a war-wise sergeant.

As daylight glimmered over the Point, the survivors of Captain Hunt's small command began to take stock of their situation. A number of men had been wounded during the night, including one good-humored Marine who had suffered a minor head wound. This character periodically doffed his cap of bandages and chortled, "Good morning, would you look at my ticket home?" Another small, wild-eyed Marine had had a hand grenade explode on his helmet. Now, his ears still ringing, he desperately sought assurance that he was not going to die. Upon being reassured, he would wander off, only to return later to repeat the question.

Swede Hanson, his arm all blue from internal bleeding, was told he should make his way back to an aid station as soon as possible. He recalled, "And I thought, yeah, how am I going to accomplish this? We're cut off up here. I can't even use a rifle anymore, and I'm just going to go through a bunch of Japs to an aid station ... like walking to a candy store."

Another Marine reported that two other men had been badly wounded in the legs during the night. Hunt turned to Hanson and said, "Swede, can you get them back?" Hanson suddenly had an idea. "I'll wade back to White Beach with 'em," he replied. Edging the two men into the shallow water, he pulled and floated them down the shoreline toward White Beach. As they neared it, he could see Marines dug in to protect the flank against enemy attack. Somebody spotted Hanson and yelled, "Here come some Japs! They're coming by the water!"

Hanson replied with a rip-roaring line of profanity, leaving no doubt he was all-Marine. To his amazed good fortune, the first person to greet him was a doctor. Within minutes, he was aboard an LCVP headed toward the ships offshore and medical care.

Back on the Point, daylight saw Hunt's men come under renewed attack. Enemy infantry had filtered in during the night and taken up positions in the trees and bushes all around. A low dip in the ground about 30 yards in front concealed Japanese mortars and grenadiers. "We could see the Japs bob up quickly, catch the fling of their arms as they hurled," reported Hunt. "Below in the rocks, we presented excellent targets for the Japs in the treetops."

Marine machine guns raked the draw, discouraging the Japanese from showing themselves too brazenly. Hunt saw a hand rise to throw a grenade— a stream of bullets "reduced it to a bloody stump." Enemy mortar fire continued to pound the Point, and Marine casualties mounted alarmingly. The Japanese began dodging in around the rocks, pressing Hunt's line.

A Marine scuttled by to snatch up a BAR from a man who had crumpled with a bullet in his chest. "Hello, five, this is control," called the radio man. "Hello, five, this is control. Do you hear me?" Hunt needed reinforcements in the worst way. A redheaded Marine, now gray with coral dust, volunteered to go for help. He scrambled down the rocks to the beach.

The line thinned as wounded Marines filtered back to the shelter of the beach, some clutching bloody arms, others sagging on stretchers. One pallid-faced victim scuttled behind a rock, blood pumping from a shrapnel hole in his back. "We must get these wounded boys out of here," shouted Lieutenant Willis. "Where in hell is the tractor?"

But the Japanese were also getting hurt in the exchange. The firing increased all along the line, grenades thudded and suddenly Hunt saw the backs of running Japanese infantrymen. The Marine riflemen stood up to better shoot them down. Moments later, the redheaded Marine arrived with some more men he found on the beach. He had also laid a phone wire across the reef from battalion. Fifteen more Marines clambered out of an amtrac, Hunt's wounded taking their place. Water, grenades and medical supplies lay stacked on the beach. The water tasted so strongly of gasoline that some of the men could not drink it, thirsty as they were. Hunt picked up the field phone and tried to ring battalion, but the line was already broken.

It was now D plus 1.

NOTES

1. One report says these were DUKWs in the sixth wave.

2. Levy was evacuated. "Several days later, he caught up with us," recalled Moskalczak, "and when asked what he was doing here, he replied, 'It is safer than on the hospital ship.' Later in the campaign, he was shot to death."

3. There is considerable confusion as to how many tanks participated in this attack. According to Colonel Tada, 14th Division Chief of Staff, Colonel Nakagawa had only 12 light tanks on Peleliu. However, two POWs, one whose platoon was assigned to ride the tanks and one a cook for the outfit, told interrogators there were 17 tanks in the unit commanded by Captain A. Mano: 3 platoons of 4 tanks each plus 5 in reserve. It would seem likely, but by no means certain, that at least 13 of these tanks participated in the attack across the airfield. Two smaller attacks later resulted in the destruction of 4 more, apparently completely wiping out the unit, since the POWs testified that none of the tanks returned, and unit personnel were subsequently organized into regular infantry units. An attempt to count the number of tanks destroyed on the airfield was unsuccessful, so thoroughly were they shot to pieces by American weaponry.

Chapter 6

The morning of D plus 1 brought still another enemy to the Marines on Peleliu: scorching heat. Shimmering off the coral, temperatures rose as high as 115 degrees, felling even strong men with heat prostration. Despite the strictest water discipline, many men had emptied their canteens by the end of the first day, and there was no readily available supply to replenish them. A tank officer reported that infantrymen in the front lines on D-Day were begging for water "like dying men."

Water brought ashore in 55-gallon drums was found to be tainted; the drums, which had originally held oil, had been improperly steam-cleaned, and now the water was barely potable. Other drums that had not been filled flush to the top had rusted in the tropical heat, also contaminating the water. Parched men choked down the blood-red liquid, finding a reside of rust like coffee grounds remaining in the bottom of their cups.

Others took dirty white water from bomb craters, including one near the scene of the tank attack the afternoon before. Two dead Japanese lay face down near the pool, and oil from a wrecked tank had seeped into the crater. "Just the same, it was water, wet and not poisoned as far as I knew," recalled one Marine who drank it. Waterholes dug near the beach yielded a brownish-red water which was purified with halazone tablets. Heated up over chunks of Composition C, it made terrible coffee but it was wet.

Already feeling the heat, although morning had hardly begun, men discarded their leggings, gas masks and blankets. A few went so far as to throw away their helmets, donning instead the soft floppy hats normally worn during fatigue duty. Some, remembering an old baseball trick, daubed mud on their cheekbones to cut the glare off the coral. In combination with the white lip salve some obtained, many of the men looked like poor facsimiles of vaudeville minstrel men.

The bright Peleliu sun also brought pause to one young artilleryman from

Rhode Island, Private Robert Biron. Back home, a fortune teller had told him he would not live to be 21. Now, only two days short of that birthday, he had plenty of reason to think the prophesy might well be fulfilled.

Chased off his gun by a Japanese tank during the attack across the airfield the evening before, Biron had taken shelter in a bombed-out torpedo storage facility. All night long, he crouched in the corner, listening to Japanese talking and moving around inside the building. At first light, he ducked outside and made his way back to his outfit—stopping en route for a satisfying look at the dead crew of the tank that had tried to kill him the day before. Whatever *his* future held, *they* would never celebrate another birthday.[1]

General Rupertus and his staff finally came ashore at about 0950. Hobbling on his injured ankle, Rupertus moved into General Smith's advance command post, burrowed into the reverse slope of the Japanese antitank ditch and took control of the operation.

A staff officer recalled that Rupertus was visibly disturbed by the reports coming from the 1st Marines. "Can't they move any faster?" he snapped into the field phone to Puller. "Goddammit, Lewie, you've gotta kick ass to get results. You know that, goddammit."

On the planning boards at least, the second day's mission was simply stated. To the south, the 7th Marines was to secure the lower part of the island where the Japanese 3d Battalion, 15th Infantry had been isolated the previous day. The 5th Marines was to seize the airfield, and the 1st Marines was directed to seize the high ground that had held them at an impasse for the past 24 hours. Orders had already been issued for all attacks to commence at 0800.

Unable to get off White 1 on D-Day, Bill Myers and his four-man crew spent the night dug in under their own tank. Artillery fire fell all night long, but Myers, utterly exhausted, slept through it all. D plus 1 began with a call from his company commander further down the beach. "Go down to the other end of the beach," he ordered. "There's a pillbox down there— some kind of gun emplacement—and they're knocking personnel boats out of the water." Learning the gun was concealed, Myers started to point out it was against the book to send a tank after a concealed weapon. The CO brushed him off. "Go down there and see what you can do," he directed.

Proceeding up the beach, Myers was lucky enough to spot the gun as it fired out to sea. A 47 mm, it had been concealed in a hollowed-out natural coral hill about 30 feet high just above the sand line. Only the muzzle protruded through a slot. Naval gunfire had not touched the position. Shooting from a wide angle, Myers's gunner tried to knock out the emplacement but could not hit the slot. "Why don't we turn on the stabilizer and run in front of it and blast 'em?" suggested Myers.

The gunner turned around, obviously less than enthusiastic about tackling a Japanese 47 mm head-on. "Bill," he said, "we in this tank are not that gung ho. Why don't I keep trying to hit it?"

"Sounds like a good idea," agreed Myers, who conceded he ran "a very democratic tank."

Moving forward a bit, the gunner finally put a round through the slot. The whole top of the hill blew off as the Japanese ammunition supply exploded. Investigating the emplacement later, the tank crew found the whole hill had been hollowed out and reinforced with concrete. Lying among the debris were the remains of about 40 Japanese killed instantly as the 75 mm round hit their ammo supply.

Moving up to attack across the northern edge of the airfield on the morning of D plus 1, Private Robert Leckie spotted two Marines still asleep in their foxhole. "Hey," he said, shaking one of them. "Wake up. We're moving out." When the man did not respond, Leckie rolled him over. There was a bullet hole through his head. The other Marine was also dead.

Three battalions were slated to attack across the airfield at 0800: 2/1 across the northern end, 1/5 and 3/5 across the lower part. The push would take the form of a wide turning movement toward the northeast, pivoting on the extreme left of the 1st Marines. Except for the shattered buildings at the northern end, there was no cover to speak of; the attack would move across the open field directly under the Japanese guns on the high ground to the north. The Marines were stuck on the proverbial billiard table.

Dug in on that high ground, the Japanese had already given the Marines a taste of things to come. At daylight, the enemy had put down an intense artillery barrage on the 5th's front lines. One shell hit the field telephone switchboard, wiping out a good part of the wire section. Another made a direct hit on the regimental CP located in a section of captured enemy trench near the edge of the airfield.

Among the casualties was Colonel Bucky Harris, who was half buried and suffered a badly wrenched knee. Exec Lew Walt returned from reorganizing 3/5 to find him lying on a stretcher, suffering considerable pain but determined to remain in command. Another man was killed, one was wounded and a member of Harris's staff, a Louisiana major who was heir to a Tabasco sauce fortune, had to be evacuated for blast concussion. In his coma, the Louisianan reverted to French. "He was parley-vooying like crazy when they carried him away," recalled a witness.

Walt and Harris soon worked out an arrangement whereby Harris would rely more heavily on his exec than would ordinarily be the case. Walt would make the less important decisions on his own. When time allowed, more important problems would be passed back to Harris for his decision. The upshot was an informally arranged joint command of the 5th Marines from 16 September until Harris recovered later in the campaign.

Lying on the hot coral waiting for 3/5 to jump off across the southern end of the airfield, Private Eugene Sledge noticed that the Japanese shelling was getting worse. American ships, artillery and planes were replying. An NCO moved past, low and fast, reiterating the creed of the assault Marine, "Keep moving out there, you guys. There's less chance you'll be hit if you go across fast and don't stop."

Out on the field, wrecked aircraft were visible here and there. Among them was a U.S. Navy carrier-type plane apparently shot down during the preinvasion softening up raids. Further out, Marines could see shattered buildings and the skeletal remains of bombed-out aircraft hangars.

An officer waved toward the airfield and shouted, "Let's go!" Covered with sweat and dust, the Marines moved out at a walk, then a trot, their lines widely dispersed. Heat waves shimmered off the runway, and a scorching wind wafted down from the hills like the breath of a blast furnace.

There was little actual resistance from the airfield area itself, but terrific fire poured down from the ridges to the north and from installations in the scrub jungle to the north and east, transforming the entire area into a terrain compartment. There was only one way to go, and that was head-on across the open field.

The attack resembled nothing so much as a World War I movie, thought one Marine advancing out in the open. The Marines moved out in open order with intervals of about 20 yards. Japanese small arms fire snapped by. "You'd hear kind of a plopping sound, like somebody shooting through a sheet on the line," recalled a 19-year-old machine gunner. "Of course, it was bullets going through bodies."

There was no place to hide. Marines stumbled and pitched forward as metal tore into their bodies. Bits of flying coral stung the living. Sergeant William Linkenfelter, who could be forgiven for thinking there were better ways to celebrate one's 22d birthday, saw his company commander sprawled out in a hole nursing his shot-up leg. The captain managed a smile as Linkenfelter passed. "Go get 'em, Link," he encouraged.

Cries for corpsmen went largely unanswered. Many of the hard-hit Marines bled to death on the hot coral runways before anyone could get to them. Amtracs protected by tanks retrieved some men; many others were less fortunate.

Lying in a shell crater as Japanese machine-gun fire swept knee high across the field, Corporal Joe Lommerse listened helplessly to the screams of a young Marine lying beyond reach in the open, blood geysering up in spurts from the wound in his body. The man cried over and over for his mother until he died.

"A lot of casualties were guys who were bleeding to death," recalled Corporal Russell Clay. "Nobody could get out there to pick them up. I know our little old platoon runner got hit in the leg as we were crossing, and they dragged him into a defiladed area. He was lucky. But once you get hit in the body, especially in the stomach . . . you just bleed out."

Also crossing with 1/5, Sergeant Flip Afflito was knocked off his feet by a shell fragment "the size of a water glass." He survived only because the fragment hit the airplane panel marker he was carrying rolled up under the pack strap on his left shoulder. "See how badly I'm hit," he said to a buddy who paused to check on him. The other Marine ripped Afflito's shirt open and laughed. The now shredded panel had absorbed the impact, leaving Afflito with only a tiny gash, a very sore shoulder and new respect for Dame Fortune. "It was only dumb luck that I put it where I did," he recalled of the panel.

Further to the south, Private Eugene Sledge was putting his faith in God. Pushing across the open field, he kept his eyes riveted straight in front, squeezed his carbine stock and recited over and over, "The Lord is my shepherd, I shall not want..." Then he was over. He had no idea how far he came; probably several hundred yards. Around him other survivors were visibly shaken by the ordeal. Even the eyes of the combat veterans betrayed their fear. Sledge suddenly felt less self-conscious of his trembling hands.

The most substantial gain in the 5th Marines zone of action was made by 1/5 under the command of Lieutenant Colonel Robert Boyd. Advance elements reached the main service apron and hangar area in about an hour, having swept the northern portion of the airfield. Here they found the Japanese dug into a large antitank ditch and several stone revetments. Heavy fighting ensued as the Marines worked to clean them out.

Crossing with A/1/5, 19-year-old Corporal Russell Clay managed to get across the fire-swept field by dashing from shell hole to shell hole. In the process, his unit seemed to melt away. His nine-man section had lost five men on D-Day. Now only he and his buddy, Private First Class Stephen Dosenczuk, made it across the open runways. They immediately piled up some rocks as cover and set up their light machine gun.

In his mid–20s, "Dozey" had been something of a father figure and good example to the younger Marines. Ironically, he did not even have to be on Peleliu. Plagued with a persistent jungle fungus, Dosenczuk had been offered a chance to return home after the Cape Gloucester campaign but had elected to remain with the division.

Now, stretched out behind their light machine gun, Clay and Dosenczuk scanned their front for targets but never found one. There was a tremendous blast as a 155 mm mortar shell landed off to their right, blowing Dosenczuk on top of Clay.

Clay didn't realize his friend was dead until he went to move him and found Dosenczuk's brains had spilled all over his jacket. A shell fragment had cleaved off the top of his skull, killing him instantly. Still in a state of shock, Clay ran to the protection of a tank trap a few yards away, where he sat down and tried to scrape the flesh and brains from his dungarees.

Flies had already begun to swarm, attracted by the carrion. Finally, Clay took off the jacket and threw it away.

Further to the north, Private Russell Davis also made it across the field to the enemy blockhouse area in a mad rush that left every man on his own. Now he joined a lieutenant and three riflemen firing on a pillbox from the rubble of some concrete foundations which had been reduced to a few broken walls by naval gunfire and Marine artillery. The lieutenant had a BAR he had picked up somewhere, and Davis noticed he did not use it very well.

A Marine tumbled into the hole. Stripes painted on his sleeves identified him as a sergeant. The lieutenant asked him if there were any flamethrowers.

"None," replied the noncom. "Only one got across and that don't work."

The others laid fire down on the pillbox slit, and a demolitions man, a swarthy, thick-bodied Italian, wriggled quickly out and placed his charge. The concussion slammed the Marines against the concrete. The pillbox stopped firing.

Also surviving the attack across the field, Private Robert Leckie found shelter in a shell crater containing about ten men. Four of them were from the 5th Marines, including a lieutenant who had been hard hit and was obviously dying. He was young, with athletic good looks, but in bad pain and "the ordeal was beginning to wear upon the discipline of his facial muscles," observed Leckie.

Whereas the 5th Marines on the right had to advance almost entirely in the open, the 1st Marines, after cutting across one corner of the airfield, entered the building area to the north. Many of the structures had been built of reinforced concrete. Blasted by heavy naval gunfire, they now lay in ruins, providing some cover for the advancing Marines—and for the lurking Japanese.

Ahead of Leckie's crater stood a blockhouse protected by a system of pillboxes. Shell fire had barely dented the structure, which spewed machine-gun fire overhead. A captain from the 1st Marines was trying to determine the source of the artillery fire slamming in all around, but without much success. "How many men here from the 1st Marines?" he asked. A half-dozen men raised their hands. "Six, eh? That ought to be enough. We'd better take that blockhouse over there. That's where all that machine-gun fire seems to be coming from. As soon as this shell fire stops, we'll move out against it."

Leckie had resigned himself to an unprofitable death when a Marine tank miraculously clanked up. The Marines attempted to attack behind it, but enemy shells drove them back to their crater.

All through the hangar area the story was the same, as individuals and small groups struggled forward to attack enemy positions with whatever they had. The assault reached the northeast side of the airfield in a little over an hour. Enemy resistance centered among the shattered concrete buildings, a large V-shaped antitank ditch and two stone revetments protecting 20 mm guns.

Using a tank as cover, a Marine platoon finally flanked the positions. The reserve company was committed, and the hangar area was taken in hard fighting. At noon, the 1st Marines reported, "Advancing slowly and receiving all types small arms, mortar and artillery. Casualties heavy."

In the center of the 1st Marines, the right company of the 3d Battalion and the left elements of Lieutenant Colonel Russell Honsowetz's 2d Battalion broke through enemy resistance and seized control of a section of the road running parallel to the eastern shore. On the right, however, enemy infantry fiercely contested the junction of the main road, which circled the base of the ridge beyond the large two-story concrete airfield headquarters building, then angled off to run up the coast. The road remained 200 to 300 yards beyond reach when the Marines stopped to set up positions for the night.

Casualties among the 1st Marines were high, but their defiance was summed up by the BAR man, who, hit in the thigh while attacking the blockhouse area, obstinately raised his middle finger to the gutted buildings beyond before crawling away, dragging his leg behind him.

Elsewhere in the twisted rubble, Russell Davis came across a big Polish Marine with half his dungarees cut away and no left arm. The stump oozed but did not bleed, and the Marine remained conscious. "Look at that," he said. "not much blood at all. No blood I can see. Maybe just a little."

Davis waited with him until he died, and the stump never did bleed.

In back of the airfield, a hot, dirty Marine slid into a shell crater and glanced around at the handful of Marines sheltering there. "Jimmy just got it," he announced.

"Where?" chorused the others.

"Through the stomach."

"Bad?"

"Bad?" echoed the first Marine. "He's dead."

Casualties had been so heavy crossing the airfield that at 1018 the 1st Battalion, 5th Marines sent an urgent message to Colonel Bucky Harris stating that help was badly needed. A Company had only 90 effectives left, reported the battalion, and B and C were in not much better shape. Harris got I Company up by 1147 to help out the battalion, easing the situation.

The story was only slightly better south of the airfield, where the men of the 7th Marines were also in action, attempting to mop up the isolated Japanese 3d Battalion, 15th Infantry. Working up through the scrub, Tom Lea came across a major sitting on a smashed log in the mud, marking a map while his radio man called over and over into his transmitter, "This is Sad Sack calling Charlie Blue. This is Sad Sack calling Charlie Blue." He sounded infinitely tired, and there was a plaintive quality to his voice as he called endlessly into the transmitter.

"The whiskery, red-eyed, dirty Marines had spent the night fighting in foxholes filled with stinking swamp water," observed Lea. "They were slimey, wet and mean now."

Some of that meanness may also have resulted from punctured expectations. A few days before the landing, the 7th Marines had been informed of "wondrous new bombs" loaded with napalm, recalled Major Waite Worden, exec of the 7th Marines. The napalm would burn off all the vegetation and incinerate "or literally suffocate any holed-up Japanese because of their appetite for oxygen," the delighted Marines were told. Now, eyeball to eyeball with some 1,500 very live and unsuffocated Japanese, the 7th's feelings about napalm were largely unprintable.

Stiffened by tank support and heavy preparatory fire, I Company, attacking eastward, fought to seize a Japanese barracks area surrounded by small pillboxes and dual-purpose antiaircraft positions. Following in the wake of the assault, combat artist Tom Lea heard the heavy slugging of the tanks, the crackling of gunfire and the answering enemy fire. The area had been overrun by the time he arrived. "Everything in it was smashed, twisted, blasted," he recalled. "There were dead Japs on the ground where they had been hit, and in two of the pillboxes I saw some of the bodies were no more than red, raw meat and blood mixed with the gravelly dust of concrete and splintered logs."

Pushing on to the east, the Marines worked along a trail littered with abandoned pushcarts, smashed ammo boxes, rusted wire, clothes and cast off gear of every description. Bright blue enamel bowls with the Japanese Navy anchor on the sides lay among a carpet of rice in a deserted mess shack, hastily abandoned as the Americans drew close.

Serious resistance cropped up again as the Marines went to ground in front of a large Japanese blockhouse. Many of the defenses in the area were built of coral chunks, but there was nothing makeshift about the blockhouse. Holed up behind reinforced concrete walls more than five feet thick, the Japanese defenders were virtually invulnerable. The fortification withstood direct hits from all infantry weapons. Naval gunfire had no effect; shells from 75 mm tank guns simply bounced off the sides. Both underground entrances and gun ports were protected by one-inch armor plate to foil flamethrower attack.

The blockhouse finally fell to gutsy demolitions teams which crept up under smoke put down to blind the defenders. The teams laid their explosives directly against the walls; they scrambled to safety, and the blockhouse went up in a blast of flame and smoke. I Company reached Peleliu's eastern shore just beyond the smoldering ruin at 0925.

The victors also poked through two big empty concrete gun emplacements on top of a nearby hill. More than 20 dead Japanese were found packed in a shelter in the wall of the emplacement. The Marines dragged them out, digging for souvenirs, drying bloody flags in the sun and examining enemy guns and gear. One man found a beautiful clean belt of a thousand stitches intended to protect the soldier from harm. That former owner was now quite dead and starting to stink, observed Tom Lea.

Meanwhile, other elements of the 7th Marines were attacking south in an effort to destroy the Japanese defenders. It was not easy. While the terrain was perhaps the closest thing to "flat terrain" on the whole island, the term was relative at best. Scrub jungle choked most of the area, hindering maneuver and turning the advance of support weapons into a major headache.

Adding to the 7th's problems, the Japanese had believed the Marines might attempt an amphibious landing in this area. From shore to shore, it was choked with defense works, most cleverly concealed and with carefully planned interlocking fields of fire. Pillboxes, casements, rifle pits and trenches had been blasted out of the coral, while attacking Marines had only what cover they could find behind natural terrain features or by building improvised breastworks of loose rocks and shell-blasted tree trunks.

There was no hope of digging into the solid coral with entrenching shovels. Their only advantage was that the installations had been built to repel an amphibious landing, so their strongest sides faced seaward, enabling the Marines to catch many of them from the flank or rear.

Reduction of the large Japanese blockhouse by the 3d Battalion opened the way for that unit's push south. K Company, advancing on the left of the 1st Battalion, battled its way through the belt of enemy installations in fighting described as "grim and deadly, but unspectacular."

The casualties of the sweep south included a good proportion of Peleliu's bird population. Although General Inoue subsequently denied it, the Marines had been informed that the Japanese would make heavy use of carrier pigeons as part of their communications network. As a result, each battalion had been allotted a number of shotguns, with predictable results. "The life of a Peleliu bird," recalled an officer, "whether parrot, marsh bird or fish hawk, wasn't worth a dime as long as we had shotgun shells."

By 1025, the company's leading elements were within sight of their final objective, the southeastern promontory. Two pillboxes defended the landward approach to the objective. The Marines wriggled forward on the scorching coral, and by 1200, both pillboxes had been turned into smoking crypts for their Japanese occupants. Meanwhile, 1/7, calling in strong artillery support, naval gunfire and air strikes, smashed its way through enemy pillboxes, bunkers and casements, knocking out four five-inch guns and three lighter dual-purpose antiaircraft weapons before noon.

The U.S. pilots were clearly visible as they made their runs; a couple waved to the infantrymen below. Two Japanese suddenly appeared, fleeing along the inner ring of the reef. Shooting badly, Marine riflemen let one of them get about 100 yards before knocking him down. The other died more quickly, taking 20 steps before a volley cut him in half and his disjoined body splashed into the surf.

Another Japanese, speaking impeccable English, broke in on the battalion's radio frequency to ask for "Captain Worden." Immediately suspicious of the misuse of his rank, battalion Exec Major Waite Worden pressed the key and replied cautiously, "Worden."

"Captain Worden, what's your strength?" inquired the voice.

Worden played along briefly, then informed the interloper that he had enough strength "to take care of him."

Despite enemy opposition, 1/7 reached the southern end of the island, opposite Ngarmoked Island, by noon. Now desperately in need of water after fighting all morning in the debilitating heat—105 degrees in the shade—the 7th Marines called a halt to the advance. Some men's tongues were so swollen from lack of water that they couldn't talk or swallow. Piling up coral rocks as shelter, the riflemen dug in to await resupply; the assault would be renewed in the morning. The assault troops were badly worn down by the heat. A dispatch from 3/7 reported, "Out of water. Troops having dry heaves."

The delay also allowed a half-track and 37 mm guns to be emplaced to fire directly into enemy installations on the promontory. Engineers ventured out to clear paths through the mines strewn across the sandy spit the Marines would have to cross during their assault the following day.

Accompanying the 7th Marines, combat artist Tom Lea heard one of the men say an LVT had arrived with some cans of water. Without even stopping to put on his helmet, Lea pulled out his canteens and set off at a trot in search of the water point. He soon spotted where the LVT had left the cans in a clearing at the top of a ridge and made straight for them. About 15 paces away, he nearly stepped in a big puddle of fresh blood; looking up, he saw three Marines carrying off another man who had been shot in the chest. A fourth Marine stood by the water cans. Lea filled his canteens without speaking to him and returned to his unit.

A moment later, as he was drinking, a Marine came puffing up with a full canteen and announced, "Goddamned snipers got two guys by me while I was pouring this. They got another guy just before that."

Lea gulped several more hot swallows, feeling peculiar.

Still clinging to the Point amid the overpowering stench of the dead, Captain George Hunt's men threw back numerous enemy probes during the morning and early afternoon. Hunt found himself responding like an automaton; death had become "as common as head colds." The roasted remains of the Japanese in the knocked-out pillbox by the water's edge were a mere curiosity, "the whites of their dead eyes shining in the dark like phosphorous." A probe to his front by two squads came to an abrupt halt when hordes of Japanese swarmed out of caves among the ridges and opened up on the Marines with grenades and rifles.

Amtracs shuttled supplies in and wounded out, while the regimental reserve, 1/1, continued efforts to punch through and link up with the beleaguered Marines by land. The Japanese fought back stubbornly from numerous camouflaged pillboxes. Much trouble was also had with one particular pillbox mounting twin 60-caliber machine guns. During the early afternoon, the last fresh troops, C Company, were committed to the assault, with a platoon from B Company in reserve. With the aid of two tanks, the Marine infantry wrested a 500-yard piece of ridge from the Japanese. Using this high ground as a lever, the remainder of B Company advanced and finally made contact with Hunt's men, who by now had spent 30 hours on their own defending the Point.

By now, too, the powers that be had recognized the precarious position of the 1st Marines on the left flank. The 2d Battalion, 7th Marines landed on Orange 3 during the morning, still in division reserve despite Rupertus's earlier concerns about the 7th's progress on southern Peleliu. Now, recognizing that Puller had the greatest need, division ordered 2/7 displaced to White 2, where it was attached operationally to the 1st Marines.

Adding muscle to the Marine beachhead, the 155 mm battalion had been landed and was ready for action by dark. Finding its previously assigned position still in Japanese hands, it set up as best it could on the ground already seized, only 100 yards from the 7th Marines' front lines. The position was so constricted—only about 200 square yards—that two of the batteries set up trail to trail, firing in opposite directions, with the third battery in march order close by.

During the day, the Marines seized their first prisoner of war on Peleliu, 18-year-old Second Class Private Tokusaburo Uyehara. An ex-fisherman from Koror, Uyehara told interrogators he had been drafted into the army three months before. He and 500 other men had undergone special counter-landing training, he said. Two hundred of this amphibious attack group had subsequently been assigned to Peleliu. Bordering on the suicidal, their mission was to swim out to American tanks and amphibious vehicles and attack them with grenades and mines during the landing. This strategy came to naught when U.S. suppressing fire kept the men in their caves until the Marines were firmly ashore.

The Japanese private knew little of military value, but he thoroughly understood the dedication of his comrades. Asked about the morale of Japanese troops on Peleliu, he replied pointedly, "*Shindemo mamoru*," translated to, "Though they die, they will defend."

As night fell on the other side of the airfield, Flip Afflito jumped into a hole about 20 feet from the rest of his group. In the darkness, he thought he smelled perfume; then someone said, "*A na hi mi hi how?*" Flip scrambled out of the hole, pulled the pin on a grenade and tossed it back at the voice. In the morning, the Marines found two dead Japanese in the hole.

Further down the line, on Orange 3, Private First Class Howard Miller also received a good scare during the night. Dozing in his hole, Miller suddenly felt something trying to get at his face. Shouting "Japs!" he leapt out of his hole in a panic before a buddy dragged him back down. Miller's "Jap" turned out to be a land crab.

By nightfall, the 1st Marine Division had enlarged its foothold on Peleliu to include much of the southern part of the island. The beachhead stretched about 3,000 yards across the southwest corner of the island and extended a mile deep in most parts, deeper in the center. The airfield had been seized, and the left flank of the beachhead had finally been reinforced and consolidated. The division's extreme left was still 100 yards short of its first objective, but gains elsewhere had been encouraging. It seemed a quick push up the East and West roads along the coasts would quickly puncture remaining enemy resistance.

These gains were well behind the projected timetable, and the cost had been considerably higher than anticipated. Private First Class Al Geirman wandered down Orange 3 during the day. "It was a mess," he remembered. "Orange Beach 3 was loaded with casualties. There was a regular hospital station there. They were giving them blood and everything. Right there, they were burying them in the sand, too. They'd just dig the hole and wrap them in a poncho and cover them up."

As is often the case with heavy combat, precise casualty figures remained vague. For D plus 1 on Peleliu, one report put casualties at 156, which a Marine historian later dismissed as "a nearly ludicrous figure." In fact, the 1st Marine Division had already taken serious losses over the first two days of battle. Especially hard hit was the 1st Marines, which reported 500 casualties on the first day, 1,000 by the end of the second. There was no question that the 1st Marines were in rough shape. Losses of 15 percent are ordinarily considered serious enough to pull a unit off the line. Puller's regiment had suffered 33 percent casualties in 48 hours.

These figures did not include many men in the line companies who ignored wounds to remain with their outfits. One of these stalwarts was Flip Afflito's buddy, Private First Class Patsy DeStefano, who had been wounded attacking a Japanese tank the previous afternoon. "We thought he was dying," recalled Afflito, who watched as his friend was evacuated. But the next day, DeStefano returned wearing only "a pair of shoes, a pair of dungaree pants, no top, no helmet, no rifle and about 15 bloody patches" all over his upper body, where he had been hit by grenade fragments. His story was straightforward. Evacuated to an offshore ship, he had hidden under a tarpaulin; he then sneaked back on the landing craft and came ashore again. "He was on his way home," Afflito recalled, still marvelling 45 years later at his buddy's courage. "He had been overseas 31 months at that time."

Such men would be sorely needed in the days ahead, for although no one knew it, the worst was yet to come.

The apparent breakthroughs on Peleliu on 16 September encouraged IIIPhib to proceed with the invasion of Angaur, only seven miles off Peleliu's southern tip. The Angaur Attack Force under the command of Rear Admiral William Blandy was even then posed off Angaur, waiting for the order to land. On 15 September, as the 1st Marine Division landed on Peleliu, the 81st Division Wildcats had feinted at Babelthuap in an effort to confuse the Japanese commander. When General Inoue failed to interfere, the convoy proceeded north until darkness fell, then reversed course for the southern Palaus and hove to off Angaur.

It had originally been planned to invade Angaur on 16 September—the night of the 15th, the assault troops enjoyed a preinvasion meal of steak, chicken and frozen strawberries—but the heavy fighting on Peleliu had delayed that timetable when concerns arose that the Wildcats might be needed to reinforce the 1st Marine Division.

Now, with the situation on Peleliu apparently in hand, pressure increased to proceed with the Angaur landing. Commanding the 81st Division, General Mueller wanted to get his men off the ships and into action. Admiral Blandy also pushed for the green light, while General Rupertus at no time indicated he might need any help from the army Wildcats.

Following a meeting between Rear Admiral George Fort, commanding the Western Attack Group and IIIPhib Commander Roy Geiger, an order was issued at 1432 on 16 September to proceed with the invasion of Angaur the following morning. Two of the division's regimental combat teams—the 321st and the 322d—would make the landing.

Also on 16 September, Admiral Halsey directed the seizure of Ulithi, 200 miles north of Peleliu, "as early as practical . . . with resources at hand." Only one regimental combat team—the 323d—remained in corps reserve, and Admiral Wilkinson decided to use the entire force, overriding Expeditionary Force Commander General Julian Smith, who advised caution in light of the fighting on Peleliu. Soon, 4,000 Wildcats of the 323d RCT—the last floating reserve immediately available to the 1st Marine Division—would be headed for Ulithi, with landings scheduled for 21 September. The Marines were on their own.

While the generals and admirals confabbed, there was little respite for Captain Hunt on the Point. The Japanese had not yet conceded its possession to the Marines, but it took until the night of D plus 1 for them to organize their strongest counterattacks on the position.

At 1600, Hunt had sent out small patrols to check the ground to his front. The Marines bumped into about 40 Japanese out in the scrub, apparently conducting an advance reconnaissance for a larger group. A sharp fight with grenades and tommy guns cost Hunt's Marines one dead and four wounded. The Japanese withdrew, but Hunt knew they would be back.

The attack came at 2200, when an estimated 500 Japanese launched a frontal assault on the Point from the facing high ground. A secondary assault struck down the narrow flat along the shoreline.

At one point the previous night, Hunt had been down to 18 men and an assault of this magnitude would surely have overrun his tiny command. By now, however, his situation had infinitely improved. Most of B Company was in position; Hunt was tied in with 1/1 and had phone contact with mortar platoons registered on the ground to his front.

Waiting in the dark, surrounded by dead men who had stiffened in rigid positions, the Marine could hear a "sort of excited jabbering" from out to their front. A Marine threw a grenade into the night; the explosion brought low squeals of pain and more jabbering. Hunt put everyone on alert and asked the mortar platoon to stand by.

Suddenly, a Marine cried, "There they are! They're comin' in on us!" and the entire line opened up at once. Japanese screams of "Banzai! Banzai!" were audible over the uproar as they pressed the attack.

Wave after wave of brown-uniformed Japanese rushed at the Marine line, disappearing in a hail of small arms, mortar and artillery fire. Flares flickered overhead, but smoke from the gunfire obscured the Marines' vision.

Lying in his foxhole, a Marine known as Duke looked up to see a Japanese hacking at his leg with a samurai sword. He had no sooner looked than a bullet whacked into his arm. Rearing up in pain and rage, Duke wrestled the attacker and finally pitched him over the cliff onto the jagged rocks below. Another man, stabbed in the shoulder and clubbed on the head by an enemy soldier who had come up behind him, swung around and shot the Japanese through the chest as he raised his arm for the finishing blow.

A Marine ran up shouting that more Japanese were coming up on the flank by the water's edge. As the threat diminished to the front, the volume of fire built up on the right. The Japanese attempting to attack along the shoreline were cut down and driven into holes along the Point. The Marines pitched thermite grenades down on them. The fugitives caught fire and, screaming with pain, ran into the water in a vain attempt to extinguish the flames. It did no good; they burned in the water like horrific human bonfires. Hunt listened to them scream; it took him a moment to realize that the shrieks were audible only because the firing had died down.

By 0200, the attack was over. Enemy dead lay sprawled four deep in the gullies facing the Point, faces frozen, eyes showing "an expression of horror and incredibility" through eyes "slimy with the green film of death." Parts of bodies hung in trees, where they had been blasted by Marine mortars and artillery. Other bodies bobbed gently in the water. The Marines later counted over 500 enemy corpses. Already a sickening, putrid stench was beginning to rise from the heat-bloated remains.

The light of dawn also revealed a 40 mm gun among the carnage. No doubt intended to enfilade the White Beaches once the Point had been recaptured, it now lay scarred by shrapnel among the torn enemy bodies. The Point remained U.S. Marine Corps' entirely.

The following morning, K Company went into reserve. Of the more than 235 men who had assaulted the island on 15 September, only 78 were left on their feet.

Joining hundreds of other casualties aboard a hospital ship that night was Private Robert Leckie, late of F Company, 1st Marines. Having survived the regiment's mad push across the upper part of the airfield, he had been too close to an ammo dump when a Japanese shell dropped in on the afternoon of 16 September. Concussion reduced him to something resembling "a life-sized doll in whom the spring had broken." Two Marines had helped him back to an aid station, where they appropriated his tommy gun before shoving off again.

It would be three days before the New Jersey Marine regained the power of speech or could make his legs walk again. Blast concussion had ended his war, but he could not shake the guilty feeling that he was somehow abandoning his buddies. He would later realize he was lucky. Peleliu was just beginning.

NOTE

1. Bob Biron not only survived his 21st birthday, but when interviewed for this book, he had reached the age of 64. So much for fortune tellers.

Chapter 7

By the morning of 17 September, D plus 2, certain characteristics of the Peleliu fighting were beginning to establish themselves. They demonstrated, among other things, that the lessons of previous defeats in Pacific island fighting had not been completely lost on the Japanese. Most significantly, there had been no wild banzai charges in the opening days of the campaign, and although the Marines continued to hope for the opportunity to slaughter their enemies in the open with superior firepower, they were not to be granted that good fortune.

Japanese counterattacks on Peleliu had been well planned—if sometimes lacking in good timing—with limited, well-defined objectives. The troops conducting these attacks included what one authority later described as "some of the finest Japan ever put in the field, under officers who had learned the futility of pitting Bushido against firepower and steadfastly refused to play into their enemy's hands."

What the Marines were discovering on Peleliu was a forerunner of what they would later encounter on Iwo Jima and Okinawa: a carefully integrated defense in depth, characterized by great strength and flexibility, manned by a stubborn enemy determined to survive as long as possible, if only to exact the greatest possible toll of American lives.

Because of this defense, the Marines relied heavily on tank/infantry teams. The bulk of the division's 30 tanks—15—had been assigned to the 1st Marines in the north. Nine had been assigned to the 5th Marines and six to the 7th Marines in the south. Used as mobile artillery, the 34-ton Shermans were invaluable in providing fire to seal caves, blast pillboxes and reduce Japanese defense works.

Just how invaluable was not always clear to the tank crews, sweltering in their steel compartments under Peleliu's blazing sun. Private First Class Larry Kaloian, a loader on a Sherman, was among the tankers working over the high ground north of the airfield—a sheer cliff face of pocked coral soon nicknamed "Bloody Nose Ridge."

"All we did was run up to Bloody Nose Ridge and throw round after round after round of 75 mm shells into all the holes we could see in the cave areas," recalled Kaloian. "Alongside all of the other tanks, while the infantry was right alongside of us. We were protecting them and they were protecting us from a banzai charge or something that might come over and throw a bangalore torpedo at us."

Kaloian never saw a live Japanese on Bloody Nose, but he had abundant evidence of their presence. When his tank crew returned to the rear to rearm each day, the crew would find "hundreds and hundreds of nicks in our tank from bullets being sprayed at us" by enemy infantry concealed in the ridges.

On another occasion, Lieutenant Lee Stack opened up a port to get some air, just in time to see a Marine field piece "go sky high." Stack, a 6'3" Yalie-turned-tank officer, did not know where the fire had come from, but his gunner had spotted the enemy artillery piece moving in and out of a tunnel in the ridge about 100 yards away from their Sherman. "Lieutenant," he said, "when that baby comes out again, it is going to take a crack at us. Permission to fire, sir."

"Hell, yes," replied Stack.

A minute or two later, the Japanese gun reappeared. Before it could fire, Stack's gunner let loose a round and knocked it out. "It was like a shootout in one of those western movies," recalled Stack. "Thank God our gunner was a crack shot."

The Shermans often had to rearm several times a day to keep up with the pace. On D-Day alone, ammunition expenditure was so high that an advance the next day had to be supplied with shells and bullets salvaged from ten damaged tanks. However, the results were good. A single tank destroyed 30 pillboxes in one day's action. Working in concert with LVTs fitted with flamethrowers, the armor proved a valuable weapon against the dug-in Japanese.

Casualties among the tankers were also higher than usual, particularly among officers who exposed themselves in the hatches to better direct the fire support. "Just about everybody that stuck their head out got it through the head, neck or someplace," observed Kaloian. Eight of the 31 officers in the 1st Tank Battalion were killed; another 15 were wounded. Only eight left Peleliu uninjured.

Repair crews also suffered losses while stripping immobile tanks of parts to keep other Shermans in operation. Through such expedients, the 1st Tank Battalion managed to keep at least 18 tanks operating at any given time, and only 9 were finally listed as total losses. Nevertheless, the Shermans left behind at Guadalcanal due to lack of transport would have been more than welcome.

Kaloian's company, assigned to the 1st Marines, arrived at Peleliu with

15 tanks. By the end of the second day, only five were operative. Casualties among the men and machinery might have been even higher but for an innovation designed to strengthen the tanks: before leaving the rear areas, the mechanics had welded spare track over the turret and front slope of each Sherman to increase resistance to armor-piercing and high-explosive projectiles. This innovation was later credited with saving three tanks from direct hits by 75 mm armor piercing shells.

On the other side of the airfield, Bird Dog Clayton spent the whole night on alert, wondering about a terrible smell wafting in from in front of his hole. Sunrise brought the answer. Ten feet in front of his position, the morning light revealed the bloated corpse of a dead Japanese.

At least Clayton's Japanese was harmless. Corporal Joe Lommerse opened his eyes on D plus 2 to see a Japanese soldier 15 feet away, reaching for his rifle. As Lommerse scrambled frantically for his own weapon, a company runner blew the Japanese off his feet with a shotgun blast.

It was also on D-Day plus 2 that the 1st Marines met the Umurbrogol, giving final lie to preinvasion reports of manageable terrain. The jungle scrub that had masked the tortured formations from aerial observation had now been stripped away by naval gunfire, baring this devil's playground of jagged ridges in all its terrible reality.

The 1st Marines regimental narrative described the ground as "a contorted mass of decayed coral, strewn with rubble, crags, ridges and gulches thrown together in a confusing maze." Marine officers were dumbfounded at the scene. General Smith recalled, "Ravines, which on the maps and photographs appeared to be steep-sided, actually had sheer cliffs for sides, some of them 50 to 100 feet high."

All of this came as a complete surprise. "We saw that roads ended at the foot of the ridge," a division intelligence officer recalled of the prevailing line of thought, "but we thought that these led to dispersal storage caves at the foot, thought probably the Japs kept their gasoline there." There had been little idea that the Japanese were deeply dug in among the ridges.

A survey later located 500 caves in the hills—200 artificial and 300 natural, but virtually all lending themselves to defense. One huge cave, punched into the ridge back of the airfield, had been finished off with cement walls, floor and ceiling and boasted entrance portals carved in rock ten feet thick. Horse-drawn ammo caissons were able to roll in and out with loads of shells, their way illuminated by a system of dome lights.

In this jungle of rock, the Japanese waited—thousands of them—for the Marines to come to them. An enemy ration statement captured on D plus 1 indicated that the week before the landing, there were slightly over 10,000 Japanese on Peleliu. Now well over 5,000 of these troops, perhaps more, were estimated to be still alive and fighting.

One of those 5,000 found Corporal Bill Myers—who had finally managed to get off the beach—jockeying his tank down a trail behind White 1 on 16 September. A veteran of two campaigns, he had never seen a live enemy point-blank in front of his tank. Now, sitting in the gunner's seat, he was stunned to see a Japanese soldier emerge from behind a coral and oil drum breastwork 25 feet away and charge directly at the tank with fixed bayonet.

Up in the commander's seat, another tanker blurted, "Do you see him, Bill?"

"Yes," replied Myers.

"Are you going to shoot?"

"Yes." Myers reached toward the actuators for the coaxial 30-caliber machine gun, but in his excitement he hit the actuators for the 75 mm. The charging Japanese literally evaporated almost in front of the tank as high explosives struck his body. Having killed his first enemy soldier at eyeball-to-eyeball range, Myers sat in his seat and shook as though palsied.

Many Marines would later refer to Bloody Nose Ridge as if it were a single geological formation, but Private Russell Davis recalled it "as a series of crags, ripped bare of all standing vegetation, peeled down to the rotted coral, rolling in smoke, crackling with heat and stinking of wounds and death . . . stained and black like bad teeth." This was the infantryman's view of the Umurbrogol faced by the 1st Marines on the morning of D plus 2. Before the attack could jump off, some reorganization was necessary. The regiment's losses—now over 1,000—forced the use of all three battalions in line: 3, 1 and 2 from left to right to provide the necessary punch.

On the right, 2/1 was the first to meet the ridges, jumping off behind artillery and naval gunfire. The Marines captured the Japanese road junction linking the East and West roads, denied them the previous day, and advanced about 150 yards before they were hit by heavy fire from a 200-foot ridge on their left, henceforth known as Hill 200. Honeycombed with caves and observation posts, the steep-sided ridge was the source of much of the fire on the airfield. Orders came down from regiment for 2/1 to take it.

Wheeling to the left, the Marines assaulted the ridge, scaling the steep coral in the face of withering small arms fire and point-blank bursts from mountain guns and dual-purpose pieces sheltered in caves. "At such close range, this fire was extraordinarily accurate," observed the official Marine Corps history of the campaign. Tanks and amphibious tractors trying to move up in support sent up plumes of oily black smoke as they were hit, one by one, by the deadly Japanese artillery. Recalled General Smith, "It was very difficult to find blind spots as the caves and pillboxes were mutually supporting. . . . The caves and pillboxes housed riflemen, machine gunners, rockets and field pieces. The Japanese technique was to run the piece out of the cave, fire and then run the piece back in before we could react."

An enlisted Marine put it another way: "When we hit them on top, they popped out of the bottom; when we hit them in the middle, they popped out of both ends."

Caught "witless and helpless" in a hole with two other riflemen, Russell Davis recalled the horror of that morning. Men were crying out all over the hill—for corpsmen, for plasma, water, artillery or air support. Some cried for God. Neither Davis nor the other two Marines even got off a shot so thoroughly were they pinned down.

In the center, meanwhile, Major Raymond Davis's 1st Battalion got off to a good start and moved "with surprising ease" for about an hour before the Marines came up short before an obstacle which, by Marine reckoning, should not have been there at all. This was an enemy blockhouse "the size of a small office building" with reinforced concrete walls four feet thick. The massive fortification was further protected by 12 pillboxes, all connected by a network of tunnels.

The defense work showed clearly on pre-landing aerial photos and was pinpointed on the map issued to all ground troops, where it was marked as a large building. But now, eyeballing this formidable structure, Marine riflemen saw naval gunfire had made no impact on it whatsoever. "The blockhouse had not been so much as nicked, much less reduced," noted the official history of the campaign with a touch of bitterness.

The Marines sent for help through division, where Rear Admiral J. B. Oldendorf's preinvasion statement that fire support ships had run out of targets was immediately brought to mind. Now, with the Marines waiting out of range, the USS *Pennsylvania*[1] sought to rectify matters by turning its 14-inch guns on the structure. Shore fire control adjusted the guns, and the blockhouse began to disintegrate under the big armor-piercing shells.

Meanwhile, smaller-caliber naval gunfire, tanks and infantry took care of the surrounding pillboxes. By 0930, the battalion CP had been established in the ruined blockhouse "mingled with the remains of about 20 freshly dead Japanese," noted Major Davis. At the doorway lay a man's hand, severed from its arm. The nearest body lay 30 feet away. Most of the Japanese, killed by the terrific concussion of the *Pennsylvania*'s 16-inch shells, did not show so much as a scratch.

A lieutenant led the remnants of two A Company platoons through the dense scrub toward the ridge. As the Marines crossed the road, a Japanese officer, pistol in one hand and sword in the other, charged at him in a frenzy. The Marine turned to his BAR man on his left and said, with a slight note of irritation in his voice, "Well, why don't you shoot him?" The BAR man promptly emptied half a magazine into the charging Japanese, dropping him in his tracks.

At about the same time, a Japanese squad was spotted setting up a heavy machine gun behind the rear platoon. The Marines opened up on them, killing all but one. He was dispatched a few seconds later by a private first class when he threw a grenade at a group of Marines. Moving on, the

Marines found about 40 dead Japanese strewn along a 300-yard stretch of the road where they had been caught by American weaponry.

Now, however, the battalion's assault took it up into the ridges, and fire from the high ground began to inflict alarming casualties. As did 2/1 on the right, 1/1 went up the only way it could: clawing and dodging up and down steep-sided gullies, losing men to enemies they never saw, hidden in caves that had to be taken by direct assault. The sharp-edged coral slashed their clothes and flesh every time they hit the deck. It was impossible to get underground, away from the Japanese mortars, and each blast threw chunks of coral in all directions, multiplying the effect of every shell.

Firing from point-blank range, a Japanese 70 mm mountain gun held up the assault for 45 minutes. Before Marine tanks and bazookas silenced the gun, it had knocked out C Company's whole machine-gun squad along with the battalion 81 mm mortar OP. A private first class had a six-inch chunk torn out of his arm, leaving the hand dangling by a small piece of muscle. Despite this injury, he helped carry another wounded man 150 yards back to battalion, then made his way to an aid station.

There was no mercy. Helping haul a wounded Marine off the ridges, Corporal Joe Lommerse and two other stretcher bearers were peppered by Japanese machine-gun fire. They stumbled and fell, dropping the wounded man off the stretcher. Manhandling him back on, they ran down the hill, but the Marine was already dead, with over a dozen bullet holes through his abdomen, stomach and legs.

By evening, 1/1 had managed to establish itself on the forward slope of the first hills, having knocked out 35 separate Japanese-defended caves in the process. Intelligence officers had suspected that there were many caves in the ridges, but they were not prepared to encounter them in such tremendous numbers. Casualties were severe, and remnants of companies, engineer troops and pioneers were used to plug gaps, while headquarters personnel formed a meager reserve.

Of Puller's three battalions, the 3d suffered least of all and managed to advance 700 yards against minor resistance along the coastal flat to the left, stopping only because it was in danger of overextending. The 2d Battalion, which had been first to encounter the ridges, was less fortunate. By nightfall, having seized Hill 200, the Marines found themselves taking fire from a slightly higher ridge, Hill 210, which dominated their positions from the west. A narrow, rock-littered ravine between the two knobs was full of Japanese, preventing the Marines from mounting an assault on the higher elevation. They could only dig in as best they could among the jagged coral rocks and take it on the chin.

Day's end found Puller's regiment with a line resembling a rough W. The 2d Battalion held Hill 200 as a salient in the enemy line, while the Japanese-held ridge to the west formed an equally deep salient in the Marine lines.

As darkness fell over Lieutenant Colonel Russell Honsowetz's 2d Battalion CP in the ridges, the field phone rang. It was Puller. He asked how things were going.

"Not very good," said Honsowetz. "I lost a lot of men."

"How many?" asked Puller.

Honsowetz said he wasn't sure. Maybe a couple of hundred.

"How many Japs did you kill?" asked Puller.

Honsowetz said he didn't know. There were a lot of bodies around. Maybe 50, he guessed.

"Jesus Christ, Honsowetz, what are the American people going to think?" blurted Puller. "Losing 200 fine young Marines and killing only 50 Japs! I'm gonna put you down for 500."

Joe Lommerse's outfit experienced one of the more bizarre incidents of the night. Setting up their machine guns to cover both sides of a road leading toward Bloody Nose Ridge, the Marines suddenly heard a motorcycle approaching from the Japanese lines. Moments later, the cycle and attached sidecar came tearing down the road, the Japanese driver and his passenger singing and yelling, apparently on a rollicking drunk. Their joy ride ended abruptly in a blast of machine-gun fire, but it provided grist for extended speculation among the bemused leathernecks.

As the exhausted Marines settled in, a more serious threat developed as the enemy discovered a gap between 2/1 and 1/1 and began to infiltrate the weak spot. To seal the hole, F Company, 7th Marines had to be committed. This outfit fought its way into position and managed to close the gap.

Japanese pressure on Hill 200 also remained heavy throughout the night. One Marine on the hill later described the experience as "a night of terror," as forward observers pulled naval gunfire down right in front of the Marine line, the huge explosions flaming orange and shaking the ground as the Marines hugged the coral.

Pressure on the hill was so strong that G Company, 7th Marines was sent up to reinforce 2/1. Luckily, the concentrations of artillery and naval gunfire prevented the Japanese from massing for an overwhelming counterattack, and the Marines managed to cling to their gains.

"Results of the day's battle were viewed with optimism," observed the regimental narrative. "Not only had the high ground been gained in the general advance along the line, but some of the stiffest opposition the Japs could put up had been dispatched."

That same night, unknown to the Marines desperately clinging to Hill 200, Colonel Nakagawa relocated from his nearby command post to one deep within the ridges on the western edge of the Umurbrogol. His original headquarters, located in a balcony-type cave distinguished by its wide horizontal mouth, had become too vulnerable. Marines later found the cave, complete with electricity and other amenities, extending completely through the ridge. But U.S. possession of the ridge did more than disrupt the colonel's CP; it transformed a Japanese salient into an American one and eliminated the heavy flanking fire on 2/1 and the 5th Marines.

Colonel Nakagawa accepted this setback philosophically. In a report to his superiors on the night of 17 September, he admitted that "under the protection of heavy naval gunfire, an enemy unit composed of two tanks and approximately two companies of infantry successfully advanced to a high spot on the east side of Nakagawa [Hill 200]."

Three days of fighting had left the 1st Marines badly battered. "Front line units had been decimated," conceded the regimental narrative. The regiment had lost 1,236 men since D-Day, according to available figures. Approximately 200 of the 473 total effectives in the 3d Battalion were headquarters personnel.

That night, Puller called division and talked with Colonel John Seldon, the chief of staff. He told him half his regiment was gone and he would need replacements to continue the attack as ordered. Seldon replied that there were none available.

"Give me some of those 17,000 men on the beach," retorted Puller.

"You can't have them," said Seldon. "They're not trained infantry."

"Give 'em to me and by nightfall tomorrow they'll be trained infantry," Puller replied grimly.

Despite that vow, he was told he would have to continue the attack as best he could without replacements.

A few minutes before noon, Private First Class James Isabelle looked up from his position to see a huge cloud of greenish-yellow smoke wafting down from the hills. All through the area, horrified Marines stopped and stared. "Gas!" someone yelled, and the alarm was raised. Like virtually everyone else, Isabelle had tossed his gas mask away as soon as he hit the beach. Now, looking at the greenish gas drifting toward him, all he could think was, "Why the hell did I throw away my gas mask?"

Private First Class Clayton saw "a total panic up and down the beach," as the cloud wafted closer. "Everybody's scroungin' to find gas masks... guys fightin' over gas masks."

Sergeant Afflito saw a yellowish haze drifting in about 200 yards from his right front. Like the others, he had long since thrown his gas mask aside—the bag now served as a repository for cigarettes and socks, which were not going to do him much good when the cloud arrived.

"There's a bunch of dead Marines over here!" someone yelled. "Go over there and steal their gas masks."

Everyone "ran over there like crazy," recalled Afflito; "we're turning these bodies over and taking their gas masks. And I put one on with a broken lens. But I didn't give a shit... I didn't care if it was no good. I wanted it on."

Seconds passed. Then minutes. Nothing.

"It's a false scare, it's false," the word was passed. Masks were slowly removed, and the men turned back to their work, some a bit shamefaced over their display of panic. It was later determined that the greenish-yellow smoke had come from an enemy picric acid shell, although witnesses would argue about the phenomenon at 1st Marine Division reunions for years to come.[2]

In the original planning for Peleliu, it had been recognized that the 1st Marines were assigned the toughest mission. However, it was assumed the 7th Marines would sweep swiftly over southern Peleliu and then be available to reinforce Puller's regiment in a quick push north within 24 hours. This had not occurred. On 18 September, D plus 3, the 7th Marines were still engaged in heavy fighting to secure the southernmost part of the island.

Plans for 17 September had called for the relatively fresh L Company to assault the southeastern Ngarmoked promontory. This attack was scheduled to jump off at 0800. Naval gunfire, followed by a preparatory air strike, sent up great fountains of flame and plumes of smoke along the length of the peninsula before engineers belatedly discovered a second enemy mine field barring the way across the sand spit.

The assault was held up while engineers, working under heavy covering fire from tanks and infantry, tackled the newly discovered mine field. The mines were cleared without casualty, and the Marine assault jumped off at 1000.

Supported by tanks, the riflemen gained a foothold on the promontory within 26 minutes, occupying enemy installations knocked out by tank fire the day before. Reinforcements were rushed up in amtracs under scattered enemy rifle fire. The assault slowly moved forward against Japanese firing from crevices and pillboxes.

Finding fire to be their most effective weapon against the dug-in enemy, a call went out for more flamethrowers to be brought up. When these arrived, progress quickened. The objective was well in hand by 1320, the last 20 or so enemy survivors being driven into the water, where Marine riflemen picked them off as they tried to escape northward across the reef. A final count showed 441 Japanese bodies scattered across the point, at a cost of seven Marines killed and 20 wounded.

The Marines of 1/7, facing the southwestern promontory, were not so fortunate. Not only was this promontory larger, but the terrain was rougher and defended in greater strength. Fortunately, one other advantage had been denied to the Japanese: the small unnamed island that had caused so much trouble on D-Day had finally been silenced. Having withstood naval gunfire and air strikes, the main gun position on the island was finally spotted from the beach and knocked out by tank fire. Apparently hoping to threaten the

Map 4.
The U.S. Scheme of Maneuver

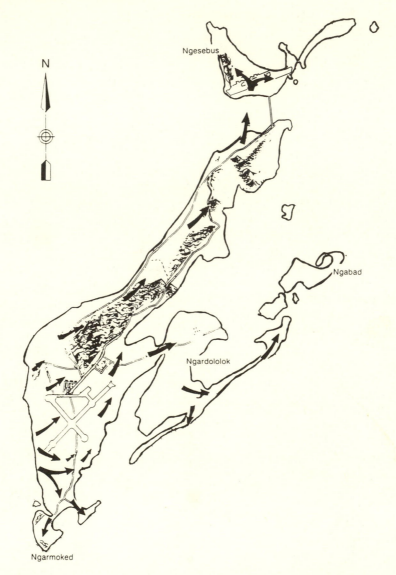

flank and rear of the Marine assault again, the Japanese had made several attempts to reoccupy the island during the night of D plus 1.

Illuminating shells caught large numbers of enemy infantry trying to wade across from the southwest promontory, making easy fodder for Marine machine gunners and riflemen. "No further trouble was experienced from that direction," an officer noted drily.

Spearheaded by a relatively fresh company, the attack on Ngarmoked managed to get one platoon and a tank across the spit during the morning. At 0835, these elements ran into the Japanese main line of resistance and "were stopped cold without being able to gain a foothold," in the words of the official Marine Corps history of the campaign.

The company asked permission to withdraw so heavy weapons could work over the ground. Permission arrived an hour later, and the Marines extricated themselves with considerable difficulty, having been badly mauled in the process—so badly that the company was sent directly back into reserve.

Artillery and mortars pounded the Japanese while all available tanks and LVT(A)s were moved up, along with half-tracks and 37 mm guns from the Weapons Company. The early success of 3/7 on the opposite promontory also freed up many of the supporting weapons attached to that battalion, as well as eliminating flanking fire from that direction.

Backed by this firepower, A Company attacked across the sand spit at 1420. Preceded by a ten-minute air strike and accompanied by three tanks, the Marines rammed through the enemy first line of defense and gained the high ground.

The Marines slugged their way southward, preceded by mortar and artillery fire, but the going was rough. "The enemy defenses were of many types," reported combat correspondent Sergeant Jeremiah A. O'Leary. "Every few yards, the Japs had coral bunkers, concrete blockhouses, reinforced foxholes, earthen trenches, caves and sandbagged positions. Every position was located to cover its own approaches and the approaches to surrounding defense works."

At least one piece of Marine equipment also proved to be a disappointment. The new Mark III offensive grenade, designed to explode on impact, proved ineffective due to its lack of fragmentation. It was also dangerous to handle. Two men of 1/7 had their hands blown off in the act of throwing them and IIIPhib subsequently recommended that it be withdrawn from service.

By late afternoon, the entire battalion had been committed to the fight for the peninsula. C Company got to the western shore, eliminating the heavy weapons that had enfiladed the Orange Beaches for three days. Attempting to push south, C Company then ran into a sizable swamp which threatened to break off contact with A Company on the right. The battalion set up a defensive perimeter for the night in the shape of an inverted U, with a shallow penetration in the swampy middle but a good hold on either shore.

The next morning, backed by armor that had been brought up during the previous afternoon and night, C and A Companies circled around each end of the swamp, linked up and drove toward the end of the promontory.

The Marines benefited greatly from a lucky find. The evening before, someone in B Company, 7th Marines turned in a Japanese map overlay detailing the defensive installations for a reinforced company on the southwestern peninsula. It was so clean and fresh that intelligence officers initially viewed it with some suspicion, but after correlating it with known positions, the map was determined to be genuine. This information saved many American lives as the Marines pressed across the peninsula.

All assault units were told to ignore any overrun Japanese hiding out in the rugged terrain and concentrate solely on pushing to the end of the promontory. Mopping up would be conducted by demolitions teams and specially designated reserves.

The impracticality of this order was soon painfully clear. C Company detached 15 men to cover suspected cave and pillbox openings in the wake of its advance. These men almost immediately found themselves pinned down "by Japanese swarming out from the underground in numbers, which, at this early stage of the operation, seemed astonishing," reported the official history. What the Marines were encountering was a demonstration of Japanese "passive infiltration" as laid out in the enemy tactical doctrine for Peleliu. This tactic proved so successful that most of the special reserve from the 3d Battalion and the Division Reconnaissance Company had to be committed to bring the situation under control.

Among the Marines thrown into the melee was a strapping 19-year-old Alaska-born private, Arthur J. Jackson. "Bull" Jackson had already pulled one stunt on Peleliu not calculated to endear him to his buddies. The night before the landing, he had pulled kitchen duty, and a tenderhearted petty officer, apparently feeling sorry for him, had presented him with a 14-pound canned ham. The idea of saving that ham for when rations ran short inspired Jackson to dump everything out of his pack except his rifle-cleaning kit.

"The only mistake I made was that I carried that dang thing clear across the island, and every time I hit the prone that darn ham like to have beat me to death," he remarked. "My steel pot was constantly being pushed down into my eyes on that little trip." Finally, Jackson broke open his prize and shared it with his squad. The problem was, nearly everyone had run out of fresh water. By the time they had finished chewing that salty, succulent ham, they were about ready to throw their benefactor into the ocean.

Since relieved of the burdensome ham, Jackson saw his platoon's left flank held up by Japanese infantry in strongly fortified positions. The newly commissioned second lieutenant and the outfit's senior sergeant were both cut down by machine-gun fire. Jackson had a reputation as a gung ho Marine; on Cape Gloucester, he had been cited for bravery for carrying a wounded man to safety under heavy fire. Now, lugging a BAR, he went forward alone to assault a large pillbox containing approximately 35 Japanese. Pouring automatic fire into the slot, he quieted the defenders long enough to toss in white phosphorus grenades and explosive charges brought forward by another Marine, demolishing the fortification and annihilating its occupants.

Scarcely pausing to admire his handiwork, Jackson then advanced to smash two smaller positions in the immediate vicinity. Harassed by Japanese fire from all sides and covered only by small rifle parties, Jackson continued his rampage, wiping out 12 pillboxes and 50 Japanese, almost single-handedly eradicating the enemy defense pocket.

Later, Jackson attributed his feat to luck and help from his buddies. "Many died all around me that day," he recalled, "and I was able to do some things like I did due to the assistance I received from many of my buddies who are no longer here."

Meanwhile, it was becoming clear that B Company, moving along the eastern edge of the promontory, had drawn the most difficult assignment, which was saying a lot under the the circumstances. Enemy defenses had been constructed to cover the entrance to the lagoon between the two peninsulas. Shore approaches were mined, and Japanese defense works choked the area. Division intelligence noted that the peninsula defenses were manned by "husky, clean-uniformed and well-fed Japs."

By 1354, the company estimated it had killed about 350 Japanese. Enemy resistance had been beaten back into a 50-square-yard area, but Marine tanks had withdrawn to rearm, and the half-tracks had bogged down.

As the Marines waited for a bulldozer to extricate the half-tracks, sounds to the front indicated that the last few Japanese diehards were blowing out their own brains. Other enemy soldiers jumped into the water and tried to get across the tetrahedrons to the southeastern promontory. These doomed men ran directly into 3d Battalion Marines, who cut down about 60 of the would-be escapees. When the position was overrun shortly afterward, 15 or 16 of the enemy dead were found to have been officers, bringing the number of estimated killed to 425.

These impersonal statistics included three Japanese who stripped to their skivvies and came out from among the rocks with their hands in the air as the Marines broke through on the causeway on 17 September. A Marine machine-gun section leader, angry over the casualties the Japanese had inflicted as his men tried to force the spit and still under fire from another machine gun to his right, turned to his gun crew and said, "Let 'em have it." The gunners cut down all three.

Called back to battalion, the unremorseful section leader was thoroughly chewed out and subjected to a quick psychological check before being sent back to his unit. Battalion's concern was more practical than humanitarian. It was felt that the killing of Japanese trying to surrender would only prolong enemy resistance—something of a moot point, since the average Japanese soldier displayed every intention of fighting to the death anyway. As a result, most Marines continued to play it safe and shoot all Japanese on sight.

By the afternoon of 18 September, the 3d Battalion, 15th Japanese Infantry was history. Colonel Hanneken notified division, "At 1520, O–1 was taken. The 7th Marines mission on Peleliu is completed."

Enemy casualties over the four days of battle on southern Peleliu totaled an estimated 2,609 dead. Not one member of the Japanese battalion had been taken prisoner. There were so many dead Japanese scattered around that black Marines from the ammo and stevedore companies had to be pressed into service to help bury them all. American losses totalled 47 killed, 414 wounded and 36 missing in action—a striking testimony to Marine professionalism.

More disturbing was the time element. Southern Peleliu had been seized . . . three days behind schedule. And this was the flat part of the island.

Pushing up along the island's eastern edge to the right of the 1st Marines, Bucky Harris's 5th Marines got some small idea of what Puller's men faced in the Umurbrogol as enemy flanking fire from the heights to their left repeatedly interfered with their advance. The situation was such that the Marines closest to the edge of the heights suffered more casualties from this flanking fire than they did from enemy forces resisting in their own sector.

The situation was somewhat better on the right of the 5th Marines, where heavy scrub jungle protected 2/5 from observation from the heights. Hacking their way through the thick scrub in a skirmish line, the Marines suffered greatly from the heat. Temperatures on D plus 1 reached 105 in the shade—what precious little shade there was—and hovered around that level as the fighting dragged on. Temperatures as high as 115 were noted, and water remained short in the opening days of the campaign. Frequent halts were ordered to rest the men, but heat prostration cases continued to rise.

Some men lost so much water that they could actually pour it out of their shoes. "By the fourth day, there were as many casualties from heat prostration as from wounds," reported *Time* magazine correspondent Robert "Pepper" Martin, one of the few civilian news correspondents to accompany the Marines ashore. Martin's observation was supported by the executive officer of 1/7, who reported that lack of water during the first three days ashore caused scores of men in his battalion "to become real casualties—unfit to fight, unable to continue . . . as many casualties as [from] enemy fire."

A few of these men had to be evacuated, but most were able to return to their units after a short rest at a forward aid station, so no firm statistics on heat prostration casualties were ever compiled. But even though most of the heat casualties soon bounced back to full effectiveness, they were lost to the division during the crucial initial assault phase.

To fight the heat, some Marines ate salt tablets like candy. As they sweated, the salt collected in caked white streaks on their dungarees until the cloth became stiff. Some men also let the camouflage covers down from the back of their helmets to protect their necks from the blazing sun, making them look like "French Foreign Legionnaires in the desert," thought a half-dehydrated mortar man.

The following day saw the left of the 5th Marines still in trouble from the heights and unable to make much progress. A Marine noted that the Japanese exercised superb fire discipline. Enemy fire ceased when the Marines stopped moving, but if the men started to group together or anyone starting moving, Japanese mortar fire was not far behind. If a general movement began to get underway, Japanese artillery fire opened up. The firing was timed to inflict the maximum number of casualties, and when the opportunity passed, so did the firing.

The right had gained 600 to 700 yards the previous day, reaching the edge of a coconut grove near the former village of Omoak—now an area of smashed Japanese barracks and utility buildings. This gain let 2/1 start off in better shape on 18 September.

Jumping off at 0700, the battalion continued to hack through the jungle, bumping into sporadic resistance. Within two hours, one company reached an unimproved road leading eastward to the Ngardololok area, referred to as the "RDF area" due to the presence of a Japanese radio direction finder. Among the booty was a brand-new, undamaged Japanese radar apparatus similar to the obsolescent U.S. SCR–268. Even the spare parts had been left untouched by the fleeing enemy. Beyond the RDF facility lay Peleliu's lower claw and the strong enemy defense works constructed to contest a landing on Purple Beach.

The road itself was constricted by swamps on both sides, presenting an unwelcome bottleneck to the advancing Marines. Aerial observation had also revealed major Japanese installations both within the RDF area and at Purple Beach. However, the sporadic character of enemy resistance indicated that the Japanese might have withdrawn from the area. A Marine patrol ventured across the causeway at 1040 without drawing fire. Subsequent efforts to cross in force were hampered by an air strike which missed its target entirely at 1245. An artillery barrage was put down instead, but as the Marines began crossing, a second air strike called down by regiment—which failed to notify battalion—mistakenly strafed them. A misplaced artillery concentration later caught other Marines approaching the causeway. This foul-up was followed by a misplaced mortar barrage on the causeway itself.

Private First Class James Isabelle's outfit lost four or five men killed by the friendly fire and several wounded, including the Marine lying next to him, "shoulder to shoulder," who had his hand blown off. Another Marine lay dead, sprawled backward over a stump, "almost in the position of a crucifix," a bandage still across his chest. "I wanted to go shoot these artillery guys," he recalled bitterly. "Here we are getting shot up, we're getting killed as it is—and our own artillery . . . it really shook me up. It's a frustrating situation. It was an accident, it wasn't deliberate, but I had that anger."

The 5th Marines obtained their bridgehead and dug in for the night, no doubt wondering which was worse—the Japanese or their own "support." Nearly all the 34 casualties sustained by 2/5 during the day had been inflicted by friendly fire.

Chesty Puller's 1st Marines were in rough shape by the morning of 18 September. The regiment had lost nearly 1,236 men, almost half its strength, in the first three days of the campaign. Reports indicated that "frontline units were decimated."

After nightfall on 17 September, some reinforcements straggled up to Puller's front lines. Under the Marine creed "every man a rifleman," regimental headquarters units were cut to the bone, as enlisted men and officers alike were sent to the front. Despite Puller's phone conversation with Seldon after the fighting on the 17th, division also managed to scrape up 115 pioneers who were promptly split up as replacements for the badly shot-up assault companies. Of the 473 men of 3/1 who jumped off the following morning, no less than 200 had been dragooned from regimental headquarters.

The badly shot-up 1st Battalion, which had fought so bitterly to take the blockhouse area on D plus 2, was withdrawn from the line by dawn. The entire 2d Battalion, 7th Marines, including two companies that had fought their way into position at nightfall, joined Puller's command. By dawn, the newly reformed line stood 3/1, 2/7, 2/1.

Surveying his lines, Lieutenant Colonel Spencer Berger, commanding 2/7 in its relief of 1/1, began to realize just how badly things were going in the ridges. As his units went into position, it was becoming increasingly clear that elements of 1/1 had either never reached points previously reported, or they had been forced to pull back before 2/7 commenced its relief. In all fairness, Berger recalled later, the horrible terrain made it very difficult to pinpoint locations on the map.

Just before H-Hour, Puller moved his command post forward to a small quarry a scant 150 yards from enemy positions. Stripped to the waist in Peleliu's terrific heat, he growled his orders around the battered pipe clenched in his teeth, his command post nothing more than a piece of old tin and a poncho set up to keep off the sun.

Puller was known throughout the corps as a hard-nose, the legend who, shown a flamethrower for the first time, had growled, "Where the hell do you put the bayonet?" By the time he reached Peleliu, he had added reason for ferocity. His brother Sam, also a Marine officer, had been killed on Guam two months earlier, a loss that left him very bitter against the Japanese, observed one of his battalion commanders.

Another officer on Peleliu recalled Puller stopping by a regimental headquarters to ask how many second lieutenants had been killed. Feeling the number too low, he supposedly bellowed, "What the hell are you doing,

having a Sunday school picnic?" To Chesty, low casualties among lieutenants indicated that the attack was not being pressed with sufficient vigor.
He believed in momentum; he believed in getting at the enemy and hitting
and hitting until his objectives were overrun. While this method lacked
tactical finesse, it suited his own aggressive nature. On Peleliu, it was also
proving expensive.

Although aware of the terrific casualties his regiment had taken, Puller
remained optimistic. The general feeling, both at Puller's CP and at division,
was that a breakthrough was imminent. The Marines had a hold on the
high ground; if past experience was any indication, enemy resistance would
collapse once a certain point was reached. The morning's objective was for
2/7 and 2/1 to erase the Japanese-held salient anchored on Hill 210.

What the optimists still failed to recognize was the true horror of the
Umurbrogol, with its jumble of ridges, ravines, caves and holes. When the
Marines jumped off at 0700 after a 30-minute preparation by planes, ar-
tillery and naval gunfire, they found themselves in a meat grinder.

Private Russell Davis's outfit came up against a steep cliff riddled with
caves and holes concealing well-armed Japanese infantry. As riflemen assembled to assault it, fire plunged down on some nearby machine gunners,
the rising screams indicating men were being hit. At 0735, the *Combat
Journal* report of 2/1 noted briefly, "We are attacking." The enemy was
replying with mortars, rockets, machine guns and a concealed large-caliber
naval gun.

Watching from below, Davis suddenly realized how heavily the regiment
had suffered since D-Day. Platoons looked like squads, and companies
looked like platoons. One platoon, ordinarily 40-men strong, had only 18
Marines left as it started up the ridge.

Clutching and clawing, the assault troops headed toward the top of the
steep cliff face. Brown-uniformed Japanese popped out of gullies and caves
to roll grenades down on the climbers. Some of the fighting was hand-to-
hand, knives and bayonets flashed in the sun. A Marine bent, then straight-
ened and kicked at something that attacked his legs. Suddenly he reached
down and heaved a Japanese soldier end-over-end down the hill. Down
below, the machine gunners yelled encouragement, but Marines were also
tumbling.

"Occasionally, a Jap popped out of his hideout and rolled a grenade
down the slope," recalled combat correspondent Sergeant Joseph Alli. "The
Marines pulled in their necks, waited for the explosion, and continued their
climb."

Only a few Marines made it to the top, clubbing and stabbing their way
over the broken coral. They were the few with the heart to go forward, no
matter what lay in front of them: the true soul and fiber of the Marine
Corps.

Up in the rocks, a youthful Texas replacement went down, hit hard by a mortar fragment. A corpsman gave him a shot of morphine, but it was no use. "I'm dyin'," the Marine said to his buddy. "Chuck, I'm dyin'."

"No, you're not, Kid," his buddy reassured him. "It's just a bad wound, that's all. You'll be all right."

"Chuck, I'm goin'," the youth repeated. "I don't want to go." And then he died.

Savage fighting by 2/1 and 2/7 finally pinched out Japanese-held Hill 210, jutting into Marine lines. The Japanese then responded by concentrating "a murderous fire" on elements of 2/1 on the forward nose of Hill 200. Weapons included mortars, rockets, machine guns and a concealed large-caliber naval gun directed at the Marines scratching futilely at the hard coral in an effort to get at least partially underground.

Following that fire with powerful counterattacks, the Japanese succeeded in pushing the battalion back. "The right two battalions were constantly calling for blood plasma, stretcher bearers and corpsmen," noted the 1st Marine report.

Up on Hill 200, 2/1 was in perilous straits by early afternoon. Severe Japanese mortar and artillery fire and fierce counterattacks pounded the Marines on the northern slopes of the hill. At 1400, the normally unflappable 2d Battalion CO Lieutenant Colonel Honsowetz called Puller and told him the situation had become desperate. Honsowetz, a 1935 University of Idaho All-American football player, was considered an outstanding officer, but Puller gave him short shrift. He directed Honsowetz to come into the flank and take the ridge.

"Christ, we can't do it," said Honsowetz in near despair. "The casualties are too much, and we've been fighting day and night."

"You sound all right; you're there," retorted Puller. "Goddammit, you get those troops in there, and you take that hill."

Honsowetz requested reinforcements and smoke to screen his positions. Puller gave him B Company—or what was left of it—which Honsowetz then threw against Hill 205, located slightly forward and to the right of the ridge, hoping it would give him access to the ridge itself. Somewhat to their surprise, the Marines took Hill 205 with only light casualties. Unfortunately, possession of the ground revealed that the hill was isolated from the main ridge system. A useful observation point, it was otherwise of limited value.

Trying to push on, B Company was thrown back before what the official Marine Corps history of the campaign would later describe as "the most formidable terrain obstacle yet encountered: an incredible complex of up-ended peaks and palisades." The area, marking the perimeter of Colonel Nakagawa's first defensive positions in the Umurbrogol, subsequently went down in Marine Corps legend in evil fame as "The Five Sisters."

Meanwhile, on the left, 3/1 had met only minor opposition. The battalion advanced a few hundred yards but was forced to stop to maintain contact with 2/7, operating with great difficulty on the higher ground. Elements of 2/1, on the extreme right, advanced across the flatter terrain below Hill 200 to the former village of Asias, where it tied in with the left of the 5th Marines.

Among the Marines fighting with 2/7 that day was a 21-year-old former mechanic and truck driver from Claude in the Texas panhandle, Private First Class Charles H. Roan. Roan was part of a squad-sized push gone bad among the exposed coral ridges. Partly cut off from the company, the squad leader ordered the men back, but Roan and the others suddenly found themselves caught up in a grenade duel with Japanese infantry located in a cave on higher ground, just to their rear. Trapped, Roan and four Marine riflemen took cover in a rocky depression, but the Texan was soon wounded by a grenade which fell close by. Another well-aimed grenade suddenly plummeted down in the midst of the Marines. Roan threw himself on the missile, absorbing the blast with his own body. His four buddies sprawled out, feigning death, and managed to escape when a tank bulldozer came up a half hour later.

Months afterward, informed that her son had won the Medal of Honor, Roan's mother failed to recognize the magnitude of the honor and declined an invitation to go to Washington to receive the award. "I didn't know it was such a high medal," she remarked after the significance had been explained to her. The medal was finally given to her on the courthouse lawn of tiny Claude "because that was where Charles was brought up," she explained.

Dusk found the 1st Marines in a shallow U with only minor gains to their credit—and an actual loss of ground on Hill 200. Even the lines on the operations maps were misleading. "There was no such thing as a continuous attacking line," recalled Spencer Berger. "Elements of the same company, even platoon, were attacking in every direction of the compass, with large gaps in between . . . there were countless little salients and counter-salients existing."

The cost of this achievement had been staggering. By nightfall on 18 September, casualties in the 1st Marines alone, not including the reinforcements it had absorbed, totalled 1,500—one half of regimental strength.

Lieutenant Colonel Lew Walt saw Puller at a command conference during the day. "He was absolutely sick over the loss of his men; he thought we were getting them killed for nothing," recalled Walt.

Those who knew Puller by reputation might have been surprised by Walt's assessment. And, despite the horrific casualties, the tone of the regimental report still bore a glimmer of hope. "Little ground had been gained, but the center of Japanese resistance had been detected and the weakest spots probed," it observed.

The restricted beachhead area raised havoc with logistic support during the first few days of the operation. Supply dumps, artillery emplacements and equipment were located helter-skelter on any available bit of space, making coordination and resupply difficult.

Visiting shortly after D-Day, Rear Admiral John W. Reeves, Jr., in charge of future base development of the Western Carolines Area, was appalled by the situation. He immediately requested through higher channels that some artillery be displaced at once to allow supply dumps to occupy their permanent locations as laid out in the base development plan. General Rupertus demurred. In light of the critical tactical situation, it would be foolhardy to move artillery already firing in support of the infantry just to simplify future base functions. Nothing came of the admiral's complaint.

As the division carved out more ground, regimental dumps were pushed forward behind the assault. On 18 September, a detachment from the 1054th Seabee Battalion began work on a pontoon causeway from Orange 3 to the outer reef. The first LST unloaded over the causeway the following day. Additional pontoon causeways soon allowed the simultaneous unloading of three LSTs. Three days later, still in need of more unloading points, the 73d Seabees started work on access roads to the eastern and southern beaches. Within two days, both beach areas were handling cargo from LSTs. Among those working in this area were several hundred black Marines of the 7th Ammunition Company and 11th Depot Company of the 16th Field Depot. Blacks had not been accepted into the Corps until 1942, and these were the first many of the whites had ever seen. Most were thoroughly shocked. "Boy, we're gettin' down to nuthin'," exclaimed one white upon seeing black Marines unloading ammunition.

Another white, a Mississippian from the 5th Marines, wounded while trying to cross the airfield on D plus 1, was startled, but nonetheless grateful, when a huge black man came to his aid. The Marine picked up the Mississippian and carried him all the way back to the aid station.

His was not an isolated example. The black Marines of the 16th Field Depot especially distinguished themselves. Working under heavy fire as stretcher bearers, the unit earned a reputation as the "volunteeringest" in the Marine Corps. One officer was embarrassed when he called for volunteers and the whole outfit stepped forward before he could explain that this was not a dangerous mission, only a burial detail.

Nor were the segregated black outfits spared their share of casualties by virtue of being "rear-echelon" personnel. The first black casualty on Peleliu was Private Dryel A. Shuler of the ammunition company, who was hit 20 September. The last was Private John Copeland, also of the ammunition company, who died 9 October of wounds received the same day. Similarly, the 11th Depot Company lost 16 wounded on Peleliu, giving the company the highest casualty rate of any black unit in World War II.

Such was their performance that General Rupertus wrote identical letters of commendation to the commanders of both companies, stating in part, "The Negro race can be well proud of the work performed by [these companies] as they have demonstrated in every respect that they appreciate the privilege of wearing a Marine uniform and serving with Marines in combat."

Medical planners at Peleliu also ran into unexpected difficulties. Three medical companies came ashore with the assault waves on D-Day: A Company was assigned to the 1st Marines, B to the 5th and C to the 7th.

Expecting a high initial casualty rate, planners had arranged for empty amphibious vehicles to carry the wounded back to the transfer line, where waiting boats took them to ships further out. On D-Day, this plan worked so well that wounded Marines were being treated on board ships within one hour of the landing—a rate that soon fell off as more and more amtracs were knocked out.

As the attack pushed slowly inland and the high casualty rate continued, the medical system became sorely taxed. In addition to the widespread demand for the remaining DUKWs and amtracs, equipment for the medical companies was late in coming ashore.

Before the operation, the number of corpsmen organic to each infantry battalion had been increased from 32 to 40, making it possible to attach a corpsman to each platoon. Ninety-six stretcher bearers were assigned to each combat team. Even with that advantage, stretcher bearers and corpsmen were unable to keep up with the constant stream of wounded and were themselves becoming casualties at an alarming rate.

Medical personnel would ultimately lose 239 men out of a total complement of 1,835. A Company took 36 percent casualties, B Company 31 percent and C Company 45 percent, most suffered during the first few days of combat.

Conditions ashore were so bad that adequate hospital facilities were not set up until D plus 5. In the interim, support troops were pressed into service to help get the wounded out.

Sergeant Kenneth Reich, a 23-year-old Chicagoan, was helping evacuate casualties brought down to the beach area, shuttling them out to hospital ships in a Higgins boat. On this trip, he already had about 15 badly wounded Marines in the boat. Another man lay on his stomach on a stretcher on the beach; a shell splinter stuck out of his back like a metal icicle, and he was noticeably blue.

A corpsman leaned over the wounded Marine. "I think this man's dead." he said.

"No, put him on the Higgins boat," said Reich. "I'll take him out."

Out on the hospital ship, the Higgins boat was winched aboard, and sailors began taking the casualties off. "Why did you bring this man back?" someone asked, glancing at the Marine with the shell splinter. "He's dead."

"He's not dead," insisted Reich against all logic. "He's alive."

A doctor interjected, "Let me look at him." He leaned over the wounded Marine. "By golly, he *is* alive. I thought he was dead because he's so blue."

Reich never learned whether the man survived, but he always hoped so.

The tremendous number of casualties also put a strain on medical personnel aboard the hospital ships. There was talk of one corpsman who dropped dead of exhaustion after working 48 hours straight in an operating room. An order subsequently went out directing medical personnel to get at least 4 hours of sleep every 24 hours.

Even so, if a man made it to a shipboard operating room, he had a good chance of surviving his injuries. Of the more than 5,000 wounded taken off Peleliu between D-Day and 14 October, only 182 died of their injuries aboard the transports or hospital ships, a ratio of about 1 man in 28.

Corporal Harlan Murray had been evacuated to the hospital ship *Pinckney* the night of the landing, a Japanese rifle bullet lodged in his right shoulder. Too busy with more serious casualties, medical personnel gave him a tetnus shot and anti-gas gangrene drops in the eyes, then hastily assigned him a bunk, where he lay drifting in and out of shock for the next 24 hours. On 17 September, two days after he had been wounded, Murray noticed a lump under his armpit. He called a corpsman over. "This might be the bullet," he told the man.

"Yeah, I think it is the bullet," said the corpsman. He called a doctor.

Running low on medical supplies, the doctors were saving the heavy-duty pain killers for the more seriously wounded. Murray quickly discovered his injury merited only a shot of novocaine. Placed on a table, the Arizonan was given a gauze-wrapped tongue depressor to bite down on. One corpsman held his good arm, another sat on his legs and a third held his head. Wielding a scapel, a navy dentist proceeded to cut him open and dig the bullet out with a pair of forceps.

Murray had never felt such pain, but once the bullet was out, he felt much better. He asked the corpsman if he could go up on deck. "Yeah, go ahead," said the corpsman.

Stepping out on deck, Murray was completely oblivious to the fact that he had no clothes on. His dungarees had been stripped off earlier, and he was now buck naked. Some sailors spotted him and asked, "Don't you have any clothes?"

"No," replied Murray.

The sailors disappeared, and when they came back they had a shirt and pants and shoes—their own personal spare clothing. The pants were big, but someone donated a belt and Murray cinched them up. Forty-three years later, the former Marine corporal recalled with heartfelt gratitude, "Those guys were the best."

Poised to seize Peleliu's lower claw on 18 September, the 5th Marines were painfully aware of the disaster befalling their buddies up in the Umurbrogol. The word came not from the top, but from the assault troops of the 1st Marines themselves, passed down the line from the left.

Survivors said any effort to move in on the mutually supporting Japanese positions hidden in the upturned coral only resulted in heavy casualties and negligible progress. The enemy weathered artillery fire in caves and then opened up point-blank on the Marines as the suppressing fire ended and the infantry attempted to attack.

One Marine reported to his buddies in the 5th of the 1st Marines survivor who "told me they got them poor boys makin' frontal attacks with fixed bayonets on that damn ridge, and they can't even see the Nips that are shootin' at 'em. That poor kid was really depressed; don't see no way he can come out alive."

The 5th Marines knew their turn would come, but first they had to seize the claw.

In this respect, the regiment's good luck of the past two days continued to hold. Despite fears that thousands of Japanese had been trapped on the islets, few enemy were encountered. The advance on the morning of 19 September encountered only scattered resistance, presumably from stragglers in the ruins of Japanese installations in the RDF area. Main units had apparently been withdrawn into the island's rugged interior, abandoning the Purple Beach fortification. The stragglers inflicted a few casualties but seemed more inclined to hide than to fight, according to Marine reports.

Reaching the abandoned defenses of Purple Beach, the Marines were glad they had come ashore on the other side of the island. The beach was heavily mined and so choked with tank traps and barricades that they had more trouble threading their way through the fortifications than they did mopping up the few remaining enemy soldiers. Mopping up on the claw and adjacent small detached islands would last until 23 September, with only minimal fighting. The entire lobster claw was cleared by 20 September. Island A and Ngabad Island off the tip of the claw were seized the following day; the occupation of an unnamed island further north and across from Radar Hill was carried out on 23 September.

Purple Beach and Ngardololok were organized against anticipated counter landings by Japanese troops from the central Palaus, and the 5th Marines settled in to await their turn at the Umurbrogol.

Up in the ridges, the stalemate continued. Shot at by day by enemies they could not see, the Marines spent sleepless nights as the Japanese attempted to infiltrate their positions under cover of darkness. Marine combat correspondent James Finan recalled one night on the line early in the campaign. The Marines took position in the coral in groups of two and three, each group about five feet from the next.

"On the crest of the ridge on the left was a man with a BAR," recalled Finan. "Next down were four riflemen, then three scouts with submachine guns camouflaged under a broken Jap ammunition cart. Three feet in front of us, to the right and a little below so as to be clear of our fire, were three men with Garand rifles, then a sturdy 50-caliber machine gun with its team. On the floor of the valley stood a half-track armored vehicle with a big 75 cannon pointed up the draw. Next to it was a low-lying 37 mm field gun; then more machine guns and rifle teams were strung up over the ridge on the right and down across the clearing on the other side."

Lieutenant Sidney Beinke moved down the line, checking positions and making sure each man knew the password. The men were lying so anyone who approached would be silhouetted against the sky. At 1810 it was dusk, and Lieutenant Beinke ordered, "Last cigarette. Pass the word. The smoking lamp is out in ten minutes."

As darkness closed down, there was some last-minute whispering and muted chuckling, then quiet as the Marines watched and listened. The equatorial moon rose behind them, and an occasional star shell popped to their front, illuminating the coral crags in a ghastly glare.

At 2350, the artillery went still. Up on the left-hand ridge, an unseen intruder slipped on a loose piece of coral and stumbled against a sapling which then snapped under his weight, each sound abnormally distinct to the keyed-up Marines. The intruder fell to the ground and chunks of coral rattled down the hill, clattering against empty cartridge cases and sheets of old metal roofing. Simultaneously, the BAR man stood up and demanded, "Give the password!"

The BAR man ripped off a burst in the direction of the noises, and it was suddenly silent again. Then something began thrashing around in the rubble, and a machine gun opened up on it from the right. Someone threw over two hand grenades which burst with red flashes out front. The noises stopped.

Two hours later, there was an outbreak of firing to the right, where a Japanese managed to get into a foxhole and cut a Marine's throat before being stabbed to death. Three other infiltrators crept down the valley and set up a machine gun in front of the lines. Their first burst caught a Marine in the head, and they kept up the fire until a half-track gunner obliterated them.

In the morning, the Marines found the cause of the disturbance on Beinke's section of the line. It was a Japanese and he was quite dead, riddled through both legs. The infiltrator wore the helmet and stained dungaree blouse of a dead Marine. The medical bag of a Navy corpsman was slung over his shoulder. After being shot, he had bandaged his wounds without battle dressings and sulfa. Then, realizing that the Marines who had shot him were on the alert, he had carefully picked his way through a draw and up a nearby valley, apparently trying to reach the half-track on the valley floor. Like others before him and others to follow, his life ran out before his determination did.

Among the most effective Japanese weapons on Peleliu were mortars. Some veterans of the campaign would later speak as if there were no other weapon on Peleliu, so lethal was the whispering mortar shell.

Japanese mortars ranged in size from the small 50 mm knee mortar to the highly effective 150 mm mortar, encountered for the first time by Marines in the Pacific. Resembling a king-sized 81 mm, the 150 mm had a tube more than six feet long and a base plate so heavy it made the device more of a static weapon. With a range of over 2,000 yards, the 150 could lob a 56-pound projectile well back into the rear areas. "And when they fired it up there in the mountains, you could hear a sound that was kind of a *boing*, you know, from the tube itself," recalled Corporal Bill Myers. "And you could look up and see that shell coming."

"We obtained our sandbags from a pile of them stacked near the beach," observed Corporal H. Kenneth Hansen. "Once, a second or two after I hoisted a sandbag onto one of my shoulders and had taken a few steps toward my foxhole, a mortar shell landed amid the pile. I and others laughed over our narrow escape. Other times after a mortar shell landed close to two or more of us, we'd laugh . . . and make comments such as, "You should have seen the fuckin' look on your face!'"

Private First Class Larry Kaloian was not so lucky. He was swabbing out the machine gun on his Sherman tank at the reloading point by the airfield on the morning of the fifth day when a 150 mm round hurtled in and detonated a pile of ordnance. The blast blew him under the tank, which probably saved his life by screening him from all the small arms ammo whizzing around from secondary explosions.

Coming back to consciousness under the tank, Kaloian thought he was going to die. His right side was completely saturated with blood. In the midst of this thought, it suddenly occurred to him that his demise might be hastened if the tank ran over him, so he pushed himself out, crawling like a snake on his left side. Then he must have passed out again, for the next thing he knew, he felt a hand on his arm. "This one's still alive," said a voice.

Kaloian underwent four hours in surgery on a hospital ship, completely conscious but numb from the waist down from a spinal. For four hours, he listened to the clink of metal as doctors pulled steel from his body and piled it in a basin. He later learned he had been lucky. Of the more than 20 others caught in the blast, many had not survived.

Another Japanese weapon, fortunately less effective than the 150 mm which put Kaloian out of the battle, was a crude type of rocket. Made by attaching a propellant charge to the base of a 200 mm naval shell, this contraption detonated with a terrific concussion—if it detonated at all. No launching device was ever found for the rocket, nor were any enemy personnel captured who would admit to knowing anything about it. Lacking stabilizing fins, the rockets were apparently aimed in the general direction of the American lines to descend "end over end, like a badly punted foot-ball," recalled an eyewitness.

Also found on Peleliu were several 200 mm naval guns with sawed-off barrels. The exact purpose of this adaptation was never determined, as the guns captured were incompletely mounted and inoperative.

Horror wore many faces on Peleliu: the mortar shell that left a man's buddy eviscerated like a slaughtered sheep; the terrible heat; the swarms of flies. Many experiences would haunt men for the remainder of their lives.

On 20 September, K Company of 3/5 pushed a combat patrol out on the lobster claw on the fringe of Purple Beach. Their mission—patently sacrificial—was to dig in, make contact with the enemy if they tried to get across the mangrove swamp between the claw and the main island and hold.

During the night one of the Marines snapped under the strain of combat. He started moaning. The moans rapidly turned to shrieks of unreasoned terror. Frantic that he was revealing their position, the other Marines tried to calm him down. The shattered man only screamed more loudly. Someone tried to knock him unconscious without success. The corpsman injected the thrashing Marine with morphine without effect. Finally, someone picked up an entrenching shovel and brought it crunching down on the man's head, killing him.

The next morning the patrol pulled out, bringing the poncho-wrapped body of their unfortunate comrade. They also brought a personal anguish, unmitigated by the certain knowledge that they had had no choice.

NOTES

1. Some reports erroneously state the blockhouse was knocked out by the *Mississippi*.

2. Sources differ on the exact date of the gas scare, but the Division Intelligence Journal seems to indicate it occurred on the afternoon of 17 September.

Poncho-covered Marine dead are identified and fingerprinted before burial. (Corporal Robert Bailey, USMC)

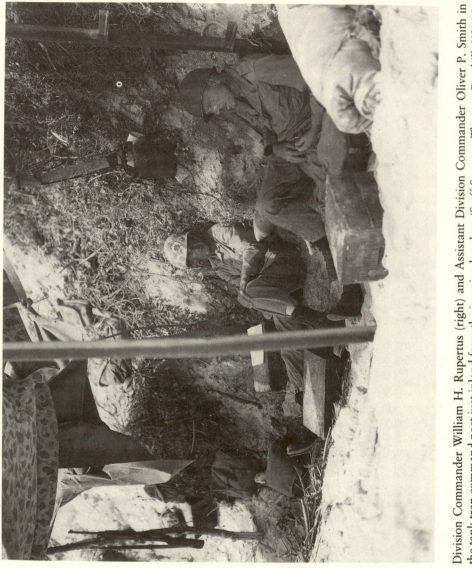

Division Commander William H. Rupertus (right) and Assistant Division Commander Oliver P. Smith in the tank trap command post just inland from the invasion beaches. (Staff Sergeant Thomas Gambill, USMC)

A Marine examines one of the Japanese tanks knocked out in the enemy counterattack across the airfield on 15 September. The tanks were no match for Marine firepower. (Staff Sergeant Harry Vasicsk, USMC)

Men of the 7th Marines take shelter behind an amtrac during the first wave landing on Orange 3, 15 September. (T/Sgt. Franklin Fitzgerald, USMC)

A Marine Corsair drops napalm on Bloody Nose during the fighting in the ridges. (S/Sgt. T. C. Barnett, USMC)

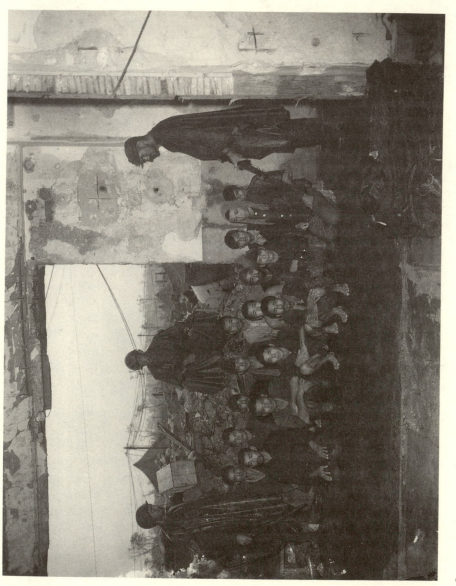

Japanese prisoners under guard. "They'd spit in your eye," said a Peleliu veteran of the Japanese regulars. (Arnold Johnson, USMC)

144

The Marine assault clings to the beachhead under heavy machine-gun fire. (Pfc. John Smith, USMC)

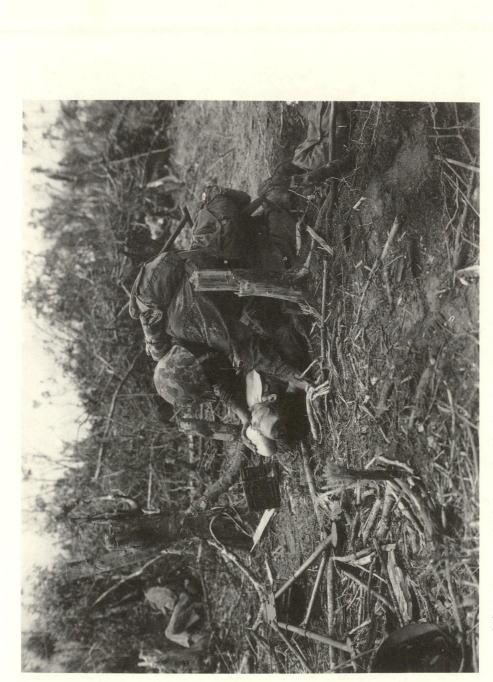

A wounded Marine gets a drink from a buddy. (Sgt. James D. Wadsen, USMC)

Wrecked Japanese aircraft litter Peleliu's airfield. Japanese airpower was not a factor in the battle. (Cpl. Max Roemer, USMC)

Tank/infantry teams tackle enemy positions in Peleliu's coral ridges. (S/Sgt. T. C. Barnett, USMC)

A wounded Marine is escorted to the aid station. (Cpl. Robert Bailey, USMC)

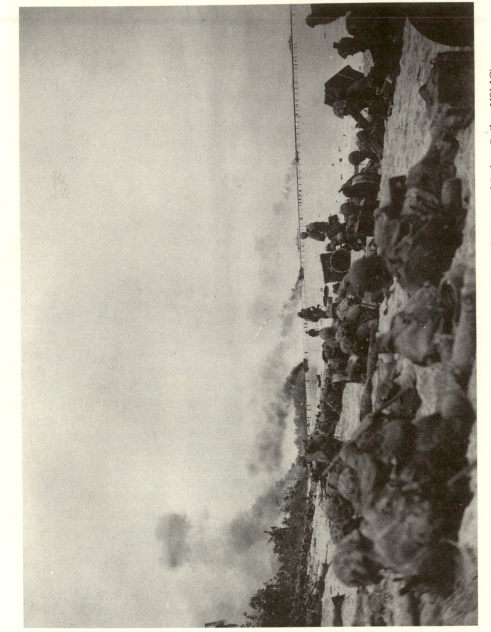

Marines pinned down on the beachhead watch amtracs burning on the reef. (Corporal Robert Bailey, USMC)

150

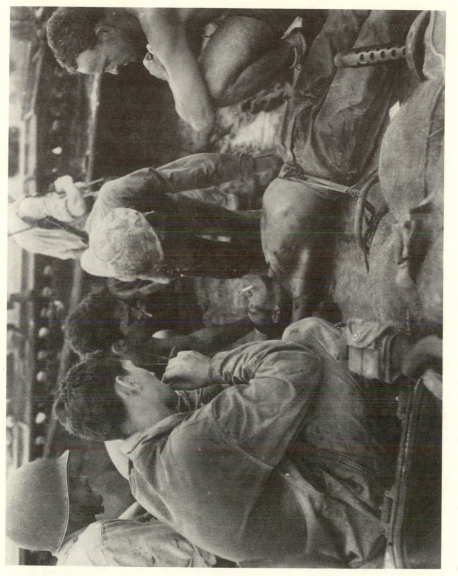

Interpreters interrogate a Japanese prisoner captured during the enemy attempt to reinforce Peleliu by barge. (S/Sgt. Harry Vasicsk, USMC)

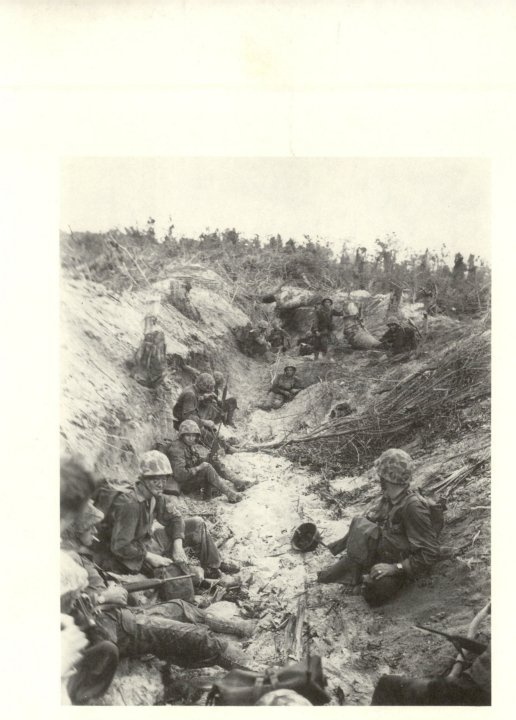

Battalion CP in a ditch just in from Orange 3 after the landing. (Cpl. Robert Bailey, USMC)

Chapter 8

Seven miles south of Peleliu, two regimental combat teams of the 81st Division landed on Angaur against light opposition shortly after 0800 the morning of 17 September. Avoiding the heavily defended beaches on the island's southern coast, the army came in over the least likely—and least fortified—beaches on the east and northeast coast while the 323d RCT staged a mock landing off the western shore.

Although unblooded, the 81st was considered a well-trained, capable division with men from every state, territory and U.S. possession in its ranks. Illinois boasted the largest contingent, followed by Michigan, California and New York. Tennessee and Pennsylvania tied for fifth place.

Organized at Camp Rucker, Alabama, the Wildcats had suffered through desert training in Arizona, amphibious training in California and jungle training in Hawaii. Now, they would get a chance to put some of those lessons to use.

Smaller than Peleliu, Angaur, the southernmost island in the Palaus, was slightly less than three miles long and just over a mile and a half wide at the waist. Also unlike Peleliu, the island was mainly flat except for a small area of 200-foot wooded ridges in the northwest corner. These would give the army Wildcats their moments of grief. The only town of any size was Saipan Town on the western coast, just south of the old phosphate plant.

The Japanese garrison on Angaur consisted of about 1,400 men of Major Ushio Goto's 1st Battalion, 59th Infantry, with attached artillery, mortar, engineer and similar units. U.S. intelligence erred in estimating there were 2,500 men on Angaur, which led planners to commit more force to the operation than necessary. Softening up by naval bombardment and air attack had been in progress since 12 September, led by the battleship *Tennessee*, one heavy cruiser, three light cruisers and five destroyers.

Against Major Goto's force, IIIPhib threw 8,000 men of the 321st and

322d RCTs. The 321st hit Blue Beach at precisely 0830 on the heels of a preliminary barrage that tossed whole trees into the air like matchsticks. Forty fighter bombers swept in over the beaches to add their muscle to the softening up, while rocket-firing LCIs moved up to provide close-in support.

Delayed by an uncharted current, the first wave of the 322d RCT landed six minutes later on Red Beach, 2,000 yards up the coast. The Angaur assault met only scattered rifle fire and a few mortar rounds. The men rushed across 20 yards of slightly sloped, rubble-strewn beach and established a temporary firing line at the edge of the jungle before pressing forward.

In their first combat of World War II, the Wildcats pushed quickly inland from the two landing beaches, separated by over a mile of rocky coastline. The feint by the 323d RCT off Saipan Town on the other side of the island apparently helped. Unsure of U.S. intentions, Goto sent a rifle company toward the eastern beaches but made no attempt to organize a full-scale counterattack. U.S. naval gunfire and aerial bombing repeatedly worked over potential assembly areas to keep the Japanese off balance.

Once off the beaches, the Wildcats had more trouble with the dense jungle undergrowth than with the light enemy resistance. The stiffest opposition was encountered by the 321st, which ran into enemy fortifications on its flanks and to its front.

Concealed in a maze of downed trees, matted undergrowth and entangling creepers, the Japanese popped away at the GIs floundering inland. Here and there, resistance was built up around a coconut log bunker or concrete pillbox, each of which had to be taken out by flamethrower and demolitions teams before the advance could resume. Supported by medium tanks, the GIs slugged their way forward, but casualties "were not unduly heavy," according to the division historian.

To the north, the 322d RCT quickly reached the 0–1 line and by midday had received the green light to push toward the objectives laid out for D plus 1. Further down the coast, the 321st RCT had more of a struggle with enemy fortifications near Rocky Point on its southern flank and Cape Ngat-pokul on the northern flank.

By late afternoon, the Wildcats had seized the designated objective line extending from the northern shore of Angaur about 500 yards southwest of Cape Gallatin to a point roughly 250 yards southwest of Rocky Point. The 321st had gained the 0–1 line in the center, but the flanks remained well behind. The 322d stood on the 0–2 line. The two regiments remained separated by a 700-yard gap, but two companies of medium tanks were ashore for added muscle, along with bulldozers and other heavy equipment. Nightfall found the two combat teams digging in with their lines bent around to protect separate beachheads.

On Koror, General Inoue, attempting to determine the overall intent of the American attacks in the Palaus, came to the wrong conclusion. The

American feint off Babelthuap by the 81st Division on 15 September, combined with reports of heavy fighting on Peleliu and the subsequent landing on Angaur, befuddled him and his staff. Inoue finally decided the Americans had planned to invade Koror and Babelthuap after they had seized Peleliu. These ambitious plans had apparently been dashed by the heavy casualties the Marines were suffering on Peleliu, preventing the main forces from withdrawing to proceed with the other landings.

The Japanese command also theorized that the Americans could not afford to ignore the threat Angaur posed to the Peleliu landing. "They were constantly harassed by the danger of being attacked by our aggressive artillery from Angaur and by counter-landing on Peleliu which may be staged by our Angaur forces," noted the general. "Because of these facts the enemy were compelled to change their plan and land their reserve forces on Angaur."

General Inoue's misconceptions saved the Marines on Peleliu a world of trouble. Concerned about U.S. attacks on Babelthuap and Koror once Peleliu was secured, he hoarded his materiel and made no significant effort to supply or reinforce Colonel Nakagawa with some of the 25,000 Japanese in the Palaus. It was just as well: the 1st Marine Division had its hands full with the Japanese already on Peleliu.

On Peleliu, the Marines continued to battle both the intense heat and fanatical Japanese resistance. "The battle against climate," noted division, "now was almost as serious as the fire fight itself." The thermometer had risen to 112 degrees on the fourth day and looked to go even higher on the fifth. The coral simply baked. One Marine compared the effect to "walking barefoot on top of a stove." A phosphorus grenade left unshaded on the coral would explode from the intense heat. Mortar men soon learned to shade their stacked shells with a piece of ammo box so they would not accidentally cook off in the bright sun.

Division asked all ships offshore to send in every available salt tablet for the dehydrated Marines. Some of the gobs also sent in cases of canned fruit juice. Private Russell Davis was among the lucky Marines who would never forget this gesture. So dehydrated he could not walk, he gulped down two cans of juice to put him back on his feet. Perhaps the most generous gesture was made by Admiral George Fort's flagship, *Mount McKinley*, which sent her entire remaining stock of beer—500 blessed cases—ashore. Divided equally among front-line troops, even a lone can boosted morale considerably.

Distillation units, along with ground wells, finally managed to relieve the water shortage, providing a minimum of 50,000 gallons a day, but the heat remained tortuous. Men ate salt tablets like candy. The normal daily dosage in the tropics was two salt tablets. On Peleliu, 6 were prescribed for each canteen of water, but many men found themselves choking down 12 to 14.

"There were fervent prayers for rain, or at least a cloudy sky to shade the sun," reported one Marine. Many of the men suffered from blistered faces and cracked, bleeding lips. The number of men forced to drop out due to heat exhaustion would never be known precisely, since most returned to their units within a short time, but the effect on combat efficiency was quite real.

Peleliu's coral—so hard it sparked when the Marines tried to dig in— also became an enemy. Unable to get below ground, the Marines remained exposed to bullets and shell fragments. "It was like sitting in the middle of a concrete parking lot," remarked Sergeant Robert Askey. All the men could do was pile up rocks for cover or find a shell hole or coral depression to squeeze into.

The effect of mortars was multiplied many times as splinters and chunks of rock ricocheted. Askey observed, "They threw a mortar in there at you and it hit that rock, there'd be rock and shrapnel and everything else flying all over the place. It almost tripled the effect of the mortar shell." Ricochets became almost as dangerous as direct fire. "I never heard so damn many richochets," remarked a machine gunner who had served on Guadalcanal. "Every two minutes there was a ricochet."

The rugged ground also caused more wear and tear on clothing than had been anticipated. Dungarees were frayed to tatters; even the soles of the heavy boondockers wore through. New clothing was flown in from Guam: 1,000 sets of dungarees, 5,000 pairs of socks, 1,000 pairs of boondockers.

Supplies were brought forward to the fighting men only through much effort. More than half the DUKWs had been knocked out on D-Day, either by enemy fire or from the wear and tear of Peleliu's wide reef. Enemy fire on the beaches also disrupted unloading. Shore party personnel suffered twice as many casualties on Peleliu than on any previous 1st Marine Division operation.

Lack of transport forced the Marines to rely heavily on their more rugged amtracs. These versatile vehicles were used not just to cross the reef, but to carry supplies right up into the front lines. It was not the safest duty. Drivers nicknamed one route up to the airport "Purple Heart Run." Another route into the ridge positions earned the title "Silver Star Run."

Peleliu's torn terrain affected even the hardy amtracs. Most drivers soon lost count of the number of trips and repairs required to keep their machines running. At times, their endurance seemed to border on the miraculous. "Why," said one driver with evident pride, "she's only running now because she's so excited."

Some amtrac drivers, their vehicles destroyed, joined the front-line infantry rather than report back to the CPs of the tractor battalions. One, a former Chicago truck driver named McCall, but known as "Fagin" due to his "propensities of borrowing," joined the 1st Marines by the simple expedient of grabbing a can of ammo and falling into line.

The platoon sergeant noticed him after a bit. "Just call me Fagin, like in the book," said McCall. "What book?" inquired the sergeant. "I don't know," grinned McCall.

Wounded and evacuated on the second day of the operation, McCall left the hospital ship, returned ashore and joined a machine-gun crew. "Fagin, just like the book," he told the sergeant. "Book, hell!" retorted the sergeant, writing "Fagin" on his roster.

A few days later, McCall was blown into his foxhole by a mortar round, and when he regained consciousness, he was on a hospital ship bound for the Admiralties. It was there that it was discovered that in addition to a wound and concussion, the indomitable Fagin was suffering from acute appendicitis.

Also finding himself on a hospital ship was Sergeant Carl Stevenson. After his brush with the huge Japanese on D-Day, he had raced back to Marine lines, suffering a bullet burn across his left wrist in the indiscriminate firing. A corpsman was bandaging his wrist when someone fired into an ammo dump "and everything turned over." Waking up on a hospital ship, Stevenson found himself surrounded by badly wounded Marines, while "me, I ain't got a damn thing but a Band-Aid on my wrist." Embarrassed, he went to the skipper and asked to return to his unit. "No," said the officer. "You get hit and you're out."

Stevenson, an old China hand, had been in the Corps too long to put up with that sort of nonsense. Going down to the chaplain's office, he found his pack among the wounded men's gear stored there. Then, he waited for the master at arms to go out for a moment and slipped in and helped himself to a Thompson submachine gun and a .45. Finally, veteran that he was, he stopped by the galley where "they had steaks just piled." Filling his pack with steaks, he went topside, boarded the next amtrac that came along and headed back to Peleliu. That night everybody in his squad ate navy steak.

Soon after the seizure of Peleliu's airstrip, hundreds of Seabees began clearing the runways of mines, wrecked vehicles and other debris. That "debris" included numerous bodies remaining from the assault across the runways on 16 September. Corporal H. Kenneth Hansen stumbled across one such pathetic scene, the dead bloated body of a Marine BAR man lying on the coral runway. His shovel lay next to him, and Hensen saw a slight indentation on the hard coral where the man had vainly tried to dig in before he was killed.

Also scattered around the field and in the shell-torn hangars were nearly 130 Japanese aircraft, none of them flyable thanks to U.S. air attacks over preceding months. Among the booty was a new model of the Type I medium bomber "Betty" and a model of another new medium bomber nicknamed "Frances."

U.S. planes soon began to arrive. On 18 September, a TBF was forced to land on the shot-up strip. The next day, two artillery-spotting planes of Marine Observation Squadron 3 (VMO–3) landed just before sundown, soon to be followed by the whole squadron. Requiring only a few hundred feet for takeoff, they were able to fly in and out as repairs continued.

Two days after the TBF made its forced landing, the Seabees received their construction equipment and within 72 hours cleared an operative strip 260 feet by 3,875 feet, complete with landing lights. The northwest/southeast strip was fixed first since it was the least damaged.

On 23 September, a B–24 with two malfunctioning engines made a successful landing on the strip. Marine air units, including fighters and transports, began flying out of the field the next day. By then, the short southeast/northwest runway had been fully repaired, and over 3,800 feet of the main runway was serviceable. Within ten days, the strip would be capable of handling any bomber with the exception of the big B–29s. Naval air support from fast carriers was secured after 28 September as Marine air took responsibility for close support.

During the early phase of the assault, navy fighters from ships offshore provided air support for the Marines. More than 300 missions were flown from D-Day through D plus 13, pilots dropping 620 tons of bombs of all types, including napalm.

This offshore support become unnecessary as the airfield was made operative. The first eight F6F night fighters of VMF(N)–541 arrived on 24 September, having staged from Emirau through Owi Island off New Guinea. Two days later, the white-nosed Corsairs of Major Robert F. "Cowboy" Stout's VMF–114 landed. VMF–122 arrived on 1 October, VMTB–134 came in five days later and VMF–121 arrived in late October.

Most of the close air support on Peleliu was provided by VMF–114. Soon after their arrival, Stout's pilots were pounding Japanese positions in the ridges in what may well have been the shortest bombing run of the war, at an average of 15 seconds from field to target. Often the pilots did not even bother to raise their wheels. So small were the distances that during the first air strike by land-based planes against Japanese in the ridges, fragments of a 1,000-pound bomb dropped on enemy positions carried all the way back to the airfield.

The air arm had already suffered casualties, primarily among the ground echelons which came in on the heels of the assault troops. During September, four aviation personnel were killed and 17 wounded. Another six were killed and nearly 50 wounded by enemy ground action during October.

Fortunately, the Japanese left the airfield largely alone, conserving their ammunition for more profitable targets. Colonel Nakagawa did send in suicide demolition squads from time to time in attempts to disrupt air operations, but none succeeded in getting through, and work on the field continued satisfactorily.

Carrier support was released on 28 September as Marine air units of MAG 11 assumed the support function—much to the approval of Marine infantry who felt (Marines being Marines) that the navy fliers made their runs from too high an altitude to be effective, while their own pilots practically got on the ground before loosing their ordnance.

The Ancient Greeks had their Seven Furies. The 1st Marines had Peleliu's Five Sisters. Only gradually, as the campaign progressed, did the true nature of the Five Sisters become apparent to the 1st Division. Even then, it was not recognized until much later that the terrain feature formed a bulwark at the core of Japanese resistance on Peleliu.

In contrast to most of the ridge topography on Peleliu, the Five Sisters lay across the island like a wall barring the way north. The southern face—the original Bloody Nose Ridge—was almost sheer, jutting up like a snaggled tooth north of the airfield. Steep drops between the five 250-foot peaks prohibited any attempt to work along the barrier from peak to peak. B Company 1/1 had hit this obstacle the afternoon of 18 September, only to be clobbered by fire from Japanese to the front and on both flanks. The following day, Lieutenant Colonel Russell Honsowetz's 2d Battalion took its turn.

Tanks, bazookas, flamethrowers, mortars and machine guns laid down heavy fire on the targets while the Marines of 2/1 rushed forward in small groups under a hail of Japanese return fire. "Losses were terrible, and the attack against the main objective got nowhere," reported the official historian of the campaign. The assault had completely folded by noon.

For the individual riflemen, the push was one prolonged horror. Private Russell Davis was hunkered down by a causeway over a swamp beneath the ridges when a Marine dashing toward the hills was shot to a skidding stop. As the man lay there in the open just beyond reach, his muddy hand opened and closed, whether in plain or in the reflex of death, Davis did not know.

Another Marine, unable to bear the sight, clambered up on the causeway to help the man. A bullet knocked him on his back, where he lay without a twitch. "Shove this," blurted a corpsman. "I'm gonna get those guys." He managed to get to his knees before a sniper shot him. Finally, a burly Marine reached up over the edge of the causeway and, grunting and sweating with effort, managed to pull all three wounded men to shelter.

One of the B Company platoon leaders, Lieutenant Alfred A. Hoover, was less fortunate. During the early morning, large-caliber Japanese shells pounded his platoon, coming in with a sound like ripping silk and exploding with a blast that could be felt 100 yards away. A shell burst on top of a revetment near Hoover, killing three men and wounding five, including a gunnery sergeant who survived, although his SLR 536 radio was blown 80 feet through the air.

Hearing a man scream, Hoover jumped up to go to his aid just as another shell tore in. A large fragment ripped through the lieutenant's utility knife, canteen and belt, tearing open his abdomen. He died on his way to the aid station.

Also among those killed during the day was Lieutenant Gordon Maples, who was leading F Company in the assault on the ridges. Witnesses later said that Maples, who had won the Navy Cross on Guadalcanal, appeared to be almost in a state of war psychosis as he recklessly exposed himself, always moving in an effort to make some progress against the dug-in Japanese. Later in the day, the young Kentuckian was shot through the abdomen and died just before reaching one of the hospital ships offshore.

Spotting a machine gun, another lieutenant grabbed an automatic weapon and started out after it. A burst caught him in the head before he had moved two steps. "He fell on me," said Private First Class Lowell E. Ralson of Marion, Ohio. "He was one of the best officers I have ever seen, but he had too much guts."

The deepest penetration the 1st Marines made on the 19th was achieved by C Company, commanded by a 25-year-old Massachusetts native, Captain Everett Pope. At about noon, Pope was ordered to seize Hill 100, a steep, apparently isolated knob which dominated the East Road and the swampy low ground to the battalion's right front.

Already reduced by casualties to just 90 men, C Company was in as good a shape for this mission as any of the depleted rifle companies. The Marines approached Hill 100—later known as Walt Ridge—through a swamp filtering forward past shell-torn tree trunks which jutted skyward like broken fingers. Reaching the road at the base of the height, they found and attacked two large pillboxes but were almost immediately pinned down by machine-gun fire from the right. Firing from only 50 yards away, the Japanese machine gunner was situated on the other side of a pond where the Marines could not get to him. Unable to move forward and taking heavy casualties from the fire, Pope requested permission to pull back, pass to the left of the main swamp area and push up the road with tank support.

The road here angled abruptly east, crossing the swamp over the narrow causeway. The single track crossing was located along the mouth of a wide draw, later known as "the Horseshoe." It then skirted the base of Pope's objective and angled northeast.

Pope extricated his men, but it was late afternoon before C Company was able to renew the push. The tank support did not live up to hopes. Trying to negotiate the causeway, the first tank slipped over the edge and stalled. A second tank ventured out to extricate the first and slipped over the other side, blocking the causeway to any more armored support.

Leaving the tanks behind, the Marines rushed across the causeway by squads, paused briefly at the foot of the hill, then started the steep scramble up, backed by mortars and machine guns. Here and there a blasted tree, stripped of its branches, jutted skyward, but there was little cover for the approach. Among the casualties were two Marines killed by U.S. tank fire as they tried to knock out an enemy machine gun.

Enemy fire from Hill 100 and surrounding heights took a heavy toll of the attacking Marines, but by sliding around to the right, some two dozen survivors made it to the summit. There, to their disconcertion, they found the maps were wrong. Hill 100 was not an isolated knob; it was merely the nose of a long ridge dominated by a higher knob only 50 yards to their front.

Pope did not need his Phi Beta Kappa key from Bowdoin College to understand he now had a major problem on his hands. Exposed to fire from the high ground to their front, as well as crossfire from a parallel ridge to the west, he was in a very precarious position.

As twilight fell, the Marines took what cover they could among the jumbled rocks. Their perimeter was very compressed—about the size of a tennis court by Pope's reckoning—perched on the edge of the cliffs. They had no real ground contact with the rear and only what ammunition they had been able to carry up in the initial assault. Noted the C Company war diary, "The line is flimsy as hell, and it is getting dark. We have no wires and need grenades badly."

At 1700, a machine-gun crew supporting C Company saw six men moving toward Japanese lines. Challenged, the strangers merely crouched down in the road. One of the machine gunners walked over to them, a belt of ammo in his hands. He was on top of the men before he realized they were Japanese. Slapping the lead Japanese in the face with the ammo belt, the Marine knocked him cold. The next Japanese fired at him but missed, his bullet striking an unlucky Marine lieutenant in the jaw and exiting through the back of the officer's head. The machine gunner shot the six Japanese, but the lieutenant was dead.

The Japanese went for Pope's men after dark, and they kept coming. At first, they tried to infiltrate the Marine perimeter; then they commenced a series of counterattacks, each made up of 20 to 25 men. How many there were and how often they came soon dissolved into a confused blur to the Marines. "The whole night was mixed up," recalled Pope.

Most of the thrusts came down the ridge. Pope had some radio contact with battalion and received some illumination. What he really needed was artillery support, but he was too closely engaged to call in fire from the big guns.

Back at a company command post, Private Russell Davis listened to the fighting over the radio. The front-line Marines were screaming for illumination or for corpsmen; men were crying and pleading for help, but there was nothing anybody could do to help them. In the CP, Davis's company commander listened to the whimpering calls from the hills, cursing monotonously and helplessly, his head down between his knees.

Up on the ridge, two Japanese suddenly materialized near the position defended by Lieutenant Francis Burke of Scranton, Pennsylvania, and Sergeant James P. McAlarnis of Kentucky. One of the Japanese ran a bayonet into Burke's leg. Burke tore into his attacker, beating him senseless with his fists. McAlarnis, meanwhile, went to work on the second Japanese with his riffle butt. They tossed the bodies over the precipice.

Pope's Marines managed to throw back the Japanese attacks, but as dawn streaked the sky, they were running perilously low on ammunition. "We used rocks," recalled Pope, "not so much to try to hit them with rocks . . . but you throw a rock and they wouldn't know if it was a grenade or not and they'd wait a minute to see if it was going to explode. Throw three rocks and then one of your remaining grenades and slow them down a bit."

As the fighting became hand-to-hand, the Marines pitched some of their attackers bodily over the steep cliffs. Spotting two enemy soldiers climbing the slope to his position, a sergeant heaved an empty grenade box at them, then opened up with his rifle. Private First Class Philip Collins of Gardiner, Massachusetts, picked up Japanese grenades before they exploded and tossed them back. "He did that until one exploded in his hand," reported Pope. "Then he picked up a rifle and used that until he was too weak to load the weapon."

Much of the enemy fire focused on the light machine gun, which was taken over by the assistant after the gunner was hit. The gun began jamming after a couple of hours of constant firing, and the gunner had to clear it by hand, exposing himself to enemy fire. "Every time he went up, they threw grenades," recalled a witness. The gun was finally blown off its tripod, but the gunner kept it in action until he was wounded and unable to continue.

By daylight, down to about a dozen men and out of ammunition, Pope received orders to withdraw. The order came just as the last Japanese assault began to sweep the survivors off the ridge anyway. There was little order. Those who could scrambled down the slope as fast as they could. There had been no question of sparing able-bodied men to evacuate the wounded during the night. Anyone who could not get out on his own was doomed.

Making their way through the light scrub at the base of the hill, the Marines dodged streams of enemy tracers whipping through the brush. Pope's radioman was killed by his side as he talked on the phone. Japanese infantry could be seen against the skyline where the Marines had been only moments before. Another enemy group came around to the right, where a couple of them proceeded to set up a light machine gun, much to Pope's discomfiture as he suddenly realized that they had singled him out personally for their attention. He kept moving—fast—until he and the other survivors found cover behind a stone wall near the causeway below.

Of the two dozen or so men Pope had brought up the hill, only nine made it down safely. Of these, many were wounded, including Pope himself. Sometime during the fighting, he had taken a spray of shrapnel in the legs

and thighs—an injury he dismissed as "not consequential." The New Eng-
lander picked the metal fragments out with a pair of pliers at the infirmary
a couple of days later. He walked off Peleliu, the only company commander
in the 1st Battalion to retain his post through the entire operation.

Pope's survivors were still pulling themselves together at 1630 when the
company received orders to attack up a ravine along the ridge they had just
lost. Pope contacted regiment and reported that he had only 15 men and 2
officers able to attack. The order was rescinded.

While Pope's company spent its lifeblood for Walt Ridge, 2/7 on the left
was trying to slug through the jumbled high ground in an effort to pull
abreast of the Five Sisters to the west. The battalion battered through stiff
resistance on 19 September to seize the forward slopes of Hills 200 and
260, a day's gain of 300 yards. Colonel Spencer Berger recalled that these
gains were not impressive on the maps at division headquarters, "but to
those of us who were on the ground and knew the terrain, it was a miracle."
Even so, it did not come cheaply: the battalion reported 87 casualties,
including 16 killed.

A Company of the 1st Marines was brought up to continue the attack
in what was to turn into a massacre. Passing through elements of 2/7 in a
turning movement from the west, A had 56 men in the assault. These few
riflemen grabbed a small piece of high ground along a ridge swept by
machine-gun fire. Struggling forward, the survivors suddenly found themselves faced with a sheer 150-foot drop—another of Peleliu's expected terrain features which regularly provided such lethal surprises. Only six
Marines managed to return unscathed to 2/7's lines.

As late afternoon shadows stretched over the jumbled coral crags, Easy
Company of the 7th began digging in for the night. Platoon leaders dispersed
their men along the crest of their newly won position. Communications
were tested, and Captain Warrick G. Hoopes of New York City set up his
CP 75 yards behind the line on a tiny plateau overlooking the beach road
and the wreckage of a Japanese officers quarters.

"Easy One calling Easy." Lieutenant Frank J. Miller, already hit twice in
the ridge fighting, was calling the command post. His right flank rested on
a ledge high over and to the right of the CP. "Unable to establish physical
contact with Fox Company on right flank," radioed Miller. "Just detected
a Jap patrol of approximately 30 strong in rear of lines."

Captain Hoopes's bull voice cut in on the phone. "Frank, draw back your
right flank a little. Cover down with automatic-weapons fire and keep me
informed."

The 25 men in the CP doubled their defense perimeter. A BAR team
moved in to support riflemen covering a trail approaching their position
from the north. An automatic weapon was also sited to cover a trail leading
west to the beach road.

Lieutenant James Sullivan, company exec, checked his watch. It was 2130. Only a few minutes had slipped by since the last flare had broken overhead with a muted pop, its brilliance fading to grotesque shadows in the hills. Now, the ridge was dark and quiet.

Stones rattled down the side of the ridge by the CP. "What's the password?" demanded a Marine. The reply came in the form of a hand grenade, lobbed out of the darkness. It exploded between the sentry and two other perimeter guards. There were screams of pain, and someone called, "Corpsman!" A pharmacist's mate crawled toward the injured Marines; he was stabbed by Japanese who had already killed the other three.

Circling around to the rear, the Japanese lobbed grenades into the command post area. "Why doesn't the BAR open up?" muttered a sergeant, already half knowing the answer. A grenade had burst close to where the BAR was set up.

Still in communication with his platoon leaders strung out along the ridge, Captain Hoopes ordered them to hold their positions. The CP would fight it out as best it could.

As grenades landed along the edge of the plateau, the defenders moved back in search of better cover. Lieutenant Francis Maybank of Long Island organized his communications people for a withdrawal, hoping to save both them and their equipment. Before they could get out, a volley of grenades landed in their midst. Maybank and his men died in the blasts, along with two navy liaison men.

Hoopes, Sullivan, Sergeant Francis Roberts and Lieutenant Jay S. Ambrose found themselves along a single line of defense. Japanese pressure was mounting, and the CP group had been cut off from their stocks of ammunition and grenades. "How's your ammo?" Ambrose asked Roberts. Before Roberts could reply that he was down to his last clip, a grenade exploded next to them. "My legs," groaned Ambrose.

"Mine too," said Hoopes. "Not bad, though," he added a moment later. The radio operator was silent—dead.

Sullivan emptied his pistol at a moving shadow. There was a scream of pain. "That's the bastard who threw it," announced Sullivan optimistically. Hoopes crawled for the communications phone and managed to get in touch with battalion. Another grenade landed. Sullivan twitched, muttered that he wanted to "check up on something" and crawled away. He never returned.

"If only we had a machine gun," Roberts whispered to Ambrose. "I'm going to try to get one from the lines."

With both legs shattered, Ambrose was unable to move. Roberts dragged the lieutenant to the edge of the plateau and rolled him off the edge to the path toward the beach road. Three enlisted men later found him and carried him to safety.

Roberts crawled back and found Hoopes and Private First Class Joseph

Rigny of Woodside, New York, firing at the sounds of men moving on the perimeter. Hoopes approved of the machine-gun idea. He got on the phone and called Lieutenant William Hudson of Birmingham, Alabama, who was holding down the ridge position most accessible to the CP. "Start a light .30 down here," he told Hudson. "We'll meet your man."

Before anyone else could move, Rigny was up and moving toward Hudson's position. By some miracle, he met Private First Class James Ojida of Bangor, New York, en route with the machine gun. Together, they carried the weapon back to the CP area.

By now, the Japanese had virtually seized the company nerve center. One enemy soldier even penetrated the battalion aid station. The assistant battalion surgeon, who had armed himself with a pistol despite his official noncombatant status, shot the intruder dead.

The few surviving Marines defending the CP position were strung out along an incline overlooking the plateau. The Japanese had taken the American ammunition supply and were now pitching Marine hand grenades at the Americans. Two landed within 20 yards of Hoopes as the three men tried to set up the machine gun. The Japanese seemed to realize something was going on but could not locate the gun. One Japanese came crawling over the coral, repeatedly whispering the recently replaced password. Rigny put a bullet into him.

Fumbling in his effort to set up the bipod on the rough coral, Roberts finally threw it over a pointed rock, and the gun was locked in place. Rigny fed in the first belt, and Roberts tripped the trigger, sweeping the command post area. Screams from the darkness told the Marines they were on target.

The gun jumped out of position. Roberts cradled it in his arms and kept firing, unaware that both his hands were blistering on the hot barrel. The gun jammed. It was cleared just as a figure lunged at them out of the darkness. The enemy soldier, a grenade in one hand and a bayonet in the other, was chopped in half only four feet from the muzzle of the gun. The fourth and last belt of ammunition was half spent when a flare popped, revealing the ground in its eerie glare. Not a movement could be seen.

Rigney peered over the ledge. "They're stacked like cordwood," he shouted, pointing to the sprawled Japanese bodies in the CP area.

They waited half an hour in the silence. The hush was nerve-wracking. It was almost midnight when Hoopes called Lieutenant Hudson to send a BAR team back from the lines to cover the withdrawal of the CP survivors. Hoopes did not know the only survivors were himself and the three other Marines in the gun position. Backed by a BAR team, the four moved into the front lines and set up a new CP. The rest of the night was quiet.

At dawn, they found Lieutenant Sullivan, badly wounded. He had apparently been hit just before he crawled out of the CP the night before, but no one would ever know for sure. The lieutenant died aboard a hospital ship.

Thirty dead Japanese were found in and around the CP area. One had been killed as he tried to operate the telephone line between company and battalion headquarters.

By now, the 1st Marines were shanghaiing every available man for reinforcements. Cooks, jeep drivers, headquarters personnel, MPs, laundry platoons, battalion clerks—all were sent into the line units. Not all were enthusiastic at the prospect.

Private Russell Davis was assigned to bring 20 of these men into the line. One of them, a heavy winner in a division poker game, offered him a bribe to let him stay behind. Davis told him to pick up his machine gun ammo and get moving.

"I'm a sergeant," the man announced.

"That's fine, sergeant," replied Davis, unmoved. "I'm a private. Let's go."

One man was killed on the way up. Others ran and hid at the first opportunity. By the time Davis got to the front, he had only 9 men left out of the original 20.

The fighting of Peleliu wore down even strong men. One enlisted Marine was shaken up to see his company commander sitting on the ground crying. "He just cracked up," remarked the Marine. "I remember thinking, 'What the hell is going on here?' This guy is sitting on the ground, and his eyes are pouring."

Some men had to be evacuated for combat fatigue. Others functioned almost like zombies, developing an unfocused "thousand-yard stare" combining shock and exhaustion. And those were the living.

The intensity of the front-line fighting was painfully evident back at the newly established division cemetery just inland from Orange 1. Grave-registration teams brought in a seemingly endless procession of dead Marines. Wrapped in canvas, they were lowered into holes as sweating burial details dug graves in the soft white sand.

Corporal Kevin Burns was assigned to the burial detail after his Sherman tank fell victim to a Japanese mine. "All I remember is white sand," he remarked later. "But we had to stay ten holes ahead of the dead and sometimes we were really digging."

Burns tried not to dwell on his dead buddies. "It was one of those things you just had to do. You didn't think much of it, you know. They were dead, and you buried 'em. It sounds kind of cold, but that's about it."

By 20 September, the 81st Division had managed to seize the entire southern part of Angaur. In the process, the GIs belatedly discovered the true size of Major Goto's small command from a badly wounded prisoner seized in a dugout on 19 September. According to the prisoner, all enemy troops—excepting only some 1,000 men of the 1st Battalion, 59th Infantry, 14th Division—had been shifted to Babelthuap in late July, a movement overlooked by U.S. intelligence analysts.

After the war, General Inoue revealed that this transfer had been executed per order of the 31st Army command, which in his opinion sealed the Angaur garrison's doom. "I knew that it was unreasonable to expect one battalion to defend such a large island," he told interrogators in 1947.

The American success had not been a complete cakewalk. Goto had executed a number of limited counterattacks, including one predawn effort on 18 September by a reinforced company which forced elements of 1/321 back some 50 to 75 yards. These helped cover his withdrawal into the northwestern hill area, where he planned to make his stand. Abandoning their heavy equipment, artillery and large stocks of supplies, the Japanese took only what they could carry on their backs as they headed into the rugged hills.

Linking up their two separate beachheads, the infantrymen worked in conjunction with tanks to smother enemy resistance. Defensive fire from cave positions was encountered as the GIs began to venture into the hill areas. During one of these skirmishes, a tech sergeant from 2/322 earned the dubious distinction of being the only known member of the division to be directly assaulted by a Japanese brandishing a samurai sword. He had just hurled a grenade in a cave when an officer dashed out and slashed at him. Although wounded by a sword cut and grenade fragments, the sergeant held his ground and gunned down his assailant.

Despite continued fighting, General Mueller considered himself firmly in control within three days of the landing on Angaur. Saipan Town was overrun on 19 September, and 24 hours later, U.S. forces had seized all but the Romuldo Hill area at the northwest corner of the island.

Just before 1100 on 20 September, Mueller informed General Geiger that Angaur had been taken. "All organized resistance ceased on Angaur at 1034," he radioed. "Island secure." He estimated that no more than 350 Japanese remained trapped on Angaur.

Mueller's announcement proved a bit premature. While the Wildcats had seized most of the island, Major Goto and some 700 Japanese—twice Mueller's estimate—remained holed up in the high ground to the northwest, where the intrepid major intended to resist to the last bullet. The 322d RCT would be engaged in rooting them out for another month.

Angaur would ultimately cost the 81st Division 264 killed and 1,355 wounded, most of the casualties occurring in the month after the island was officially declared secure. These losses were not inconsequential, but by Peleliu standards, Angaur was practically a skirmish.

One result of Mueller's announcement on 20 September was that the 321st RCT could now be shifted to reinforce the hard-pressed Marines on Peleliu, while the 322d remained behind to mop up. The 321st was sorely needed, but it would receive a mixed reception from the proud Marines.

Still hoping that one last push would break Japanese resistance at the Five Sisters, the 1st Marines—or what was left of it—gathered for another try on the morning of D plus 5 (20 September). The main objective was Walt Ridge, scene of Captain Pope's doomed stand the night before. This was to be an all-out effort utilizing every resource Puller had left. Every man left available to the regiment was thrown into the line, including a provisional company made up of cooks, wiremen and supply handlers who were put on 12 machine guns in support of the assault. A battleship from offshore worked the ridge line over with 16-inch shells to soften the opposition.

After five days of some of the most vicious fighting of the Pacific war, Puller's men did not have much left to give. The right battalion, 2/1, was so shot up by this time that when 1/1 was attached to it, they still did not add up to a full battalion. The highly specialized Division Reconnaissance Company was added in an effort to fill out the ranks. The line for the assault was, from left to right: 3/1, 2/7 and 2/1 and 1/1 combined.

An old, red-faced sergeant watched his men stumble slowly out of their holes to make the assault, and he turned away wiping sudden tears from his eyes. "Let's get killed on that high ground there," he said finally. "It ain't no good to get it down here." The men followed, stumbling along behind him. "That's the good lads," said the sergeant gently.

Private Russell Davis saw one man move forward dragging his blanket like some bizarre personal talisman. Another had his head covered with his poncho so only his eyes peered out, like those of some small, cornered animal. A small radioman staggered in a circle, determined to move but unable to orient himself. Another Marine pointed him toward the ridge.

They were the hard core, the ones who would die before they quit. Others could not make themselves move. "I got nothing more inside," said a sergeant crouching in his hole. "Nothing. I don't even know anybody who is still alive. They're all gone, boy. Done, the whole lash-up."

Rank meant nothing. Those who could, went forward. Privates with something left inside led sergeants with nothing. Men went forward alone and in pairs. It did not matter. Japanese fire hurled them back down the slopes. They got nowhere.

Among those hit was Corporal Joe Lommerse. Now more riflemen than machine gunners, the 17 survivors of his outfit started crawling up the ridge through the broken coral as mortar and artillery rounds burst around them. Three or four rounds fell nearby before Lommerse suddenly felt "stabbed in the back," as fragments ripped through his dungaree jacket near the spinal column.

Looking around, Lommerse saw his wounded buddies lying in all directions. As one of the least hurt, he helped drag them back to an aid station. Later that day, doctors operated on Lommerse aboard a shop offshore, using a table in the chief's mess as an operating table. Peleliu was over for him, but he was lucky to be alive; the fragments had just missed his spinal cord.

Several hours after the aborted attack, Colonel Nakagawa reported to General Inoue. "Since dawn, the enemy has been concentrating their forces, vainly trying to approach Higashiyama [Walt Ridge] and Kansokuyama [Hill 300] with 14 tanks and one infantry battalion under the powerful aid of air and artillery fire. However, they were again put to rout receiving heavy losses." Some of the Marines were killed so far forward that their bodies would not be recovered for days.

The only gain was made by 2/7, which advanced almost due east, struggling against sheer cliffs and heavy enemy fire. By mid-afternoon, F Company on the right managed to gain the crest of a ridge—then designated as Hill 260—facing the Five Sisters from the west. Between them lay the mouth of a narrow, steep-sided ravine, an area soon to be dubbed "Death Valley."

It may have been one of the casualties from this fight who was found by Pharmacists Mate Reeder Paker of Lexington, Alabama, in a search among the rocks. The badly wounded Marine was in pain but had not cried out. He lay quietly with his face to the sky, and he seemed to be thinking.

Paker and another corpsman lifted him onto a stretcher and headed for the beach. It was grim going. Machine-gun fire continued to rake through the thinned trees, and mortar fire was still hitting near. They worked along, bending over when possible, while the young Marine watched their progress from the stretcher. Suddenly, the other corpsman dropped without a sound. Paker could see he had been hit in the head and instantly killed. The wounded Marine saw it too, and he became visibly distraught. "I am sorry he got it trying to get me back," he blurted. "It's no use taking me back, because I am dying anyway."

Paker stayed there with him, unable to go on. The wounded Marine prayed for the dead corpsman and he prayed for himself. Finally, he took off his watch and asked Paker to give to to a friend of his in the 7th Marines, laboriously writing the name on the white side of a cigarette pack. He gave the plastic cigarette case to Paker. Scratched on the surface were the names and addresses of some girls in Southern towns. "I want you to have this as a souvenir," he said. "Take it, it's got some good addresses on it. Really good ones." Then he died.

Back on the beach, Paker told a *New York Times* correspondent about the young Marine, calling him "the bravest man I ever saw." Before he left, he handed the cigarette pack to the reporter. "You take it," he said. "I'm married. I can't use those addresses."

That afternoon, the shattered remnants of the 1st and 2d Battalions, 1st Marines, were relieved by 1/7. 2/7, now down to 60 men, was relieved by 3/7 and straggled back to be fed the first hot meal since the landing.

Moving up with A/1/7, Private Tom Boyle spotted a familiar figure shuffling along all by himself. It was a buddy with whom he had enlisted in

Memphis at the start of the war. The other man had gone into the 1st Marines and by the looks of things had been having a bad time of it. "Tommy, stay out of there," he told Boyle now. "I lost all my men." Boyle gave him a quart of Japanese whisky and a half-dozen oranges he had scrounged out of an enemy officer's mess and pensively watched him shuffle away toward the beach area.

Also leaving Bloody Nose was Private Russell Davis. Picking up the rifle of a dead Marine, he had gone forward with the rest earlier in the day, spending the afternoon on the scarred hillside with no feeling anymore, content just to shoot at anything that moved in front of him, friend or foe, it did not seem to matter. He just wanted to be as far forward as the next man when his turn came.

Davis never remembered coming back down the hill. When he finally came to his senses, he was sitting by the roadside in tears.

The 1st Marines were finished.

On 21 September, General Geiger, accompanied by members of his staff, visited Chesty Puller's CP to get a better idea of what was happening. Optimistic reports from division notwithstanding, it was clear something had gone very wrong.

Talking with Puller, Geiger realized almost immediately that the colonel was "very tired." Puller was unable to provide a very clear picture of his situation. When asked what he needed in the way of help, he said he was "doing all right with what he had," recalled one of Geiger's staff officers incredulously.

Proceeding to the division CP, Geiger reviewed the casualty reports. Their significance was inescapable. During five days of incessant fighting, the 1st Marines had sustained nearly 1,700 casualties, or more than half of its original strength. In his estimation, Geiger told Rupertus, "the 1st Marines were finished." The regiment should be relieved and replaced by an army combat team.

Geiger's appraisal was supported by the division assistant chief of staff, Lieutenant Colonel Lewis J. Fields. "They weren't fire-eaters anymore," he recalled of the 1st Marines. "They needed to be replaced, if we could replace them." He told both Rupertus and Geiger that he felt the army troops were definitely needed. Incredibly, General Rupertus demurred. Completely out of touch with the reality of his predicament, he became greatly agitated and argued that his division could secure Peleliu in another day or two without the aid of the army.

Over the past few days, Geiger had refrained from imposing any particular line of action on Rupertus, although he had occasionally been tempted. Now, openly critical of the way the 1st Marines had been handled, he remained firm. He ordered that preparations begin to evacuate the 1st Marines to the Russells. A regiment of the 81st Division was to be attached to the 1st Marine Division immediately.

The reluctance of General Rupertus to use army troops to help his sorely pressed division was later the subject of much speculation. The decision was actually long overdue; reinforcements could have been used much earlier in the campaign. The 1st Marine Division had suffered nearly 4,000 casualties by 22 September. With these losses came a corresponding decline in combat efficiency, which had dropped from "excellent" on 15 September to "very good" by 18 September.

Rupertus died before the end of the war, so his precise reasoning was never adequately addressed. It has been speculated that he opposed the use of army troops out of what a former company commander bluntly termed, "that damn Marine Corps pride." His own men would do the job alone no matter what the cost. He may also have questioned the quality of the army troops.

Even General O. P. Smith, who agreed that fresh troops were needed, had doubts about using army personnel. "What was needed was another regiment to finish the job," he wrote later, "but what we needed was a fresh *Marine* regiment." But of course, there was no fresh Marine regiment.

Rupertus also apparently believed, quite mistakenly as it turned out, that the Japanese were close to the breaking point and that the campaign would soon be concluded. The general himself never explained his reasoning. Whatever his motives, his reluctance to employ the Wildcats almost certainly cost Marine lives.

Late that same afternoon at 1625, General Geiger radioed General Mueller of the 81st Division: "Can you spare me one RCT complete for combat movement to Peleliu immediately?" Within 45 minutes, Mueller replied that the 321st Infantry would be ready as soon as it completed its resupply. Shortly before midnight, the 321st received orders directing its movement to Peleliu.

Private First Class Arthur Jackson, late of the 14-pound ham, could be pardoned if he thought the Japanese were out to settle his personal hash. Hunkering down in his hole after his outfit relieved 2/7 in the center of the ridges on 20 September, he waited as night fell. The deep darkness combined with clouds "made things really spooky to say the least," he recalled. There were no challenges. Anyone moving around in the dark just got shot.

At some point in the wee hours, four Japanese came out of the night after Jackson. The young automatic rifleman killed three of them in front and clubbed the fourth to death as he attempted to jump in the foxhole with him. But Jackson was also hit. Four cursing men carried his 210-pound frame off the cliff to the beach at 0400 the next morning. Only later did he learn that he had been recommended for the Medal of Honor for his action on southern Peleliu on 17 September. He was one of only three Peleliu awardees who survived to wear his medal.

On 21 September, only a few hours after Jackson was lugged down from the ridges, the 1st and 3d Battalions of the 7th Marines received their initiation to the Umurbrogol. It was not a pleasant experience.

1/7, which had relieved 1/1 and 2/1 the previous afternoon, jumped off in a morning attack directed at the 1st Marines' old nemesis, Walt Ridge. Since tanks were late coming up, the attack did not get off until 0800, giving artillery and air good opportunity to pound the target area thoroughly.

At 0800, C Company, with A Company just behind, pushed up East Road toward the ridge. Initial opposition was described as light. Masked by smoke and shell concentrations from the battalion's 81 mm mortars, C pushed over the causeway past the two Sherman tanks immobilized there since 18 September and reached the point where the road skirted the base of the ridge. Here, the riflemen were joined by tanks which had bypassed the blocked causeway by circling north around the swamp area.

Any encouragement the Marines might have felt quickly vanished as they came abreast of the ridge. Enemy fire intensified, and when the Marines started up the slope, the Japanese blanketed them with a mortar barrage. Enemy infantrymen in caves sprayed the assault troops with automatic-weapons fire and rolled grenades down on them as they scrambled up the coral slope. Japanese artillery, cleverly camouflaged on nearby high ground, also joined in, cutting the Marines down like so many duckpins.

Laying down covering fire, Tom Boyle's machine guns suddenly came under fire from Japanese knee mortars. A shell exploded under one of his guns, killing both operators and wounding three or four other men. Not realizing he had been hit too, Boyle walked over and kicked at the ruined gun in anger and frustration. Only then did he see the blood squirting out of his calf. A few minutes later, his leg tightly bandaged, Boyle turned his back on Bloody Nose and walked down to the beach and away from Peleliu forever.

Staggered by heavy losses, the assault folded up. The Marines pulled back to their own lines, unable to make an impression against the well-protected Japanese.

Meanwhile, in the center, 3/7 jumped off from positions deeper in the ridges. The assault followed naval, air, artillery and mortar preparation. Three medium tanks and an LVT flamethrower were in support, but they proved of little use because of the rugged terrain.

The attack got off to a fast start with I and K Companies reporting gains of 100 yards at 0918. Then, Japanese resistance gelled, and "the advance for the rest of the day was slow and tedious and measured in yards," noted the report.

The 7th Marines resumed the attack on 22 September. The 3d Battalion hit a stone wall of resistance. The maximum gain for the day was only 80 yards—even less on the flanks. This failure affected the efforts of 3/1 on the extreme left. Operating in the high ground, the right flank of 3/1 had the usual troubles, which hindered its left on the coastal flat. Finally, after a daylong battle, L Company managed to seize a crucial bit of high ground to anchor the defense for the night.

By now 3/1 was so badly shot up it was necessary to stiffen it with 1/1, which was itself reaching the point of nonexistence. Moved up in reserve, the 1st Battalion had been reorganized into only two pathetically under-manned companies totalling 74 men.

In the center of the ridges, the exhausted men of 2/7 did not attempt any offensive action. Further to the right, however, the still comparatively fresh 1st Battalion spent most of the day preparing to seize the Five Sisters from the southwest. Artillery concentrations pasted the target, and a platoon of tanks accompanied the infantry when the battalion attacked at 1445.

B Company, followed by A in close support, approached the objective under a smoke screen laid down by Marine mortars. Attempting to confuse the Japanese as to the direction of the attack, the Weapons Company put fire down on Walt Ridge.

For once, the plan seemed to be working. Over the first 250 yards, over ground so rocky the tanks were slowed to a crawl, the Marines received only "moderate" sniper fire. Then it all came apart, as machine guns on the ridges rattled away at the assault companies.

Pushing ahead into the worsening machine-gun fire, the Marines reached the mouth of a narrow draw, soon to be known—quite aptly—as Death Valley. This was a northerly extension of Hill 200, called Nakagama by the Japanese. The crest was occupied by the 2d Battalion, but the drop was so steep that they were unable to get to the enemy guns emplaced in the cliff face.

The sheer walls on both sides of the funnel-shaped draw were honey-combed with Japanese gun emplacements and rifle pits. Large coral boulders and rubble littered the floor of the draw. Stripped of their branches, blasted tree trunks jutted up among the rocks like the quills on a porcupine. The Marine tanks, unable to enter because of mines and the rugged terrain, fired white phosphorus and HE shells into the caves while riflemen pushed into the draw.

It was a meat grinder. B Company suffered such severe casualties from the murderous fire that a platoon from A Company was pushed forward to help. The assault had not gone far when the Marines found that they were in a box canyon; the north was also blocked by a sheer cliff, also full of Japanese.

Although they did not know it, the Marines were actually within 100 yards of Colonel Nakagawa's CP. It was as close as they would get for weeks, for their position, now under fire from heights on three sides, was clearly untenable. "The depleted units found themselves in a topographical funnel, with sheer sides from which mutually supporting dug-in enemy positions covered the low ground with fire from every angle and which were impervious to infantry assault," noted the official Marine history of the campaign.

A withdrawal was ordered. The canyon was blanketed with smoke, and A Company provided covering fire while the forward Marines extricated themselves. By 1830, the survivors of the 1st Battalion had been pulled out. Having begun the action with only 60 percent strength, there was not much left of the organization.

During the night, a Japanese crawled into a hole in the 3/7 sector. A Marine grabbed him and hollered until his buddy came over and killed the infiltrator with a shovel. I Company scouts reported that the Japanese were booby-trapping Marine dead. Word went out to all hands to exercise caution.

Holed up in the Umurbrogol, the Japanese had reason to feel confident in their new tactic of attrition after one week of battle. They had lost their immediate grip of Peleliu's airfield, but they were killing a lot of Marines. According to Japanese estimates, the 1st Marine Division had suffered over 5,000 casualties since 15 September. It was believed that over 120 tanks and tracked vehicles had been destroyed, along with approximately 15 artillery pieces.

Marine reports confirmed Japanese estimates of high casualties. A total of 3,946 men were listed as casualties as of this time. However, Japanese estimates of equipment losses were highly inflated. One 105 mm howitzer had been lost to enemy action (three others were lost when DUKWs sank on D-Day). Nineteen out of 30 tanks remained operative, with only 6 being complete losses during the 1st Tank Battalion's participation in the operation. Breakdowns among amphibious tractors affected the number operative at any given time, but only 22 LVT(A)s were permanently knocked out during the entire operation.

While Marine casualties had been painfully high, the 1st Marine Division had captured virtually everything of strategic value on Peleliu. The airfield, which was the main objective of the assault, had been seized, along with all of the island south of the Umurbrogol. New roads were already under construction with the occupation of the Purple Beach area on the eastern coast. LST landing ramps, pontoon causeways and a new road transformed that beach into the most important unloading point on the island, helping to ease the arrival of supplies.

It was estimated that two thirds of Colonel Nakagawa's original garrison had been destroyed, but this was largely guesswork. Not until 20 September did the Marines seize another POW, only the second man captured since the landing five days before.

Kanasuke Uehara, a 42-year-old Okinawan laborer, was captured in a dugout near the former village of Asias, where he had been hiding since being wounded by a grenade three days before. He had not eaten or had anything to drink for four days, he told interrogators. Upon being captured, he requested the Marines to kill him and was astonished when they demurred. He had no military training, but he said he had been issued a rifle and told to fight to the death. Significantly, the former fisherman requested that his name not be forwarded to his homeland as a POW.

A few other hungry stragglers were picked up over the next few days. On the run for over a week, they knew little of value to American intelligence.

Nevertheless, the Japanese were far from broken. Concluded a 1st Marine Division report at this time, "There is no indication that the morale of the enemy is not still high as he holds to his positions with determination."

From the shelter of the ridges, the enemy controlled all northward movement along both the East and West roads. Communication between enemy units was conducted primarily along East Road, since it was generally defiladed from naval gunfire and artillery. The airfield was in American hands, but all activity was under enemy observation and subject to harassing fire. Counterattacks from the estimated 25,000 Japanese garrisoned on the northern islands of Babelthuap, Koror and Eil Malk remained a continual threat.

Despite the sometimes overoptimistic tenor of his reports to Koror, Colonel Nakagawa could have had few illusions as to the ultimate outcome of the battle. He could delay the inevitable only temporarily. The colonel accepted this like the professional soldier he was, advising General Inoue against attempting to reinforce the garrison. It would be futile, he observed, to "pour our military into Peleliu."

The army had come to Peleliu. The 4,000 men of the 321st RCT began debarking at Orange Beach at noon on 23 September. With the Angaur fight behind them, the soldiers considered themselves combat-tested veterans. They were "sure of their abilities and anxious to demonstrate the prowess of combat infantrymen to the Marines," noted the Wildcat unit history.

In fact, the three-day fight on Angaur had been just the tempering the Wildcats needed. They had defeated the enemy; they had seen their own dead and wounded; they now knew what enemy fire sounded like, and the trigger happiness typical of all green troops had noticeably diminished. Morale was good and confidence high.

Commanding the 321st RCT was Colonel Robert Dark, an officer of wide experience. A former enlisted man commissioned from the ranks, Dark was a combat veteran of World War I, having commanded an infantry company, and later a battalion of the famed 4th Division through four major campaigns. Cited for bravery in action, he had remained in the army after the war, moving up through the ranks until he received command of the 321st in 1942. In the interim, he had seen varied service in the Philippines and stateside.

Dark had reported to General Geiger aboard the *Mount McKinley* on 22 September, and his regiment now moved smoothly into place. Immediately upon landing, the 2d Battalion of the 321st Infantry moved up and relieved the 1st Marines in position at 1500. The 3d Battalion followed in immediate support. The 1st Battalion was designated as regimental reserve.

The Marines cynically noted that the army CP was considerably further back than Chesty Puller's old command post. For their part, the Wildcats noted that the Marines were "not reluctant to pass to the Wildcat regiment the burden of further advance into this area."

The 1st Marines had been shattered. In 197.5 hours of combat, the regiment had sustained 1,672 casualties according to official figures, the most severe losses suffered by any Marine regiment in the Pacific war up to that date. The 1st Battalion, with 71 percent casualties, had been virtually destroyed. Of the nine rifle platoons in the battalion's three companies, only 74 men—and not a single one of the original platoon leaders—remained. The 2d Battalion had taken 56 percent casualties; the 3d Battalion, 55 percent.

"You the 1st Marines?" a newsman asked as the exhausted leathernecks came out of the line.

"There ain't no more 1st Marines," came the weary answer.

Puller had good reason to be proud of his Marines. "I went over the ground he captured, and I didn't see how a human being had captured it, but he did," remarked General O. P. Smith. In the fighting on Peleliu, the 1st Marines had killed an estimated 3,942 Japanese, seized 10 defended coral ridges, 3 large blockhouses, 22 pillboxes, 13 antitank guns and 144 defended caves.

Sent to Purple Beach to recoup, the remnants of the 1st Marines had barely settled in when Puller told them they would go back into action after a three-day rest. This news was not well received. A combat rifleman has just so much luck, and these men figured they had already overextended theirs.

They need not have worried. As Puller must have realized, division had no intention of sending the 1st Marines back into the Umurbrogol. "There were no replacements available, and losses in the rifle units had been so heavy, particularly among the officers and noncommissioned officers, that the units were no longer effective," noted a staff officer in the clinical jargon of his trade.

Among the "ineffectives" was Puller himself. Commanding 1/1, Major R. G. Davis recalled that the Guadalcanal shell fragment lodged in Puller's leg crippled him up so badly during the campaign that his men were carrying him around on a stretcher. It was Davis's considered opinion that the shrapnel saved Puller's life, since it prevented him from indulging in his usual habit of getting as far forward as possible—which, on Peleliu, probably would have gotten the hard-nosed CO killed.

The 1st Marines would remain on Purple Beach, seeing only sporadic action against Japanese stragglers and the odd sniper. Some patrols were sent out to search for bypassed Japanese, but most of the men did only three things while recuperating: they ate, slept and looked to see who was alive and who was not.

That same day, the 81st Division's 323d Regimental Combat Team secured Ulithi Atoll with nary a shot.

Located 260 miles northeast of the Palaus, well sited in relation to most strategic points in the Western Pacific, Ulithi Atoll was made up of about 30 small islands forming a large lagoon. As one of the best natural anchorages for large vessels in that part of the world, Ulithi had been the only Stalemate objective Bull Halsey had considered worth seizing, and he had wasted no time getting the process underway.

As early as the morning of 16 September, while the Marines fought desperately for the airfield on Peleliu, Halsey had alerted Admiral Wilkinson to prepare a regimental combat team from corps reserve "for possible early employment" to capture Ulithi. That evening, he issued a formal order for the seizure of Ulithi, overriding General Julian Smith, who felt the regiment might be needed in the Peleliu fighting. Advance parties left the Palaus on 19 September, with the main body following two days later.

For two days, starting on the afternoon of 21 September, U.S. recon parties scouted the atoll, only to discover the Japanese were gone. Apparently underestimating the value of Ulithi as a fleet anchorage, higher headquarters had directed the Japanese garrison to move to Yap late in the summer. Now only a few solitary graves and a heavily mined lagoon remained behind to attest to their former presence.

Also easily gained by the U.S. Navy was Kossol Passage, north of Babelthuap. Ammunition supply vessels for Peleliu and Angaur reached it on 21 September. Minesweeping operations were concluded within a week, and a good-sized flotilla of ships was soon safely anchored.

The 323d RCT spent the next few months occupying small islands and atolls in the Western Carolines. Good weather, friendly natives and lack of Japanese made the experience unusually enjoyable. Only at Fais, where the Wildcats suffered half a dozen casualties, was there anything approaching enemy resistance—in sharp contrast to the situation in Peleliu.

Ironically, Ulithi, which fell without a shot, was to prove far more valuable in the coming months than either Peleliu or Angaur and all their cost in blood. Seabee battalions soon began work on the anchorage and construction of an air base. A huge rest and recreation complex also took shape with a hospital, baseball diamonds, clubs for officers and enlisted men, beautiful white bathing beaches and similar facilities.

Although enemy-held Yap was only 60 miles away, it was indicative of Japanese confusion that it was 7 October before a Japanese submarine reported the American presence on Ulithi. In late November, a raid by five suicide midget submarines called *kaitens* sank the fleet oiler *Mississinewa* with 400,000 gallons of aviation gas. A suicide plane raid the following March damaged the carrier *Randolph*, causing casualties totalling 34 dead and 125 wounded. It was an almost negligible price to pay for such a valuable prize.

Meanwhile, back on Peleliu, the fighting dragged on.

Chapter 9

With the relief of the shattered 1st Marines, a new strategy went into effect on Peleliu. Belatedly recognizing the futility of a continued slug-fest against the incredible terrain of the Umurbrogol, General Rupertus and his staff now contemplated an end run around the fortress.

Fairly early in the campaign, the Marines had realized that if the Japanese had a weakness, it lay along the flat ground on the western coast. Here, along this narrow strip ranging from 50 to 75 yards in width, enemy defenses lacked the advantage provided by the rugged ground just to the east, and resistance was less solid. Protected by a low ridge line paralleling the road, 3/1 had consistently made headway along the coastal flat, only to be held back by the lack of progress by Marine units fighting in the rugged high ground to their right.

Now it was decided to take advantage of this situation. Instead of beating themselves with direct assaults on the Umurbrogol, Marine and army units would contain the Japanese in their natural fortress while elements pushed 6,000 yards up the coastal flat and seized the northern end of the island to isolate the enemy in a pocket.

Field Order No. 4, issued 25 September, noted that "intelligence reports give every indication that a swift move to the northern portion of Peleliu would be successful," and if it did succeed "all that would remain would be a small area in the vicinity of Umurbrogol Mountain, with the enemy surrounded therein."

Hopefully, the plan would reduce the soaring casualty rate. It would also allow the Marines to launch a ship-to-shore amphibious landing against the off-lying island of Ngesebus. The half-completed fighter strip there had been one of the major objectives of the invasion; now, with the assault far behind its original timetable, it seemed expeditious to use whatever means were necessary to secure the airstrip as soon as possible.

If there was any doubt about the wisdom of sidestepping the Umurbrogol and securing northern Peleliu and Ngesebus, it was quickly dispelled by the 23 September discovery that the 14th Division was reinforcing Colonel Nakagawa's garrison. As early as 18 September, two Japanese barges and one sampan had been spotted unloading on the northwest coast. Aside from that small effort, U.S. air searches to the north had shown no indication that the Japanese were reinforcing Nakagawa from the 25,000 troops stationed in the Palaus.

General Inoue had good reason for not rushing to reinforce Nakagawa's beleaguered force. He continued to believe Koror and Babelthuap would be invaded once the Americans finished with Peleliu. Nevertheless, he finally decided to send the 2d Battalion, 15th Infantry Regiment "for the sake of the garrison at Peleliu and to bolster the morale of the troops there."

Previous to the American invasion, Inoue's headquarters had requested 300 small boats from the 31st Army, intending to use the craft to transport reinforcements over Peleliu's reef. Those boats had not been forthcoming, and now the 14th Division was forced to rely on larger, slower barges to get through to Nakagawa.

Under cover of the first sustained rains since D-Day, the Iida Battalion, named after its commander, Major Yoshio Iida, set out by barge from Babelthuap on the night of 22 September. Some confusion exists as to the success of these landings. At the time, U.S. naval forces claimed to have destroyed most of the reinforcements at sea, but Japanese accounts indicate that most of the troops made it safely ashore, justifying Inoue's confidence in Iida, whom he described as one of his best majors.

According to U.S. reports, the destroyer *H. L. Edwards* detected seven enemy barges approaching the vicinity of Akarakoro Point on Japanese-held northern Peleliu at about dawn on 23 September. The destroyer opened fire and sank one barge. The others reached the beach, where they were taken under fire by naval vessels and shore-based artillery and aircraft. By 0845, the cruiser *Louisville* reported all barges had been destroyed.

At about 0230 on 24 September, another group of barges was detected and brought under fire by naval vessels and LVT(A)s. Shore-based artillery also fired on the barges, illuminated by star shells from attacking destroyers. The *Edwards* fired so many star shells over the next half hour that she depleted her stores and had to switch on her searchlights.

By 0536 the *Edwards* reported having sunk 14 barges, some of which were still burning at dawn as Japanese survivors struggled in the debris. During the morning, other survivors were fired on by naval vessels and strafed by planes as they attempted to wade ashore. Final tallies claimed 11 barges sunk or disabled. What few survivors managed to get ashore probably arrived without equipment or supplies, according to U.S. estimates.

A captured survivor, identified as a member of the engineer unit of the 2d Battalion, 15th Infantry, revealed that the convoy had included 13 barges and a motor sampan. The barges shot up the previous night had carried most of the battalion's supplies, he reported. The second convoy had carried mostly troops. The prisoner estimated 600 Japanese had gotten ashore, either on northeastern Peleliu or on small islands in the area.

Despite American claims, Japanese reports made no reference to any losses during the first landing effort. "The advance detachment, part of the 2d Battalion, 15th Infantry Regiment, made a successful landing at 0520 under command of First Lieutenant Murahori," noted Japanese reports.

The second landing on 24 September was only slightly less successful, according to Japanese reports. Leaving Babelthuap on the night of 23 September, nine barges arrived safely at Peleliu. Six others were shelled and burned when they took the wrong landing route. "Most of the personnel of these were able to land by walking through the shallows," noted Japanese records.

Lending credence to the Japanese claim, subsequent U.S. intelligence indicated 300 to 600 men of the 2d Battalion, 15th Infantry were fighting on Peleliu—evidence that the reinforcement was at least partially successful.

In an effort to prevent any further reinforcement of the enemy garrison, amtracs were detailed to patrol the northern reefs, too shallow for conventional naval vessels. Air search and destroy missions were also implemented to sink all visible barges and other craft in the Central Palaus. But despite these precautions, it was clear that the surest method of denying reinforcements to Colonel Nakagawa was to seize northern Peleliu.

The plan to sidestep Japanese resistance in the Umurbrogol by attacking up West Road got off to an auspicious start.

Relieving the survivors of 1/1 and 3/1 by 1500 on 23 September, 2/321 found itself 700 yards north of the airfield. As soon as the relief had been completed, the battalion sent out patrols to scout north up the coastal flat to Garekoru Village—or what naval gunfire had left of it—about 1,200 yards beyond the battalion front. Marine patrols had scouted this area earlier, encountering negligible opposition. Now, traveling mostly to the left of the road near the coast, the GI patrols also encountered little Japanese resistance, although fire was received from the ridge system east of the road.

The Wildcats found Garekoru had been heavily mined with aerial bombs jury-rigged as land mines. There were also a few Japanese defensive positions at the village, but these were not manned in strength. At 1700, the patrols reported the entire area north of the battalion to Garekoru was generally free of Japanese.

Upon receiving this information, General Rupertus directed the 321st Infantry to advance as far as it could before dark. The 2d Battalion started the push at about 1700.

The GIs soon discovered what the Marines had found in similar forays up the road: any advance to the left of the road, where the ground was

Map 5.
Northern Peleliu

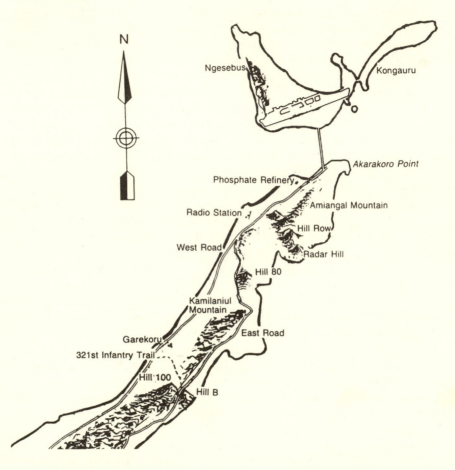

masked from the enemy-held ridges by a slight incline to the east, was largely unopposed. However, any infantry company trying to advance over the open ground to the east of the road was subjected to a deluge of enemy fire from the ridge system on the flank. Quickly pinned down, the Wildcat company assigned to this area found it impossible to keep up with the unit on the far left. With darkness falling, the effort was called off, and the Wildcats dug in along the lines of departure.

24 September opened bright and cloudless to the thunder of a 75-mile naval, air and artillery bombardment directed at the western side of the ridges. Also taken under fire were suspected enemy defensive positions near Garekoru. The 2d Battalion jumped off at 0700. The northern tip of Peleliu lay only about 6,000 yards away.

On the left, where elements of the advance enjoyed the partial defilade, progress was excellent. At about noon, the leading assault elements discovered a well-defined trail about 300 yards short of Garekoru Village. Angling east from the main road, the trail crossed a swamp and disappeared into a ridge system. The Wildcats overran a few lightly manned defense works at the junction, capturing one antitank gun, three machine guns and a partially emplaced naval gun.

Leaving the rear elements to exploit the potential of the trail, G Company pushed on through Garekoru, reaching the 0–4 line, just beyond the wrecked village, at 1535. The soldiers stopped and prepared positions to defend their gains. "The entire area was strewn with wreckage resulting from the aerial bombardment and naval gunfire of the previous nine days," noted the division operations report.

Meanwhile, the assault on the right of West Road had run into trouble. Army troops had been detailed to clear a low ridge paralleling the route and dominating the low ground. In some spots, the ridge was only 50 yards away from West Road and had to be secured to ensure the success of the penetration along the coast.

This critical need was obvious to the 3d Battalion, 7th Marines, which had been detailed to trail the advance in column along the ridge. "It was perfectly obvious to anyone who stood on that ridge that its control by the Japs would have been disastrous to the whole effort," observed battalion CO, Major E. Hunter Hurst.

Unfortunately, as the Wildcats detailed to secure the ridge encountered Japanese opposition, they veered down the slope to follow the easier path below. "They moved forward along the ridge for a few yards until they encountered the first enemy positions, then gave it up as a bad idea and bore sharply to their left front to the coastal road below," Hurst noted with thinly veiled contempt.

Hurst watched a young army major make several fruitless attempts to get a Wildcat company back on the crest. Finally, convinced he would have to secure the high ground himself, a disgusted Hurst committed I Company on the left of K to sweep the high ground. At 1310, he informed regiment: "3 Bn. 321 has withdrawn from the hills leaving a gap on the left flank of 3/7 undefended. The Japs reoccupied the hills and 3/7 is fighting to retake them." The ridge was seized at a cost of 17 Marine casualties. Among the dead was the commanding officer of I Company, Captain Carl D. Ferguson.

Within hours, the army captain who had failed to secure the ridge was relieved of his rifle company and banished to graves registration duty. His exec was also relieved, and temporary command fell on a mere platoon leader. As far as the Marines were concerned—lugging their dead and wounded down the ridges—the damage was already done.

Meanwhile, patrols from 2/321, backed by Marine and army tanks and LVT(A)s mounted with flamethrowers, pushed north from the fourth phase line almost 2,000 yards to the fifth phase line. Moving up another 200 yards, the soldiers spotted the towers and sprawling concrete building marking Japanese radio installations a few hundred yards beyond. Many caves, pillbox, bunkers and other enemy defenses were also seen along the road and at the radio station. However, opposition to the patrols was negligible, and the GIs withdrew to Garekoru before dark without interference.

The lack of stiff resistance on northern Peleliu was encouraging. It appeared that the Japanese had concentrated their main strength in the southern part of the central ridges, where they had been battling the Marines for the past week. If this was the case, U.S. forces might be able to slip by and seize the rest of the island without serious opposition.

While the bulk of the 321st Infantry secured the coastal flat, E Company pushed eastward over the trail discovered just below Garekoru. This path, soon to be dubbed "321st Infantry Trail" in honor of its discoverers, passed over a swamp before meandering over a narrow, relatively low section of the ridge system north of the center of enemy resistance in the Umurbrogol.

The Wildcats immediately recognized the potential of the trail. Other potential gateways into the ridges had turned out to be blind canyons. If the track ran through the ridges to East Road on the opposite shore, its seizure would isolate the Japanese in the Umurbrogol, cutting Colonel Nakagawa off from reinforcement, supply or escape. While narrow and almost impassable in spots, it appeared that the trail could be improved to support vehicles. But first, access would have to be ensured by seizure of a knoll, designated Hill 100, which reared up just as the trail entered the ridges.

Recognizing the tactical importance of Hill 100—which also marked the northern extremity of the Umurbrogol Pocket—E Company moved quickly to seize the height before the Japanese to the south recognized the threat and moved to reinforce the height. Pushing rapidly forward against "scattered but stubborn resistance," the company clambered up the rugged slope and gained possession of the summit before dark. Other units linked up on the right, extending the line back along the trail to West Road.

The Japanese finally managed to regroup. At about 1700, a strong counterattack struck G Company at the Fourth Phase Line on the coastal flat beyond Garekoru. The Wildcats reeled back 200 yards in places but failed to break, and the ground was quickly retaken. An hour later, as enemy forces appeared to be regrouping, the Wildcats called in artillery fire and the attack, if that is what the Japanese had in mind, never materialized.

Japanese infiltrators also jabbed at the 7th Marines during the night. One enemy soldier, killed ten feet in front of a half-track, was found the next morning, a Molotov cocktail tied to one leg, explosives fastened to his back, his pockets full of grenades.

Hunkered down among the coral heads on Hill 100, E Company Wildcats passed an uneasy night. Now and again, automatic weapons ripped in the dark as Japanese—real or imagined—tried to filter in through their lines.

Between 0100 and 0300, Japanese from Hill B, east of the road, tried to cross over and reoccupy Hill 100. Spotted by alert eyes, the effort folded as E Company swept its front with automatic-weapons fire. Fifteen dead Japanese remained strewn along the road at daybreak, but any wounded had apparently been able to crawl away in the darkness.

Daylight found a radically changed tactical situation on Peleliu as U.S. forces sidestepped the core of Japanese resistance in the Umurbrogol. The capture of Hill 100 marked a major accomplishment. Overlooking East Road on Peleliu's opposite shore, it gave the Wildcats a glimpse of the goal that would cut Peleliu in half, completely isolating Colonel Nakagawa in his coral stronghold.

It was not going to be that easy. At this point, East Road passed through a saddle bounded on the west by Hill 100 and on the east by a second, slightly higher hill known as Hill B. This well-fortified position would have to be seized if the Wildcats were to cut the island in two.

The Wildcats' second day of battle began at 0700 as E Company stormed down the eastern slope of Hill 100 in a drive toward East Road. Braving "moderate" rifle and machine-gun fire from dug-in enemy infantry on Hill B, the soldiers reached East Road by 1030.

The volume of fire from Hill B indicated that it was going to be a tough nut. E Company halted so the 3d Battalion, attacking on the right, could come up and assist in a coordinated assault. But the 3d Battalion already had more problems than it could comfortably handle. Attacking the central ridge system just south of E Company, these Wildcats were getting their first real taste of the Umurbrogol, and it was not a pleasant experience.

"Strong enemy fire was encountered from a series of pillboxes and emplacements built on promontories and protected by steep walls and sheer cliffs," observed the division operations report. "Gains for the day were unappreciable."

Luck was with at least two men that day. Droning overhead in an artillery liaison plane, they were apparently brought down by enemy fire and forced to crash-land behind enemy lines. Lieutenant Gordon B. Costello of F Company, 321st Infantry volunteered to lead a patrol out in an attempt to rescue any survivors. The GIs got to the downed plane before the Japanese, found both fliers injured but alive and brought them out of the area.

Action to the north on 25 September brought better results, weak resistance indicating that the Japanese were not prepared to seriously contest the northern end of the island. Based on information gathered by reconnaissance the previous afternoon, a strong combat patrol made up of infantry, tanks and LVT flamethrowers pushed up West Road to destroy enemy positions.

The patrol advanced 1,200 yards, destroying four pillboxes and two supply dumps and capturing one prisoner, a Korean laborer. Although 30 enemy were reported killed in this foray, the lack of real resistance reinforced the view that Colonel Nakagawa intended to remain holed up in the rugged central ridges where U.S. forces would have to dig the Japanese out, one by one.

At mid-morning, General Rupertus, now operating out of the battered former Japanese administration building at the northern end of the airstrip, ordered northern Peleliu divided into two separate sectors. The 5th Marines would secure the ground west of the height known as Kamilianlul Mountain and East Road. The 321st Infantry would complete its drive over the 321st Infantry Trail and take the ground east of the 5th Marines.

The 5th Marines were quickly gathered from their positions around eastern Peleliu and sent up West Road. The division order covering the movement was not issued until 1030—the regimental order at 1100—but the 1st Battalion, pulled from the vicinity of Ngardolok Village, was in position to launch its attack at 1300, an impressive display of organization and movement by Bucky Harris's regiment. The 3d and 2d Battalions followed soon after.

As they moved up through the army line, the Marines could see that Japanese machine guns were raking the crest of the ridges to their right. Bluish-white tracers floated overhead. The terrain was flat and sparsely wooded. Enemy small arms, mortars and artillery fire emanated from the high coral ridges to the right and from enemy weapons emplaced on Ngesebus Island a few hundred yards north of Peleliu proper.

Pushing forward with the 1st Battalion in the lead, the Marines ran into spotty resistance. As always, the Japanese fought fanatically when found, but the overall defense of the northern area seemed to lack professional cohesiveness. This was probably due to the lower quality of the enemy naval and construction units facing the Marines. The flatter terrain was also well suited to the use of tanks and LVT flamethrowers, which helped the advance considerably.

Advance elements had seized the East/West Road junction by 1700, killing 20 Japanese trying to block them from a ridge dominating the road forks. The battalion then drove another 100 yards, seizing the shot-up Japanese radio station by dusk. A C Company platoon took the sprawling concrete structure, going through windows and doors "just like you'd see as a model of street warfare," recalled the company commander.

Regimental Exec Lew Walt was ramrodding the assault, maintaining contact with Colonel Harris, who was still suffering from his knee injury. At nightfall, Walt and Harris made a bold decision. Concerned about overextending their lines, but also unwilling to relinquish their gains, they decided to break off contact with the 321st Infantry and set up a night perimeter facing east.

The 3d Battalion set up its perimeter across East Road, which angled in at this point to its northern juncture with West Road. 1/5 held the perimeter to the north with its flank on the beach, while 2/5 held the southern perimeter with its flank anchored on the beach a hundred yards north of Garekoru.

This rapid deployment took the Japanese by surprise. After dark, as the I Company CO stood on the road determining his defense with a captain from the adjacent company, an outpost passed word that enemy troops were coming. The Marines took cover and soon spotted a group of about a dozen Japanese Naval Guards coming down the road. This was clearly no counterattack. The CO noted that the Guards were completely oblivious to the U.S. advance, for they "approached making a great deal of noise." Surprise was total as the concealed Marines suddenly opened up on the Japanese, annihilating the entire group.

With darkness, the Japanese directed most of their attention to 1/5, which had penetrated the farthest north. The battalion's forward position lay only 300 yards from enemy-held high ground. Two Japanese 70 mm guns and numerous mortars put down heavy harassing fire on the Marines. Additional fire came from two Japanese 37 mm guns on off-lying Ngesebus. Small arms fire poured in from three directions.

The Marines countered by firing on selected areas with their artillery. If enemy return fire seemed to diminish, the shelling was continued on that area slowly and irregularly through the night. This experiment seemed to work and allowed the Marines to hold the forward positions, despite some initial doubts.

Under cover of darkness, the Japanese launched three strong counterattacks against 1/5. There were numerous casualties, including a C Company Marine chopped down by a sword-swinging Japanese. Another man was killed by a phosphorus grenade, and two were burned by Molotov cocktails.

Although the counterattacks were pushed vigorously, all were beaten off without loss of ground. At 0200, a platoon of C Company launched a counterattack of its own and succeeded in destroying two bothersome machine guns.

Infiltrators also plagued the Marines. Further south, near East Road, Private Eugene Sledge suddenly saw two shouting Japanese rise up from a shallow ditch, "arms waving wildly, yelling and babbling hoarsely." One, dressed in shorts and armed only with a bayonet, jumped into a two-man foxhole in front of Sledge's position. A Marine who jumped out of the hole was cut down by one of his buddies, who mistook him for a Japanese. The second Marine, who was supposed to have been on watch but apparently had nodded off, woke up in time to shoot the infiltrator dead.

The second infiltrator angled off and jumped into another hole down the line. Agonized, prolonged screaming arose from the hole as the desperate Marine, losing his weapon, jammed his forefinger into the other man's eye socket and killed him.

Further south, near Hill 100 overlooking East Road, the Wildcats were also taking some pressure from patrols and infiltrators. Manning a hole on the perimeter, Private First Class Joseph Broffman spotted a Japanese rifleman approaching his position just before dawn. Broffman cut the man down with his automatic rifle, awakening the other two men in the hole. None of them saw the second Japanese, who had crawled within ten yards of their position, until it was too late. The enemy soldier lobbed a grenade into their midst. Unable to find the grenade in the poor light of dawn, Broffman threw himself in its general direction, absorbing the full impact of the explosion. His two buddies escaped harm. Broffman lived, but both his legs were subsequently amputated.

Another E Company man, Private First Class Junior Williams, occupied a foxhole with a badly wounded companion. One by one, eight Japanese grenades landed in the foxhole during the course of the attack. Each time, Williams managed to hurl the grenade back down the slope before it exploded. At daylight, he was still alive and in one piece.

The 321st Infantry renewed its assault on Hill B at 0700. The 2d Battalion attacked from the west, while the 3d attempted to close in from the south and southwest. The effort broke down when the 3d Battalion drive stalled under heavy fire from two heights later dubbed Wattie and Baldy Ridges.

After two or three hours of this, the attack plan was revised. A separate group under the command of Captain George Neal, 2d Battalion operations officer, was organized to circle around to strike Hill B from the north. Dubbed the Neal Task Force after its commander, this group consisted of 45 infantrymen from F Company, 7 medium tanks, 6 LVT(A)s and an LVT flamethrower.

Starting north from the Garekoru area at 1000, Neal Task Force moved 2,200 yards up West Road to its junction with East Road in the zone of the 5th Marines, then headed south down East Road, clearing roadblocks as it went. The force moved rapidly along the road on the east side of Kamilianlul Mountain within 150 yards of Hill B. The most serious resistance materialized at about 1500, when a group of 15 Japanese soldiers launched a suicide charge on the armored force. They were quickly cut down, and the task force moved up to provide support for the 2d Battalion's assault from the west.

While Neal Task Force made its end run, Companies E and F had maneuvered into positions along the ridges along East Road just south and southwest of Hill B. 1/321 had taken over positions vacated by 2/321 at Garekoru. K Company had relieved E on Hill 100.

At 1600, white phosphorus smoke enveloped Hill B, blinding the enemy as the Wildcats converged from three directions. F Company struck east, while E Company attacked north and Neal Force attacked south through the gorge. Fighting stubbornly through the broken terrain, Companies E and F slowly made their way to the top of the hill. Advance elements secured the summit by 1645, and all but a few enemy riflemen had been mopped up by dark. As usual, the Japanese defenders fought to the death, although a few Korean laborers managed to surrender to the Wildcat infantry.

Infiltration and raids would continue to be a hazard. That same day, Japanese infiltrators armed with rifles and machine guns attacked the 321st Infantry CP, creating havoc and inflicting heavy casualties while losing 35 of their own people. But the breakthrough had been made. Colonel Nakagawa's main forces were isolated in the Umurbrogel Pocket.

While the Wildcats strove to secure Hill B, the 5th Marines was attempting to clear the northern end of the island. The 3d Battalion in the center of Colonel Harris's perimeter jumped off at 0600 in a drive on Hill 80 rising along the eastern shore. Fortunately for the Marines, this hill was isolated from any of the ridge systems. The battalion stormed up the sides, and by 0830, the Marines were looking down on a large swamp which marked Peleliu's eastern shore at that point.

Just to the north, 1/5 found itself in much rougher circumstances. The situation could be expressed in a word: terrain. The high ground on Peleliu's northwestern peninsula featured three main components. To the south lay the most formidable high ground, Umurbrogol Mountain.[1] Adjoining this terrain feature about midway up the peninsula was Kamilianlul Mountain, a lower, less rugged continuation of the same formation. Finally, there was Amiangal Mountain, the northernmost formation, separated from the Kamilianlul by a broad saddle.

The Amiangal formation was shaped like a crude letter L. Beginning at the shore below Akarakoro Point, a spine of narrow ridges ran southwest along the axis of the peninsula for about 1,000 yards. The formation then abruptly changed direction at nearly right angles to cross nearly the whole width of the peninsula.

This curious formation, later dubbed "Hill Row," was made up of four steep, semi-independent knobs known as Hills 1, 2 and 3 and Radar Hill. The latter, rearing up like a huge wart from a low flat near the eastern shore, was the tallest and earned its name by virtue of the installations the Japanese had constructed on its domed summit.

The hill formation, which contained some of the largest and most complex cave systems on Peleliu, was manned by about 1,000 Japanese. Most belonged to the 346th Independent Infantry Battalion, an outfit organized a few months earlier from former service and transportation troops. There were also some naval troops and personnel from miscellaneous outfits.

Attacking north along West Road, 1/5 came under heavy fire from Japanese on Hill 1. Enemy weapons included everything from small arms to 75 mm and 37 mm guns, mortars and machine guns dug into caves and holes on the 140-foot height. Fire also poured in from enemy positions on

Ngesebus. Unable to suppress the fire, even with the help of tanks and LVT flamethrowers, the Marine advance stalled.

Attacking east of the road, B Company had better luck, managing to claw its way up the less imposing Hill 2 by 1400. Among those involved in this fighting was Sergeant Flip Afflito. With most of B Company's officers already casualties, his platoon was now under the command of Lieutenant Joseph H. Widseth, a burly Minnesotan who had been sent over from a mortar platoon. Widseth was no fool. Already he had drawn Afflito aside, confessing, "Look, Flip, you know all about a rifle platoon. I know all about mortars. So I'll get the orders, give 'em to you and you try and get 'em carried out."

As the Marines fought their way up Hill 2, mortar fire began falling among them. Afflito saw Widseth yell into the radio, "Knock off that goddamn mortar fire!" Then the lieutenant was down. A tiny splinter had punched into his chest just under the heart. He was dead by the time Afflito got over to him.

Though losing a few men to mortars, the company got to the top of Hill 2. Using this position on the flank, the Marines knocked out one 75 mm and two 37 mm guns on Hill 1. With this help, C Company gained a foothold on the knob before dusk but withdrew to set up night positions.

Darkness saw the regiment settling down in a somewhat odd configuration. Due to its forward progress and the problems with Hill 1, Major Gordon D. Gayle's 2d Battalion was out of contact with the 1st, so Gayle set up his own perimeter with both flanks on the beach. The 1st Battalion stopped partly athwart Hill Row and tied in with the 3d Battalion on the right. Its left was refused, hooking around the summit of Hill 2. The 3d Battalion, now under the command of Major John Gustafson, posted I Company to hold the high ground captured that morning and be ready to move to the support of the others if necessary.

Meanwhile, up on Hill 2, Afflito got a new lieutenant—this one from an engineer battalion. "Christ, he didn't know shit from shineola about running a platoon," recalled Afflito.

The engineer officer soon suffered a minor wound, and when he left to have it attended to, never to return, Afflito got on the horn to his company commander, John Wisdom Holland, trying to get a bona fide infantry officer up to his unit. "There aren't any," Holland told him. "How about you taking over?"

"Okay, fine," said Afflito. He was now in command of 40 men, the combined survivors of two badly shot-up platoons.

What was not fully appreciated in the directive to seize northern Peleliu was the complexity of the cave systems constructed in the ridges. It was here that the Japanese 214th Naval Construction Battalion, made up of former miners and mining engineers, had tunneled into the coral like so many moles. Caves were constructed with multiple entrances and one or more staggered levels.

Secure in such defenses, the Japanese blasted away at the Marines below. With evident frustration, the 5th Marines regimental narrative reported that "tank guns, firing point-blank directly into caves and tunnels, did not even temporarily cause the enemy to cease fire."

Over subsequent days, various unit reports would list certain caves as neutralized, only to see the same caves mysteriously return to life. Only belatedly was it realized that "individual caves" were more often than not the multiple entrances to complex tunnel systems. Under pressure, the occupants would merely retreat deep into the ridge, reappearing at will to fight from "neutralized" positions.

Frustrated Marines clinging to the hilltops could sometimes smell the aroma of cooking fish and rice wafting up from literally beneath their feet, sometimes on three or four separate levels. The Japanese were dug in so deeply that one of the more frequently "reduced" caves was not finally cleaned out until the following February.

Fortunately, Hill Row lacked the lateral depth that contributed so much to the horror of the Umurbrogol further south. Built by naval personnel, often as shelters or storage areas, the positions also lacked the mutual integration of the army-designed defenses, making them more vulnerable to infantry assault.

During the night of 26 September, Weapons Company, 7th Marines killed three Japanese, one of whom carried a machine gun. One of the Japanese also bore a crudely printed message:

American Brave Soldiers: We think you are much pity since landing on this island. In spite of your pitiful battle, we are sorry that we can present only fire, not even good water. We will soon attack strongly your army. You had done bravely your duty; now abandon your guns, and come in Japanese military with a white flag (or handkerchief) so we will be glad to see you and welcome you comfortably as we can well.

At 0800 on 27 September, an American flag was raised in a simple ceremony in front of General Rupertus's command post, the battered two-story concrete administration building at the northern end of the airfield. Rupertus, his three regimental commanders and other high-ranking officers looked on as artillery fire thudded in the ridges to the north.

That same day, the island was declared "secure," a pronouncement that presumably would have mystified the men still battling fierce resistance to the north. In fact, the term was purely technical, marking passage of overall command from Vice Admiral Wilkinson to Rear Admiral George Fort.

Certainly, the flag raising brought no respite for 2/5 in the attack along the flats. The Marines had halted the night before at a large antitank ditch. The ditch had been built to impede any assault on a still more formidable position: the reinforced concrete foundation of the ruined phosphate plant. Gun ports had been cut in the thick concrete, sheltering numerous weapons sited to interdict the road and any further push to the north.

A bad omen arrived with morning in the form of extremely accurate Japanese mortar fire. 2/5 had established its CP in the gutted enemy radio station near the island's northern tip, after clearing out the corpses of the former tenants. During the morning, the Japanese laid several rounds of mortar fire on the building with such accuracy that two of them went through the second-story windows—fine shooting by anybody's standards. Another barrage that same morning came down on the CP with devastating effect. Battalion CO Major Gayle had men killed all around him but escaped with only sand blown in his eyes. His helmet was riddled: fortunately, noted a witness, he was not wearing it at the time.

Now Gayle turned his attention to the antitank ditch. Of the three tank dozers (medium tanks equipped with bulldozer blades) that had come ashore with the 1st Tank Battalion, only one remained operational. This battered treasure now labored to fill in the deep trap barring the way to Marine armor. Under a hail of enemy fire which knocked out its periscope and pinned down the officer guiding the work from outside, the dozer pushed rubble into the ditch.

Meanwhile, E Company, at the tail of the attack, sent patrols into the high ground to the east. The crest proved to be lightly held, and the Marines rapidly occupied the entire top. This victory, as tended to be the general case, was only partial, as the Japanese continued to remain immune in their caves positions on the slopes.

The armored tank dozer completed its work at the ditch at about 0830, allowing an LVT flamethrower to work close enough to douse the makeshift blockhouse with jellied gas. Resistance folded abruptly. More than 60 Japanese corpses were later found in the smoking rubble.

During the morning, F Company also managed to seize the two ridges at the northwest of the Amiangal system. Observation posts were established on the crests, but Japanese remained dug into caves halfway up the hill. Trying to exterminate them, the Marines used hand grenades, five-gallon cans of gasoline, Composition C wrapped around 81 mm WP mortar shells, flamethrowers, even direct 155 mm fire. The Japanese continued to fire out of the caves and throw the grenades back out at their assailants.

"It was hard to believe that a 70-pound compo charge wrapped around an 81 mm mortar shell, which, when set off, fairly rocked the OP on the top of the hill, did not kill the Nips in the caves," noted the battalion operations officer with incredulity.

At noon, even this labored progress came to a sudden halt as the Marines encountered the largest, most elaborate cave/tunnel complex on Peleliu.

With multiple entrances facing in three directions from the nose of the island's northernmost ridge, this mini Gibraltar dominated West Road and the reef approaches to Ngesebus, and had been occupied at one time by more than 1,000 Japanese, according to subsequent testimony by a prisoner.

So elaborate was this cave system that many Marines believed it to be the mine that supplied the ore for the phosphate refinery located nearby. Actually, the old phosphate diggings lay further to the south near Asias Village, where mining had been by the open-pit, rather than the tunneling, method. This cave complex was the handiwork of the 214th Naval Construction Battalion, which originally located its headquarters in one of the cavernous wings.

The seaward tip of the complex reared directly above the roadway, which narrowed at this point between hill and shore so that a single tank could barely squeeze past. The first Marine tank to try was promptly hit. Infantry attempting to neutralize the positions from the low ground took a beating— not only from weapons in the ridge itself, but also from enemy positions on Ngesebus and Kongauru off the northern shore. Attempts by aircraft and Marine artillery to silence the fire from Ngesebus were unsuccessful. It was later discovered that the weapons were deeply emplaced in caves in a low ridge west of the Ngesebus fighter strip.

The 5th Marines responded with an outstanding demonstration on the use of combined resources. "Harris," said one division staff officer, "used supporting fires more fully and more wisely than any of our regimental commanders at Peleliu."

Artillery put down a barrage on Ngesebus while naval gunfire pounded Kongauru. Nine medium tanks moved up along the shore below the old phosphate plant and fired smoke shells on the Ngesebus beach. With the island position effectively blinded, five LVT(A)s mounting 75 mm guns churned out into the channel and clambered up on the reef about 300 yards due north of the ridge nose, where they "poured shells into the mouth of the cave." Tanks then edged up the road past the cave entrance, which was hosed down by an LVT flamethrower.

The Marines believed that they had bypassed a series of caves. Few could have imagined the extent of the cave/tunnel complex or that it would continue to pose a threat not for hours or days, but for weeks and months.

While 2/5 fought its way to Akarakoro Point, 1/5 spent most of the day securing Hill 1, which proved to be rotten with enemy caves and tunnels. While waiting for help from that lone tank dozer, then on its way back from 2/5's tank ditch, a patrol ventured southeast along a road or trail running parallel to the base of Hill Row. It found a scattering of Japanese dead, who appeared to have fallen victim to artillery fire. The trail was also heavily mined. This information was passed back, and a squad of engineers went out early in the afternoon to clear passage.

The arrival of the tank dozer put 1/5 back in motion against Hill 1. The attack jumped off at 0930 as Companies B and C converged on the height from two directions. Recalled Flip Afflito of the fighting in this area, "It was bad because they were trying to catch us in the valleys. We'd go up one hill and down another, and they'd hit us with grenades and machine-gun fire. You see, once you got down in there, it was very tough getting out."

Progress was painfully slow, but at 1700, C Company had secured night positions on top of the hill. Among the weapons destroyed were four 75 mm guns, four 37 mm guns and numerous automatic weapons. Demolition charges thudded as engineers systematically sealed every opening that even remotely resembled a cave mouth.

Just to the south, the 321st Infantry was also in action as the 1st Battalion pushed north from Hill B to close the long gap between the 321st Infantry Trail and Hill 80, an elevation located in the saddle between the central and northern ridge systems. One company headed north along Kamilianlul Mountain. Two others pushed up East Road, now lying constricted between the mountain on the west and a swamp along the shore to the east.

To their surprise—not to mention relief—the Wildcats encountered no resistance of any consequence. By 1235, the battalion had advanced 1,000 yards, passing through abandoned Japanese defenses and storage areas. Conjecture that the Japanese had withdrawn to the hilly area on the northern end of the island was confirmed by prisoners, who said 500 Japanese were concentrating north and east of the East/West Road junction. But for now, the advance was slowed mainly by the rough terrain on the crest of the ridge and by the swamp to the right of the road.

This good fortune continued until late afternoon, when infantrymen on the road were pinned down by a Japanese pillbox located at a sharp bend about 100 yards north of Kamilianlul's nose. By the time armor arrived to help out, it was nearly dark, so the attack on the pillbox was put off until daylight.

Also in action during the day was 2/321, which moved south from Hill B at 0700 in an attempt to push up to the central ridge system. According to the sketch map, their objective was a new line less than 650 yards south along the edge of what was believed to be the heart of Japanese resistance in the central ridges.

K Company (attached to 2/321), on the west, advanced along the ridge line to the right of East Road, while F Company advanced along the road itself, supported by Neal Task Force. E Company stayed to guard Hill B, where it suffered casualties throughout the day from machine guns firing from the Umurbrogol.

K Company had it worst in the push south. The terrain in its zone was sharply furrowed with ridges, deep valleys and defiles which the Japanese used to full advantage to inflict casualties on the exposed GIs. Enemy caves were attacked with direct fire by tanks using phosphorus shells and by LVT flamethrowers and demolition squads.

One of the demolitions men, Private Jerry Reynolds, was moving toward a cave with a portable flamethrower when four Japanese charged out. Calmly holding his ground, he torched his attackers one by one, a burst of flame catching the last man less than a yard away from the nozzle.

More typical of the fierce enemy resistance was the experience of Staff Sergeant Frank W. Nicholson's platoon, which was caught by heavy machine-gun and rifle fire while crossing a deep ravine in an effort to link up with another unit. Three men were killed and others wounded in the hail of bullets. Nicholson, directing the evacuation of his wounded, was also hit. He survived being carried out of the ridges but succumbed to his wounds on a hospital ship two weeks later.

Noon found the 2d Battalion bogged down 200 yards from its objective, dubbed the O-X line. Among the day's casualties was the K Company commander. As day wore on, a withdrawal was ordered to less exposed positions. It would require another day of hard but unspectacular fighting before the Wildcats reached the O-X line.

Resuming its attack north in the morning, 1/321 again encountered stiff resistance. Supported by two medium tanks and flamethrowers, A Company struck at the pillbox that had halted the advance the evening before. Japanese resistance was stubborn. Not until 1100 did the reinforced company overrun the positions.

Meanwhile, some elements of the 321st Infantry were fighting over ground already seized by the 5th Marines. The fact that the Wildcats did not realize that they were actually engaged in a large-scale mopping up was hardly surprising, considering the number of Japanese who emerged to greet them— yet another demonstration of "passive infiltration" and the broken nature of the terrain.

Among the worst spots was Hill 80, first seized by L Company, 5th Marines at 0830 on 26 September. On 28 September, B Company of the 1/321 found it necessary to fight its way back up the hill—nearly 1,000 yards behind Marine lines along Hill Row.

Where the defenders came from was not clear. They may have been bypassed in the initial assault and remained hidden in accordance with the new tactic of passive infiltration. It is also possible that some elements of the 2d Battalion, 15th Japanese Infantry reoccupied the hill the night of 27 September while attempting to move south and join Colonel Nakagawa. They could have filtered in unopposed, since the Marines had abandoned the hill.

In any event, B Company fought until noon to secure the hill and surrounding ground first taken by 3/5 two days earlier, and it was not an easy job.

During the day 84 Koreans and seven Japanese were taken prisoner in the fighting, more than seven times the total captured in the entire period since the landing. Most of the POWs were laborers. The few captured Japanese regulars were typically hard cases. One, a second class navy machinist's mate, slashed his wrists and died a few hours after capture.

"They'd spit at you with the muzzle in their mouth," observed a Marine of the Japanese regulars. "Haughty types of people. They'd just give you the old evil eye like they were going to get you somewhere down the line."

Thousands of other Japanese would never "get" anybody again. First Marine Division intelligence estimated a total of 7,975 Japanese had been killed over the past 12 days. Casualties in the 1st Marine Division totalled 768 killed, 3,693 wounded and 273 missing, for a total of 4,734. The army's Wildcats had lost another 46 killed, 226 wounded and seven missing, for a total of 279.

In return, U.S. forces had seized the bulk of the island. According to Korean laborers who surrendered to elements of 2/321 in the vicinity of Hill B, there remained 3,000 Japanese in the rugged central pocket and 500 more in the high ground on the northern end of the island.

The next step, now that Colonel Nakagawa was isolated in the Umurbrogol, was to seize that dagger in the side of the 5th Marines, Ngesebus Island.

Nearly 1,000 miles away at a field hospital in the Admiralty Islands, Swede Hanson awoke as some medical personnel came into the ward and began calling out names. His name was among those called.

"Where am I going?" Hanson asked.

"To the airport," said one of the army medics.

"For what?"

"We're flying you to Guadalcanal to Fleet Hospital 108," came the reply.

"Why?" insisted Hanson.

"Mac," said the medic, "your arm may have to come off."

NOTE

1. The title "mountain" in each case is a misnomer.

Chapter 10

General Rupertus, his optimistic schedule in a shambles, issued verbal orders to the 5th Marines late on the afternoon of 27 September, directing the regiment to seize Ngesebus.

Once linked to Peleliu by a wooden causeway, since broken, Ngesebus lay 600 yards from the main island across a shallow strait. Possession of the off-lying island would give the Marines the half-completed Japanese fighter strip there, put an end to the fire from enemy positions on the island and further seal off Peleliu itself from the possibility of reinforcement from the islands to the north.

At low tide, the water between Peleliu and Ngesebus was no more than four feet in depth, and a man could easily wade the gap. The small island was defended by several hundred Japanese. Perhaps another 100 Japanese occupied Kongauru, a smaller island just to the east, and a third, even tinier island still farther to the east.

Twenty-four hours before, 13 swimmers from UDT 7 had braved Japanese small arms and mortar fire from both islands to examine the strait. Diving and porpoising in evasion, the team swam steadily eastward for a mile and a half, taking soundings and searching for obstacles. They turned only when Japanese concealed on the old causeway began taking close-range potshots at them. The lucky 13 returned without casualty to report the safest, shallowest paths for tanks to cross.

With the Marines now in possession of Peleliu's northern shore, an island-to-island assault was directed. The assault would be made by 3/5 at 0900 on 28 September, set to coincide with the lowest ebb of the tide so the tanks could cross unassisted. Support would be provided by a battleship, a cruiser, two destroyers, division and corps artillery, a tank company, a company of LVT(A)s and a company of LVTs.

Naval gunfire, air and artillery began pounding the Japanese on Ngesebus at 0800. The weather was cool and cloudy, broken by intermittent rain squalls. Waiting in their amphibian tractors at the water's edge, the Marines watched smoke, flame and dust rise from the off-lying island. Marine F4U Corsair fighters from VMF–114, which had landed on Peleliu airfield two days earlier, winged overhead. The navy also contributed four missions as its aerial participation in the campaign drew to a close. "We're gonna have a lot of support for this one," remarked a Marine happily.

In another amtrac, an argument arose over whether the assault would entitle participants to a separate battle star. The consensus was against.

The gull-winged Corsairs hit the beaches with machine guns, bombs and rockets 50 feet off the deck, pulling out of their dives at the last possible instant, it seemed to the watching Marines. The riflemen cheered and waved their fists as dirt and debris shot into the air. Huge shells from an offshore battleship rumbled overhead like freight trains to crash with awesome blasts on the island.

Just after 0900, the tractors churned into the water. Huddled in a crowded amtrac, Private Eugene Sledge spent the six-minute crossing squeezing his carbine stock and praying quietly. His fervent hope was that the beachhead would not be a repeat of Peleliu on 15 September.

It was not. Despite a technical misunderstanding that caused naval gunfire to be lifted prematurely, the enemy failed to react. The Marine Corsairs continued their strafing runs until the assault force was almost on the beach.

The first wave swarmed ashore at 0911, overrunning the stunned defenders in their beach defenses. A Japanese officer taken prisoner said the strafing by Corsairs had been terrifying and had given his men no chance to defend the beach.

LVT(A)s blasted several pillboxes on the beaches. Marines fired into other pillboxes and bunkers and dropped grenades through the slots, obliterating any survivors. Not a man of 3/5 was hit during the actual landing.

By now the 1st Tank Battalion had 19 operative Shermans, 16 of which participated in the crossing. Three of them swamped on the way over, but the rest arrived 12 minutes later to aid in the annihilation of the 50 or so Japanese beach defenders. Air spotters reported that the Marines were crossing the airfield at 0922 against meager resistance, and the eastern part of the island was reported secured within an hour and a half.

Sledge, with K Company, had pushed as far as the airstrip when he and a fellow Marine were pinned down by a light machine gun. Flattened shoulder to shoulder behind a small rock, Sledge heard a sound like a stick snapping. "Oh, God, I'm hit!" his buddy screamed, grabbing his elbow and thrashing in pain.

Quickly realizing the Nambu was firing high and they had been targeted by a sniper, Sledge dragged the wounded Marine to better shelter and called for a corpsman. Two other men sidled out after the sniper. They returned a few minutes later and waved. "We got the bastard; he ain't gonna shoot nobody else," reported one.

The going got a little tougher on the left as K Company confronted a series of ridges flanking the western shore. The Japanese were dug into caves and had to be rooted out by tank/infantry teams. Among the wounded was 3/5's new CO, Major John Gustafson, hit by a piece of shell as his men tackled the ridge.

Out on his platoon's flank, Private First Class Joe Moskalczak moved up along the shoreline. The tide was out, leaving a five- or six-foot bluff on his right. The assault up above stalled as the Marines worked to neutralize a particularly troublesome bunker.

"The shoreline where we were held up is shaped like a J, with a large piece of coral jagging out, making a small island," recalled Moskalczak. "To my surprise, two enemy soldiers were coming down the shoreline. The one closest to me I shot dead; the other one I wounded, and he ran for the small coral island. As I approached, I heard a Jap grenade go off; he had held the grenade to the left side of his chest."

Searching his victims, Moskalczak retrieved two wallets. Among the contents, each yielded a condom tied with an identical red ribbon "just like a bow tie," observed the Pennsylvanian. He pocketed them as souvenirs of their fatal encounter.

The Marines also encountered the new Japanese tactic of passive infiltration. Setting up near a supposedly vacant bombproof shelter near the airstrip, a group of K Company mortar men heard Japanese jabbering away inside. A burst of fire through the slot brought a flurry of grenades in return. The Marines began dropping their own grenades into the ventilator shaft, then pulled back to await flamethrowers and an amtrac with a 75 mm gun. Suddenly, three Japanese bolted from the structure. Incongruously, each carried his bayoneted rifle in one hand and held up his pants with the other. The Marines cut them down as they ran.

As the LVT(A) clattered up, several more Japanese scurried from the pillbox. Some held their rifles in both hands, but others imitated their predecessors, clutching their rifle in one hand and holding their pants with the other. Riflemen and the machine gunner on the amtrac knocked them over like so many rag dolls.

The amtrac blasted a hole through the bombproof building. A Japanese appeared with a grenade in his hand. His determined expression turned to agony as a Marine shot him through the chest. He collapsed in a flurry of gunfire, and the grenade went off at his feet.

Another Marine turned his flamethrower on the structure. There was a whoosh, followed by muffled screams as the flame darted inside. The Marines found seven enemy dead inside and ten more outside. Incredibly, one Japanese inside still lived. Playing possum, he was quickly shot dead.

Further forward, another big pillbox was taken on by Private Raymond G. Serna of Los Angeles, who pumped in two bazooka rounds, killing ten Japanese. "Ten others ran out," recalled Serna, "and the men with me opened fire and killed them."

Buzzing overhead, the pilot of an L–5 observation plane spotted a Japanese officer, replete with sword and white gloves, directing the emplacement of a mortar. Unable to resist such a tempting target, the pilot returned to his field, obtained several hand grenades and promptly headed back over Ngesebus for a run on the mortar. The grenades were dropped with undetermined effect. The Japanese replied with a flurry of machine-gun fire, putting a bullet through the pilot's leg. He made it back to base, but the wound ended his career as a self-appointed bombardier.

As 3/5's advance swept north, one platoon of L Company, supported by two tanks and three LVT(A)s, turned to the east and overran the semiconnected island of Kongauru and the unnamed islet just beyond.

Private First Class James Isabelle's L Company team moved along the shoreline on Ngesebus, checking caves. The Marines had a standard technique for this: they would fire into the cave mouth, then shout a Japanese phrase they had been taught to command any occupants to surrender. Approaching a cave by the water's edge, the Marines fired and shouted *De-te koi*! Two Japanese suddenly emerged, hands high, stripped to the waist. As Isabelle, a Massachusetts teenager on his third campaign, helped escort the prisoners down the beach, he absently noticed one of them was slipping off his split-toed sandals. Suddenly, the Japanese made a break for the water. It was a futile hope: A Marine BAR man cut him down in his tracks.

As Isabelle watched, bemused, a crewman climbed down from his tank, drew his .45 and pumped another round into the already riddled corpse. The other prisoner, obviously expecting to be shot too, fell to the ground and groveled at Isabelle's feet, pleading in Japanese and clutching a photo of his family. Isabelle handed the terrified man a cigarette before escorting him to the rear past his riddled buddy.

Elsewhere, the advance was also proceeding rapidly. By 1700, all of Ngesebus had been secured except for an area a few hundred yards square at the rugged northern end of the island and a few enemy-held caves in the ridges. Settling down for the night near the still-burning bombproof shelter, Private Sledge's squad could hear Japanese grenades and ammunition cooking off in the heat. All night, occasional shifts of wind brought the nauseating odor of burning flesh wafting over their positions.

As 3/5 exterminated the Ngesebus garrison, 1/5 continued its grinding assault against Hill Row. By morning, the Japanese had been compressed into a pocket slightly more than 2,000 yards long containing Hill 3 and Radar Hill. Enemy infantry also held out from tunnels in the northern leg of the Amiangal ridge, although Marines occupied the crests.

The Marines were intent upon sizing Hill 3, now exposed to attack from two directions: north from Marine-held Hill 2 and west from the parallel trail discovered the day before.

Neither approach was a cakewalk. After an hour-long mortar preparation, bazooka men and demolitions teams tackled the caves systems under covering fire. A Sherman tank also joined the fray, its ingenious crew backing it into a depression to obtain enough angle to bring the higher slopes under direct fire. Among the tank's victims was an especially bothersome machine gun which had been firing on the Marines from the southern slope of the hill.

Before noon, 1/5 had gained a foothold on the crest. The Japanese attempted a counterattack in early afternoon, but they were frustrated by a well-placed mortar barrage. By 1600, the Marines had seized Hill 3, capturing 15 Koreans and isolating Radar Hill just to the south.

Elsewhere on northern Peleliu, G Company was in action around the northern ridge nose which had offered so much trouble the previous day. Backed by three tanks, the Marines secured the end of the peninsula, then deployed for an assault southward on the flank of Hill Row. Here the terrain was more or less flat and open, a widening area of coconut groves yielding to a strip of swampy ground along the eastern edge of the hills. The area was full of Japanese in elaborately prepared positions. However, professional Marine eyes quickly saw the Japanese were not fighting with the determination of their brethren to the south. Subsequent intelligence revealed most of these troops were personnel from naval construction battalions and from the 346th Independent Infantry Battalion, made up of former transportation and service personnel. Their inexperience showed. In sharp contrast with the fierce resistance displayed by members of the vaunted 14th Division, most of these Japanese allowed themselves to be killed with only token resistance or simply hid, abjectly awaiting death.

A further reflection of the low morale among these units is indicated by the fact that the 5th Marines captured 45 POWs on 28 September, including the 23 on Ngesebus. Many more simply died where they stood. During that morning, 2/5 alone killed about 150 Japanese. In one gruesome spectacle, mop-up crews flushed some 70 Japanese from the northern ridge position. The enemy mob attempted to flee across the reef but was easily caught by three LVTs carrying Marine riflemen. Some of the Japanese surrendered; the rest were gunned down and left bobbing in the shallows.

Quickly overrunning this halfhearted resistance, G Company pushed south, stopping only when it could bring Radar Hill under fire from infantry weapons. The hill was now the last ridge of the Amiangal system still entirely in Japanese hands. Meanwhile, other Marines were laboring to seal the countless cave openings in both faces of the northern ridge. During the afternoon, a platoon also followed up in the wake of G Company's advance to mop up Japanese stragglers.

After a wet, but relatively quiet night, 3/5 resumed the attack on Ngesebus. The Marines made good progress cleaning out the remaining Japanese in the push to the north. At 0850, Major Gustafson received word from the front: "There are flocks of dead Japs up here. The advance is going well." At 1000, another messenger reported, "One hill on the point is holding us up. We have only 50 yards to go."

Moving up, Marines eyed a bizarre sight. A Japanese machine-gun squad had been killed in place. The gunner sat beside his weapon, the top of his skull gone, his helmet lying by his side like a riddled tin can. The assistant gunner lay sprawled by his side. Ammunition carriers lay strung out at intervals behind the gun, where they had been caught by Marine fire, each man with a box of ammo still on his back.

Hardened to such gruesomeness, one Marine sat nearby, idly pitching pebbles into the dead machine gunner's open skull. Each time a pebble landed on target, it made a little splash in the rainwater that had collected in the cavity.

Progress remained good until early afternoon. Tanks had already knocked out a large naval gun, but as the Marines approached the tip of the island, a 77 mm opened up at point-blank range, so close that the muzzle blast jolted them. Terrified men hit the deck, shouts for corpsmen revealing some had been hit. The gun got off a number of rounds in quick succession before tanks wheeled and knocked it out.

Stunned riflemen picked themselves up and looked to their casualties, including the gunner on an LVT(A) who had a chunk of meat shot out of his thigh when he lost a point-blank shootout with the enemy. He was luckier than some. A quick-thinking lieutenant wrapped the wounded Marine's belt around his leg, stopping the gush of blood before it was too late. Another Marine was hit too hard. As his buddies tried to lift his unconscious form onto a stretcher, the man's body came apart in their hands.

The remaining organized Japanese resistance soon folded. Ngesebus was declared secure at 1500. An hour later, 2/321 arrived to complete the mopping up.

The seizure of Ngesebus had cost the 3d Battalion 15 men killed and 33 wounded. A total of 470 Japanese had been killed and 23 captured, a ratio attributable to good Marine tactics and the island's more open terrain. Lieutenant Colonel Walt subsequently remarked that a less capably handled force would have required two to three days and probably would have lost better than 100 men.

Ironically, one of the original reasons for seizing Ngesebus, the airstrip, proved to be a white elephant. Built on a foundation of loose sand, it was too soft to support U.S. aircraft. It was subsequently decided not to try to upgrade the facility to U.S. standards, and so the strip was never used. On the other hand, the capture of Ngesebus eliminated the fire plaguing the

Marines from the flank and denied the Japanese a potential staging point for reinforcements moving down from the Central Palaus.

Meanwhile, in the Umurbrogol Pocket, Colonel Nakagawa had lost contact with units on Ngesebus. He reported this to Koror, adding it was "my guess" that heavy fighting was still going on there.

Although the Wildcats would subsequently mop up another 100 or so Japanese on Ngesebus, Nakagawa was indulging in wishful thinking.

The fighting on northern Peleliu reached its climax on 29 September as 1/5 took on Radar Hill with flamethrowers, bazookas, demolitions, sweat ... and their own precious blood.

Marine seizure of Hill 3 had isolated Radar Hill 150 yards to the southeast, but the height turned out to be a major obstacle in its own right. Darting in and out of intricate cave systems, the Japanese contested every inch of the coral knob.

Patrols from 1/5 scratched their way up Radar Hill and settled in on the summit without opposition. However, Japanese continued to occupy the interior of the knob, fighting from a large cave against the Marines outside. The mouth was protected by a large stone and log revetment, which baffled frontal attack. Frustrated Marine demolitions teams finally climbed the hill and sealed the entrance from above, using explosives to start a landslide over the position.

Elsewhere on the northern ridge leg, attempts to mop up the rabbit warren of Japanese tunnels and caves rapidly turned into a waking nightmare. Marines working warily along the crest tackled cave mouths on both sides of the ridge, sealing four openings to no avail; the Japanese inside soon blasted them open again and resumed fire. The enemy also cleared openings to two previously sealed caves on the western side, allowing them to fire on the west and east beaches.

Similarly, G Company Marines facing the slopes were suddenly taken under fire from the rear from positions supposedly sealed the previous day. A platoon swept the area again, driving the enemy stragglers out onto the reef where Marine amtracs gunned them down in the bloody water.

By now, it was also strongly suspected that the cave openings in both flanks of the ridge above the phosphate plant were part of one huge underground system. For two days, Japanese had continued to inflict casualties along West Road despite the close attention of Marine flamethrowers and direct artillery fire.

Working on the theory that the caves comprised one huge system, E Company posted a detail armed with machine and submachine guns to cover the eastern face of the ridge while a 155 mm gun fired directly on the western cave mouth only 200 yards away—so close that the crew had to take cover from the back blast of their own shells.

Enemy small arms and machine-gun fire killed two cannoneers and wounded three before the position could be adequately sandbagged, but the gun had the desired effect. No sooner did the shells begin exploding than Japanese began scurrying out through the cave openings on the east, where the Marines cut them down. "My God, it was like shooting fish in a barrel," recalled a tank lieutenant. "We could see our machine guns turning those poor guys into mincemeat."

Stunned Japanese could also be seen trying to crawl out through the rubble knocked down by the shell bursts. One round set off a munitions cache in the cave which blew out through the main entrance in three successive blasts, the last accompanied by a large smoke ring. The ridge was soon sealed, along with any live survivors who chose to remain inside.

Previously upbeat about the fighting to the north, Colonel Nakagawa now faced the hard truth. After fierce fighting, the enemy had finally succeeded in occupying the northern end of Peleliu, he reported on 30 September. "Our surviving forces are attempting to dash southward, cutting through the enemy in order to join the main force," he observed.

On D plus 13 (30 September) the U.S. command declared that organized enemy resistance was at an end. That assessment would prove premature.

During the afternoon, the 5th Marines were relieved on northern Peleliu by the 1st Battalion, 321st Infantry. The Marines reported that they had killed or captured 1,170 Japanese around Amiangal Mountain in four days of combat. This total sharply contrasted with previous intelligence estimates of 27 September, which put the number of Japanese defenders in the area at about 500.

Despite these numbers and despite assurances from a Marine commander that organized resistance had been broken, the arriving Wildcats were due for a nasty surprise. Anticipating only minor mopping up, they soon found themselves in the throes of what could have passed for a full-fledged battle.

The action began when B Company moved up to take over Hill Row. One platoon started up Radar Hill about 1330. Coming off the hill, the CO of C Company, 5th Marines expressed doubts that a lone platoon would be able to hold the position if the Japanese managed to dig their way out of the sealed cave. The Marine officer volunteered to carry word to that effect to the army platoon's battalion operations officer, but the Japanese moved first. As the platoon moved on to the pocked coral knob, it was overwhelmed by a fierce counterattack. Still full of fight, the Japanese had burrowed their way out of the cave.

The Wildcat platoon tumbled back down the slopes, and the whole company was soon involved in what took on the proportions of a fairly sizeable action. An hour and a half later, aided by artillery, mortars and tanks, the Wildcats finally pushed the Japanese back into their caves. Forward elements of B Company set up night defenses at the base of the hill. "They were also verbally working over the Marines," recalled an officer.

Other elements of 1/321 fared better, but they too encountered enemy opposition in some strength. A Wildcat company moving into the northernmost part of the battalion area encountered Japanese who had reoccupied pillboxes and caves in previously mopped-up areas. The opposition was particularly severe in the ridge running southwest from the vicinity of Akarakoro Point and the palm grove area to the south.

At daylight on 1 October, the 1st Battalion resumed the task of clearing the Japanese from the northeastern sector. C Company killed 40 Japanese in the vicinity of the palm grove alone. Of these, five were gunned down by Private First Class Raymond A. Brock, who saw them moving in to attack his patrol from the rear. Brock was fatally wounded in the exchange.

Patrols and demolition teams scaled Radar Hill, destroying many caves along the slopes. The Wildcats also pinpointed the cave area where the main body of Japanese had dug in for a fight to the death. This force was backed by several machine guns and at least one heavy-caliber gun in the caves.

At 1600, a rifle platoon from B Company, accompanied by an engineers demolitions squad, tackled this hotbed of resistance. The Japanese swarmed out in a counterattack, inflicting heavy casualties on the platoon. Among those killed was the officer in charge of the demolitions team.

The casualties might have been worse had it not been for the courage of Private Harvey Haynes. When the counterattack threatened to cut off the platoon, Haynes stuck to an exposed position, gunning down 12 of the brown-uniformed Asians and wounding others as they swarmed forward. His stand disorganized the Japanese attack long enough for the Wildcats to scramble back down the slope. Reinforced by a platoon from the Cannon Company, B Company established a cordon around Radar Hill for the night. Colonel Dark, seeing the amount of resistance remaining, also directed a company from Ngesebus to join in the attack the following day.

Japanese infiltrators caused some casualties during the night. Among them was Staff Sergeant William Sherry. When an enemy grenade landed in his foxhole, Sherry smothered the explosion with his own body to protect his two companions. He died in the blast.

Aided by fire from tanks and a battery of Marine 155 mm guns, the Wildcats resumed the attack on Radar Hill at 1000. The riflemen climbed hand over hand along the cliff faces, using ropes and makeshift ladders to get at the enemy in their warren of caves and tunnels. Engineers attached explosive charges to ropes and lowered them over the cave mouths to blast the positions shut.

The hill was finally declared secure at 1700. Personal count by the B Company CO revealed approximately 100 Japanese dead among the defenses on the hill. Many were found in the main cave, apparently killed by the force of the heavy demolitions used in the assault.

On 2 October, the survivors of Chesty Puller's 1st Marines left Peleliu. It was raining, and the sea was running in heavy swells as the Marines boarded the hospital transports *Pinckney* and *Tryon* for the long voyage back to Pavuvu. Two or three of the DUKWs overturned, spilling the men into the sea, but no one was lost, cheating Peleliu of a last bitter joke.

Also leaving the island were the exhausted platoons of the 1st Tank Battalion and the two pack howitzer battalions of the 11th Marines. The constricted area made use of massed artillery fire dangerous, so the gunners were leaving. The rugged terrain also made it unlikely that the tanks would be of much use in future action. In fact, withdrawal of the Marine tank battalion would prove to be a serious miscalculation, although its departure was somewhat compensated for by the arrival of the Army's 710th Tank Battalion.

There was no such question concerning the wisdom of relieving the worn-out 1st Marines. Peleliu had cost Puller's regiment 1,700 casualties. In practical terms, this meant that most men had more buddies who had been hit on Peleliu than they did friends who came off in one piece. Puller himself, his thigh swollen to nearly twice its normal size from the Gaudalcanal shell fragment, hobbled aboard only with assistance.

Among the survivors boarding the *Tryon* was Private Russell Davis. Ironically, he had survived Bloody Nose without a scratch, only to be wounded by an infiltrator while standing guard the first night on "quiet" Purple Beach. The infiltrator took a burst in the chest from Davis's tommy gun; Davis took one small grenade fragment in the lower back. He would have used it to get off the island, but he was going anyway.

Many of his comrades were so worn out that they could scarcely get up the cargo nets. Sailors stood at the rail, helping the Marines over. Some, clearly shaken at the shape the Marines were in, tried somewhat inadequately to offer an encouraging word. "You gave it to 'em real good, boys," said one of the sailors.

A clean, starched, young naval officer approached with other thoughts in mind. "Got any souvenirs to trade?" he asked a ragged leatherneck. The Marine contemplated this curious creature for a moment, then reached down and fervently patted the seat of his dungarees. "I brought my ass out of there, swabbie," he replied. "That's my souvenir of Peleliu."

Chapter 11

With the seizure of northern Peleliu on 30 September, the "short but rough" campaign had already gone into its fifteenth day. But if Peleliu was not turning out to be short, it had more than lived up to the prediction that it would be rough.

Casualties in the 1st Marine Division through 30 September totalled 5,044, including 843 killed, 3,845 wounded and 356 missing. Of the missing, many would later turn up in hospitals throughout the Pacific, having been hit in the early part of the invasion when casualties were high and record keeping spotty. During their brief time on Peleliu, the 81st Division Wildcats had lost 46 men killed, 226 wounded and 7 missing, for a total of 279.

By contrast, it was estimated that as many as 9,000 Japanese had been killed on the island by the end of the month. Prisoners, mostly Okinawans and Koreans, totaled 180. Even accounting for the 600 to 700 Japanese of the 2d Battalion, 15th Infantry who had managed to slip ashore by barge the week before, there were now less than 2,500 enemy soldiers left on the island according to American estimates.

Except for the diehards being mopped up by the 321st Infantry on northern Peleliu and a few in the rugged ridge area of Ngesebus, most of the Japanese were concentrated in the central pocket, where they had been contained since the 321st Infantry began its end run up West Road on 24 September. By the end of the month, this pocket measured about 1,900 yards long on the eastern side, 1,200 yards on the west. It averaged about 550 yards wide. However, the area had room vertically, the highest elevation being 300 feet, and the Japanese were deeply dug in.

Korean laborers who surrendered near Hill B at the northeastern tip of the pocket on 27 September estimated that 3,000 Japanese remained in the Umurbrogol ridges. They were contained on the north by U.S. forces along

Phase Line X, which roughly paralleled the 321st Infantry Trail before angling southeast to the northeastern tip of the pocket.

To the east of Walt Ridge, the pocket was bordered by an extensive swamp, considered so inaccessible that no American troops were committed to the area. U.S. units did man the southern side of the pocket facing the Horseshoe, the line serving as a buffer between the airfield and infiltration from the ridges.

A containing line to the west was manned by a variety of units, including pioneers, engineers and former artillerymen who wryly referred to themselves as "infantillery." Recognizing that the terrain was too jumbled for practical attack, these troops manned a line just far enough inland to buffer West Road against enemy fire.

No offensive action had been taken against the Umurbrogol Pocket from 22 to 27 September. Elements of the 7th Marines and 321st Infantry had merely settled in to contain the Japanese while the northern end of the island and Ngesebus were secured, but even that relative inactivity had exacted a price. Between 21 September and the time it came out of the lines on 2 October, 2/7 suffered about 150 casualties, including 33 men killed. This was without major offensive action.

One of the dead was a 20-year-old private first class from Mobile, Alabama, John D. New, who had enlisted in the Marines the day after Pearl Harbor. The first from his city to enlist to fight the Japanese, he was pictured on the front page of the *Press-Register*. Shortly after noon on 25 September, New and two other Marines were hunkered down on a small ridge north of Garekoru, calling in mortar fire on enemy positions. Suddenly, a Japanese burst from a bypassed cave directly below them and hurled two grenades. One missed; the other landed next to New, who threw himself on it, saving his two comrades at the cost of his own life.

On 29 September, 1/7 relieved elements of RCT 321 on the northern perimeter of the pocket. The depleted 7th Marines also held down the southern and western sides; the eastern side was effectively contained by the dense swamp. The initial offensive plan called for 1/7 to push south along East Road and the ridges alongside. Elements of the 3d Battalion would cooperate on the right.

The fact that the Marines would have to come after him suited Colonel Nakagawa just fine. The terrain within the pocket was ideal for defense; even a small number of well-dug-in Japanese would be able to inflict heavy casualties on the Marines as they scrambled up the open slopes.

A geologist would have viewed the Umurbrogol with professional fascination as an ancient coral-encrusted sea floor forced above the surface by subterranean volcanic activity. The highest elevation was only about 300 feet, but that was nearly straight up. Ridges, cliffs and jagged rock jutted up in haphazard profusion amid a litter of boulders and coral debris in what one Marine veteran of the fighting called "a nightmare's nightmare if there ever was one."

Cracked and buckled by pressures endured thousands of years before, the coral limestone was riddled with faults and fissures like some sprawling, leprous creature. Erosion had created caves in all shapes and sizes throughout the pocket. Nakagawa's original command post on the southern perimeter had been located in one of these caves, complete with all the comforts of home: wooden floors, electric lighting, a well-equipped kitchen and partitioned quarters with built-in bunks. The colonel had unhurriedly vacated these lavish quarters on D plus 2 in the face of Puller's continued assaults and withdrawn deeper into the ridges. His new CP was a deep, two-chambered cave 40 feet down a vertical shaft near the northern end of the China Wall, a steep rock facade about 750 yards long.

Unknown to U.S. intelligence—and never suspected throughout the campaign—Nakagawa also had constant telephone communication with General Inoue on Koror over a suboceanic cable. On 28 September, he reported that his main force was approximately the size of two and a half battalions.

Nakagawa's men had adequate food and ammunition. Water shortages were occasional problem until heavy rains arrived at the end of the month. A godsend to the Japanese, this rain was collected and hoarded in underground cisterns, although lack of water would continue to be a problem.

Seeing but unseen, the dug-in Japanese exercised superb fire discipline. A Marine officer recalled it was possible to stand at the mouth of the Horseshoe in broad daylight and study at leisure the pocked slopes "almost physically aware of the weightless impact of scores of hostile eyes." Occasional small patrols operated here and elsewhere with impunity, but if an important target was approached or enough men gathered to present a profitable target, "a fury of fire" would descend on them from weapons concealed in the ridges.

It was difficult to determine how many of the enemy were being killed. General Smith inspected one two-entrance cave near Death Valley which had fallen victim to simultaneous flamethrower attacks on both mouths. Sixty-five dead Japanese were found inside. However, there were also many attacks that yielded no enemy dead as the Japanese retreated to the safety of laterals, descended to other levels or escaped through secondary entrances to continue the fight.

Efforts to entice the Japanese to surrender by use of leaflets and broadcasts brought the usual disappointing results. As a last resort, a captured navy antiaircraft man, 19-year-old Seaman First Class Akiro Maeda, was sent into the pocket to talk the defenders into surrender.

Maeda had been captured in the water between Peleliu and Kongauru by an LVP operated by the 5th Marines. Now, outfitted in a newly captured uniform and loaded down with candy bars and cigarettes, this "rather bright little character from a naval AA unit volunteered to approach the caves in person as living evidence of the Americans' kindness to their captives," recalled a Marine officer.

The emissary approached the first cave and started his spiel, only to have one of his former comrades hurl a grenade at him. The emissary hit the deck and wormed out of range under Marine covering fire. With a "toothy grin and a nonchalant wave of the hand," he then approached another cave, where he was greeted by a burst of automatic fire.

Approaching the basement of a concrete blockhouse, he was seen to talk to the occupants a while, then he vanished inside. Minutes passed, and the waiting Marines were speculating as to whether he had gone back to his own side or been killed when the emissary suddenly reappeared leading nine laborers, all with hands held high and anxious to surrender. But the bulk of the Japanese had no intention of giving up. Enemy documents captured on 1 October indicated that the Japanese thought the Marines seemed "exhausted" and were "fighting less aggressively."

Unable to use tanks and support weapons to their fullest advantage in the rugged terrain, the Marines and Wildcats had only one option: take the caves one by one, sealing each mouth discovered. It was a slow process, expensive in American lives... but it was the only way.

Combat soldiers are only people. Some are brave, some not; some are foolhardy, some cautious; some lucky, some not. Most are thoroughly acquainted with fear. It is also an axiom of battle that the combat rifleman may have more in common with his enemy counterpart than with his own countrymen only a couple of thousand yards to the rear.

"I remember on East Road... Oh, God, that was way back," recalled Sergeant Carl Stevenson. "We'd gone around there for some damn thing ... walking up that road. About 15 Japs just stepped out and looked at us ... and we looked at them. And both of us turned and walked the other way. I don't know why. It was probably the best thing. The point is if one of them or one of us had shot, we would have had a lot killed right then. Hell, we had a squad. We just turned around and walked away."

Moving out under heavy rains and a low-lying fog the morning of 30 September, B Company, 7th Marines seized a high ridge just west of East Road as part of a plan to drive south on the pocket. As visibility cleared, A Company leapfrogged through and attacked down East Road. Supported by a tank and an LVT flamethrower, the Marines jumped off after a mortar barrage. Others struggled through the rugged high ground to the right. "Hey, we got the best job," hooted their buddies down below.

Out on point, Sergeant Stevenson's squad pushed down the road with the tank. Passing a burning Japanese tank truck, the Marines rounded a corner and found themselves at the edge of a wide pullover built to facilitate the flow of traffic on the narrow road.

The tank pulled up. Stevenson, who was following along behind, stopped, glanced down at his feet and was startled to see five scared Asian faces looking back at him. Dug into the coral, the Japanese had let the Marines walk right into the position, apparently hoping to ambush the company.

Stevenson cut them down with his tommy gun, then jumped back and tried to get the tank crew's attention. Suddenly "a little fat Jap" jumped from behind a rock with a grenade in each hand. He popped them on his helmet and pitched them at Stevenson. Stevenson dove for the ground. Seeing one grenade land by his leg, he kicked at it frantically. It went off with a bang, and for a moment he thought it had taken his leg with it. He gave a pull on his knee, saw the leg wiggle, and decided, "Hell, I'm good."

Backing up, the tank mangled Stevenson's tommy gun, but he had hung on to his .45 and a bag of grenades. He pulled a grenade and went to throw it. Only then did the excruciating pain in his shoulder tell him he had been hit there too. Switching hands, he started throwing grenades and directing the fire of his men as they fought the trap.

The platoon sergeant scuttled up to find out what was happening. Bullets were whizzing everywhere as the Marines shot it out with Japanese concealed among the rocks around the wide spot. "Are you all right?" asked the platoon sergeant.

"No, I'm hit," replied Stevenson. "I'm going to get out of here." Oblivious to the humming bullets, he walked down the road, back around the corner, and sat down on a rock. A corpsman was busy working on two other wounded Marines, so Stevenson cut off his pant leg to find a hole spurting blood in the middle of his calf. For lack of anything else, he stuck his finger in the hole until the corpsman finally came over and bandaged his wounds. He asked Stevenson if he needed a stretcher.

"Hell, no," replied the Arizonan. "I walked this far, I can get out of here." He stood up and fell flat on his face. They finally took him out in a jeep. Stevenson survived, but years later he would still carry 28 pieces of metal in his leg from that "little fat Jap." He was lucky. The one piece that probably would have killed him, a chunk of metal as big as his thumb, tore into his pack in the middle of his back and penetrated three quarters of the way through his Bible before losing its momentum.

Despite Japanese resistance, the 7th Marines managed to push 300 yards down East Road before halting for the night. Also during the afternoon, a Marine patrol from 3/7, groping through the rain and fog, came up against a rocky knob on the northern end of a long, narrow ridge directly south of Phase Line X. This knob, soon to be dubbed Baldy Ridge,[1] turned out to be one of the northern anchors of the Japanese pocket. As the Marines explored potential openings for attack, they sighted a number of Japanese on the hill. Soon after, taken under heavy mortar fire, the Marines withdrew for the night.

Baldy showed its teeth the next morning by keeping the advance at a standstill all day. Plagued by rain and high winds, L Company had not moved more than 75 yards when the Marines came under such heavy rifle and machine-gun fire from the hill that any attempt at frontal assault just fell apart. Supporting fire from 155 mm guns also had to be cancelled because fragmentation was kicking back into friendly lines.

By now, the 7th Marines had been thoroughly ground down. A check of 1/7 revealed only 90 men fit for duty. Many of the men had been so stricken with diarrhea that they could hardly walk. Major Hurst's 3d Battalion, which was in the best shape, reported combat efficiency below 50 percent. Lieutenant Colonel Berger reported combat efficiency in the 2d Battalion at 30 percent. "The men are very tried," he reported.

Fatigue showed in a certain degree of carelessness. O. P. Smith later recalled watching tanks run up into a ravine. Riflemen nonchalantly sat down in their lee and lighted cigarettes, waiting for the armor to advance. "It is a common observance," remarked Smith, "that in a long campaign, men tend to get more careless about taking cover as the campaign progresses, partly due to fatigue and partly, I suppose, to fatalism."

Despite their deplorable condition, the remnants of the 7th Marines were to make one final push against the pocket. The plan for 3 October called for the 7th to seize the remainder of East Road and its dominating ridges. By changing the main effort from the north to the southeast, General Rupertus hoped to avoid another stalemate and gain ground to launch flank attacks against the Japanese pocket, which had proved such a hard nut to squeeze from the north and south. Seizure of East Road would also ease the resupply of units and the evacuation of the wounded.

The plan called for 2/7 to attack and seize Walt Ridge from the south, while 3/7 drove from the north to capture Boyd Ridge. When the crests had been seized, the Marines would face west toward the pocket. To the south, 3/5, back from the Ngesebus assault, would also be involved. That battalion would attack the Five Sisters after relieving 2/7. Weapons Company, backed by army tanks, would move into the Horseshoe and up East Road in support.

Among the men moving into position was Private Eugene Sledge's mortar outfit. The Marines coming out were stooped and hollow-eyed, weary to the bone. Sledge inherited a mortar pit where two Marines had been badly cut up by a pair of Japanese infiltrators the night before. Both Japanese had been killed, their bodies tossed into some nearby bushes, but one of the Marines had died, and the other was in bad shape. Inside the pit, the white coral was splattered and smeared with the blood of the two Marines, more fodder for swarms of already bloated flies.

Commanding 2/7, Spencer Berger had witnessed the bloody repulses of 2/1 and 1/7 at Walt Ridge, where Captain Pope had made his stand nearly two weeks before. Attacking across low open ground, exposed to fire from the eastern face of the ridge, the Marines had been chopped to pieces. "It was just plain murder to throw these battalions in the attack in that manner," he recalled.

Now, hoping to give his own men every possible chance of avoiding a similar fate, Berger made extensive use of both air and ground reconnaissance to find the best route of attack. He ultimately decided to approach over the trail through the swamp—the same trail over which Captain Pope had withdrawn when thrown off the ridge on the morning of 20 September.

The American preparations had not been overlooked by Japanese eyes in the hills. "It seems the enemy acted as if preparing for an attack on our surrounded garrison units in the central hills," reported Colonel Nakagawa.

At 0700, following an intensive half-hour barrage by 155 mm guns and the massed fire of 81 mm mortars, the Marines moved out in single file under cover of smoke. For its part, 2/7 encountered only light resistance on the trail. By 0730, the leading platoon of G Company had clambered to the top of Walt Ridge. Other elements of the assault were close behind. Any jubilation they may have felt was tempered by the scene that greeted them on the crest. Scattered about the ridge top were the decomposed remains of C Company Marines killed during Pope's stand two weeks earlier.

Up to this point, 2/7 had taken no casualties, but now, as the Marines attempted to expand their hold on the ridge, they came under heavy fire from the Five Brothers on the other side of the Horseshoe and from the heights to the north. The deteriorating situation was registered at the regimental CP with increasingly urgent calls to send up stretchers.

Tanks and half-tracks moved into the Horseshoe in an effort to suppress some of the crossfire from the Five Brothers. Discovering a large cave with a concrete front at the foot of one of the Brothers, the tanks promptly killed its 60 occupants but could do nothing about fire from Japanese on the other side, in the pocket itself. One half-track was hit, and the positions continued to plague the Marine assault from the other flank.

E Company was ordered through G's right, but at 0900, the assault northward along the crest bumped into what was described in reports as "a slight saddle." Covered by a murderous crossfire from the Five Brothers, the saddle was a death trap.

"Two out of every four men attempting to get across were hit," reported the battalion. Among the casualties was the CO of G Company.

Clinging to the ridge top, the assault riflemen waited for ropes and ladders. Engineers were also called in to blast a covered approach along the eastern face of the ridge, which fell off in a vertical 90-foot drop. As they consolidated, purple smoke rose from their northern flank, signaling 3/7 to start its own push south.

Spotting the smoke, 3/7 jumped off at 1020. The Marines progressed well until the advance riflemen climbed down into the draw separating them from Boyd Ridge. One squad of K Company's lead platoon, nine men commanded by Lieutenant Charles Hickox, Jr., managed to get across before the Japanese reacted, pinning the rest of the platoon down with fire channeled down through the draw from positions higher on the ridge. Tank support failed to make a dent in the volume of enemy fire, although the arrival of the two tanks and an LVT flamethrower, which had to travel up and down three quarters of the peninsula to reach the battalion, marked the first successful attempt to use the direct line of communication along East Road from the south.

The lead company, K, finally quit trying to force the draw directly under the enemy guns and detoured through a swamp just east of the road. Pushing through the dense growth and muck proved slow but gave the advantage of concealment and some defilade—saving casualties. Hickox, who remained in radio contact with battalion, was also able to place his men in advantageous positions to aid the attack. At 1530, the Marines were through, and Boyd was in U.S. hands.

Meanwhile, 2/7 had expanded its hold on Walt Ridge. Contact between the two battalions was established at 1600 by patrols venturing into the swampy draw between the two ridges. The cost was 24 killed and 60 wounded for the 2d Battalion, which figured it had killed about 130 Japanese. The 3d Battalion lost 4 killed and 25 wounded but killed about 22 Japanese.

For his part, Colonel Nakagawa apparently took leave of reality in his report on this action. Noting that numerous tanks and "about two infantry battalions" attacked the position from the north and south, he informed Koror, "Our garrison units repelled them and withdrew. In this district about 100 enemy troops infiltrated our front lines secretly but were exterminated during the evening." The report concluded with the comment that the attackers, "estimated at about five infantry battalions," were "believed to be Marines with one part of the Australian Army."

While the 7th Marines battled for the ridge, 3/5 attacked the pocket from the south. This push was intended mainly to divert Japanese attention from the 7th Marines' assault, interfere with any efforts to reinforce the eastern perimeter and possibly gain positions to support the 7th's push directly.

The 5th's objective was that bitter palisade, the Five Sisters, which had held up any advance since Puller's 1st Marines had first encountered the system two weeks before. Gruesome evidence of that fighting remained scattered among the rocks. Private First Class James Isabelle's outfit saw it on the way up. "I remember going down this causeway . . . this thing was left and right full of shell holes," he recalled. "And the first time I'm running down here, I'm looking left and right and all I see is dead Marines in these holes. And the shock of it is just . . . jeez."

Moving up in the lead of K Company, Private First Class Joe Moskalczak came across a large pile of Japanese shoes heaped there as if a truck had dumped them off in a hurry. With his own boondockers in shreds, Moskalczak poked through the pile until he found a pair that fit and put them on.

"*Bang*, a bullet misses me," he recalled. "I got down behind a large piece of coral. I made a dash for a bale of hay. *Bang*, another miss. Now I am pinned down. Finally a tank came by. We got behind the tank and made our way to the pocket. The ridge on the right was a cliff about a hundred feet high, and this is where the sniper was." An LVT flamethrower finally burned the sniper out, but not before he managed to kill a Marine lieutenant.

The assault battalion found the approach very difficult, as it paralleled a ridge on the left where many Japanese were still holed up and harassed the Marines from the flank. Lieutenant Tom "Stumpy" Stanley, exec of the lead company, later compared this experience to going up a narrow street lined with six-story buildings. Only these "buildings" were full of heavily armed Japanese.

Despite the difficulty of the terrain, the assault drove forward. The Marines reached the base of the hills at about noon, and L Company ascended Sisters 1, 3, 4 and 5. On the far left, a platoon supported by a tank moved into Death Valley to try to get at Sister 2, which lay to the north of the others. Difficult terrain and enemy resistance thwarted that hope.

Meanwhile, the other Marines found themselves in possession of the crests of the other Sisters but with no place to hide. Their success showed that the Marines were not the only ones suffering on Peleliu—the fact that they even reached the peaks was presumably the result of two weeks of steady attrition on the Japanese defenders, as supporting installations and positions on the Five Sisters were knocked out. Even so, there were plenty of Japanese left in the area, and most of them seemed to be shooting at the Marines on the crests.

By late afternoon, it was clear that the cost of holding the hills would be prohibitive. Exposed to fire from positions they could not locate, unable to dig into the hard coral for cover, the Marines wisely withdrew. The defense line for the night was set up only 100 yards beyond where the battalion jumped off earlier the same morning.

"The enemy unit that attacked Kansokuyama, our main post in the southwestern hills, was its best picked company," chortled Nakagawa. "However, more than half of them were killed."

Although Nakagawa again exaggerated his success, the night of 3 October found the containing lines in nearly the same position they had been that morning, with the important exception of the gains made by the 7th Marines on Boyd and Walt Ridges on the eastern perimeter.

Men were not the only victims of Peleliu. By the end of September, both war dog platoons assigned to the 1st Marine Division had also been pretty well shot to pieces.

Elements of the 4th War Dog Platoon—made up of three squads, each with 12 dogs and 20 men—had landed only 60 minutes after H-Hour on 15 September, but they were of little use in the first 48 hours of battle. Many of the handlers were put to work as stretcher bearers, although other teams provided security for command posts and guarded against infiltrators.

The 5th War Dog Platoon landed late in the day of 16 September after the airfield had been seized. One dog, a German shepherd named Duke, soon distinguished himself by carrying some 20 pounds of maps, papers and other data across the airfield under heavy mortar fire, successfully delivering the material to intelligence officers. Other dogs, placed on the line for night security, alerted the Marines to Japanese infiltrators, which led to several kills.

The dog platoons were most successful working the scrub jungle with the 5th Marines. On 20 September, Boy, a Doberman pinscher handled by Corporal Harold Flagg, was patrolling in front of I Company when he detected an ambush of about 20 Japanese armed with two machine guns and other automatic weapons. Picking up the presence of the Japanese 75 to 100 yards beyond the point, the dog undoubtedly saved the company from walking blindly into the ambush.

Similarly, on 20 September, the 4th War Dog Platoon reported that one of its dogs "alerted [detected] a Jap sniper at about fifty yards distance and killed him." The following day a dog by the name of Pardner was reported to have "chased a Jap sniper approximately 150 yards before the sniper was killed."

But all in all, hindsight indicated that the war dog platoons were badly misused on Peleliu, suffering tremendously from the cut-up coral and the constant mortar and artillery fire. As early as D-Day, the 4th Platoon lost a dog to shell shock. The following day, the platoon reported, "Dogs becoming very nervous under heavy mortar fire."

On 19 September, Rusty 222 attacked his handler and had to be destroyed; two other dogs, Prince and Major, were killed by mortar fire, and Max 5E07 was badly shell shocked.

On the 20th, the platoon reported, "Dogs feet bruised and cut from coral." That same day, Private First Class Dyer was killed by mortar fire and his dog, Arko, was badly shell shocked. Rex B21 was also shell shocked, became uncontrollable and had to be destroyed; Max 5E07, badly shell shocked the day before, also had to be destroyed.

By 21 September, reported the 5th Platoon, "Dogs were becoming exhausted, and had feet badly cut by coral." That same day, the platoon reported four dogs with evidence of severe shell shock. Those reports were echoed by the 4th Platoon, which noted, "Nemo J01 and Bingo 241, who had been shell shocked and wounded, became completely uncontrollable and had to be destroyed. Dog used for night security—completely tired out and of little use."

On 26 September, the platoon reported, "The following dogs were evacuated to the rear as being either wounded or suffering from concussion and deafness: Tuffy 67E1, Prince 217, Mr. Chips 309, Baron 00E5, Duke 221, Buddy A215, King 216, Phi A296, Major E757."

Also listed among the casualties was Duke Z876, the German shepherd who had crossed the airfield with the load of maps and papers on 17 September. The messenger dog died of wounds on 25 September while serving with the 5th Marines near Hill Row on northern Peleliu.

Virtually decimated, the 4th War Dog Platoon left Peleliu on 1 October. Remnants of the 5th Platoon stayed in action until 18 October, primarily running security patrols along Purple Beach. Survivors left Peleliu on 21 October.

By early October, the weather had become consistently rainy. The rain was welcomed by the Japanese, who had been running seriously short of water, but for U.S. troops, the weather was a mixed blessing, helping somewhat to break the heat but also interfering with combat operations. Rain and high winds forced the cancellation of air strikes on the pocket and interfered with supply. The strain of resupplying the Marines was too much for the lieutenant colonel charged with supervising the unloading of materiel. His nerves shattered, and on 3 October, he killed himself with a fellow officer's .45.

On the morning of 4 October, strong winds and high seas nearly reached typhoon proportions. Two LSTs tied to the pontoon causeway constructed by Seabees off Orange 3 were driven ashore. No other craft were able to get to the beach with supplies. With only four days' rations on the island, troops were temporarily reduced to two meals a day.

Using about 75 C–16 and C–47 transport aircraft, MAG-11 flew in 42,000 ten-in-one rations. Transports also began flying casualties out on 4 October. In five days, VMR–952 alone evacuated 247 wounded to Momote in the Admiralty Islands.

When supplies of aviation gasoline ran low at the Peleliu airstrip, gasoline in drums was floated over the reef and guided to shore by swimmers. Forty-five–knot winds tugged at VMF–114's ready tent, shredding maps and whipping over the waiting pilots. Overcast skies turned the whole island gray, adding to the general gloominess.

On Koror, General Inoue and his staff prepared to move four battalions—three on Babelthuap and one on Koror—to Peleliu around 2 or 3 October. The Japanese had predicted a typhoon would strike the Palaus at about that time. The plan called for the troops to move by barges under cover of the storm, avoiding the prying eyes of American carrier planes. But American air, which for the past weeks had been searching out and destroying anything in the Palaus that could float, had done its job too well. Now, even with the willingness to send reinforcements to Peleliu, Inoue could not scratch together enough barges to transport the men.

The threat of Japanese reinforcement from the northern islands would continue to worry American planners throughout the campaign. Efforts to seal off Peleliu prompted the seizure of Garakayo, north of Ngesebus, on 9 October. Garyo, Ngemelis and Arimasuku, still further north, were seized two days later. But Inoue had shot his bolt; Nakagawa was on his own.

One of the more peculiar aspects of the campaign on Peleliu was the disparity between the front and rear lines, scarcely a rifle shot apart. On the airfield, a scant 100 yards from Bloody Nose, hundreds of Seabees, stripped to the waist, guided grading equipment over the runways. The post office was only 300 yards south of the ridges; movies were set up only a little further away, the nighttime features marred only by the rumble of heavy artillery pounding the ridges. Tents and shelter halves sprouted along the edge of the field. Private Eugene Sledge recalled passing some of these men on his way to the front. The rear echelon men, neat, clean shaven and relaxed, eyed the haggard, filthy assault Marines curiously "as though we were wild animals in a circus parade," observed Sledge.

But there were heroes here, too. Private First Class Henry Dearman recalled sitting in the front line surrounded by five dead Japanese in an advanced state of decomposition when someone shouted, "Hey, Marines, don't shoot!" Looking back, he saw someone in a white undershirt duck out of sight. The man popped up and repeated, "Hey, Marines, don't shoot!"

Beckoned forward, the man approached carrying a large silver container. It developed that he was a cook from one of the ships offshore; he had brought steaming hot dogs and corn ashore to pass out to the Marines. The Marines held out their steel helmets, liners removed, and the cook, unarmed and still in his kitchen whites, doled out their portions. Then, with a "Good luck, Marines!", he was on his way. Even to men accustomed to bravery, the cook was something special.

The presence of so many rear-echelon troops and the proximity of the front lines resulted in a major nuisance as hordes of souvenir hunters wandered to the front. The problem was compounded by the departure of the 1st Platoon, 1st MP Company with the 1st Marines in early October. The MPs could have exercised some restraint and control.

Disgusted front-line Marines did not much care to act as chaperons to such innocents. Not a few souvenir hunters were killed or wounded as a result of their curiosity. Others, coming up for a brief "tour" of the lines, found themselves pressed unceremoniously into service by exasperated front-line officers short on both men and patience.

One of the more hard-nosed practitioners was Major Joseph Buckley, CO of Weapons Company, 7th Marines. A former enlisted man, he had been promoted from captain to major during the second week at Peleliu, an elevation he regarded with some astonishment. "Imagine me a fucking major," he remarked over and over. Any man found in Buckley's area without a legitimate reason was seized, handed a weapon and placed in the line—held there by force if necessary. If they behaved themselves, Buckley notified their unit commanders of their whereabouts; recalcitrant "recruits" were simply held as long as he pleased.

Not everyone came forward out of idle curiosity. As the fighting dragged on and casualties mounted, many rear-area troops grew restless, even guilty, and came forward for no other reason than to lend a hand to their fellow Marines. At one point in the fighting, word came back to the airfield that some Marines had been trapped in a ravine near Bloody Nose Ridge. A sergeant recalled, "Nobody ordered nobody. Right out of nowhere everybody just grabbed their damn weapon and hauled ass up there and just started shootin' the mountain up and got all the wounded out. I don't know who was up in there, but hell, we had sailors, we had Marines, we had tankers, we had everybody."

Other volunteers brought up supplies, served as stretcher bearers, manned front-line positions and pestered combat outfits to let them help "in any way," recalled a battalion commander. They included Seabees, aviation personnel and service troops. A combat correspondent was wounded while commanding a machine-gun section. A messman won the Silver Star. A staff captain, slammed across the back with a samurai sword, killed the owner but lost the prized souvenir to a sharp-eyed private first class, who somehow got to it first in the darkness and confusion.

Among the more unusual volunteers was Carpenter's Mate First Class Leslie Griggs, a 43-year-old Seabee who was practically a living fossil compared to the young Marines on the line. A former National Guard gunnery instructor, he had lost his own son earlier in the war. Determined to exact revenge, he headed for the front lines the first chance he got.

The would-be warrior was stalking along a trail when a Marine sergeant spotted him. "Hey, you souvenir-huntin' Seabee sonofabitch!" he yelled. "Come over here and get a load of this ammo!"

A few minutes later, Griggs, loaded down with belts of 50-caliber machine-gun shells, was staggering up the ridge. Suddenly, a Japanese machine gun opened up, and the detail went to ground. Soon afterward, the Marines spotted some Japanese sneaking out of a cave onto a ledge, apparently oblivious to the presence of the Americans. "Hold it," whispered the sergeant. "Let them all come out."

The Marines opened up when eight enemy soldiers showed themselves on the ledge. They killed all eight. Griggs shot one. "Say, this goddamn Seabee can shoot," remarked the sergeant with new respect.

From then on Griggs made trips to the front every chance he could get, sniping at the enemy and rigging booby traps at the mouths of caves. One trap yielded five dead Japanese. His only injury occurred when a Japanese bullet hit his full canteen "and the damn thing blasted an acre of skin offa my tail," he recalled. "The Marines guyed me and said I ought to get a Purple Heart for being shot in the tail by my own canteen."

Now and again, some Marine, braver or more foolhardy than the rest, ventured into the Japanese cave system. "One of the old boys [Carter] come around kinda late one evening," recalled Platoon Sergeant William Linkenfelter, "and said, 'Let's go hunt for souvenirs.' I wasn't much of a souvenir hunter, you know. He says, 'Ah, we'll just go up here a ways, we won't go far.'

"So we walked for a half hour or so and found a cave. He said, 'Let's go in there and see what we can find.' I said, 'Well, I'm right behind you; I'll back you up.' So here we go crawlin' into this damn cave. And we go back in the cave; it goes and goes and goes. We thought, Damn, where's the end of this thing? Finally I smelled something. And I said, 'Hey, Carter, do you smell what I smell?' He says, 'It smells like shit to me.' 'Well, that's what it is, I got it clear down the front of me here.'

"So I said, 'What do you see up front?' He says, 'I can't see very far, there's a curve up here.' I said, 'Well, I don't know how in the hell they got back here, but there's probably somebody in front of you.' So that didn't stop him. We get on up, get around the curve a little bit, and there was a little shiny ration can sittin' up on a little ledge of rock. We were still crawlin' now, there wasn't room to turn around or nothin'. So we saw this little shiny ration can there, and there was water dripping in it. And you could hear *drip, drip, drip, drip, drip*. So I said, 'Whaddya see up in front of you?' He says, 'I can't see nothing. It looks like it turns right up here.'

"So we go a little farther, and he says, 'Hey, Link.' And I said, 'What?' He said, 'There's somebody up here.' I said, 'Yeah, I figured that.' He said, 'He's covered up with a blanket. I see two white socks stickin' out. He must be asleep.' I said, 'Well, make sure he's asleep.' So *bang bang bang bang bang bang* went that .45 automatic, and then I heard. '*Ooohhhmmm*.'

"So that was the end of that guy, he was the only one in there. At the end of the [tunnel] there was a cut-out place that was, oh, about 10 or 12 foot in diameter and big enough to stand up in. He had his rations in there ... and he had a rifle right there beside him, loaded, ready to go. He had to be asleep, 'cause if he hadn't a been he could have fired that thing right head on and hit both of us, you know? You couldn't even turn around in there. Man, if that guy had just fired one time with that big, long rifle he had in there, he'd 've killed both of us with one shot."

On 3 October, the 1st Marine Division lost its highest ranking casualty on Peleliu, Colonel Joseph F. Hankins. Hankins, a former battalion commander, was then in charge of the Division Headquarters Battalion. Among other duties, he was responsible for security on West Road.

For the previous day or two, Japanese snipers had worked their way into the high ground dominating a section of road—promptly dubbed "Dead Man's Curve"—less than 2,000 yards north of the airfield, where they began harassing traffic from the cave-pocked cliff face. On the afternoon of 3 October, Hankins, a member of several famous Marine Corps rifle teams, picked up an M–1 and a pair of binoculars and set out to snipe the snipers. The colonel's plan suffered a setback as soon as he arrived at the ill-famed curve. An LVT and three trucks were jammed up on the road under heavy small-arms fire from the nearby cliff face only 50 yards away. The men had deserted the vehicles to find cover, leaving the road blocked.

Unmindful of the enemy fire, Hankins strode to the middle of the road to restore order. He had just gotten the crews back on the vehicles when a bullet thwacked into his chest, killing him. Among the most distraught over his death was the POW Hankins had adopted a few days earlier as a sort of mascot. The POW wept bitterly and insisted on the privilege of digging Hankins's grave before being led off to a proper POW facility.

Following Hankins's death, a Marine company was sent into the area to clean up the high ground near Dead Man's Curve. They managed to put a temporary halt to the sniping, but it later became necessary to place three medium tanks at the curve. The crews blasted the cliffs whenever snipers became bothersome, which was frequently.

The day after Colonel Hankins's death, the 7th Marines suffered one final horror in a campaign full of them. With Boyd and Walt ridges now firmly in hand, the Marines still had not completely freed East Road. Enemy fire directed through three major gaps—the Horseshoe, the draw between Walt and Boyd and a still narrower draw between Boyd and an unnamed ridge to the north—continued to interfere with use of the road. Fire coming through the draw was partially negated by using tanks to shield stretcher parties and the thin-skinned supply and ammo vehicles, but passage remained perilous. On 4 October, the 3d Battalion was directed to clean up the two draws north of the Horseshoe.

Aided by tanks and the cooperation of elements of 2/7, I Company managed to mop up the southern draw lying between Walt and Boyd. This achievement did not come cheaply. Two officers were killed, and the company came out of the action with only one officer and 31 men fit for duty—a company in name only. Meanwhile, L Company tackled the northern draw, which was dominated by three rocky knobs ranging from 60 to 90 feet high. These rose just to the north and northeast of Ridge 120, "a steep-sided razorback." Just to the west of 120, Baldy Ridge reared its ugly head, still lethal after resisting Marine attacks from the north for the past several days.

This incredible jumble of cliffs, knobs and coral boulders lay practically in one gigantic heap in geographical terms. The nearest knob was only about 100 yards from East Road; Ridge 120 was less than 150 yards away. Even a mediocre rifle shot would have little trouble hitting a target at that distance. The Marines jumped off from Boyd Ridge at 1430, ordered to seize the three knobs. To their astonishment, this was accomplished without casualty within 45 minutes. Enemy resistance was so light as to be almost negligible.

Apprised of this development, the CO of 3/7, Major Hunter Hurst, saw what appeared to be an ideal opportunity to seize the initiative. Just beyond the knobs lay Ridge 120, the perfect springboard for future assaults against recalcitrant Baldy. Hurst sent an engineer company to hold the knobs and directed L Company to press the attack on 120.

Commanded by 230-pound Second Lieutenant James E. Dunn of Duluth, Minnesota, a 48-man platoon moved out at 1415. Picking their way through a ravine with 100-foot walls, the Marines drew fire from Japanese in a draw running perpendicular to the route of advance. Two men were hit and sent to the rear, while the remaining Marines sprinted by twos and threes to the base of the ridge. By 1605, a platoon had clambered up the northern nose of the elevation, scrambling over fissures and crevices and clinging to roots and vines. Several enemy positions were knocked out.

Surprised by the lack of opposition, the gasping riflemen lay among the scattered scrub brush on the coral, catching their breath. Above them, Old Baldy reared menacingly among the forest of coral crags and spires. Ravines yawned on all sides. Their nearest friends—K Company—were located on the ridge to the southeast, separated from Dunn's platoon by a deep, 100-foot-wide gorge.

As the Marine riflemen began scouting the ridge south, one man dropped like a sack of old laundry with a bullet through the head. The Japanese rifleman was killed, but within minutes the platoon began taking fire from Baldy. Suffering several casualties, the Marines took cover on the eastern slope. This maneuver brought them under the guns of Japanese positions still untouched on the lower slopes of Boyd Ridge. Other Japanese, deeply dug into the lower slopes of the newly seized knobs and into Ridge 120 itself, covered the exits.

Only now, as death stalked them on the open ridge, did the Marines realize the enormity of the trap they had entered. Maintaining the strictest fire discipline, the Japanese had waited until the platoon was fully committed on the open crest before cutting loose with everything from rifles to 20 mm machine cannons and mortars in a savage crossfire.

The senior noncom, Gunnery Sergeant Ralph Phillips, was hit and killed almost immediately by a machine-gun burst. Two others were killed soon after. Three navy corpsmen accompanying the platoon tried to aid the wounded, but efforts to evacuate casualties were nearly impossible due to the sheer slopes. The only feasible way out appeared to be down a steep drop from a ledge on the eastern precipices. Dunn lowered himself over the edge in an effort to lead his men out. Quickly hit by enemy fire, the young Minnesotan plummeted to his death on the rocks below.

As K Company tried to help with fire from parallel Boyd Ridge, the platoon slowly disintegrated. Wounded men were hit again and again. Some just lay there soundlessly, the life leaking out of them; others cried for help and begged their buddies not to leave them. Corpsmen dragged some of the wounded to the ledge. "Take it easy!" shouted one of the navy men. "Bandage each other. Get out a few at a time—" A bullet ended the sentence and his life.

Men who could still move dropped their weapons to attempt the climb down the cliff face. Some were hit and tumbled to the floor of the ravine.

Watching from below, L Company CO Captain James V. Shanley shouted, "For God's sake, smoke up that hill!" He called for a tank, and the vehicle ventured as far into the draw as terrain allowed before stopping and searching futilely for targets.

As men on Boyd hurled white phosphorus grenades into the ravine, smoke wafted up around the ledge. Some of the trapped Marines decided to take their chances and just drop off the edge, figuring it could not be any more dangerous than the Japanese bullets sweeping the slopes. Five Marines chanced the leap into space and escaped to the protection of the tank. Their departure left six wounded and four dead on the ledge, guarded by three able-bodied riflemen and one corpsman—the last survivor of the three "docs" who had accompanied the attack. Higher up on the slope were three more live Marines, whom the Japanese had apparently left for dead. The wounded urged their able-bodied buddies to jump. "You've done all you can for us," sobbed one of the men. "Get outta here."

In a last desperate effort to save their wounded, the able-bodied Marines rolled them off the ledge into the ravine. One casualty, his foot caught in a vine, endured the added horror of dangling helplessly upside down in the open until someone kicked him free and he fell into the draw. Then it was the turn of the Marines playing possum higher up the slope. One was killed instantly as he got to his feet, but the other two scrambled down to the ledge and tumbled over.

Nearly all those still alive had gotten out when Shanley, peering through the thinning smoke, spotted two wounded Marines staggering toward him as bullets powdered the coral around their feet. One put his arms around the other, and they hobbled desperately toward the tank. Thirty yards away, their strength gave out, and they collapsed. The Japanese opened fire on them as they lay helplessly on the coral.

Shanley, a native New Yorker who had won the Navy Cross for heroism at Cape Gloucester, could not stand any more. A lieutenant tried to restrain him, but Shanley shook him off and sprinted into the open draw. Grabbing one of the wounded Marines, Shanley dragged him back to the tank, then dashed out after the second man. He never made it. A mortar shell burst in the draw, sending its splinters slicing through the captain's body. As he fell, his executive officer, Lieutenant Harold Collis of Tulsa, Oklahoma, charged into the smoke to help, only to pitch forward dead at Shanley's side, cut down by an antitank round. His promotion to first lieutenant had arrived at regimental headquarters that same morning, but Collis never learned of it. Shanley, still breathing, was evacuated but died later that night.

Shanley was not alone in his heroism. Two of the Marines who had escaped the trap immediately volunteered to return to the foot of the ledge for the wounded. Both were killed.

By 1730, it was all over. In 3 hours and 15 minutes, Shanley's company had virtually ceased to exist. Of the 48 men who had scaled the ridge, only 11 survived. Of these, only 5 escaped unscathed. Companies I and L combined—normally boasting an authorized strength of 470 Marines—could muster only 80 men between them.

The massacre in the Umurbrogol marked the finish of the 7th Marines as a regimental unit on Peleliu. Its relief by the 5th Marines began the next day. Aside from a few limited combat missions, the 7th would remain in general reserve.

The relief came too late for a 21-year-old Kentucky farmboy, Private Wesley Phelps. Phelps was stationed with another Marine manning a .30 caliber machine gun that night when the Japanese launched a counterattack on the remnants of K Company. Suddenly, a grenade flew out of the darkness and landed in their hole. Shouting a warning, Phelps rolled over on the missile, absorbing the blast with his own body. He was among 12 Marines killed in the nightlong action. The Japanese left 52 of their own strewn among the rocks. Phelps's Medal of Honor went to his mother.

The Japanese were also suffering. On 14 October, a Wildcat patrol discovered a cleverly hidden Japanese medical aid station in Hill Row. It was concealed in a large cave partitioned into two rooms, each approximately 50' x 15' x 10'. Of the three entrances into the cave, one was protected by a Lewis gun with an antiaircraft mount. Cautious GIs venturing inside found a lighting system and radio station in one room. Fifty dead Japanese lay in the aid station, the majority having suffered gunshot wounds to the head. Very few medical supplies and bandages were found.

Enemy personnel captured in early October told of surviving on rainwater and cave seepage. A seaman blinded by smoke and captured in a cave said he had been in a hospital cave with about 40 other patients, two doctors and five or six medical personnel when the patients were all ordered back to their units. A Korean laborer said he and the others in his unit had each been given a stick of dynamite and told to kill themselves rather than be captured. Most of the men had thrown the dynamite away but were cut down by U.S. tanks before they could surrender, he reported.

Although heavy rains now fell regularly on Peleliu, the air remained heavy and muggy. The reek of death and corruption hung over the island, a combination of rotting rations, uncovered feces and the thousands of Japanese corpses putrifying among the rocks. Hardened to such sights, Marines used the heat-bloated corpses for target practice.

By 4 October, the 1st Marine Division had lost 1,327 killed, 4,304 wounded and 249 missing, for a total of 5,580. The division estimated that it had killed slightly over 10,000 Japanese. A total of 214 Japanese and Koreans had been captured. Perhaps 300 to 600 enemy troops remained, according to Marine estimates. (The estimate would later prove to be far wide of the mark: as late as 13 October, Colonel Nakagawa would report a total strength of over 1,150 men, including naval personnel.)

American bodies were removed to the rear whenever possible. Very rarely was a dead Marine left uncovered. Standard practice was to cover the man with his poncho. Failing this, at least his face would be covered from the sun, rain and ever-present swarm of flies until he could be interred in the expanding cemetery behind Orange 1. Marines coming into a section of the line could tell what to expect by the number of poncho-wrapped corpses lined up behind the position awaiting removal by graves-registration teams.

All of the dead bloated quickly in the terrific heat. "The bodies would blow up within a day," recalled Private First Class Al Geierman. "Yeah, they'd blow up and then they'd turn brown, then the skin and the uniform would turn brownish-orange—an oily brownish color—and then *pop*. Within two days, there'd be nothing left but the cartridge belt and the shoes." The stench was beyond belief.

Private First Class Howard Miller drew the loathsome task of picking up Japanese bodies for mass burial. Besides the terrible condition of the corpses, there were booby traps to worry about. "We had one body we were suspicious of," he recalled, "and we got a hold of some communications cord and tied it around his shoulders—we were going to pull the body before we removed it, you know. And of course he's decomposed and everything, and we pulled his arms right out of the sockets. It made me sick."

Proper field sanitation was an impossibility in the ridges. "There wasn't too much movement going on once you got up there," remembered Corporal Russell Clay. "You had to crawl or move quickly. You didn't stand around."

Unable to dig into the hard rock, troops were forced to leave feces uncovered, adding to the already stupifying stink. Huge, bloated flies proliferated in the filth, their greenish-blue bodies so swollen some could scarcely fly. They swarmed on everything, making no distinction between a putrifying corpse and a man's C rations.

Thousands of Marines and GIs learned to eat by spooning food into their mouths with the right hand while picking sluggish flies out of the concoction with the left. A disgusted GI was only half joking when he remarked, "One time our kitchen served us raisin bread. I have often wondered about those raisins."

Dysentery soon became rife in many units. Everyone seemed to be suffering from "the runs." Coral cuts infected rapidly and refused to heal. Many men developed multiple open sores. About the size of a dime, the sores formed under the arms, around the belt and on the inner parts of the legs.

Mosquitoes were a nuisance, but none were of the malaria or yellow fever carrying types. Even so, they were not to be taken lightly. Corporal Robert Anderson recalled a patrol up the island. "We were attacked by a large horde of very large mosquitoes," he remembered. "They were so ferocious they completely covered our arms and faces, and we beat a hasty retreat out of there. What the Japs couldn't accomplish, the mosquitoes did."

Also causing extreme discomfort were multitudes of tiny gnats which were vicious biters. They were most bothersome during the early morning and late afternoon and evening hours, often appearing in great numbers. Their bites caused small red papules to appear. These often became infected and in extreme cases reached the ulcer stage. Some men slept with their cuffs tightly buttoned in hopes of keeping the gnats out, but short of draining the mangrove swamps where they bred, there was little hope of controlling the pests.

In an effort to curb the exploding fly population, lavish use was made of the newly developed insecticide DDT. Mixed with diesel oil, it was sprayed liberally on breeding spots and other areas. Added to kerosene, it was used to saturate jungle hammocks, nets and similar gear.

Among the more novel experiments was the use of three 15-man sanitary squads. Equipped with portable knapsack sprayers, the squads followed close behind the combat teams spraying corpses, rotted food, latrines and stagnant pools in an effort to control flies and other pests. A large power sprayer was also mounted on a truck, while later in the campaign, DDT was sprayed from aircraft. One Marine recalled that the shooting seemed to taper off during the aerial spraying. "Everybody just kind of let it go," he remarked. "Including the Japanese."

These measures did help to control sickness and disease on Peleliu, although they by no means eliminated the problems. One discovery was that DDT was lethal to adult flies but had virtually no effect on their larva. As a result, flies continued to pose a major nuisance well into the second week of October, when the numbers peaked and then began to go into decline.

NOTE

1. Not to be confused with Hill 300, referred to by the Wildcats as Old Baldy, on the southern end of the pocket.

Chapter 12

THE UMURBROGOL POCKET

One Marine, searching for words to impart the alien quality of the pocket, described it as looking like "the face of the moon defended by Jap troglodytes."

Dug deeply into the coral ridges, the Japanese were indeed like some modern-day—and far more lethal—breed of cave dweller. Safe underground, they waited out American artillery fire and air attacks, emerging only to pick off the exposed Marine riflemen scrambling up the slopes in assault. A Marine officer later described that experience as like fighting along the ridge of a house—only these houses ranged over 100 feet high.

The frustration of knowing the Japanese were sometimes literally underfoot and not being able to do anything about it tried the nerves of even patient men. "Once you got on top of a hill...it was like gettin' on top of an ant nest," remarked a Texas corporal. "You thought you had it made once you were on the hill, but then at night they'd crawl out and try to crawl in the hole with you."

Hungry Marines, perched on the crests, grumbled as the tantalizing aroma of cooking fish and rice drifted up from the cave systems below. "It was damned provoking smelling that Jap food," recalled the CO of 3/7, Colonel Spencer Berger. In Berger's case, irritated Marines finally tied a charge of TNT to a rope and swung it into the cave mouth, blasting it shut along with its well-fed occupants.

But the Japanese were always dangerous. Enemy small-arms fire was particularly accurate, indicating Nakagawa's men had been well drilled in rifle marksmanship. Marines and GIs often were killed or wounded by riflemen 200 to 400 yards away—good shooting under combat conditions.

Close calls were commonplace. Digging into his pack for a jar of instant coffee, a mortar man in Sergeant Linkenfelter's outfit found only powder and shattered glass. Examining his pack more closely, he discovered six bullet holes—in one side and out the other—shot straight through as he hunkered down with his pack on his back. He had not even noticed, there was so much firing going on.

Private First Class Howard Miller recalled two Marines picked off by a sniper as they came through his position in the western ridges. "There was a bush—it was the only bush that was around," he remembered. "We were in a little pillbox, a shell hole right in the ledge, and we told the first guy to come up. He was supposed to put a telephone in this cave...and we told him to get up there and go around that doggone corner [to the cave] and just keep going. Don't stop, you know? Guy stopped, peeked through this bush. He got it. *Boom*, he's dead. We hauled him out. Then, I don't know, it was the next day or a couple of days later, a guy—*boom*—exactly the same thing. Got him right between the eyes."

Assigned to the holding line on the high ground along West Road, two men in Sergeant Robert Askey's artillery outfit also made the mistake of relaxing their guard. "I don't know if they were dozing off or if they weren't watching," recalled Askey, "because we'd been up there maybe four or five days, you know, and nothing had happened. Oh, they'd occasionally take a shot at us or lob a grenade up or something, but nothing physical where they were coming in close contact with us."

For one of the two Marines, the lapse brought sudden death. Armed with a bayonet, a Japanese crept up a 90-foot cliff in the dark and stabbed the artilleryman—a teenaged replacement—right through the eyesocket. The other man in the hole—a veteran who had been with the outfit since Guadalcanal—picked up the Japanese and threw him bodily over the cliff to his death. It was too late for the young recruit.

The Marines retaliated by searching for air vents. The preferred method upon finding one of these was to pour a five-gallon can of gasoline down the hole, followed by a grenade. "That would create quite a little stir," remarked Corporal Vincent Clay, who fought in the ridges with the 7th Marines.

Nevertheless, as the frustrated Marines quickly discovered, the ground was almost entirely in favor of the defense. In military parlance this type of terrain is called "cross-compartmentation." In Peleliu's case, remarked a veteran of the campaign, "criss-cross-compartmentation" would have been a more accurate description of the jumble of ridges, gulches and knobs facing the assault troops.

The parallel ridges allowed concealed Japanese on one ridge to lay down murderous fire on Marines exposed on the crest of an adjacent height. The volume of fire was unbelievable. "It was just *crack crack crack* cracking all over," recalled a sergeant. The steepness of the ridges also prevented the Marines from getting at their enemy in the slopes directly below. There

Map 6.
The Pocket, 17 October

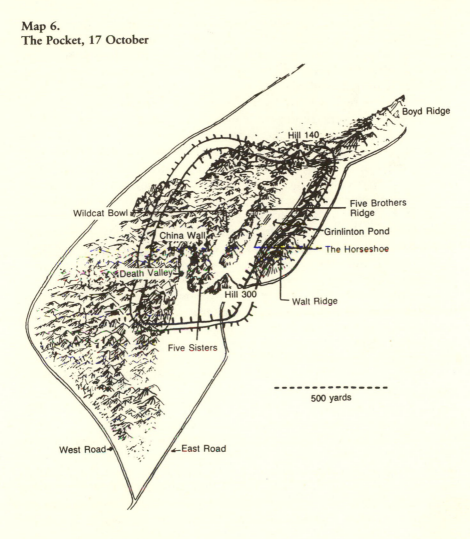

were numerous instances of demolitions teams lowering explosives on ropes over cliffs in an effort to blast caves shut, only to curse as the Japanese reached out and cut the ropes.

Recalled Private First Class James Isabelle of the cave fighting, "We'd get in there with the flamethrowing tanks...seal the damn thing up and dynamite it, and they'd just open another one. Rarely did you see a live Japanese come out. Very, very rarely."

Flat trajectory naval gunfire was useless in this terrain. Massed artillery had little effect on enemy soldiers holed up in deep caves. "It was just like throwing a handful of bee-bees against the wall for all the good it was doin'," remarked a cynical Marine rifleman. A frustrated Marine officer later recalled how an artillery battalion fired 20,000 rounds of 75 mm at a cave 200 yards in front of the 1st Marines "without disturbing appreciably anything below the foliage and topsoil."

Direct fire from individual heavy weapons worked better on caves—there was one bizarre report of a 75 mm gunner sighting in on a lone Japanese soldier at a cave mouth, cutting the man in half at 300 yards—but the battle area was so compressed that the back blast was often more dangerous to the Americans than the actual explosion was to the Japanese. Tanks and LVT-mounted flamethrowers were invaluable, but all too frequently they were unable to operate in the rugged terrain where they were needed most. Pack-type flamethrowers were used so extensively that 4,500 pounds of hydrogen had to be airlifted in to replenish supplies.

Grenade launchers would have been useful against the caves, but most of the men had thrown theirs away after finding the cartridges had been spoiled by the humidity. Division flew in 200 new launchers from the rear echelon and distributed them to the men in the ridges.

Some use was made of Garrett 60 mm shoulder mortars, 27 of which had been distributed to the division for testing. Although somewhat successful, the heavy recoil made them unpopular. The short effective range—not over 125 yards—also made it difficult to get the weapon in a position where it could be used effectively.

The Marines much preferred the lighter bazooka. Detonation problems experienced due to the soft ground during the Cape Gloucester campaign were not a problem on rocky Peleliu, and the Marines used bazookas lavishly against the dug-in Japanese, sometimes in unorthodox fashion.

On one occasion, Corporal Russell Clay's outfit faced a Japanese-held ridge 50 or 60 yards away. Individual Japanese, probably trying to maintain liaison or resupply themselves, had a habit of dodging for cover behind a particular coral boulder. Finally, the Marines targeted a bazooka on the rock, and the next time a Japanese jumped behind it, the bazooka man let loose with a rocket. The boulder shattered "and this Jap helmet flies up in the air about 20 feet," much to the delight of the watching Marines, recalled Clay.

The air arm tried to help. Between D-Day and D plus 14, pilots dropped 62 160-gallon napalm tanks and 25 58-gallon napalm tanks, fired 3,996 rockets and unloaded 157 1,000-pound bombs, 968 500-pound bombs, 307 250-pound bombs and 2,071 100-pound bombs. On a single day—8 October—VMF 114 dropped 35 1,000 pounders on its target area in the pocket.[1]

Unfortunately, the bombs had little material effect on the Japanese deep in their holes. Prisoners taken later said their only effect was to make a big noise. Napalm was equally ineffective, although its sometimes lavish use did not go unnoticed. "The enemy plan seems to be to burn down the central hills post to ashes by dropping gasoline from airplanes," reported Colonel Nakagawa's headquarters.

There was one report of the intense heat driving a small group of the enemy into the open, where they were shot down. Probably the main value of the napalm, however, was that it burned away what was left of the vegetation in the pocket, revealing enemy positions.

As far as the Marines were concerned, the strikes often terrified friend as much as foe. "We were up on the ridges as the navy fighters would come over, and they would release these belly tanks full of napalm, and no precision to them they would just lob-lolly any way," recalled Private First Class M. L. Clayton. "And we were always scared to death they were gonna get on us instead of where they should have been."

Due to the constricted area, some accidents were inevitable. Sergeant Flip Afflito recalled one incident when he and one of his men were talking and watching a plane make a run on the ridges. Afflito saw something come off the airplane. The object—the tail fin of a rocket—hit the other Marine right in the helmet, crushing his skull, not 12 feet away. The dead man had been in Afflito's platoon for two and a half years.

Later, going through the battalion casualty reports, Afflito saw that the Marine's death had been attributed to mortar fire. "You know, it's like the joke about how they gave our cooks chickens and steaks," he remarked, "and by the time we got it, it was hash."

The same terrain that made it so tough to close with the enemy also raised havoc with efforts to evacuate casualties. Very often the carriers on one end would have to hold the stretcher handles over their heads while those on the other held theirs almost to the ground in an effort to keep the stretcher level on the steep slopes.

No one entertained any illusions about Japanese mercy. One day, Eugene Sledge passed by a shallow defile containing three Marines lying on stretchers where they had apparently died before their unit was forced to pull back. Even an advanced state of decomposition could not disguise that the bodies had been badly mutilated by marauding Japanese. One man had been decapitated. His head and severed hands lay on his chest; his penis had been cut off and stuffed in his mouth. The adjacent corpse had been treated similarly, while the third had been chopped to pieces. Scenes like these not only infuriated the Marines, but spurred them to go to any length to save their wounded.

It was in an effort to recover wounded Marines that an 18-year-old Minnesotan won the eighth and last Medal of Honor awarded for action on Peleliu. On 5 October, Private First Class Richard E. Kraus and three other Marines volunteered to try to evacuate a wounded man from the front lines. Making their way forward, the volunteers penetrated some distance before the enemy opened up with an intense barrage of hand grenades, forcing them to take cover and abandon their mission. While returning to the rear, they saw two men approaching who appeared to be Marines. When they demanded the password, one of the "Marines" threw a hand grenade into their midst. Kraus immediately threw himself on the grenade, absorbing the blast and sacrificing his life to save his three buddies.

Unable to maneuver on any large scale within the pocket itself, Colonel Nakagawa resorted to infiltration and small-scale counterattacks to keep his enemies on edge. "We are attempting to defeat the enemy by using our close-quarter combat tactics to the utmost," he informed General Inoue on 30 September.

The persistent attempts at infiltration forced a change in Marine security procedures. The division had originally set up a simple password system whereby the challenge would be any make of American car, with the response being any other make. Thus, a man might challenge, "Ford!" and receive the friendly reply, "Chevrolet." But the Japanese quickly caught on to the system, forcing a return to the old practice of a new password coined for each day.

Tight security and the use of personnel from headquarters, service outfits and other units to reinforce the line at night kept the Japanese away from the most lucrative target—the airfield. Despite at least one report from Colonel Nakagawa stating that his infiltrators set fire to the air base on 6 October and "threw the enemy into confusion," there is no evidence that enemy soldiers ever succeeded in reaching the airfield. Most of the demolition groups were stopped short of the lines, many being blown to pieces by their own explosives.

It was different up in the ridges. "They were pretty active at night," recalled Corporal Russell Clay, "so you didn't get too much sleep. That was one of the problems. We tried to pair up at least a couple of guys in the holes so one could stay awake for a while. But you didn't sleep all that soundly. If you dozed off 30 minutes, it was almost like a night's sleep."

One group of front-line Marines, continually harassed by Japanese who crept in close and threw grenades, devised a novel defense. They covered their foxholes with downward-sloped ponchos. When they heard grenades thump onto the makeshift roofs, they would merely wait until the grenades rolled back off toward the Japanese and then emerge to throw grenades of their own.

One benefit of the high casualties, recalled a Marine, was that there were plenty of spare weapons lying around for the taking. Some kept four or five loaded rifles at hand in their positions, which saved valuable reloading time when things got hot. Anybody moving around after dark was a fair target. "At night, just to keep everybody on their toes, we'd throw grenades just for the hell of it," recalled Corporal Clay. "The Japs . . . if crawling up, well, we'd roll a few grenades down there periodically . . . sometimes you'd hear 'em holler."

A tough kid from Georgia in Clay's outfit actually enjoyed closing with the Japanese hand-to-hand. "He said he was glad we weren't fighting fat-necked Germans, cause he said these little skinny-neck Japs, you could grab 'em by the Adam's apple and it was just like twistin' . . . you know, picking cotton. He'd grab 'em by the arm in kind of a hammer throw and then throw them down the hill. He said if we were fighting fat-necked Germans, we'd a been in trouble." The tough kid from Georgia was killed shortly afterward. The Japanese had some tough kids of their own.

The inexperienced replacements were particularly vulnerable to infiltrators. Assigned four pioneers as replacements in the bitter ridge fighting, Clay put all four in the same hole, figuring they could take care of themselves. During the night, the pioneers apparently all fell asleep—Clay was never certain. What was certain was that a Japanese infiltrator crawled in with a bayonet and hacked three to death before the fourth realized what was happening and managed to shoot him dead.

At daylight, Clay went over to check on the pioneers and found the lone survivor sitting "bug-eyed out of his skull," surrounded by his three dead buddies. The man was in such a state of shock he had to be evacuated.

As the fighting continued on Peleliu, regimental commanders came under increased pressure from division to speed up the operation and put an end to it. General Rupertus, his earlier prediction of a short campaign now a bitter joke, seemed at a loss on how to deal with the protracted enemy resistance. Lieutenant Colonel Harold Deakin, the division personnel officer, came in one day to find the general sitting on his bunk, his head in his hands, apparently in the midst of a deep depression. "This thing has just about got me beat," he lamented. Deakin, previously the butt of Rupertus's eccentric behavior and no great admirer of the general, suddenly found himself with his arm around his superior's shoulder, comforting him.

Bucky Harris, whose handling of the 5th Marines had been superb, later recounted an even more startling incident. Called to Rupertus's headquarters on 5 October, he said he found Rupertus in tears. "Harris, I'm at the end of my rope," said Rupertus. "Two of my fine regiments are in ruins. You usually seem to know what to do and get it done. I'm going to turn over to you everything we have left. This is strictly between us."

Nothing came of the offer—Rupertus could not have turned over his command in any case—but it spoke volumes about the division commander's mental state and left Harris a very thoughtful man.

As the fighting dragged on, Rupertus badgered Harris and his exec to hurry the advance. "Don't lose momentum!" he insisted. For their part, subordinate commanders tried to resist pressure to speed things up, hoping to save already depleted units from further losses that would serve no good purpose. "The men and officers were superb during this last phase, but very, very tired," recalled a staff officer of the 5th Marines.

"Of course you're scared," remembered Private First Class James Isabelle. "Sometimes the fear was overwhelming, but as you're moving forward, your thought is, I'm going to get to cover, and you momentarily lose that fear. And once you're back of the lines, you've got some protection, you know, you'd relax and you'd be so drained—emotionally drained—and just lay there kind of like in a stupor. And then your next thought is when are you going again."

The Marines knew what had to be done, and they did it, but their innocence was long gone. "Every Marine fighting in those hills is an expert," remarked 2/5 commander Major Gordon Gayle. "If he wasn't, he wouldn't be alive."

Fate. She could be good . . . or she could be bad.

"I know the biggest shock I had there," recalled Private First Class Howard Miller of the fighting in the ridges. "We had a boot that came into our outfit before Peleliu, you know, a replacement. His name was H. U. Miller, and I met the kid in the chow line or something. Nice young kid.

"And when I came down out of the hills everybody says, 'Miller, we thought you was dead.' I says, 'What do you mean, dead?' 'Well Miller, you were listed as killed in action.' Well, H. U. Miller got killed.

"It kind of gives you goose pimples, you know? Well, you thank God: I'm glad I'm H. H. Miller, 'cause I'm alive and H. U. Miller's dead. But I still felt . . . my heart went out for this kid. I was 21 years old and this kid was maybe 17, and to me he was just a baby yet, you know?"

Rhode Island artilleryman Private Robert Biron recalled another man in his outfit who had been "hit through the ass." The wound did not appear to be serious, and the injured man was ebullient. "Yo, Jug!" he yelled at Biron. "Yo, Jug! I'm goin' stateside." Biron left him under a tree near some other casualties awaiting evacuation from the beach. When he came by a short time later, the man was dead.

At 0900 on 6 October, within half an hour of arriving in position to relieve elements of the 7th Marines, E Company, 5th Marines launched an attack into the pocket. Colonel Bucky Harris had decided to make his main push from the north, where 2/5 now faced Baldy Ridge and supporting knobs and ridges. The front taken over by 1/5 included Walt and Boyd ridges to the south, which spread the Marines thinly over some 1,200 yards; 3/5 had temporarily been withdrawn to a bivouac area.

Jumping off, E Company pushed westward into the devilish terrain where Captain Shanley's men had met disaster two days earlier. The weather had cleared, and the island was beginning to dry out after the spate of heavy rains. E succeeded in recapturing two of the previously abandoned knobs, but the Japanese took them under fire from other positions. "Not only was further advance impossible, but the men risked having their heads blown off if they so much as raised them above the knob's crest," noted the historian of the campaign.

Bulldozers soon began cutting out an access track for tanks and flame-throwers in preparation for the next push south. At the same time, G Company launched a frontal attack against Baldy's leprous slopes. Harris ordered the attack "only under pressure and with considerable reluctance," fearing unwarranted casualties.

Surprisingly, a platoon-sized group of Marines made it to the top. There, they could not be reinforced because the area was too small to accommodate more men. Armed with nothing heavier than a BAR, the platoon would have been in dire straits after dark. Recognizing the position as untenable, the battalion CO ordered the men back down. "It didn't have any future," he commented laconically.

On 7 October, 3/5 ventured into the Horseshoe following a two and a half hour artillery preparation. Six tanks of the Army's 710th Tank Battalion fired into as many enemy positions as could be located. Several of the tanks were hit by return fire from heavy weapons, but none was seriously damaged. Encouraged, the tanks withdrew at 1045 to replenish fuel and ammunition before returning for another crack at the Japanese.

The second push jumped off at 1215, as Marines protecting the tanks and supported by two LVT flamethrowers attempted to move into a draw off the Horseshoe. Later dubbed "Wildcat Bowl," this area was described—by men who were experts—as "possibly the worst death trap on the island."

The Japanese reacted violently from their positions on the high ground, and the push stalled. Unknown to the Marines, Colonel Nakagawa's head-quarters lay near the northwestern end of the bowl in a deep dual cave in the China Wall. It would be weeks before American forces penetrated far enough to threaten him again.

Meanwhile, Marine/tank teams operated in the Horseshoe itself, knocking out as many enemy caves and positions as possible. There was no intention of trying to hold the Horseshoe—that was patently impossible—but it was hoped that caves containing heavy weapons that had been firing on the airfield and southern perimeter could be knocked out. The teams penetrated 200 yards—the furthest advance into the pocket yet from that direction—before the tanks ran short of ammunition and the force pulled out.

Over the next couple of days, the Marines of 2/5 also prepared method-ically to seize the ground around Baldy. E Company's surprising success on 6 October indicated that the Japanese used the height primarily as an ob-servation post. However, the wooded ridge extending south from the hill was held in force, judging by the amount of fire emanating from this vicinity.

As access was bulldozed for LVT flamethrowers to come up and burn off the vegetation, mortar concentrations were laid down on enemy positions in hopes of softening up the opposition. One of the more novel engineering feats occurred near the northern perimeter. Faced with a sheer cliff blocking approaches from that angle, the Marines bombarded the obstacle with heavy shells. Blast after blast gradually knocked the cliff into a steeply inclined ramp, allowing access from that quarter.

For two days, these preparations continued as engineers labored on a trail to bring tank guns to bear on Ridge 120 and the western face of Boyd. Air attacks with napalm and 1,000-pound bombs also blasted the pocket. Harris continued to resist pressure from division to speed the assault. He was, he liked to say, lavish with his ammunition but stingy with his men's lives.

Evidence of the constant pressure on the pocket was duly noted by 81st Division troops holding down the northern end of the island. Japanese, alone and in small groups, were detected in increasing numbers during the first week of October trying to slip out of the battle area.

The night of 3 October, a Wildcat machine-gun section on the eastern shore north of Radar Hill cut down 20 Japanese who were apparently trying to escape along the reefs to the east. Two nights later, another eight enemy solders were killed. Between 4 and 8 October, the 321st Infantry killed 171 Japanese and took one prisoner.

Meanwhile, Marine Corsairs from VMF–114 scattered leaflets over the ridges on the slim possibility that some Japanese officers could be persuaded to surrender their men:

Officers of the Japanese forces

As you can see if you look at the planes, the material and the ships, your best efforts are not impeding our work. American planes not only bomb you at will, but they also bomb Babelthuap and the other islands north of here. Perhaps you can see the flames. Your comrades to the north have all they can do to help themselves, so how could they help you?

You honor and respect your men, but how can they honor and respect you if you make them die needlessly? Thousands of brave Japanese soldiers before you have realized the futility of death in such circumstances; they will live to raise families and help build a new Japan.

You still have this choice—raise a white flag and come out unarmed. We will give you water, food, shelter and medicine for your wounded.

For all practical purposes, Colonel Nakagawa's force was no threat beyond the pocket itself. There was half-joking talk of simply stringing barbed wire around the pocket, classifying it as a prisoner of war enclosure and ceasing further assault operations. Appealing as this idea might have seemed to the front-line riflemen, it was not to be. The grind against the pocket would continue until the Japanese were completely broken.

Human nature being what it is, the fighting on Peleliu was not without its moments of humor, often black. In the fighting north of the airport, Private Davis witnessed one of the most ridiculous scenes of his combat career when an unflappable forward observer confronted half a squad of very live Japanese with an empty carbine. The observer raised his rifle and clicked the empty chamber. "Bang, bang, I pass," he remarked, turning to the astonished Davis. Another Marine gunned down one of the Japanese; the others disappeared.

Sergeant Carl Stevenson remembered a short, stocky Mexican in his outfit who dressed up in a Japanese sailor's uniform. Then he decided to make a game of it. Making a mock movie camera out of a shell casing and a surveyor's tripod, and fitted with a huge pair of paper buck teeth, the prankster stood by the side of the road, grinding away on his "camera."

"Oh God, I stood right there and just roared," recalled Stevenson. "Well, these trucks would come up with all these Marines on 'em, and he'd be there with his teeth...windin' away...and the damn trucks would come to a screechin' halt and guys hollerin', 'Don't shoot! Don't shoot, dammit! Don't shoot!'"

Sometimes humor came out of sheer terror which suddenly proved unfounded. Plagued with diarrhea, a Marine rifleman got up to relieve himself one morning and stepped squarely on the back of a concealed Japanese. The Marine brought his carbine to bear on the Japanese and squeezed the trigger, only to be rewarded with a hollow click. The Japanese threw a grenade and, when that failed to explode, started after the Marine with his bayonet. The weaponless leatherneck fled toward a BAR man, yelling, "Shoot him!" After what seemed like an eternity, the automatic rifleman emptied most of his magazine into the Japanese at about the belt buckle, nearly cutting the man in half. The terrified, winded Marine asked the BAR man why he had waited so long and was informed by the latter that he wanted to let the Japanese get close enough to see if he could cut him in half. His grim humor found a receptive audience among the other marines, particularly when they found out that the enemy soldier's near victim had filled his skivvies during his mad dash for safety.

Similarly, some of the men in Private Robert Leckie's outfit got a big laugh out of one of their buddies, hit high in the leg by a mortar fragment. Terrified that he had lost the "family jewels," he pleaded with the corpsman, "Are they all right? Quick, tell me—are they all right?"

"Take it easy," replied the corpsman. "It wasn't even close. You got plenty of sack time ahead of you."

The wounded man lay back, smiling. "He was so relieved you'd think he only cut his finger or something," recalled a witness. "I swear he'd have begged the corpsman to shoot him if it had been the other way."

But the classic line—a play on the far-traveling, influential Mrs. Roosevelt—had to have occurred the night Sergeant William Linkenfelter was peering into the darkness up in the forward positions. A couple of Japanese infiltrators tried to move in on the Marines, and Linkenfelter called for an illumination round. As the flare popped greenly to the front, someone a short distance down the line shouted, "Who ordered that flare?" Like an echo, somewhere far down the line, another voice responded, "Eleanor!"

The morning of 9 October, a platoon commanded by Second Lieutenant Robert T. Wattie scaled the pulverized cliff face off West Road and got to the top of a narrow ridge forming the western spur of Baldy. This height, subsequently dubbed Wattie Ridge in honor of its young conqueror, provided direct access to Baldy. In Japanese hands, it also provided a clear field of fire to West Road.

Wattie led his men south along the hill for about 100 yards. They knocked out several Japanese positions before pulling up under heavy fire. This fire came from the ridge to the east and from a large cave located at the head of the box canyon separating the two. Wattie pulled back to let artillery and air work over the cave. Air attack proved too dangerous, due to the proximity of the Marines, but the artillery had better luck. The shells set off a landslide, sealing the cave as effectively as a demolitions team.

As a grim reminder of earlier attempts to penetrate the area, patrols operating in the gulch discovered the rotting remains of 12 men from the 321st Infantry. The group had apparently been caught and massacred more than two weeks before when the Wildcats were trying to find a practicable route of attack to isolate the pocket from northern Peleliu. These 12 had gone in and never come back.

On 10 October, the Marines returned to the attack, supported now by a battery of 105 mm howitzers and an army M–10 mounting a 75 mm and a 37 mm gun which had been bulldozed within range. The preliminary softening up included an artillery barrage which began at dawn and lasted until shortly before 1100.

Returning to the ground they had relinquished the previous day, Wattie's men worked down the ridge and over Baldy, where they ran into a block of Japanese positions. Hand grenades and bullets winged back and forth until the Marines rushed the position and annihilated the Japanese. They then swept the crest, burning out scattered opposition. The entire ridge and Baldy itself were secured by noon.

Wattie's success ended the flanking fire that had destroyed Shanley's men on Ridge 120. Now E Company, launching its assault at 1215, was able to seize that ridge with relative ease. Ridge 3, a semidetached razorback south and slightly east of Baldy, was secured by elements of G Company.

With these successes, the 2d Battalion had managed to seize some of the most difficult terrain in the pocket. Less than four hours later, 50 enemy holdouts came through the lines and surrendered.

Also during the day, a minor mystery was solved. For several days, artillery shells from some unknown point had been landing on Peleliu's southern tip. Reported as enemy, it was now discovered that the projectiles were "friendly." Fired into the pocket from positions on the northern end of the island, some of the shells were apparently ricocheting off the ridges and landing on the southern end of the island.

During the night, interdictory fire was put down as close as 25 yards from the Marine lines to keep the Japanese from closing in on the newly won ground. No enemy counterattacks materialized.

The survivors of Sergeant Flip Afflito's B Company platoon came out of the ridges on 10 October. Nobody was smiling. It had been raining, and the skies were as leaden as their mood. They trudged through the cement-like coral mud, hollow-cheeked and vacant-eyed, beaten down to their socks. The BAR man, a 240-pound Irishman from the state of Washington, was particularly dejected; taking off his cartridge belt, he exposed a four-inch-high red ring around his waist where the skin had chafed completely away.

Afflito took a piece of string and knotted it like a long tie, letting it hang to his ankles. A twig placed in the shoulders of his shirt added to the rude facsimile of a zoot suit. He had thrown his helmet away; folding back the brim of his soft hat, he launched into an exaggerated jitterbug for the men coming off the ridge. The Marines started laughing. Some were crying. Then they were laughing and crying at the same time. Spirits picked up noticeably.

"Flip," remarked Afflito's company commander, "if there was a medal I could give you for boosting morale, I'd give you the highest one."

Afflito shrugged it off. "I made an asshole out of myself just to get a smile out of these guys," he said later. "You know, when you're in charge, it does something to you."

The next morning, 2/5 seized the remainder of Baldy Ridge, then jumped off against Hill 140. Attacking through a ravine, F Company bypassed the strongly defended northern slope and worked its way up the height from the west. The Marines made rapid headway and managed to secure the height by 1500.

The hill was considered important since its possession would allow a heavy weapon to place direct fire on the nearest of the Five Brothers and part of the Horseshoe. It would also allow fire down the draw between Walt and Boyd, possibly converting it into an avenue into the heart of the pocket.

2/5 spent the rest of the afternoon mopping up enemy caves overrun in the attack. This resulted in a good scare when an LVT flamethrower inadvertently detonated a 12-inch naval shell in one of the caves. What it was doing there was anybody's guess, but the resulting blast blew away a good-sized chunk of the hillside. Fortunately, only one Marine was injured.

"The enemy was very thick throughout our newly occupied areas, and the mopping up was a bloody procedure. Sixty of the enemy were killed in a very short time," according to the battalion operations report. While not escaping unscathed, 2/5 made out fairly well in the assault. All told, the battalion lost only two killed and 10 wounded taking Hill 140, a small price for such a key position—unless, of course, you happened to be one of the men hit.

Aware of the value of Hill 140, the Japanese staged a counterattack that night, but now the Marines held the heights on the northern perimeter, and the attack was beaten off without undue difficulty. On the morning of 12 October, exhausted Marines of 2/5 were relieved by their only slightly less fatigued buddies in the 3d Battalion.

The relief did not go smoothly. The line held by 2/5 was in the form of a deep salient, and the Japanese had the positions under heavy sniper fire. Twenty-seven-year-old Captain Andy "Ack Ack" Haldane, the well-liked commander of K Company, found the troops he was to relieve so pinned down that the machine gunners were sighting along the underside of the barrel. Haldane raised his head to examine the terrain and died instantly as a bullet pierced his brain. Before the movement was complete, 22 Marines had been hit, and the Japanese had managed to reinfiltrate some areas.

Just to the west, the Marines were also hard-pressed as a platoon from 3d Battalion tried to relieve a 2/5 platoon in the high ground above West Road. The Japanese waited until the platoon moved in, then enfiladed both units with heavy rifle and machine-gun fire. The Marines withdrew under cover of smoke grenades.

At 0800 on 12 October, General Geiger moved his CP ashore and declared the assault and occupation phases of the operation at an end. The announcement marked the passage of command from the task force afloat to an area commander—in this case, from Rear Admiral George Fort to Admiral J. H. Hoover, commander of the Forward Area Forces. CinPac directed that the Marines were to be relieved. 81st Division troops would liquidate the remnants of Colonel Nakagawa's garrison.

The directive from CinPac presumably came as a relief to Geiger. According to one source, he had been after Rupertus for days to replace the battered 5th Marines with fresh army troops. Rupertus continued to demur. Geiger could have ordered Rupertus to comply—or relieved him outright—but at this late date, either course would have caused a furor and ruined or seriously jeopardized the division commander's career. Ironically, within a year, the question of Rupertus's career and reputation would become a rather moot point.

Two other significant developments occurred on 12 October. The first was a new map which showed the terrain in the pocket as it actually was, not as it had appeared to be in the old aerial survey taken when the ridges were obscured by vegetation. A hurried sketch job put together by the intelligence section of the 5th Marines, the map suffered from inaccuracies concerning relative elevations and deceptive contour lines. Still, it was reasonably accurate on the horizontal plane and far superior to anything the Marines had had in hand previously.

Now, place names began to become more standardized, although some injustices occurred. For instance, Boyd Ridge, seized by Major Hunter Hurst's 3/7, was named after Lieutenant Colonel R. W. Boyd because he was occupying the elevation when the mapping party happened along a week later. Similarly, Walt Ridge was named after Lieutenant Colonel Lew Walt, although the ridge had been the site of Captain Pope's heroic stand on D plus 4 and was finally seized by Lieutenant Colonel Berger's 2/7 on 3 October. According to Berger, "comment was pungent" when his men learned of the ridge's new name. Pope, arguably the most legitimate candidate for the honor, dismissed the whole question as trivial. "I couldn't care less," he remarked later.

The other significant occurrence was the positioning of artillery on the high ground. With plenty of sweat, rope and tackle, 68 artillerymen spent eight solid hours hauling a disassembled 75 mm pack howitzer to the top of Hill 140. One part of their burden weighed over 300 pounds; the lightest was 75 pounds. Once up the ridge, the gun was muscled forward, reassembled just before night fell and dug in behind sandbags to fire on the western base of Walt Ridge and into the Horseshoe. In honor of their CO, Major George Bowdoin of Baltimore, the Marines dubbed their position "Bowdoin's Bump."

That night, Japanese infiltrators crept up the face of Hill 140 to within a few feet of the gun, tossing grenades at the crew until daylight. One Marine's leg was blown off—it was hours before he could be evacuated down off the ridge by basket stretcher—but morning found the crew still in possession of the gun.

Laying the piece on the entrance of a cave at the foot of Walt Ridge, the Marines were unable to dig the trail into the hard coral, so they piled some rocks on it and fired their first round. It hit the cave, but the gun recoiled sharply, injuring one man and slipping out of position. The gunner sent for sandbags, packed the gun in tightly and subsequently fired 11 rounds into the cave.

A second gun was placed in the southeastern sector manned by a scratch group of troops who referred to themselves as "infantillery," commanded by Lieutenant Colonel Edson A. Lyman. Marines had noticed what appeared to be high-ranking Japanese on the opposite point from time to time. Replete with white gloves, these officers had been seen studying the terrain through binoculars. This led to the suspicion that the Japanese command post was located in the vicinity.

The first rounds seemed to verify that theory. The fire "routed out a covey of Nips," reported Lyman. About a dozen Japanese were seen jumping and sliding off the eastern side of the hill to escape the shelling. Soon after, the gun crew was taken under heavy small-arms fire from a distance of only 75 yards.

The Marine crew kept shooting, but by the time it had fired 40 rounds, one man had been hit and, as Lyman noted, "it was deemed expedient to secure." Two more Marines were picked off at daybreak—shot through the head by Japanese snipers from just across the canyon—and it was decided to halt further artillery operations from the position.

Another novel maneuver on 12 October occurred at the Five Sisters at dusk. This took the form of a small combat patrol which attempted to counter-infiltrate and go into concealed positions on the Five Sisters. Led by Lieutenant Roy O. Larsen of C Company, 5th Marines, the patrol moved out as artillery attempted to distract the Japanese by shelling the Horseshoe. The plan was to get onto the hills and dig in for the night. The patrol managed to creep up to a saddle between Sisters 1 and 2 when it bumped into a group of about 35 Japanese. An enemy grenade scattered the Marine patrol.

By now, the Marines were having serious doubts about the wisdom of their foray. "There were a great many more Japs in the hills, as they could be heard talking and sliding around in the coral," reported the regimental war diary.

With his force scattered and facing large numbers of Japanese, Larsen discretely withdrew.

Over the previous nine days, the Marines had managed to push 200 yards deeper into the pocket and narrow the north-south axis by something like 400 yards, reducing the pocket area by 30 to 40 percent. Pressed into an area measuring less than a half mile square, the generally optimistic Japanese were also beginning to admit the worst. "At present a fierce combat and severe artillery fire is taking place with results unknown, "Colonel Nakagawa notified General Inoue. "A unit of the enemy penetrated into Suifuzon [Boyd Ridge and the northern perimeter of the pocket]. They also attacked with flamethrowers attached to tanks."

Despite that admission, the Japanese survivors retained considerable muscle. On the evening of 13 October, Nakagawa reported his troop strength at 1,150, including naval personnel. This force possessed 13 machine guns, 500 rifles with 20,000 rounds of ammunition, 12 grenade launchers with 150 rounds, a 20 mm automatic gun with 50 rounds, an antitank gun with 350 rounds, a 70 mm howitzer with 120 rounds, 1,300 hand grenades and 40 antitank mines.

Their strategy remained simple but effective. As 14th Division Chief of Staff Colonel Tada later remarked, "The situation closely resembled a contest between a large man armed with a spear and a small man armed with a short sword. The man armed with the short sword must crowd in close to the large man so that his spear is useless. We had to attempt to infiltrate into the American lines to render American air attacks, naval bombardments and tank attacks ineffective. We did not believe that this method of attack could defeat air and sea power, but we believed that the great number of American losses would cause them to think that the price was not commensurate with the value of [Peleliu] and therefore withdraw."

The Marines of 3/5 greeted the morning of 13 October with bleary eyes. Enemy attempts to infiltrate and retake Hill 140 during the night had been turned back, the Japanese leaving another 15 dead among the carrion in the rocks.

Overhead, high above the stench of rotting bodies, Captain Earl J. Wilson circled in a grasshopper observation plane, waiting to view a napalm strike on the pocket. With the safe drop area measuring only 300 by 100 yards, the airmen sweated every strike, knowing a three-second error would put the flaming gas on their own people.

Napalm was a fairly new innovation, and no one wanted to take any chances with the volatile mixture. As Wilson observed, orders to the air crews directed, "If you can't get rid of your bomb, get off the island and hit the silk. Don't land with that stuff."

Looking down, Wilson could see the Marines in their holes and behind barricades waiting for the strike. Just to the south—over what seemed an impossibly short distance—the Marine Corsairs were taxiing into line, ready to take off. The first ship charged down the runway and lifted into the air, its belly tank fire bomb plainly visible beneath. The others rose and circled over the target area for a last look before the strike.

The first ship, piloted by Robert F. "Cowboy" Stout of Fort Laramie, Wyoming, a six-plane ace and skipper of the "Death Dealers" squadron, barrelled in at better than 140 knots. Making a sharp banking turn, he slid in over the target at less than 150 feet. When it looked as if he would scrape his belly on the sharp coral, he slid the Corsair to the side and cut his bomb loose. The oval cylinder tumbled end over end in the air, hit the top of the ridge, skidded for half a second, then blew.

Watching from the grasshopper, Wilson noted, "A wall of fire boiled down over the face of the cliff, while hundreds of fiery balls rushed furiously out from the impact. At the same time, a mass of thick greasy smoke coiled up into the air and hung like crepe over Dead Man's Gulch." Plane after plane roared in until the entire ridge seemed to be bathed in flame.

Then came trouble. Lieutenant Nicholas J. Virgets of New Orleans could not get his bomb loose. Flying out over the ocean, he pushed his Corsair into a dive at better than 400 knots, succeeding in attracting a couple of patrol planes which made two passes at him before getting the word. A destroyer waited below, while a Black Cat rescue plane hovered nearby. Waiting back at the airfield, pilots and air crews heard Virgets's voice over the radio. "Here goes nothing. Hope that [destroyer] has ice cream and cake for supper."

Virgets got out of the cockpit and popped his chute. The pilotless Corsair zipped by him, made three wobbly *chandelles*, missed the waiting destroyer by about 30 feet and exploded into the water. Three sharks cruised by before the Louisianan was picked up and brought aboard the destroyer, where he was read the riot act for nearly sending the ship to the bottom with his pilotless plane. Putting that behind him, he was just reaching for his ice cream when the crash boat arrived to take him back to the beach.

Meanwhile, the 5th Marines were following in the wake of the napalm attack. On the heels of the strike at 0915, K Company pushed a patrol into the jagged terrain near the West Road line. Protected by artillery and mortar fire, the patrol ventured 75 yards into this previously unexamined terrain without meeting resistance. A patrol from I Company also pushed 150 yards without resistance.

Basing their plans on this reaction—or lack of it—I Company attacked on 14 October, moving against the western section of the pocket, where patrols had been unopposed the previous day. The attack was preceded by a napalm strike and heavy mortar barrage. Now alert, the Japanese subjected the advance to heavy small-arms fire, but the Marines advanced 250 yards by late afternoon, pulling abreast of the northernmost of the Five Brothers, 150 to 200 yards west of the China Wall.

Meanwhile, supported by LVT flamethrowers, what was left of Lieutenant Colonel John J. Gormley's 1/7 had advanced west of the Five Sisters, parallel to the containing line. On the next day, the battalion penetrated 50 yards into Death Valley and on the third day advanced up the next draw to the west. As a result of these combined pushes, the Umurbrogol Pocket was reduced to an area about 400 yards wide and less than half a mile long.

This accomplishment marked the end of major fighting on Peleliu for the battered Marines. Orders called for the relief of the 5th Marines effective 0800, 15 October. The U.S. Army was taking over.

Up in the Umurbrogol, the Wildcats filed past a mortar position manned by the 5th Marines. Squatting on his helmet, one of the grimy leathernecks cast a skeptical eye over the newcomers. An awful lot of the dogfaces seemed to be wearing glasses, he observed to his buddies. Eyeglasses were unusual among front-line Marines.

"We sure are glad to see you guys," a mortarman remarked to one of the passing riflemen.

The man grinned tightly. "Thanks," he said with an obvious lack of enthusiasm.

Also watching the relief on Hill 140 was Lieutenant Tom Stanley, who had taken command of K/3/5 after Captain Haldane was killed on 12 October. Stanley was appalled at the quality of the men in the 81st Division.

"They were old men," he recalled, "they were 15 years older, on the average, than the men they were relieving. I felt sorry for them. Some of them wearing eyeglasses. Some 115, 118 pounds—well, hell, our own kids were no bigger than that, but they'd been in the middle of a 30-day campaign. But these guys that relieved us, I thought it was a crying shame. They had no more business being on that island than the man in the moon."

That afternoon, Stanley's outfit finally got out of the ridges after 30 days of combat. The outfit took its last casualty on the way out when an unlucky private first class from Lumberton, Mississippi, was cut down by a Japanese mortar shell as he left his position to go to the rear. He died on the spot.

Over the next two weeks, the 5th and 7th Marines were taken off Peleliu for the voyage back to Pavuvu. Off in the distance, the Marines could hear the rattle of machine-gun fire as the 81st Division kept up the pressure on the pocket.

3/7 and 1/7 boarded the *Sea Sturgeon* at Purple Beach and left for Pavuvu on 22 October. 2/7 was less fortunate: their vessel, the old Dutch merchant ship *Sloterdyke*, left on time only after the weary Marines helped with the loading. The 5th Marines sailed for Pavuvu on 30 October on the *Sea Runner* and two smaller vessels. If they had not quite finished the job, they had done as much—or more—as could be humanly expected.

"On 12 October, we had everything on Peleliu that was ever used by anybody," observed General O. P. Smith. "We had the beaches, we had the airfield, we were using everything that we ever wanted to use. All we didn't have was this damn pocket."

Afterward, someone with a mind for statistics totaled up the amount of ammunition the 1st Marine Division expended on Peleliu:

13,319,488	rounds of .30 caliber (carbine, rifle, BAR),
1,524,300	rounds of .45 caliber (pistol, submachine gun),
693,657	rounds of .50 caliber (machine gun),
97,596	rounds of 60 mm mortar,
55,264	rounds of 81 mm mortar,
13,500	rifle grenades,
116,262	hand grenades,
65,000	rounds of 75 mm pack howitzer,
55,000	rounds of 105 mm howitzer,
8,000	rounds of 155 mm howitzer,
5,000	rounds of 155 mm gun.

According to those figures, to kill each of the over 10,000 Japanese soldiers on Peleliu required approximately:

1,331   rounds of .30 caliber,
  152   rounds of .45 caliber,
   69   rounds of .50 caliber,
    9   rounds of 60 mm mortar,
    5   rounds of 81 mm mortar,
    1   rifle grenade,
   10   hand grenades,
    6   rounds of 75 mm pack howitzer,
    5   rounds of 105 mm howitzer,
    1   round of 155 mm howitzer,
  1/2   round of 155 mm gun...

or a statistical average of 1,589 1/2 rounds of heavy and light ammunition.

The Japanese exacted a heavy price in return. Upon leaving Peleliu, the 1st Marine Division reported losing 1,252 killed in action, 5,142 wounded in action and 73 missing in action and presumed dead. Of the rifle regiments, the 1st Marines had suffered most heavily with 1,749 casualties, followed by the 7th with 1,497 and the 5th with 1,378. The rifle battalions had lost a total of 385 officers dead or wounded.

Commanding C Company, 5th Marines, Captain John McLaughlin had landed on Peleliu with 6 officers and 230 men. When C Company left, it numbered only 40 men and McLaughlin was the sole remaining officer. Tragically, the last casualty in the 5th Marines was a sergeant accidentally shot in the stomach by a Marine who had neglected to unload his submachine gun before embarking on the transport vessel. The noncom died.

Private Eugene Sledge's company had only 85 men left unhurt out of a normal complement of 235—a 64 percent casualty rate. The survivors were hard, a few callous beyond belief. Some carried gold teeth they had pried from the mouths of their dead enemies. One Marine had carried around a shriveled hand severed from a Japanese corpse before his comrades finally persuaded him to toss it away.

Sledge was deeply affected by his experiences on Peleliu. The memories would haunt him for years afterward. Now, staring at Peleliu's malevolent ridges from the rail of the merchant troopship *Sea Runner*, he asked Gunnery Sergeant Elmo Haney what he thought of the campaign.

Sledge half expected Haney, a veteran whose experience went back all the way to World War I, to retort with some old salt put-down. Instead, the old gunnery sergeant looked at him and blurted, "Boy, that was terrible. I ain't never seen nothin' like it. I'm ready to go back to the States. I've had enough after that."

And still it wasn't over.

NOTE

1. During its 37 days of action on Peleliu, General James Moore's 2d MAW flew 1,174 sorties and dropped 186 tons of bombs on enemy positions.

Chapter 13

On 14 October U.S. personnel stripped a notebook from a dispatch case on a decayed Japanese body 1,200 yards northwest of Peleliu's former airport administration building. It had belonged to Platoon Sergeant Ineda of the 346th Independent Battalion. Entries listed the 17 men and 8 laborers in his command. The last entry, dated 18 September, reported in commendable detail that three had been killed, one hit in the stomach and two in the face. Four more had been wounded, one in the right front thigh, one in the left upper thigh, one in the right chest and one in the lower stomach. Sergeant Ineda had not been able to enter the next statistic—his own death—and the notebook remained on his corpse until found almost a month later.

Ineda's notebook was evidence that the Japanese were being hurt, even though that fact might not have been obvious to American troops scrabbling in the upturned coral. A 27-year-old Japanese corporal captured on 10 October confirmed heavy loses. Only six men from his company of the 2d Regiment had survived to escape into the hills, he told interrogators. Those who could not walk out under their own power had killed themselves with grenades.

Other information indicated that the commanding officers of both the 1st and 2d Battalions, 2d Regiment had been killed in action by 6 October. Some supplies and equipment were also running short. A directive from a Major Iida commented on a lack of helmet covers and directed close assault personnel without covers to obtain them from injured comrades before going into combat.

"Since hand grenades are to be conserved," added the major, "and we should have faith in our ability to hit the target the first time, no man should carry more than three grenades in hand-to-hand combat."

Still another document, this one emanating from the 15th Regiment, indicted that some Japanese liaison personnel were attempting to avoid combat by returning to headquarters without consulting their officers.

Nevertheless, the Japanese were far from finished. The action of the 5th and 7th Marines from 29 September through 6 October had compressed the pocket into a rough oval. While relatively small—about 300 yards east to west and 450 north to south—the nightmarish terrain made it "a natural fortress," as the 81st Division historian so aptly pointed out.[1]

To deal with the perimeter, the 81st Division deployed 3/321 to the east along the crests of Walt and Boyd ridges, with positions extending south to the entrance of the Horseshoe. 1/321 held Hill 140 along the northern perimeter, a line roughly parallel to West Road. Finally, 1/323, which arrived 14 October from Ulithi, was subsequently assigned to hold the southern edge in the area of the Five Sisters and Death Valley.

The Wildcats had already had a bitter taste of Peleliu. During the period from 23 September to 20 October, when command of the operation officially passed to the 81st Division, the 321st Infantry lost 98 men killed and 468 wounded. The Wildcats had killed more than 1,500 Japanese and captured 108.

The actual number of Japanese still waiting in the jumble of ridges, gullies and caves was unknown. Pressed by the 81st Division staff for a rough estimate, the 1st Marine Division staff put the number at about 500. Other guesses ran to a maximum of perhaps 1,200 enemy holdouts.

The latter number appears to be the most accurate. Japanese sources indicate that the Marines killed between 850 and 1,000 enemy from 29 September to 16 October, leaving about 1,000 Japanese alive in the pocket as the 321st Infantry moved back in. On 13 October, Colonel Nakagawa reported a total strength of 1,150 men, including naval personnel. Three days after the Wildcats took over the perimeter, he informed Koror, "Our total garrison units number about 700 soldiers, including the slightly wounded." Six days later he reported, "Garrison units number about 500 still able to fight." No one doubted that they would.

The Wildcats did not get off to an auspicious start after taking over from the Marines. At about 1500, 16 October, 2/321 attempted to seize Brother 1 with an assault from its positions on Hill 140. This was the next peak south of Hill 140 and the northernmost of the Five Brothers.

The mission was assigned to a G Company platoon under covering fire from F Company, located on a ridge just west of Hill 140. Clambering down into the deep ravine, the platoon reached the valley floor, where it was swept by withering machine-gun and rifle fire. The Japanese positions were in defilade from the Wildcats' supporting weapons, rendering the covering fire useless.

The platoon quickly lost three killed and a dozen wounded, including the company commander, Lieutenant Jack Smith, who had come forward to ramrod the attack. The infantrymen pulled out in a hurry, leaving behind some of their dead and wounded. A sergeant led two men out and retrieved two of the wounded who were lying exposed to enemy fire. The noncom then returned to cover the withdrawal with an automatic rifle.

Staff Sergeant Harry Courtemanche was less fortunate. Observing that Smith had been seriously wounded and was in great pain and in need of medical attention, he scrambled through the hail of enemy fire to obtain aid. While returning with medical assistance, he was fatally wounded. Smith survived, but the dead and some of the wounded could not be retrieved until after dark, so fierce was the enemy fire sweeping the draw.

Indicative of the Marines' diminishing role in the campaign, tactical command of operations in the Umurbrogol passed to Colonel Dark of the 321st Infantry at midday on 17 October. General Rupertus remained in overall command, but his departure was clearly drawing near.

1/321 was already in action when the transfer became official, having attacked south at 0700. By noon, the leading elements had gained a little more than 100 yards against light resistance. The first significant resistance cropped up in the early afternoon. The lead company had struggled forward another 50 yards when fire from a Japanese pillbox and nearby caves stopped the push. Efforts to suppress the positions, located on the second of the roughly parallel ridges behind Hill 140 and West Road, exposed the Wildcat flank and rear to weapons emplaced on the Five Brothers. Compounding the infantrymen's problems, some of the caves appeared to be protected by sliding steel doors. The effort to advance was speedily abandoned.

Meanwhile, 2/321 again failed to get across the ravine to Brother 1. When this effort stalled, other elements of the battalion, supported by tanks from the 710th Tank Battalion, ventured into Mortimer Valley[2] through the draw between Walt and Boyd, hoping to reduce Brothers 1 and 2 from the east.

As a bulldozer scratched a tank road through the draw, a Japanese soldier rushed up and slapped a magnetic mine against the vehicle, blowing himself to pieces in the process. Another such attempt was thwarted when Private Jeff Rhodes wrested a magnetic mine away from another suicidally minded Japanese. As Rhodes dashed away to get rid of the mine, his companions dispatched the Japanese.

No significant progress was made, but tanks and flamethrowers knocked out some caves along the western base of Walt Ridge and the eastern side of Brother 1. An estimated 40 Japanese were killed. Shortly after dark, the enemy retaliated with a mortar barrage on Hill 140, causing a number of Wildcat casualties.

The Wildcats made an all-out effort against the Five Brothers on 18 October. Tanks and LVT flamethrowers again crawled up the gap between

Walt and Boyd Ridges. A platoon of the 88th Chemical Weapons Battalion plastered the ridge with 4.2-inch and 81 mm mortar fire to keep the Japanese in their holes.

Following the mortar barrage south, E Company scrambled to the top of Brother 1. About 45 minutes later, elements of the company also made it to the top of Brother 2, 75 yards to the south. Hoping to exploit his gains before the Japanese regained their balance, the CO of 2/321, Colonel Peter Clainos, sent F Company past E to seize Brother 3. This was accomplished at 1315. Then the roof fell in.

As F Company tried to organize its position on the open crest, it was firmly pinned down by machine-gun and mortar fire from Brothers 4 and 5, the southwestern tip of Walt Ridge and the Five Sisters. Artillery fire and napalm had long since blasted off any vegetation on the knobs. Without cover, unable to dig into the hard coral and without time to bring sandbags forward, the Wildcats now found themselves frightfully exposed.

At 1450, a Japanese counterattack was observed advancing northward from Brothers 4 and 5. Despite an effort to get reinforcements forward to help F Company, the Japanese were not to be stopped. The counterattack hit Brother 3 at 1600 and by 1700 had sent 2/321 scrambling back down from all three knobs.

Some of the Wildcats fled by sliding down the steep slopes to the Horseshoe below, then worked out through the draw. The others withdrew northward and set up defenses at the base of Brother 1 for the night. Volunteers, including ammunition carriers, ventured back to the fire-swept ridge and rescued what wounded they could find. Those who could not be found contributed to the 321st's casualties for the preceding 24-hour period: 15 enlisted men killed, 46 men and two officers wounded.

While the Wildcats took their first blows around the Brothers, the 3d Battalion, 7th Marines also suffered through a last piece of bad luck in the final Marine ground action on Peleliu.

Late the preceding afternoon, General Rupertus had committed I Company, just south of the pocket, to clear up some infiltrators sniping from caves they had reoccupied in the area of Company E, 1st Medical Battalion. Going into combat on such short notice, I Company was not fully supplied with ammunition. The Marines entered into a brief fire fight, then remained in place to protect the service troops.

At 0630 the next morning, L Company replaced I. Four and a half hours later, L reported that the enemy was infiltrating the area in greater strength than anticipated and had taken position in 12 cave sites. A tank was sent to help out. Just before 1400, the tank struck a mine and burned. Two of the crew, both badly burned, managed to escape, but the rest died. Among the casualties was Captain Harry W. Jones, the L Company CO who had taken command following the death of Captain Shanley. Jones was killed while directing the tank's fire on enemy cave positions.

His death continued the run of bad luck suffered by 3d Battalion rifle company commanders. Of the four who served in that capacity during the Peleliu operation, three were killed in action and one was badly wounded.

During the afternoon, 37 mm guns were brought up to knock out the enemy positions, but some Japanese continued to resist as night fell. The next morning, L Company was relieved by army troops. Five days later, the battalion was at sea, headed away from Peleliu forever. Behind them, Captain Jones lay in the sands of Peleliu's still-expanding cemetery, the last Marine infantry officer to be killed during the campaign.

Among the few Japanese military personnel captured on Peleliu was Superior Private Takeo Sugimara, seized near the sunken barges off the island's northern tip on 16 October by Marines of 2/5. A former chicken farmer from Osaka, the 24-year-old had arrived on Peleliu in May as a member of a grenade-launcher squad of the 2d Platoon, 2d Company, 1st Battalion, 2d Regiment. His platoon had subsequently been trained to ride the garrison's tanks into battle. Only the grenade-launcher squad was exempted from this duty, a circumstance that undoubtedly saved Sugimara's life, since none of the tanks nor infantry riders returned from the counterattack across the airfield on the afternoon of 15 September.

His squad was subsequently taken over by the maintenance platoon and organized into a close-assault unit. In that capacity, Sugimara took part in one raid against U.S. tanks. Their success was apparently less than anticipated, for he and other stragglers soon found themselves dodging U.S. patrols in the mangrove swamps off Purple Beach. Moving by night and hiding by day, they finally emerged by a road, where they waited two nights without seeing any American tanks, although they heard the sound of tank engines.

Out of food, the stragglers crept up into the ridges and found shelter in a cave with about 200 other men. On 23 September, Sugimara was wounded in the right foot and immobilized. The next day, tanks attacked his cave and killed 50 to 60 of the men hiding inside. Most of the rest died soon afterward in an attack against American tanks and machine guns, leaving only enough men to defend the cave itself, which was built on two levels and had two entrances.

On 8 October, having regained use of his wounded foot, Sugimara left the cave with three companions. One was killed just as he left the cave mouth, the other two were killed in the water when Sugimara was captured.

Sugimara was the rare exception—a Japanese who gave up voluntarily. Hopes that Japanese morale might be cracking remained unfulfilled as the Wildcats faced their cornered enemy on Peleliu. Surrender leaflets dropped on the enemy facing the 1st and 2d Battalions brought no results: the enemy presumably put them to the same "sanitary" application that Marines reserved for Japanese leaflets.

A laborer captured during the second week of October said he had occupied a cave with about 100 Japanese officers and men. The officers had killed themselves as the Americans closed in. U.S. propaganda leaflets and voice attempts to induce surrender were laughed at by the army regulars, who were determined to fight it out or commit suicide, said the POW. The POW's assessment would prove correct, although efforts continued to persuade holdouts to surrender.

Linguists were called in again on 18 October, when a Japanese was spotted in front of 1/321 with what appeared to be a white flag. The Wildcats brought up an interpreter with a loudspeaker, but while the Japanese suspended fire during the broadcast, none came forward to surrender.

The enemy's obstinance could be attributed to the famous Japanese fighting spirit, but fear may also have played a role: POWs told a Nisei interrogator that Japanese soldiers on Peleliu had been warned that they would be castrated and subjected to other tortures if captured by the Americans.

During 19 and 20 October, the Wildcats confined themselves primarily to sealing caves and reorganizing for another attempt to seize the Five Brothers. A volunteer patrol from the 3d Battalion ventured up the knobs to recover any weapons that might have been left and to be sure that all the wounded had gotten out. If any wounded had been left, they were long dead by the time the patrol arrived.

Colonel Clainos also requested Marine Corsairs to drop napalm on the Brothers. Due to the proximity of the GIs, 16 Corsairs dropped 16 unfused tanks, each containing 30 gallons of incendiary fluid. After the Corsairs droned off, 4.2 white phosphorus and high explosive mortar shells were lobbed into the area to ignite the tanks. "The napalm was very effective against Japanese snipers hiding in trees," noted the division operations report.

The heat drove some Japanese into the open around Brothers 3 and 4, where they were picked off, but it did not soften up the opposition long enough to permit a successful ground assault against the Five Brothers.

During the night of 19 October, a Company E platoon commanded by Lieutenant William Sutherland witnessed a bizarre scene. Dug in along the base of Hill 140, the Wildcats heard a fife or flute from up in the hills. Soon afterward, a U.S. flare revealed two or three small animals passing from one cave to another along the side of Walt Ridge. Sutherland woke members of his platoon, and all observed the animals, which were thought to be monkeys. It was speculated that they were being used by the Japanese to facilitate their defense—a bizarre development if true—but no satisfactory explanation was ever found. That same night, a few miles to the south on Angaur, Major Ushio Goto finally met his end.

For nearly a month, Goto and a dwindling band of survivors had been resisting from a pocket of broken high ground on Angaur's southwest corner. For individuals, some of the fighting here had been as difficult as anything on Peleliu. On 22 September, Colonel Benjamin Venable, CO of the 322d RCT, had his arm nearly severed by enemy antitank fire. The captain in command of B Company was killed leading his troops on 5 October; the CO of 1/322 was killed by a sniper on 17 October; while there was also a steady toll of noncoms and lower ranks.

But the grinding American assault was having its effect. Outnumbered and outgunned, able to hold out only by virtue of the strong natural defensive terrain, the Japanese were being gradually worn down. The few Japanese prisoners taken said the survivors were short of food, reduced to obtaining drinking water from the brackish marshes and from pools of rainwater. Ammunition was also running low.

Seeing the flash of weapons and hearing the sounds of heavy combat across the water, Colonel Nakagawa reported to Koror on 10 October that "judging from the flare bombs and other indications, it is certain that our garrison units in the northwestern [Angaur] hills are annihilating the enemy in close-quarter combat." Eight days later, Major Goto's survivors had been backed into an area less than 5,000 yards square.

On the nights of 18 and 19 October U.S. forces destroyed two feeble counterattacks. Among the corpses was Major Goto. A prisoner revealed that the major had ordered his few surviving men to slip through American lines to the shore and construct a raft to make an escape attempt.

The Japanese were finished. The casualty rate said it all. On 21 October, the Wildcats killed 29 Japanese, took 10 prisoners and watched four others commit suicide at a cost of only two Americans killed and three wounded. More stragglers were mopped up over the next couple of days, and by 23 October, the Angaur Pocket had been secured.

The price paid had been low from day to day, but far from inconsequential when totaled. During the fighting for the Angaur Pocket from 1 to 23 October, 58 officers and enlisted men had been killed and 386 wounded, bringing the total for the campaign to 196 killed and 1,480 wounded. But enemy losses were more severe. Between 1 and 23 October, approximately 225 Japanese were killed and over 50 prisoners were taken. Final estimates of Japanese casualties were 1,338 killed and 59 captured, a figure that tallied closely with garrison strengths listed in captured documents—including Goto's defense plan and diary—which were picked up by U.S. intelligence.

Meanwhile, development of Angaur as a base was already well underway. The first plane, a C–47, landed on the new airstrip on 17 October. Bombing raids on the Philippines, the main reason for seizing the island, would soon begin.

On Peleliu, Colonel Nakagawa had received no direct word from Major Goto since communications between the two islands were broken on 22 September. Nevertheless, the colonel continued to inform Koror of the heroic deeds of the Angaur garrison for several weeks thereafter. Not until mid-November did Nakagawa finally admit that continued resistance on Angaur was just "his surmise."

At 0800 on 20 October, official responsibility for the ground defense of the Southern Palaus and destruction of the remaining Japanese forces on Peleliu passed from IIIPhib to the 81st Division. General Geiger and his staff departed by air to Guadalcanal at 0830. General Rupertus, with some elements of division headquarters, left by air at 2300. His "quick but rough" campaign having turned into a prolonged nightmare, both were glad to leave Peleliu behind.

"I'm glad it's finally over and the Marines can leave," one of Geiger's aides remembered the corps commander saying upon learning the army would take over.

"I am too," replied Rupertus.

General Mueller, viewing the Peleliu campaign now as a major siege operation, determined to reduce the pocket slowly, cautiously, step by step, with a minimum of casualties. No life would be spent that could possibly be spared.

During the period from 23 September to 20 October, the 321st RCT had lost 98 killed, 468 wounded in action. It had killed 1,500 Japanese and captured 108 prisoners by division estimates.

Mueller, who had won a Silver Star as an infantry officer on the battlefields of France in World War I, left no doubt that the army was in charge now. Talking with General Smith, who remained behind to oversee remaining Marine personnel, he commented that he was just beginning a new campaign and undiplomatically opined that the Marines had not done much with the Japanese in the pocket.

Smith refused to be baited until Mueller asked for an overlay showing the position of all the Marine machine guns on the island. "Look, General," he replied pointedly, "we have been attacking, and we don't make overlays for machine guns when we are attacking, we keep them moving."

To Smith's eternal amusement, the first thing the army did was sandbag the old administration building, former 1st Marine Division Headquarters, and title it "Advanced Operations Center of the 81st Division." Mueller himself moved the division CP over to the vicinity of Purple Beach on the east coast of Peleliu, which provided a more scenic environment surrounded by palms. The army was settling in for the long haul.

The Wildcats resumed the assault against the Five Brothers on 21 October, following on the heels of another napalm attack delivered by Marine Corsairs from VMF–114. Sixteen aircraft participated in the morning attack, guiding on smoke pots set out to mark the end of the Horseshoe and its western approaches.

Despite the burn-over, 1/321 immediately encountered automatic-weapons fire from two caves on the western slope of Brother 3. This marked the beginning of stiff resistance which held the battalion to gains of less than 100 yards for the day. The GIs registered a couple of small successes: At 0900, a patrol located a Japanese machine-gun nest and killed its three-man crew. A mortar position and another machine-gun nest were also reported destroyed in the slow chipping-away at enemy defenses.

While 1/321 banged its head against Brother 3, a patrol from the 2d Battalion ventured out with orders to capture Brother 1, the northernmost of the Five Brothers. The Wildcats were dispersed by enemy fire from the hill's eastern slope. Soon afterward, direct fire from 75 mm pack howitzers and 37 mm guns unmasked the two Japanese caves and silenced the occupants, but the battalion's morale had already dropped a notch as a result of the setback.

Battalion commander Lieutenant Colonel Peter D. Clainos had a habit of exploring targets with a small patrol of volunteers before moving in. Now, to his complete disgust, no volunteers were forthcoming. No shrinking violet, Clainos made sure that all the men knew about it, then struck off toward Brother 1 by himself. His solitary attack may have astounded the Japanese, for he drew no fire until he reached the lower slopes and a concealed Japanese threw a grenade at him. "I rushed uphill to the nearest rock pile," recalled Clainos, "caught my breath and looked back over the flat plain I had recently traversed and saw the prettiest sight of my life—about a dozen of my GIs, with rifles at the port, were coming toward Five Brothers and me!"

By the time the "reinforcements" arrived, Clainos was already halfway up the hill. He issued instructions, and the patrol moved out, but it was soon pinned down by rifle fire and grenades. Clainos looked back and saw his whole battalion moving toward him, each man carrying a full sandbag on his shoulder in addition to his rifle and ammo.

By 1700, the volunteers were in control of the northern part of Brother 1. E Company, waiting at the foot of the hill with sandbags, rushed reinforcements up. Forming a human chain, the Wildcats passed sandbags up to the crest. Recalled Clainos, "In less than an hour . . . I was walking back to my accustomed OP, telling myself that I was the most stupid commander in the U.S. Army—but a happy one!"

By nightfall, the infantrymen were "dug in" behind their sandbag barricades and prepared to stay.

The Japanese struck back after dark. Enemy patrols repeatedly tried to throw the Wildcats off the hill, working close to lob hand grenades into the American positions. The Wildcats tossed the grenades back, adding some of their own for good measure. The Japanese also struck L Company on the western edge of Walt Ridge, but again without success.

Field Order No. 7, issued by the 321st Infantry late on the afternoon of 21 October, called for a coordinated assault by all four battalions at 0645 the next morning. 1/321 was directed to seize the high ground overlooking Wildcat Bowl from the northwest; 2/321 was to take the remaining four Brothers; 3/321, supported by tanks and LVT flamethrowers, was to secure the remainder of Walt Ridge and occupy the Horseshoe; 1/323 was to close with the enemy on its section of the western perimeter.

The day began with a 15-minute mortar concentration, followed by an air strike. The infantry assault jumped off at 0645 around the perimeter of the pocket.

The attack against the Brothers made relatively good headway, considering past experiences. By 0900, E Company had seized the remainder of Brother 1. A platoon promptly advanced across Brother 2 to 3 in order to keep the enemy occupied while sandbag barricades were erected on 2.

The attack was also supported by a platoon of tanks from Company A, 710th Tank Battalion. Under the command of Second Lieutenant Brooke P. Halsey, the tanks were attempting to reduce Japanese caves in Death Valley east of Brother 4 when one of the Shermans lost a track to a mine. Pinned down by enemy fire from a cave directly to their front, the tank crew remained buttoned up in the sweltering compartment all afternoon. After dark, Halsey led another tank crew and a maintenance party into the valley. The crew repaired the track, enabling the Sherman to withdraw before the Japanese could come down from their caves and finish off the cripple and its trapped crew.

Throughout the day, carrying parties from headquarters and service units worked with the combat infantrymen under enemy rifle fire, lugging sandbags up the steep slope. When darkness fell, both Brothers 1 and 2 were snugly fortified, and 3 was under effective control.

Attempts to push further along the ridge were turned back. Meanwhile, 2/321 had sent I Company into the Horseshoe, backed by the not inconsiderable punch of two platoons of medium tanks, three M–10 tank destroyers and two LVT flamethrowers. Covered by fire from its armored support, I Company made extensive use of flamethrowers and demolitions to neutralize all the caves it could locate.

By 1100, the company had completed its sweep and turned west to tackle the caves at the base of the Five Sisters. Midway up the valley in the vicinity of a marshy sinkhole—later dubbed Grinlinton Pond in honor of a Wildcat officer killed in the area—the Japanese had occupied defensive positions near the water's edge. Infantry rooted them out, going from hole to hole. Among the dead was a Japanese shot trying to place a mine under the tread of a tank. By actual count, 35 Japanese, including two officers, were killed in this sweep. How many died unseen in the caves was not known.

As afternoon waned, the company boldly erected a defense of tanks, sandbags and spotlights, jury-rigged from vehicle equipment, to defend positions located in the Horseshoe along the base of Walt Ridge. The Japanese response to these encroachments began as the sun went down. At 1800, Japanese riflemen on Brothers 4 and 5 began to direct accurate rifle fire into K Company's positions on Walt Ridge. Fifteen minutes later, a Japanese patrol tried to break into I Company's position on the floor of the valley. The attack failed. Eight Japanese armed only with grenades and bayonets were killed.

Shortly before 1900, the Wildcats noticed a signal light flashing from a cave on the northern side of Brother 5. Five fires, possibly some sort of signal, were also spotted in the vicinity of Hill 300.

Half an hour later, Japanese infantrymen armed with American grenades smashed into a platoon of 1/323, forcing it back about 100 yards to West Road from the southern end of the pocket. Artillery fire broke up the attack, and the ground was regained the next morning. U.S. casualties totaled one killed and nine wounded.

More serious was a simultaneous attack on the battalion's left flank, which pushed the left platoon of A Company back to West Road. This puncture opened a gap between the 321st and 323d Infantry Regiments. A few determined holdouts such as Privates First Class Ellis Smith and Lacy Pack of E Company managed to prevent the breakthrough from becoming even more serious. Although wounded early in the action, Smith and Pack held their position on the flank and, with automatic-rifle fire, prevented any further Japanese advance. The gap was plugged in the morning.

A fourth enemy attack developed at 0430, when a platoon of Japanese attacked in an attempt to retake Brother 2. Twenty or more were killed in the exchange before the attackers withdrew.

Several Japanese moving alone were also killed at various points. These activities indicated that the enemy was repositioning some of his strength while counterattacking and was also reoccupying caves and emplacements that had previously been knocked out or abandoned.

The following afternoon, E Company jumped off from positions on Brothers 1 and 2 and secured a hold on Brother 4. Before darkness fell, the Wildcats had occupied and sandbagged positions on the northern, eastern and southeastern slopes of 4.

Twice during the night, at 1930 and at 0200, Japanese from Brother 5 tried to drive the Wildcats off 4. These attacks developed into grenade duels. Ten Japanese remained sprawled on the slopes at morning, while E Company escaped unscathed.

The Wildcats spent the next day strengthening their defenses on Brother

4. One innovation—the brainstorm of a Tech 5 with the medical detachment—saved incalculable difficulties. The GIs rigged up a cable basket tram
powered by a quarter-ton truck. This first rig, set up along West Ridge, was
about 100 yards long on a 20-degree incline. Upon occupying the Five
Brothers, the 2d Battalion implemented another cable tram to supply troops,
bring up sandbags and evacuate the wounded.

Another, more gruesome task involved cleaning up the rotting corpses
around Grinlinton Pond, scene of the stiff fire fight three days before. Crews
sprayed gasoline on the decaying Japanese bodies and torched them; a
graves-registration group came in with the unenviable task of retrieving the
remains of Americans killed five days before.

During the night, a babble of Japanese voices was heard at the southern
end of Mortimer Valley. This led to the hope that some of the enemy wanted
to surrender—a supposition that was dashed when an interpreter using
loudspeakers received no response after an hour and a half of talking into
the dark. However, nighttime activity by the Japanese during this period
also indicated that some of the holdouts were running short of water. The
GIs, who consumed an average of 2.9 gallons of water per man per day
from their shallow wells, cordoned off the major source of fresh water,
Grinlinton Pond at the base of Walt Ridge. On the night of 23 October, a
group of Japanese, apparently intent on obtaining water from the big sinkhole, attacked the Wildcats at the base of Walt Ridge. Nineteen Japanese,
including a warrant officer, were killed by Wildcats firing from the protection of sandbag barricades.

This attrition would continue night after night, as individual Japanese
and small groups were driven into the open by thirst or the impulse for
self-destruction. Nevertheless, Japanese infantrymen would retain their grip
on the southernmost of the Five Brothers, Number 5, for another month.

Backs to the wall, the beleaguered Japanese infantry remained obdurate
even when caught well behind U.S. lines.

On 23 October, Sergeant Clayton E. Shockley and Private First Class
Jack R. Musolf of the 81st Signal Company were troubleshooting a phone
line near the "safety" of Purple Beach when the line abruptly disappeared
into a swamp. Suspicious, Shockley cautiously followed the wire and came
across an enemy soldier, whom he promptly killed. Returning to his jeep
for additional ammunition, the sergeant and Musolf reentered the swamp.
The Japanese disclosed their position by lobbing grenades, and the two
signal men eliminated three more Japanese and wounded another in the
subsequent skirmishing.

On the morning of 25 October, two other Japanese were trapped in a
cave on the west wall of Walt Ridge. When a Nisei interpreter and two
lieutenants approached the cave entrance, they were pinned down by a

sniper. The interpreter, one of two Nisei assigned to the 323d Infantry, was shot through the thigh, and all three were forced to withdraw hastily.[3]

Another incident brought better results when a Japanese POW revealed the location of a cave where he had hidden with 40 others until the officer in charge threw him out because he could not control his dysentery. When he tried to return, the officer beat him and forced him out again.

Using interpreters, the Wildcats tried to talk the occupants into surrendering, but without result. After dark, during a heavy rain, some of the Japanese tried to escape one by one. GIs shot down seven—one was thought to have escaped—and in the morning blew the cave mouth, sealing any survivors inside.

On 25 October, the 321st Infantry received a well-deserved rest as its sister regiment, the 323d, came forward to take over the grind against the pocket. To that date the 321st had lost 146 men killed and 469 wounded on Peleliu. Records of each casualty revealed that most had died in unspectacular fashion, falling victim to bullets, mortars or grenades.

- Corporal LeRoy McNoel. Wounded on Radar Hill on 2 October when a grenade fell in the midst of his squad, he died at an aid station.
- Private First Class William R. Phillips. Killed by a mortar shell on 25 October when he stood up as his company was being relieved.
- Private First Class Walter Gorkiewicz. Killed by small-arms fire during an attack by Company C on 21 October.
- Tech 5 Philip Griego. A cook who volunteered to work with a front-line rifle squad, Griego spotted a sniper late on the afternoon of 18 October. He and the sniper fired at each other simultaneously, each man killing the other.
- Sergeant Frank Casteel. Died on 13 October of wounds when rocks hurled by an explosion fell through a table under which he had taken shelter and inflicted fatal head injuries.
- Staff Sergeant Harry J. Taylor. Killed by a sniper on 18 October as he rose to leave his position during a relief.
- Private First Class George O. Hall. Accompanying a demolition squad that successfully placed explosives at the mouth of an enemy-held cave, he was killed in the ensuing explosion.
- Private First Class James Madigan. Killed on 27 September while administering first aid to a wounded GI.
- Private John W. Morgan. Killed instantly by enemy fire on 22 October while scouting in front of his squad.

The 323d, commanded by Colonel Arthur P. Watson, was directed to "maintain constant pressure on the enemy by offensive action both day and night to annihilate the Japanese force from Peleliu Island...the regiment will contain the enemy force within a constantly decreasing perimeter until destroyed . . . exits of escape from perimeter will be blocked with barbed wire and covered by automatic weapons fire. The regiment will be especially alert to destroy a banzai counterattack."

By now, enemy strength in the pocket was estimated at "anywhere between 300 and 1200." Japanese sources would later confirm that estimate, reporting a total of only 700 effectives still alive, including lightly wounded men.

It was believed that the 321st Infantry had killed about 400 Japanese in the pocket over the past ten days. The pocket itself had been reduced to an average north-south length of about 600 yards. It remained about 475 yards wide at the northern extremity, but deep salients had been driven into the guts of the position down the Horseshoe and along the Five Brothers. To the south, the pocket had been reduced to a width of about 350 yards.

These gains had been made with some ingenuity. In the absence of any natural cover, the Wildcats continued to rely heavily on sandbags for protection from enemy fire. First used by the Marines, the lowly sandbag was refined by the Wildcats into a major assault tool. Filled at Peleliu's beaches— the only available source of loose sand—the bags were trucked to the ridges, then lugged up to the front lines, where they provided cover for men trying to hold positions on the open slopes. At times, the sandbags were also used as portable walls, the GIs moving them forward as they advanced behind.

"In effect," noted the Wildcat history, "the sandbags had to be used instead of armor in ground too rough and steep for tanks. Without sandbags the troops, on the sides and tops of the ridges and peaks, were completely exposed to enemy rifle fire."

A typical instance occurred on 23 October, when 1/321 advanced behind sandbag barricades. At times, it was necessary to push the sandbags forward with poles under the heavy Japanese fire, so a first layer could be placed to protect the men who crawled forward to finish the work. In this way, the Wildcats edged up on their enemy literally inch by inch until they were close enough to destroy him.

Two Japanese were wounded in front of Wildcat lines in the Horseshoe on 26 October. Blinding the enemy with a smoke screen, the GIs managed to capture both. After first aid treatment, one of the enemy soldiers stated that there were 15 or 16 wounded Japanese in the cave in which he had been hiding. They had only a grenade apiece for weapons and were being attended to by two medical officers. The soldier also believed that there were about 60 men armed with rifles and grenades in two adjacent caves. He thought there were 500 to 600 Japanese in the entire pocket. About 300 of this number were sick or wounded and lacked medical attention. All had orders to fight to the end.

During the five days from 26 October through 1 November, heavy rains, fog and the resulting poor visibility severely restricted operations around the pocket. Amphibious patrols stepped up their watch over the outlying islands in case General Inoue tried to use the weather to cover a reinforcement attempt, but they found no evidence of such an effort.

The 323d Infantry began its combat duties with patrol action on all fronts and the demolition of caves in rear areas to prevent reoccupation by the Japanese. They also worked on improving their own positions.

One newly arrived Wildcat recalled picking his way through the ridges when one of the GIs saw something move in a cave. "Japs!" he yelled. An enemy soldier ran out in an effort to flee, only to fall riddled by a BAR burst. The GIs took cover as five other Japanese set up a machine gun at the mouth of the cave. Engineers finally managed to set off a charge at the entrance, and the GIs rushed the position to find the dazed Japanese groping for their weapons. They were all quickly shot dead.

Another mop-up effort ended in tragedy. Coming into the line shortly after noon on 26 October, E Company was clearing caves on the southern edge of the Umurbrogol when a deafening blast engulfed the GIs. Screams of pain and fright arose from the rocks. "Many of our closest friends could not be recognized," recalled a GI. Dazed from concussion and bleeding from wounds, men staggered blindly down the hill.

It was later determined that an aerial bomb rigged as a controlled mine had been detonated from a remote Japanese observation post. Nine GIs died and 20 were wounded in the explosion. The area was found to be thickly mined with similar bombs, either booby-trapped or rigged to explode on impact.

On the evening of 25 October, a Japanese radio broadcast reported that the U.S. fleet had suffered terrific losses in a naval battle off the Philippine Islands. Although largely discounted by American troops on Peleliu, lingering apprehensions were dispelled the following morning when an announcement from the White House reported that the Japanese Navy had suffered a great defeat from which it would never recover.

Two days later, some of the Wildcats experienced Japanese "naval power" in the Palaus firsthand when an LCI and destroyer escort detected Japanese boats about 6,000 yards off Purple Beach. As tracer bullets skipped off the water and through the encampment, the Japanese flotilla was dispersed, but the previously peaceful division command post got a good scare.

It was later learned that the attackers consisted of five landing barges from Babelthuap. Fitted with improvised torpedo-launching equipment, they had been sent in an effort to sink shipping off the coast of Peleliu.

The raid was a dismal failure. One barge was sunk, its crew captured. No damage to American shipping or personnel was sustained, although a single Japanese torpedo somehow managed to worm its way through scores of ships to beach itself harmlessly near division headquarters. Later, a midget submarine was spotted near Peleliu, and it was speculated that the enemy was trying to evacuate personnel trapped in the pocket.

Further evidence of General Inoue's interest in Peleliu came on the night of 29 October, when a Japanese float plane was spotted circling over the island. The plane dropped two parachutes. A Wildcat patrol recovered one. A supply chute 16 feet in diameter, it contained 60 hand grenades packed in a wicker basket.

A second air drop was attempted on the evening of 31 October, when a Japanese float plane, pursued by a Marine night fighter, passed directly over the 321st Infantry CP. Front-line infantry units reported that Japanese in the ridge system threw out lighted flares in an apparent attempt to signal the aircraft. Seven to a dozen large cargo parachutes were dropped. Several of these were recovered by U.S. troops and found to contain radio batteries, tubes and insulated wire.

It was later learned that the delivery was intended for General Murai, who had requested radio batteries since his were almost run down. Much of the material was damaged in the drop, aimed in the general vicinity of the West Coast Ridge, where Nakagawa and Murai were believed to be holed up. The enemy aircraft also scattered crudely lettered propaganda leaflets addressed to "Poor Reckless Yankee-Doodle," claiming that "19 Aeroplane carriers, 4 Battleships, 10 several Cruisers and Destroyers" along with "1261 ship aeroplanes" had been destroyed by the Japanese in a great naval battle. The leaflet threatened "cruel attack," adding, "Thanks for you advice notes of surrender. But we haven't any reason to surrender to those who are fated to be totally destroyed a few days later."

The most immediate object of destruction was the enemy plane itself, shot down in flames by a Marine night fighter from VMF(N) 541 near Arimasuku Island. The pilot, Major Norman L. Mitchell, earned the distinction of shooting down the only Japanese aircraft destroyed in the air by Marine aviation squadrons in the Palaus.

Back on Koror, General Inoue was also feeling less than victorious. Since arriving in the Palaus, he had felt as if the heat and humidity—if not the Americans—were robbing him of his powers of concentration. Now, toward the end of October, his appendix had become inflamed, "but because of the gravity of the situation, I neglected it," he recalled.

Around 1 November, the general's appendix burst. It was immediately removed, but Inoue began what was to be five months of recuperation.[4] His duties and overall direction to the garrison at Peleliu largely devolved on his able chief of staff, Colonel Tokuchi Tada.

NOTES

1. The 81st Division estimated the size of the pocket at 400 yards by 850 yards, but this appears to be erroneous, as it would include some areas supposed to be under U.S. control.

2. This was the same area the Marines referred to as the Horseshoe.

3. It is worth noting that of the dozen or so Nisei assigned as translators to the 81st Division, at least seven had families confined in U.S. internment camps.

4. Lieutenant James Wickel, who interviewed General Inoue in 1947, recalled, "At this point, the subject unbuttoned his shirt, pulled back his garments, and revealed a scar about six inches long and one inch wide. The appendix seemed to have been removed with a bayonet."

Chapter 14

Preparations to renew pressure on the pocket were completed on 1 November when 1/323, commanded by Lieutenant Colonel Hugh K. Forsman, was directed to capture Hill 300 and the Five Sisters the following day.

According to a captured medical officer, Japanese forces had been badly whittled down in weeks of fighting. The officer, who emerged with a white flag, was "effusive," noted U.S. interrogators, "wanting to talk and help—anxious to survive, he said, for the sake of science and research, to which he always devoted himself." Speaking fluent English, he told interrogators he had been informed in regimental headquarters that 800 to 1,000 Japanese remained in the central combat zone, but gave as his own estimate a strength of perhaps 400 to 500. The survivors had two weeks of food left, but water was again in short supply, despite help from the rain.

It is an indication of the deterioration of Colonel Nakagawa's command that the American attack on the morning of 2 November met with quick success. Jumping off at 0630 after a 40-minute mortar barrage, the assault, spearheaded by G Company, seized Hill 300 and Sister 4 within an hour. Among the discoveries on Hill 300 was a Japanese OP reached by ladders from the interior cave system—one more reason the enemy had been able to hang on as long as it had.

By 0830, all five of the Sisters were in Wildcat hands. As the Japanese tried to sweep the heights with fire from further north, American infantry hustled to fortify the hills. The cave entrances on Wildcat Bowl could now be kept under constant surveillance, and inter-cave communication became more hazardous for the Japanese.

Assuming Japanese attention was now firmly focused on 1/323, Colonel Forsman ordered Lieutenant Colonel Arthur Hutchinson's 3d Battalion to strike south toward the China Wall. Despite Forsman's hopes, progress proved slow against bitter Japanese resistance. The rate of progress was determined by the speed sandbags could be brought forward to protect the creeping advance.

During the night, as expected, the Japanese made an attempt to reoccupy Hill 300 and the Sisters. The assault, launched shortly after midnight, was repulsed. Thirty-eight bodies were found the next morning at the base of the cliffs. Fifteen other Japanese were killed as they tried to work through the lines on the west.

Colonel Nakagawa admitted the situation was becoming grim. The Americans had gained footholds on the China Wall and Hill 300, he reported, and the GIs were observed to be strengthening their newly won gains with sandbags and wire entanglements. "Our defense unit attacked this enemy unit every night but to no avail."

The deteriorating condition of the Japanese was verified by prisoner statements. Of four prisoners seized by GIs on 3 November, one, armed with three grenades and a mess-kit knife, was captured by an artilleryman after a brief tussle in a headquarters latrine. The prisoner said he had been living in the swamps and subsisting on land crabs and coconuts for the past 45 days. The other three, including a sergeant major seized on Hill 300, stated that rations and other supplies in their area were nearly exhausted.

The American successes led to the first apparent rift between Colonel Nakagawa and his adviser/liaison, Major General Kenjiro Murai. Murai, who apparently had remained in the background until now, felt the situation now warranted an all-out banzai attack on the airfield, and he proceeded to contact Koror for approval to launch the suicide charge. Permission was denied.

"It is easy to die but difficult to live on," came the reply from Koror. "We must select the difficult course and continue to fight because of the influence on the morale of the Japanese people. Saipan was lost in a very short time because of vain banzai attacks, with the result that people at home suffered a drop in morale." Peleliu's defenders would stay in their caves.

Seizure of Hill 300 and the Five Sisters was followed by another hiatus. From 3 to 12 November, no major gains were made by any unit, although there was occasional heavy fighting. During the morning of 3 November, a detachment of about 20 Japanese was detected in the beach area west of the main combat zone. Scattered by fire from a field artillery unit, 18 of the enemy were subsequently hunted down and killed by Wildcat combat patrols. A prisoner later revealed that the detachment had been sent out to raid army positions.

Shortly after noon on this same day, a tank/infantry reconnaissance patrol from 2/323 ventured into Death Valley. A similar patrol on 29 October had met with little resistance, but this time the Japanese responded in force. Moving into the draw, four men of F Company's 1st Platoon clambered up to investigate a cave, only to pull back hastily as they came under fire from Japanese inside. Flamethrower and demolitions teams tried to close in on the position without much success.

Platoon medic Gerald Colby rushed out and dragged one wounded man to the cover of a fissure, then went back to retrieve the man's rifle and water. As others fell wounded, Platoon Leader Lieutenant Harold Cox ordered his men to withdraw. Then Colby was hit. Covered by a tank, the others tried to carry the medic out, but as they placed him on a stretcher, he was killed by a burst of automatic-weapons fire. A corporal was also killed.

Also hit while tackling the China Wall were Staff Sergeant Luther Burbank and Private First Class Chris Kortman, both of F Company. Burbank was killed outright, while Kortman was badly wounded. Four other men were wounded trying to rescue the private first class, who lay on a ledge above them. Kortman died before help finally arrived.

Under the leadership of Captain Oscar "Buck" Luttrell, the Wildcats worked desperately to retrieve their wounded and dead, but they were repeatedly thrown back by enemy fire. Among the hardest hit group was a 13-man E Company patrol. Trapped front and rear, it lost five men in the valley. One of the missing was Private First Class Woodrow W. Hodges. Seriously wounded, he waved away all efforts to reach him, telling the survivors to get out of the trap. He and the other four were subsequently listed as killed in action.

While fierce Japanese resistance stonewalled Wildcat thrusts into Death Valley, the lack of progress on the rest of the perimeter was partly due to the return of heavy rains which began falling on 4 November and culminated in a typhoon that did not blow itself out until 8 November.

Japanese continued to be killed, both individually and in small groups. A fairly typical instance occurred around midnight on 6 November, when GIs in K Company, 323d Infantry killed two Japanese coming over a ridge near Hill 140. One of the dead Japanese had been wounded in the right side sometime earlier but was still fighting. He was carrying a bag of rice and biscuits, four grenades, a canteen of some reddish liquid and a position sketch.

Another reconnaissance party fell victim to two F Company GIs before dawn on 5 November. Private First Class Rusty Restuccia had just asked his buddy the time when the other GI opened up to his front with everything he had. Restuccia saw "three sparks" coming right at him as Japanese returned fire. The shooting lasted ten minutes. Morning revealed three dead Japanese, who were found to be carrying papers with information about the Wildcat positions.

Japanese headquarters on 5 November reported 350 men of the Defense Unit still able to fight. This included men with minor wounds. Another 130 men were alive but too seriously injured to participate.

Water shortages had been alleviated by the heavy rains, but now, for the first time, the Japanese survivors were running seriously short of ammunition. Only two months supply had originally been stored on Peleliu, and these stocks were being rapidly depleted as the fighting dragged on beyond earlier expectations. Colonel Nakagawa cut the normal allowance of small-arms ammunition by half, but he conceded darkly, "It was tentative as to whether it would last until 20 November."

The ever-present possibility of help for Nakagawa was underscored on 9 November when a Japanese force estimated at 100 men came ashore on Ngeregong, a small island about nine miles northeast of Peleliu. The small army garrison withdrew under covering fire from 20 mm and 40 mm guns. Over the next few days, patrol craft, destroyers and a flight of 47 navy aircraft pounded the island.

The shooting was not entirely one-sided. On the morning of 10 November, a flight of 51 navy planes bombing and strafing the island reported receiving light machine-gun fire. One of them crashed into the lagoon near the island. An amphibian tractor patrol was unable to locate the wreckage or any survivors. Nevertheless, the Japanese activity was apparently not conducted in great strength. When the Wildcats finally retook the island on 15 November, they found only some abandoned ordnance equipment and three rather ripe Japanese corpses.

On 8 November, 13 Japanese were killed and one captured as they attempted to flee the pocket to the northern islands. These attempts at flight could only be interpreted in one way: enemy morale was beginning to crack.

Some small gains were made in the nine days following seizure of the Five Sisters, but most of the U.S. effort was devoted to preparing for the next push. Armored bulldozers ventured 100 yards into Death Valley to construct a tracked vehicle route over the broken valley floor, and sandbags and supplies were brought up to the front lines. Action against caves also continued. One on the eastern slope of Hill 300 yielded 16 dead Japanese after it had been thoroughly worked over by LVT flamethrowers.

During the night, the Wildcats stayed in their holes, alert for infiltrators. Lavish use was made of illumination: one observer counted as many as three 60 mm illumination shells in the air at a time. Anyone who had to defecate stayed put and used an empty mortar or bazooka casing. Some of the more enthusiastic GIs hurled the full containers down the slope toward the enemy—accompanying the missile with the shout, "Tojo eats shit!"—but most found the whole procedure a nuisance. Nuisance or not, it was far safer than trying to move around in the dark at the risk of being shot by friend or foe.

Attacks on the Umurbrogol Pocket began in earnest again on 13 November as 1/323 pushed east from the ridges west of Death Valley and 2/323 moved north in Death Valley and Wildcat Bowl.

The movement into Wildcat Bowl was made by tanks and an LVT flame-thrower along a trail cut out by an armored bulldozer. Meanwhile, other Wildcats descended from the Five Sisters to seize the China Wall, while still others ventured into Death Valley to attack from the east.

Possibly because the Japanese were distracted by the armored patrol assaulting caves along both sides of the China Wall, initial enemy resistance to the infantry was negligible. This respite ended at 1000, when strong enemy fire from the northern part of the China Wall and the west wall of Death Valley stopped the Wildcats after they had seized 75 yards of the former. The Wildcats pulled up and began to sandbag their gains, having pulled off a major success.

From his command post in the China Wall, Colonel Nakagawa reported to Inoue that ammunition, food, water and radio batteries were running low. The latest American attack, he added, was stubbornly resisted, "but the enemy force successfully penetrated the defense line" with the aid of flamethrowers.

That night, there were further signs of deteriorating Japanese organization. Thirteen Japanese were killed in the area of 3/323 as they walked around in the open in "a carefree and jovial manner, singing and laughing." It was suggested that they were drunk on sake, but they may have just snapped from combat fatigue. In all, 42 Japanese were killed during the night.

Between 17 and 21 November, tanks and LVT flamethrowers operated throughout Wildcat Bowl and Death Valley, pounding enemy-held caves at the base of the Five Brothers and the China Wall. Following in the wake of the tanks, infantrymen and engineers attacked the caves with flame-throwers and demolitions. Also used was a jury-rigged long-range flame-thrower which used booster pumps and a fire nozzle to pump oil through 300 feet of pipe into enemy positions. The oil was ignited with phosphorus grenades. Armored bulldozers then sealed the entrances to prevent reoccupation by enemy infiltrators.

The Japanese seemed bewildered by these bold thrusts into the heart of the pocket and put up little resistance. During the night of 17 November, there was even a wholesale effort to escape the pocket. Thirty-three Japanese were killed in the attempt.

By 20 November, however, the last hard-core survivors seemed to have regained their balance. Resistance stiffened, and U.S. patrols came under fire from positions that had been bypassed or overlooked in previous sweeps.

One last effort to help Colonel Nakagawa at this time was made by Japanese forces on the islands to the north. Shortly before midnight on 17 November, lookouts observed a number of peculiar-looking objects floating toward the ships of LCI Flotilla 13 in Schorian Harbor some 4,000 yards north of Peleliu. A searchlight snapped on, its harsh glare revealing some three dozen flotation bladders bobbing in the water.

Machine-gun fire ripped out from the ships, deflating the bladders and exposing the Japanese who had been using them to approach the ships. Most of them were quickly gunned beneath the surface. A survivor who was fished out of the sea revealed that the force had consisted of 35 men. Armed with five hand grenades each and a total of five demolition charges, they had been sent to raise confusion in the American anchorage.

When their attack was completed, explained the survivor, they were to continue south to Peleliu to look for a suitable place to land reinforcements from Babelthuap or the other northern islands.

Two of the demolition charges were found a few days later fastened to LCT gunboats. Each had a 50-kilogram aerial bomb as the principal explosive, the charge being packed in a waterproofed wooden box. Both were disarmed without incident.

Typically, Japanese snipers remained ever-alert to pick off U.S. officers. So it was on 17 November that Lieutenant Colonel Raymond S. Gates, commanding 1/323, was studying enemy positions from an advanced observation post when he was picked off by an enemy rifleman. Gates was the highest ranking officer lost by the 81st Division on Peleliu.

By 23 November, it was apparent that Colonel Nakagawa had withdrawn the bulk of his survivors from the Wildcat Bowl area. The remnants of his force were now dug into the China Wall for their final stand. Much of the recent night's movement, which had cost numerous Japanese lives, had apparently been part of this consolidation.

With the end clearly in sight, General Murai renewed his pleas for a final all-out attack against the Americans. Again, 14th Division headquarters on Koror managed to dissuade him. The Japanese were to stay in their caves and kill as many Americans as possible.

Marking the painstaking progress of the Wildcats, General Mueller offered backhanded praise for the enemy tactics. "The Japs don't indulge in banzai charges anymore—at least not on Peleliu," he told news correspondents. "We wish they would. We would rather shoot them in their tracks than have to go in and burn them out." Even with Japanese forces surrounded and compressed into a small area, Mueller estimated that the mopping up would last into early December.

Although the pocket had now been reduced to an area approximately 285 yards long and 125 yards wide, the China Wall constituted a formidable defensive position. Inaccessible to all vehicles, it provided protection from tanks and LVT flamethrowers while allowing observation all over Peleliu. Actually two razor-backed ridges, the depression between the two sides of the wall offered shelter from direct rifle and gunfire and served as a death

Map 7.
The Last Cave Holdouts, 24 November

Death Valley

China Wall

Wildcat Bowl

The Horseshoe

Hill 300

Last Cave Holdouts

trap for anyone entering. Infantry could approach only by scaling the precipitous cliffs from east or west. "Eight or ten well-placed enemy sharpshooters could hold off a company trying to climb the cliffs from the east or the west," noted the division historian.

The northern and southern approaches, still highly defensible, were somewhat more negotiable, and it was this avenue that the Wildcats chose for their attack.

Previously, 3/323 had been unable to reach the China Wall in its drive to the south. Strong enemy opposition and difficult terrain had held the battalion at a standstill. Now, the regiment ordered F Company through Wildcat Bowl to seize positions on the northern end of the wall.

At 0700 on 22 November, an F Company platoon guide said curtly, "Okay, men, let's get ready to go," and the company descended into the southern end of the bowl. Preceded by scouts, two of whom lugged a .30 caliber machine gun and wore belted ammo around their shoulders, the Wildcats moved north, staying close to the eastern cliff of the China Wall. At the same time, tanks entered Death Valley to distract enemy defenders in positions on the western side of the wall.

Forty-five minutes later, F Company had reached the northern end of the bowl and was climbing the wall. Suddenly, the 3d Platoon came under heavy fire. The commander, Lieutenant Leon W. Szetela, fell dead. "The damn little bastard hit me!" a sergeant shouted in pain and surprise, clutching his wounded wrist. Despite the casualties, the company managed to seize a prominent peak just south of the furthest previous southern advance by the stalled 3d Battalion. Work began immediately to sandbag the height. Enemy fire caused several casualties, but by late afternoon the peak was fully fortified.

Over the next days, the Wildcats slowly chipped away at Japanese defenses in the China Wall. Enemy resistance was clearly cracking. Attacking from the northwestern boundary, one company advanced a whopping 75 yards after burning out the area with the improvised pipeline flamethrower. Watching his defense literally go up in flames, Colonel Nakagawa reported that his men were on the verge of collapse.

His pitiful situation was detailed by a Japanese soldier captured on 23 November. He reported that 60 to 70 men remained in the 1st Battalion position, while approximately 150 remained all told in the 323d's area. Most of these survivors were said to be wounded. All were weak from hunger and thirst and were losing their will to resist.

Despite their pitiful condition, the survivors had been ordered to remain at their posts until killed, reported the prisoner. Colonel Nakagawa believed that the longer they resisted, the more it would benefit their comrades now fighting new American thrusts in the Philippines. A last-ditch attack was not planned, so far as the prisoner knew.

That same day, Wildcat patrols from Brother 4 found the once formidable Brother 5 deserted. The peak was immediately seized and fortified, falling with scarcely a whimper after being a knife in the U.S. side for a month.

The next day, 24 November, the Wildcats began construction of an earth ramp from the northern end of Wildcat Bowl to the top of the China Wall. This ambitious project would make the inside of the China Wall accessible to tanks and flamethrowers. Even before the ramp was completed on the afternoon of 25 November, the Japanese held an area only about 150 yards long and were trying to fend off attacks from all directions.

Symbolic of the seemingly inexorable U.S. advance, when the bulldozer building the ramp up to the China Wall ran over an unexploded shell and lost a track, engineers put a new one on in the record time of only 65 minutes. Fiercely though the Japanese might fight, American power would eventually crush them.

From his headquarters deep in the China Wall, Colonel Nakagawa could see that the end had come at last. On 24 November, the colors of the 2d Infantry Regiment were burned to keep them from falling into enemy hands. Koror was advised that the final collapse would be signalled by the coded message "*sakura*" (cherry) repeated twice.

"Our defense units were on the verge of being completely annihilated; therefore the unit destroyed the 2d Infantry regiment flag," reported Nakagawa. "All documents were burned."

Nakagawa also reported that there were 56 Japanese survivors under the command of a Captain Nemoto. These were now divided into 17 teams and directed to hide out by day and raid the American lines at night. The survivors would shout "banzai" three times, wishing continued prosperity to the Emperor, before launching their final breakout. The wounded would commit suicide. "This will be the last message we will be able to send or receive," advised the Peleliu operator over the sub-oceanic phone cable.

At 1600, 24 November, the Japanese operator on Koror recorded one last message from Peleliu: "*Sakura. Sakura.*" The battle was over.

Shortly afterward, having defended Peleliu to the best of their abilities and earned the grudging admiration of their enemies, Nakagawa and Murai took the honorable exit. Deep in their cave, surrounded by U.S. troops, they shot themselves. As a measure of their hard-fought campaign, both were posthumously promoted to the rank of lieutenant general in the Imperial Army.

That night, 45 Japanese, including two officers, were killed in what a prisoner later revealed was an attempt to break out of the pocket to assemble and organize raiding parties behind the American lines. The prisoner also advised his interrogators of the suicides of Nakagawa and Murai.

At 0630, 26 November, tanks and LVT flamethrowers entered Wildcat Bowl from the south and moved north to the 306th Engineer Ramp. Thirty minutes later, they began to grind their way up the ramp into the China Wall fortress.

In spite of fairly heavy enemy fire, the armor was in place by 0745. It then coordinated its attack with the infantry to seize the entire eastern ridge of the wall.

At 0700 the next morning, the Wildcats set out to exterminate the remaining Japanese holed up in part of the China Wall and the northern end of Death Valley. "Resistance to this multisided attack seemed to disintegrate completely," noted the division operations report.

Three and a half hours later, the red-eyed Wildcats of the 2d Battalion driving north met with the 3d Battalion driving south. A few yards away, the men of the 1st Battalion could also be seen, perched on the rim of Death Valley. The pocket was no more.

The link-up took place amid an eerie stillness near the cave that had served as Colonel Nakagawa's final command post. The badly decomposed bodies of the colonel and Murai were not found until much later, when Wildcats finally ventured into the 40-foot-deep crypt. Identified by a former headquarters noncom who recognized Murai's personal effects, the general and a body presumed to be that of Nakagawa were given an honorable burial. The remains of Admiral Itou—Colonel Nakagawa's bugbear in the weeks before the U.S. landing—were apparently not located, nor were the circumstances of his death recorded.

At 1100, Colonel Watson informed General Mueller that organized resistance was definitely finished on Peleliu. In the words of the operations report of the 81st Division, "The enemy had fulfilled his determination to fight unto death."

News of the victory failed to make the front pages of American newspapers, by now filled with headlines about American successes in the Philippines, bombing raids in Tokyo and fighting in Europe. Somehow, the quiet end to the Peleliu fighting seemed almost fitting—a tired old wreck which had finally tottered to its inevitable conclusion.

One last unintentional irony was supplied by Rear Admiral J. W. Reeves, Jr., commander of the Western Carolines Sub-Area, who notified the weary Wildcats: "Please accept my hearty congratulations on successfully and efficiently liquidating organized enemy resistance on Peleliu, well ahead of estimated completion date."

Victory came 73 days after General Rupertus had gone on record with his prediction that Peleliu would be rough but short—two days, three at the most.

Chapter 15

Back on Pavuvu, the 1st Marine Division was being rebuilt.

By now, Pavuvu was a well-established base. Mess halls were screened and lighted; beer rations were issued regularly; and there was plenty of recreational equipment for baseball, boxing, basketball and even horseshoes. Every area now had showers, and most units had a laundry.

More novel still were three Red Cross girls who arrived to dispense donuts and charm. The most immediate effect of their presence was an order that all hands must wear trunks when swimming. Recalled an officer, "Division set down to tackle the latest tactical problem—how to find sufficient bathing trunks to shield the nakedness of 18,000 Marines from the modest gaze of three American women whom most of them would never get close enough to talk with."

Veterans exchanged visits to check up on the fate of buddies, brothers or cousins in other outfits. All too often, the news was bad. "You didn't really know until you got back to Pavuvu how many of your buddies were gone," recalled a corporal. "Up to then, you kept telling yourself that they'd turn up back at Pavuvu, that they were only slightly wounded, or not even wounded at all, just lost from their units. But at Pavuvu you couldn't fool yourself any longer."

Among the missing was General Rupertus. Shortly after the division returned to Pavuvu, Rupertus was relieved by Marine Corps Commandant A. A. Vandergrift, who assigned him to command of the Marine Corps schools. Few in the division mourned his departure. Command of the 1st Marine Division was assumed by the highly respected General Pedro Del Valle, who began readying the Marines for their next operation.[1]

Vandergrift, who later referred to Rupertus as one of the Marine Corps' "finest officers" and one of his own "finest friends," gave no indication that the relief was in any way related to Peleliu. In fact, the new assignment clearly marked the end of Rupertus's professional aspirations. Vandergrift soothed the sting of that reality by awarding his friend the Distinguished Service Medal for his service on Peleliu.

On Pavuvu, each survivor had to come to grips with the disaster in his own way. Referring to his own confusion, Private Russell Davis remarked, "Either I can't sleep or I can't wake up. I don't know which."

Another Marine had an eerie experience while rowing across the bay. Far from shore, he came across another Marine "sort of struggling along, half-swimming, half-floating, not making much headway." The oarsman leaned over and asked the swimmer if he wanted a lift. The man looked up, a strange, blank look in his eyes, and shook his head. The Marine repeated the invitation. "I guess not," replied the swimmer. The other man rowed away.

"Now I've thought about this a million times since then," he recalled. "I must have been as crazy as he was. But I know that day I said to myself, 'The guy's trying to figure out something for himself. Leave him alone.' And I know now, or maybe I'll just come out and say now, that what the guy was trying to figure out was whether the hell to stay up or let himself go down."

Limping off the hospital ship at Guadalcanal, Private Tom Boyle stood on his one crutch wondering how he was going to climb into the back of the 2 ½-ton truck provided to take the wounded to the hospital. As he stood there perplexed, a Red Cross girl came up and handed him a chocolate bar.

"I thought, 'Boy, this is really all I need,' " recalled Boyle. "What gratitude, huh? Well, they don't know how you feel. The last thing I wanted was a damn bar of chocolate. What we called 'pogey bait' in the Marine Corps. If she'd had a bottle of beer, she'd a been the greatest thing in town."

By the time Tom Boyle got to Guadalcanal, Private First Class Harlan Murray, hit on the first day at Peleliu, had been in Fleet Hospital 108 for some time.

"That was the worst hospital I've ever been in in my life," he recalled, "and I've been in a lot of 'em. The nurses were more concerned about playing badminton. . . . I'm not that bad. I mean, it hurts, but God Almighty, when you look at one guy that's got his leg half there . . . somebody else is missing an arm . . . how the hell can you bitch about your own problems?

"The guy next to me, he had a cast on his leg. They put these casts on a lot of times while the wound is still open and later they're to be changed. But this damn thing stunk and he kept telling them, 'It hurts, it hurts. I can't stand it. Take it off.' 'Yeah, yeah, okay, uh huh.' They didn't pay any attention to him. And he kept asking them to do something and they wouldn't do anything. By the next day he was so mad he couldn't stand it; he told 'em either take it off or he was going to take it off himself. They finally cut it off . . . it's so full of gangrene they gotta cut his whole leg off. It was needless. Stupid.

"My wound was hurting there, too, and I told 'em, 'I feel great. I want to go back to duty.' I just wanted to get out of there. My wound was still open. And they said, 'Yeah, no use hangin' around here,' and they gave me permission to go back."

Back in the Russells, Murray walked into an infirmary. "And I said, 'Will you please change the bandage on my wound?' And the guy took the bandage off and boy, he called the doctor over and the doctor says, 'Where you from?' And I told him and he said, 'Well, you mean they let you out of the hospital like that?' And I said, 'Yeah, it hurts so damn much I can't stand it.' And it did.

"They had to cut into my wound and take everything . . . it wasn't healing like it should . . . so they cut that damn thing out and I went back to the rear echelon of the 1st Division. And they had a couple of corpsmen, they took over from there, fixed me up. Been fine every since."

Also in Fleet Hospital 108, Swede Hanson managed to keep his arm, although he had gone from 169 pounds to the low 90s in the process. By that time, he would have considered himself comparatively fortunate even if amputation had been necessary. The wing was filled with seriously wounded men. One had both eyes shot out. Another, hit in the head, could only speak three words: yes, no and goddammit. Still another Marine was so badly shocked that he could not tolerate the weight of a sheet over his body.

One day, a navy doctor told Hanson that they had decided to leave the shrapnel in his arm. Removing it would only cause more damage.

"Okay," said Hanson. "When can I go back to my outfit?"

"You're not going back to your outfit," replied the doctor. "You're going Stateside."

Hanson demurred. He wanted to go back to his outfit, he said.

"I don't know what's the matter with you crazy guys," said the doctor. "As a doctor, we try to do the very best for you, but you keep fighting us instead of going back to the States where you should get more treatment. You want to go back to that hell and fight more."

"No," said Hanson. "It's to be with my buddies."

"Okay, you're going back to your outfit," replied the doctor in exasperation.

Back on Pavuvu, Hanson rejoined his outfit. Many of the old faces were gone. Over 4,400 replacements had joined the division during his absence. They looked "just like a bunch of little kids to me," he recalled, although they were probably only a year or so younger.

"I'll never forget one cocky little guy," remarked Hanson. "He says, 'You old guys are just a bunch of has-beens. We're here now. We'll show you how it's done. We'll take care of you all.' And I couldn't help but kinda smile and say, 'Yup, here we go again. We got another bunch of guys that are going to go straight forward. They say *charge* . . . and up the hill they're going to go.' "

The 1st Marine Division went "up the hill" again six months later on Okinawa, where it again suffered heavy casualties in its last campaign. After the war, the division did duty in China before shipping home.

The 81st Infantry Division saw no major combat after the Palaus campaign. General Mueller was formally relieved of responsibility for defense of the sector on 13 January 1945. Garrison duty was subsequently taken over by the 111th Infantry. The 81st Division was assembled on New Caledonia before staging out for the Philippines in late April 1945. Assigned to mopping up Japanese stragglers on Leyte, the Wildcats were preparing for the invasion of Japan when the war ended in August.

The formal announcement that Peleliu had been secured did not signal a complete end to the fighting. Numerous enemy stragglers remained holed up in caves, where they posed a nuisance for months.

Now and again, some forlorn, half-starved soldier foraging for food would surrender or fight a futile one-man battle with an American patrol. As many as 30 stragglers remained holed up in the huge navy-built cave on northern Peleliu. Deep within the elaborate maze of partially collapsed tunnels, the Japanese picked off a number of careless souvenir hunters who ventured inside. Demolitions men and flamethrower teams gradually killed most of the occupants, but as late as February 1945, a captured Japanese revealed that a handful of his comrades still lived.

The last significant combat event occurred shortly after 0200 on 18 January 1945, when the Japanese mounted an amphibious landing against the garrison on Peleliu. Armed with an odd assortment of rifles, improvised grenades, incendiaries, demolitions and spears, 64 Japanese raiders landed in two barges, one near Purple Beach and the other at the White Beaches, under the command of a navy lieutenant junior grade named Hori.

The enemy field order noted that since U.S. forces were now heavily engaged in the Philippines, Peleliu was vulnerable to a suicide attack which "will crushingly attack the enemy on the spot." The raiders were directed to destroy aircraft, kill personnel and blow up supplies, ammo dumps and the U.S. headquarters. "Every participant will fight with special valor to the death if called upon to," directed the order.

Instead, the 64 were quickly bottled up by a force of infantrymen, artillerymen, amtrac crews and support personnel. Two Japanese were captured; the rest were killed. Found among the corpses were two Japanese in U.S. uniforms who had apparently come out of hiding to join the raiding party.

Under interrogation, the two prisoners, both of whom landed with the

White Beach force, told a bizarre tale. Both men, one an army enlisted man, the other a navy machinist's mate, had escaped from Peleliu during the fighting in September.

The soldier, 28-year-old Yutake Kawahara, had been in the hospital on Peleliu on 26 September and was evacuated with 29 other patients, including two officers, by barge to Babelthuap. Chiyoshi Takeuchi, 42, said he had fled from the airfield when the Marines landed in September and subsequently made his way to Babelthuap by swimming and wading along the reefs.

Further interrogation revealed that all of the raiders—a mix of army and navy personnel—had escaped from Peleliu during the campaign. This included Hori, who had been evacuated to Babelthuap due to illness.

According to the POWs, all the escapees had been held in isolation at a detention compound on Arakabesan upon their return from Peleliu. Kawahara said the men were considered to have deserted their posts by escaping. Sent back on the raid, they had been told not to return again. Takeuchi supported this statement, adding that he had been issued only a spear for the attack, although he had "asked and pleaded" for a rifle.

After the war, both General Inoue and his chief of staff, Colonel Tada, proved extremely reluctant to discuss this incident. Inoue indicated that the whole attack might well have been a matter of honor, explaining that the raiders "may have been a group of navy personnel returning to Peleliu after having once fled unsuccessfully." The chief of staff noted curtly, "I'd rather not speak about this because it would be a grave insult to the navy." Despite their silence, the inference was clear that the raiders were military personnel who had originally fled Peleliu and were now ordered back to atone with an honorable death.

Eight months after the raid, General Inoue, commanding Japanese forces in the Palaus, surrendered unconditionally. At the time of his surrender, 18,473 Japanese soldiers, 6,404 naval personnel, 9,750 civilians and 5,350 natives came under U.S. control.

Bypassed by war, the thousands of Japanese stranded on Babelthuap were ultimately repatriated to Japan, and peace came to the Palaus. By then, the scrub jungle had already begun to thicken again on Peleliu's blasted ridges.

Peleliu did not come cheap. The 1st Marine Division ultimately posted casualty figures of 6,526, of whom 1,252 were killed or died of wounds and 5,274 were wounded but survived. The 81st Infantry Division lost 1,393 officers and men, including 208 killed. Another 334 were killed and 843 wounded on Angaur and the smaller islands off Peleliu.

A rough comparison of the Peleliu statistics indicates that U.S. forces suffered one casualty for every Japanese killed. Considering that the average loss ratio for Pacific battles factored out to one Allied soldier to 2.3 Japanese, Peleliu was clearly one of the hardest fought actions of the Pacific war.

Some senior Marine officers later compared Peleliu to Iwo Jima—smaller in scale, but equally fierce. "The only difference between Iwo Jima and Peleliu," remarked General Geiger, "was that at Iwo Jima, there were twice as many Japs on an island twice as large, and they had three Marine divisions to take it, while we had one Marine division to take Peleliu."

Although it hardly seems conceivable, Peleliu could have been much worse. Under interrogation after the war, General Inoue said he had had only six months to prepare for the invasion. The Marine officer who interviewed the general reported, "He stated that he fully believed that if he had one year instead of six months, he would have completely repulsed us. . . . He further stated that he was really prepared for us in Koror and Babelthuap, and was positive he could have defeated us there."

Exactly how many Japanese died on Peleliu will never be known. The best estimates put the number around 10,900, even assuming a few of the defenders escaped to Japanese-held islands to the north.

An indication of the high state of enemy morale on Peleliu appears in the breakdown of prisoners taken during the operation. As of 20 October, a total of 302 enemy personnel had been captured on Peleliu. Of these, less than a third—92—were Japanese. The remainder were non-Japanese laborers, mostly Koreans. More significantly, of the 92 captured Japanese, only 7 were members of regular army units; 12 were naval personnel, and the remaining 73 were Japanese laborers. At least insofar as regular Japanese forces were concerned, the garrison had fought almost literally to the death.

Sadly, hindsight indicates that Peleliu was in no way worth the price the Marines and army paid. As a threat to MacArthur's flank during the invasion of the Philippines, the Palaus were largely a paper tiger. Without ships or aircraft, they posed little danger. As bases to launch air attacks against the Philippines and to neutralize the remaining Western Carolines, Peleliu also seems to have been of little or no value. The last-minute decision to bypass Mindanao and speed up the Philippines invasion schedule effectively negated much of the operational role originally intended for the Palaus. Angaur was subsequently developed into a bomber base, but the first attacks against targets in the Philippines were not launched until 17 November, nearly a month after U.S. forces invaded Leyte.

The Peleliu airfield served primarily as a stop for transient air traffic to the Philippines and as a base for routine antisubmarine patrols and bombing and rocket missions over Koror, Babelthuap and Yap. Between October 1944 and June 1945, 28 Marine planes were shot down on these missions. A total of 16 pilots and 2 crewmen were killed, including VMF–114 CO Major "Cowboy" Stout, who was killed by antiaircraft fire over Koror on 4 March 1945.

It was also from the Peleliu airfield that a PV–1 Ventura patrol craft from VPB–152 spotted hundreds of survivors from the torpedoed cruiser *Indianapolis*, struggling in the water on 2 August 1945. Torpedoed the night of 29 July after delivering atomic bomb parts to Tinian, the cruiser sank in 12 minutes and was not missed for three and a half days. Not until the fourth day did the Ventura from Peleliu accidentally spot the survivors in the water. Of the 1,196 crew members, only 316 survived. Most were brought to the 1,000-bed Base Hospital 20 on Peleliu. Two of them died there.

Ironically, it was Ulithi Atoll, seized by the 323d RCT without a shot on 22 to 24 September, that proved the most valuable prize of Stalemate II. This anchorage served the U.S. Pacific Fleet as a major asset during operations in the Philippines and later as a staging area for fleet and amphibious forces in the Okinawan campaign.

Admiral Bull Halsey, who had opposed the Peleliu assault almost from its inception, felt vindicated by the results. "I felt [the Palaus] would have to be bought at a prohibitive price in casualties," he wrote after the war. "In short, I feared another Tarawa and I was right."

Admiral Oldendorf, whose vessels had provided fire support for the landing, was even more outspoken, writing, "If military leaders (including naval) were gifted with the same accuracy of foresight that they are with hindsight, undoubtedly the assault and capture of the Palaus would never have been attempted."

Adding to the sting of Peleliu was the slow realization among the Marines of the 1st Division that the battle remained almost unknown back in the States. The huge airborne Market-Garden assault in Holland had been launched the same day they landed on Peleliu; later, U.S. landings in the Philippines usurped the headlines. Then, too, Rupertus's prediction of a short campaign had discouraged reporters from following the action in any great detail. "It was the 1st's luck again that it had fought and lost so much and gained so little esteem in the doing," remarked the division historian with a tinge of bitterness.

Army troops were also resentful, feeling the Marines garnered the lion's share of what little credit trickled down for the seizure of the island. "The relationship of my division to the Marines during the Palaus operation was generally satisfactory," wrote 81st Division Commander General Mueller to a fellow officer after the war. "Certainly the senior Navy and Marine commanders gave us due consideration and expressed the highest praise of the division's accomplishments in combat." Nevertheless, Mueller added, he did not feel his Wildcats had been accorded the general credit due them.

In later years, many Marine and army veterans of the Peleliu campaign would express similar bitterness that so many of their buddies died for so little purpose. Captain Everett Pope, who won the Medal of Honor on Walt Ridge, was more philosophical. "I suppose you could refight the whole Pacific war and decide you shouldn't have taken this island, but we were quite well aware that if we didn't take that island, we would take another one instead," he remarked 43 years later. "It wasn't a question we'd go home and rest. I guess the answer is it didn't make much difference to us if we took Island A or Island B."

Private Tom Boyle, evacuated for wounds suffered on 21 September, also remained philosophical. "I tell you what, you look at these things, it's got a lot of good stuff in it," he remarked. "It's miserable, too. All in all though, it'll round out your life. But I don't recommend it for everybody. There's not enough survivors to do that."

NOTE

1. Rupertus unfortunately never had the opportunity to detail his personal view of the Peleliu operation. He died of a heart attack on 26 March 1945.

Epilogue

One night late in March 1947, two native boys finished work at Peleliu's small naval compound and started home through the scrub. Suddenly, gunfire erupted around them. The boys dived for cover, escaping uninjured.

For weeks, the small U.S. naval and Marine detachment on Peleliu had seen signs of Japanese activity. A raft loaded with stolen Marine rations had been discovered floating in one of the swamps. Then, a Marine sentry fired on intruders looting a warehouse of captured Japanese weapons and was answered by rifle fire and a volley of grenades.

Twenty-six more Marines, armed with flamethrowers and 60 mm mortars flew in from Guam, bringing the strength of the detachment to about 100. By day, the Marines crawled cautiously among the ridges. By night, they established cossack posts in an attempt to ambush guerrillas who sneaked out for food and clothing.

Finally, on 3 April, a Japanese straggler emerged from the ridges and surrendered to two Marines on patrol in a jeep. He identified himself as Superior Seaman Tsuchida. According to him, there were 33 stragglers hiding in the Umurbrogol: 21 Japanese Army personnel, 7 navy and 4 Okinawan workers under the command of army Lieutenant Ei Yamaguchi.

"Tsuchida expressed amazement on his surrender when he was informed that the war ended and there was such a thing as the atomic bomb," observed a news report of the incident. He also reported that the 33 survivors were "torn by suspicion and dissension."

On a more ominous note, Tsuchida revealed that the Japanese survivors might be planning a last-ditch banzai attack on the main Marine camp and naval installation surrounding Peleliu airstrip. This information prompted the garrison commander, navy Captain Leonard Fox, to move some of the 110 naval personnel and 35 dependents from the airstrip to a more secure area further from the ridges. Armed guards with machine guns were posted on the rooftops, Marine patrols were doubled and 25 more leathernecks were brought in from Guam to reinforce the 100 already on Peleliu. Also flown in from Guam, where he was a war crimes witness, was Rear Admiral Michio Sumikawa, who came in hopes of persuading the holdouts to surrender.

In the end, however, it was Superior Seaman Tsuchida who averted more bloodshed. When Sumikawa's broadcasts brought no response, Tsuchida went back into the ridges with letters from the holdouts' families in Japan and from former officers in the Palaus, assuring them that the war was over and that they would be repatriated.

On 21 April, 26 of the holdouts formally surrendered to U.S. forces (the remaining seven gave up the following day). Led by Yamaguchi, the Japanese, looking well fed, marched ceremoniously to the front of the former Japanese headquarters building. As 80 Marines in full battle kit stood at attention, Yamaguchi bowed low and handed his sword and battle flags to Captain Fox.

Except for the memories, it was over.

Bibliography

The Peleliu campaign has not received the public attention lavished on Pacific battles such as Iwo Jima, Tarawa or Guadalcanal. However, the battle has given rise to three classic personal narratives: George Hunt's *Coral Comes High*, Russell Davis's *Marine at War* and the most recent, Eugene Sledge's fine memoir, *With the Old Breed at Peleliu and Okinawa*. The official Marine Corps monograph, *The Assault on Peleliu* by Frank Hough, is also invaluable, as well as quite hard to come by in the original.

Marine Corps records of the Peleliu operation, available through the Marine Corps History Center, fill several large cardboard boxes. There are literally hundreds of after-action reports, unit journals, intelligence reports, interrogation summaries, photo studies, plans, bulletins and directives—far too many to enumerate in any detail—relating to the III Amphibious Corps and the 1st Marine Division. Among the more interesting are three large "Peleliu Comment" files amassed by Colonel Hough in preparation of his monograph. Various officers offered their recollections and comments—some of them pungent—on the operation. The special action reports for the various units are also invaluable. I referred to all of this material in researching *The Devil's Anvil*. The center also has a fine library, where I found Peleliu-related articles and information in issues of *Leatherneck* and the *Marine Corps Gazette*. Also invaluable to the researcher is the oral history collection at the center, where officers such as General O. P. Smith recorded their recollections in interviews.

The Operation Archives of the Navy Historical Center was also of much assistance, particularly in providing the details of the fated *Burrfish* reconnaissance and other naval actions. The "Report of the Island Commander" on file at the archives contains an illuminating account of the bizarre Japanese raid that occurred in January 1945. Also on file is a detailed study of Japanese cave types on Peleliu.

The U.S. Army Military History Institute has a variety of material on file concerning the role of the 81st Division in the Peleliu and Angaur campaigns. Rosters of 81st Division units are available, along with unpublished unit histories, action summaries and regimental journals. Brief typewritten histories of the 323d Infantry, some ranging down as far as platoon level, are on file. General Mueller's papers include a few hundred copies of commendations issued to men of the division. There is also a poignant grouping of letters from the relatives of men killed while serving with the division; most of them thank the general for his letter of condolence, and many seek further details on the death of the soldier. Of particular interest are two reports, held by the archives branch, detailing interviews conducted by Lieutenant James Wickel with General Inoue and Colonel Tada shortly after the war.

PUBLISHED MATERIAL

Asprey, Robert B. *Once a Marine: The Memoirs of General A. A. Vandergrift.* New York: W. W. Norton and Co., 1964.

Berry, Henry. *Semper Fi, Mac.* New York: Arbor House, 1982.

Blakeney, Jane. *Heroes, U.S. Marine Corps 1861–1955.* Washington, D.C.: privately published, 1957.

Davis, Burke. *Marine! The Life of Lt. Gen. Lewis B. (Chesty) Puller.* Boston: Little, Brown and Co., 1962.

Davis, Russell. *Marine at War.* New York: Scholastic Book Services, 1961.

Falk, Stanley. *Bloodiest Victory.* New York: Random House, 1974.

Gailey, Harry A. *Peleliu: 1944.* Annapolis, Md.: The Nautical and Aviation Publishing Co., 1983.

Garand, George, and Truman Stobridge. *Western Pacific Operations, History of the U.S. Marine Corps Operations in World War II.* Vol. 4. Washington, D.C.: Historical Division, Headquarters, U.S. Marine Corps, 1971.

Halsey, William F., and J. Bryan III. *Admiral Halsey's Story.* New York: McGraw-Hill Book Co., 1947.

Harrington, Joseph D. *Yankee Samurai.* Detroit: Pettigrew Enterprises, 1979.

Hayashi, Saburo, and Alvin D. Coox. *Kogun: The Japanese Army in the Pacific War.* Quantico, Va.: The Marine Corps Association, 1959.

Hough, Frank O. *The Assault on Peleliu.* Washington, D.C.: Historical Division, Headquarters, U.S. Marine Corps, 1950.

———. *The Island War.* Philadelphia: J. B. Lippincott Co., 1947.

Hunt, George. *Coral Comes High.* New York: Harper and Brothers, 1946.

Isely, Jeter, and Philip Crowl. *The U.S. Marines and Amphibious War.* Princeton, N.J.: Princeton University Press, 1951.

Kennard, Richard C. *Combat Letters Home.* Bryn Mawr, Pa.: Dorrance and Co., 1985.

Leckie, Robert. *Helmet for My Pillow.* Garden City, N.Y.: Nelson Doubleday, 1979.

———. *Strong Men Armed: The United States Marines against Japan.* New York: Random House, 1962.

McMillan, George. *The Old Breed: A History of the First Marine Division in World War II.* Washington, D.C.: Infantry Journal Press, 1949.

Manchester, William. *Goodbye Darkness: A Memoir of the Pacific War.* Boston: Little, Brown and Co., 1979.

Merrill, James M. *A Sailor's Admiral: A Biography of William F. Halsey.* New York: Thomas Y. Crowell Co., 1976.

Morison, Samuel Eliot. *History of United States Naval Operations in World War II.* Vol. 12 (Leyte). Boston: Little, Brown and Co., 1958.

Newcomb, Richard F. *Abandon Ship!* New York: Henry Holt and Co., 1958.

O'Sheel, Patrick, and Gene Cook. *Semper Fidelis*. New York: William Sloan Associates, 1947.

Potter, E. B. *Bull Halsey*. Annapolis, Md.: Naval Institute Press, 1976.

Pratt, Fletcher. *The Marines' War*. New York: William Sloane Associates, 1948.

Roscoe, Theodore. *United States Destroyer Operations in World War II*. Annapolis, Md.: United States Naval Institute, 1953.

———. *United States Submarine Operations in World War II*. Annapolis, Md.: United States Naval Institute, 1949.

Ross, Bill D. *Peleliu: Tragic Triumph*. New York: Random House, 1991.

Shaw, Henry, I., Jr., and Ralph W. Donnelly. *Blacks in the Marine Corps*. Washington, D.C.: History and Museums Division, Hq. U.S.M.C., 1975.

Sherrod, Robert. *History of Marine Corps Aviation in World War II*. Washington, D.C.: Combat Forces Press, 1952.

Sledge, E. B. *With the Old Breed at Peleliu and Okinawa*. Novato, Ca.: Presidio Press, 1981.

Smith, Robert Ross. *United States Army in World War II: The War in the Pacific (Approach to the Philippines)*. Washington, D.C.: Center of Military History, United States Army, 1984.

Smith, S. E. *The United States Marine Corps in World War II*. New York: Random House, 1969.

Thacker, Joel D. *First Marine Division, 1941–1945*. Washington, D.C.: Historical Division, Headquarters, U.S. Marine Corps, n.d.

United States Army. *The 81st Infantry Wildcat Division in World War II*. Washington, D.C.: Infantry Journal Press, 1948.

———. "Reno v. Outline Plan for Operations of the Southwest Pacific Area to Include the Reoccupation of the Philippines." n.p., June 1944.

———. *Reports of General MacArthur: The Campaigns of MacArthur in the Pacific, Vol. I*. Washington, D.C.: GPO, 1966.

———. "The 321st Infantry Regiment from Camp Rucker to Guadalcanal, Angaur, Peleliu, New Caledonia, Leyte and Japan." Typescript, n.d.

———. "Unit History—321st Infantry: Operations against the Japanese on Peleliu Island, Palau Group." Typescript, n.d.

United States Marine Corps. "3d Amphibious Corps Report on Palau Operation." 3 vols. n.p., n.d.

United States Navy. *Combat Connected Naval Casualties in World War II by States*. Washington, D.C.: GPO, 1946.

———. *Navy Department Communiques 301 to 600*. Washington, D.C.: GPO, 1945.

———. "3d Fleet: Comments on Operation Report Palaus Operation of the III Amphibious Corps." n.p., n.d.

United States Strategic Bombing Survey. *Interrogations of Japanese Officials*. Vol. 2. Washington, D.C.: GPO, 1946.

———. *The Campaigns of the Pacific War*. Washington, D.C.: GPO, 1946.

Warner, Denis and Peggy. *Sacred Warriors*. New York: Van Nostrand Reinhold Co., 1982.

Willock, Roger. *Unaccustomed to Fear: A Biography of the Late General Roy S. Geiger*. Princeton, N.J.: privately published, 1968.

Y'Blood, William T. *The Little Giants*. Annapolis, Md.: Naval Institute Press, 1987.

UNPUBLISHED DOCUMENTS

Wickel, Lt. James J. "Interrogation of Lieutenant General Sadae Inoue," May 23, 1947.
———. "Interrogation of Colonel Tokuchi Tada," May 24, 1947.

INTERVIEWS

The following veterans provided extended interviews and/or written recollections for this book.

Sgt. Walter Afflito, B Company, 5th Marines
Cpl. Robert P. Anderson, K Company, 1st Marines
Sgt. Robert S. Askey, 11th Marines
Cpl. Burton A. Bilharz, K Company, 1st Marines
Pfc. Robert A. Biron, 11th Marines
Pfc. Thomas R. Boyle, A Company, 7th Marines
Sgt. Kevin Burns, 1st Tank Battalion
Col. Peter D. Clainos, 321st Infantry
Cpl. Vincent R. Clay, A Company, 5th Marines
Cpl. M. L. Clayton, A Company, 5th Marines
Cpl. Dan Coughlin, A Company, 5th Marines
Cpl. Emil Droule, 26th Marines
Capt. John I. Fitzgerald, Jr., 6th Amphibian Tractor Battalion
Pfc. Al Geierman, 11th Marines
Sgt. Wilfred G. Hanson, K Company, 1st Marines
Cpl. Joseph P. Hendley, K Company, 1st Marines
Pfc. James Isabelle, L Company, 5th Marines
Pfc. Arthur Jackson, 7th Marines
Pfc. Larry Kaloian, 1st Tank Battalion
Plt. Sgt. William C. Linkenfelter, A Company, 5th Marines
Pfc. Joseph G. Lommerse, F Company, 1st Marines
Pfc. Howard H. Miller, 11th Marines
Pfc. Joseph J. Moskalczak, K Company, 5th Marines
Cpl. Harlan J. Murray, K Company, 1st Marines
Cpl. William N. Myers, 1st Tank Battalion
Capt. Everett P. Pope, C Company, 1st Marines
Sgt. Kenneth W. Reich, 1st Marines
Lt. Thomas Stanley, K Company, 5th Marines
Sgt. Carl R. Stevenson, A Company, 7th Marines
Lt. Raymond G. Stramel, K Company, 1st Marines
Cpl. George B. Uptain, 2d Radio Intelligence Platoon
Pfc. Norman L. Zimmerman, 8th Amphibian Tractor Battalion

Index

About the Author

JAMES H. HALLAS is publisher of the *Glastonbury Citizen*, a newspaper in Glastonbury, Connecticut. He has published articles in *American History Illustrated* and *Yankee Magazine*.